Subjectivity, the Unconscious and Consumerism

Marlon Xavier

Subjectivity, the Unconscious and Consumerism

Consuming Dreams

palgrave
macmillan

Marlon Xavier
University of Caxias do Sul
Caxias do Sul, Rio Grande do Sul, Brazil

ISBN 978-3-030-07257-5 ISBN 978-3-319-96824-7 (eBook)
https://doi.org/10.1007/978-3-319-96824-7

Softcover re-print of the Hardcover 1st edition 2018

Cover illustration: Tetra Images/gettyimages

This Palgrave Macmillan imprint is published by the registered company Springer Nature Switzerland AG
The registered company address is: Gewerbestrasse 11, 6330 Cham, Switzerland

Note on Translations and Gendering

I have tried to employ gender-neutral language; however, I did not modify quotes that were originally gendered. At times "their" is used as an alternative to "his" and "her"; at other times singular masculine and feminine pronouns were used alternately. All the translations (of dreams and quotes) into English are my own, unless noted.

Preface

As a prologue to the oneiric theoretical and empirical discussions that follow, it seemed necessary to put forward just a few introductory remarks so as to generally situate the reader in relation to this present book, derived from my doctoral dissertation for the PhD program in Social Psychology at Universidad Autónoma de Barcelona. The proposal it offers may be most succinctly and broadly defined as an interdisciplinary outlook on the regime of capitalism-consumerism, and its psychological subject, through the *dream*—as a general idea or motif, a *lens* through which we shall look at our objects, but also as the empirical material for research. Historically, such proposal is not without some antecedents: the concept of "dream" already appeared as an important trope for analyses of capitalism in some classical social authors, like Marx and Althusser, for instance, who used it mainly as a negative metaphor for the ideological, unreal character of capitalism.[1] However, the main antecedent and inspiration for this work is Walter Benjamin (1999), in whose archeological, monumental, and unfinished study of capitalism, *Passagen-Werk*, the concept and language of dream have a central, pivotal role. Moreover, in it Benjamin put forward a proposal that came to define this enterprise: the

[1] As Althusser (1971) comments upon Marx's usage of the idea of dream: "The dream was the imaginary, it was empty, null and arbitrarily 'stuck together' (*bricolé*), once the eyes had closed, from the residues of the only full and positive reality, the reality of the day. This is exactly the status of philosophy and ideology (…) in *The German Ideology*" (as quoted in Cohen, 1995, p. 53).

idea of complementing a critique of capitalism-consumerism (as a collective dream) with the illumination and understanding of the night dreams of the individual (and their historical and collective character). Such idea appears in different *loci* within the *Passagen-Werk* but is most concisely put thusly: "(…) to shed light on the dreams of the individual with the help of the doctrine of the historical dreams of the collective" (Benjamin, 1999, p. 908). His heritage summarizes this work: "I want to tell you a dream before it fades away[2]" (Benjamin, 1916/1982, p. 151).

In tandem with the leitmotif of dream, this work sees the *ethos* of the regime of capitalism-consumerism through the ample concept of *imaginary*. Before reaching such definition of a general conceptual approach to such regime, however, I endeavored to establish relations and build dialogs with many major authors who wrote about its *spirit* from different perspectives, especially authors from the tradition of sociology, such as Max Weber (1905/1958), Daniel Bell (1976), Richard Sennett (1998, 2006), and Boltanski and Chiapello (1999). They were indeed relevant for this work, yet ended up not appearing much in its final version. Analogously, the process of constructing this study involved a preoccupation with developing an interdisciplinary dialog with other authors from sociology, philosophy, anthropology, and psychology, ranging from classic authors to old, quasi-forgotten works, to well-known postmodern names.

Besides its interdisciplinary effort, there are two other distinct features that mark this work. The first regards its subjective character, or, put differently, the multifarious importance that *subjectivity* has for it. Having *dream* as its leitmotif and empirical material, it could not be otherwise: although it can also be perfectly objective, the dream is by definition a very subjective experience and phenomenon, of a peculiar qualitative and symbolic nature. Furthermore, a hermeneutic approach is required in order to reveal and comprehend such subjectivity contained in the dream; and its interpretation is always subjective to a certain extent. Moreover, the psychology that grounds this work, C. G. Jung's analytical psychology, is also distinguished by the import it gives to acknowledging and understanding that which is subjective and individual—which includes recognizing and stating explicitly the inalienable role that subjectivity plays in psychology as a field of knowledge, which always includes the subjective viewpoint of the

[2] "Voglio raccontarti un sogno prima che svanisca."

researcher, be it of a conscious or unconscious nature, viewpoint or horizon that must be considered and relativized in order to apprehend, interpret, and understand the *other*, the "object", in its singularity. Indeed, Jung's psychology may be characterized by a plea for full consideration and confession[3] of what William James (1890) called the *personal equation*. Taking all these factors into account, I have decided for writing in the first-person singular form and actually rendering very explicit my personal standpoint, or personal equation. Such decision is already apparent in the Introduction that follows these initial words, which interweaves my personal trajectory, motivations, and inquietudes with the more objective justifications, arguments for relevance, and rationales for this work, all of which were equally important for its making and constitute its background.

The second distinct feature of this study consists in the fact that, since its very inception, it was conceived as an *attempt* to innovate and offer something original, to present different points of view and theories, and to generate reflection. Such endeavor at originality demanded elaborating different concepts and theorizations, whose meanings and particular definitions may be hard for the reader to grasp at first. Also, my utilization of an interdisciplinary theoretical framework essentially based on two authors (Jung and Baudrillard) whose conceptualizations may be deemed complex and "difficult" can present the same problems for the reader. In order to try to alleviate such possible difficulties, at the end of this work is a concise Glossary with brief definitions of a few of the main terms or concepts used here.

Finally, I shall let the reader decide whether such attempt at innovating was a successful one. Yet, maybe the main value of this work simply consists in revealing and trying to understand what goes on in the forgotten, deep recesses of the souls of a few people—in comparison with our contemporary situation. As Fernando Pessoa (1924/1995) put it, "Everything is illusion. To dream is to know it" (p. 100). And also Maffesoli (2008): "According to Fernando Pessoa, it was important to decipher the secret laws that govern society. Laws that allow us to recognize the relationship between the dream

[3] Jung (CW18) formulated such plea thusly: "I consider my contribution to psychology to be my subjective confession. It is my personal psychology, my prejudice that I see things in such and such a way. But I expect Freud and Adler to do the same and confess that their ideas are their subjective point of view. *So far as we admit our personal prejudice, we are really contributing towards an objective psychology*" (§275; e.a.).

and what is called reality. The reality of a social life in which ideas, illusions, phantasms and, in one word, the imaginary, have a central role" (p. 156). Thus, and to paraphrase T. S. Eliot (1925),[4] we ought to dare meet and in fact *see* through the eyes of the dream.

Rio Grande do Sul, Brazil Marlon Xavier

References

Althusser, L. (1971). *Lenin and Philosophy* (B. Brewster, Trans.). London: Monthly Review Press.

Bell, D. (1976). *The cultural contradictions of capitalism*. New York: Basic Books.

Benjamin, W. (1982). L'arcobaleno (1915–1916). In G. Agamben (Ed.), *Metafisica della gioventù: Scritti 1910–1918* (D. Regenbogen, Trans., pp. 151–158). Torino, IT: Einaudi. (Original work written 1916).

Benjamin, W. (1999). *The arcades project* (H. Eiland & K. McLaughlin, Trans.). Cambridge: The Belknap Press of Harvard University Press.

Boltanski, L., & Chiapello, E. (1999). *El nuevo espíritu del capitalismo*. Madrid: Akal.

Cohen, M. (1995). *Profane illumination: Walter Benjamin and the Paris of surrealist revolution*. Berkeley, CA: University of California Press.

Eliot, T. S. (1925). *Eliot's poems: 1909–1925*. London: Faber & Gwyer.

James, W. (1890). *Principles of Psychology*. New York: Holt.

Maffesoli, M. (2008). *Iconologías: Nuestras idolatrías postmodernas* (J. Terré, Trans.). Barcelona: Península.

Pessoa, F. (1995). *Poesias* (15th ed.). Lisboa: Ática. (Original work published 1924).

Sennett, R. (1998). *The corrosion of character: The personal consequences of work in the new capitalism*. New York: W. W. Norton.

Sennett, R. (2006). *The culture of the new capitalism*. Yale: Yale University Press.

Weber, M. (1958). *The Protestant ethic and the spirit of capitalism*. New York: Scribners. (Original work published 1905).

[4] I am referring to Eliot's famous lines "Eyes I dare not meet in dreams", from his poem *The Hollow Men*.

Acknowledgments

I would like to take this opportunity to express my gratitude and indebtedness to some people for their help, support, and encouragement, without which this work would not have come to fruition. My sincere *agradecimientos* must go first to Dr. Josep M. Blanch i Ribas, my dissertation director, for his patience and wisdom, for welcoming, teaching, criticizing, and motivating me, and for being the humane person that he is. My heartfelt thanks also to Dr. Patrícia Martins Goulart, for her friendship, joie de vivre, and incentive—and for making this Barcelona journey possible.

I must also express my deep gratefulness to all professors, workers, and colleagues at the Departamento de Psicología Social at UAB. Among them, I would like to thank particularly my colleagues and friends Adriano Beiras and David Castillo (in memoriam), Roberta Rodrigues, Domenico Hur, and Rafael Diehl, and express my sincere gratitude to Isabela de Melo Mussi, Antonio Stecher, and all from the coLABORando research group, for their friendship and manifold contributions; Diana Hermoso Lloret and Genís Cervantes deserve a special *moltes gràcies!* for their unswerving support and help.

Further acknowledgment and *muchísimas gracias* must also go to Dr. Miguel Sahagún, Dr. Enrique Santamaría, Dr. Félix Vázquez Sisto, and Dr. Lupicinio Íñiguez, for their advice, guidance, and support. Many thanks to Dr. Mark Davis, at the University of Leeds and the Bauman

Institute, for his friendly welcome and stimulating thought. In Brazil, my deep gratitude to Professor Dr. Maria Lucia Tiellet Nunes, who has been helping me ever since my graduation course, for her unbound generosity.

My appreciation also to some friends who helped me in so many ways along the way: Fernandito Martín Yagüe, Francisco Netto da Costa, Ines Chacón, Victor Grosman, and Leticia F. Cestari who deserves special cheers for reviewing my manuscript and for her many insightful comments.

Finally, I would like to express my most profound gratitude to some people who are very special to me: first, my father Edgar, for his support and love, his ethics and courage, for being who he is, for everything; my mother Beatriz, who gave me life; and my aunts Ana and Mercedes, for the example and all the help. André Guirland Vieira—I am grateful to you for so, so many things.

Thank you.

Florianópolis
May 2018

Contents

Abbreviations

Works by C. G. Jung

CW — *The Collected Works of C. G. Jung*, edited by Sir Herbert Read, Michael Fordham, Gerhard Adler; William McGuire, executive editor; trans. R. F. C. Hull (New York and Princeton, Bollingen Series 20 and London, 1953–1983), 21 vols.[1]

DAS — Jung, C. G. (1984). *Dream Analysis: Notes of the Seminar Given in 1928–1930 by C. G. Jung* (W. McGuire, Ed.). Princeton: Princeton University Press.

MDR — Jung, C. G., & Jaffé, A. (1989). *Memories, Dreams, Reflections.* New York: Vintage Books. (Original work published 1963)

MHS — Jung, C. G. (Ed.) (1964). *Man and His Symbols.* New York: Anchor Press/Doubleday.

SCD — Jung, C. G. (2008). *Children's Dreams: Notes from the Seminar Given in 1936–1940 by C. G. Jung.* Princeton: Princeton University Press.

[1] When quoting or referencing a work that is part of Jung's Collected Works, for reason of space only the volume number is indicated, together with the acronym "CW". Instead of providing the page numbers in quotations, I chose to give the paragraph number (§), which is invariable in all translations. (For instance, "CW11, §40" refers to the Volume 11 of *The Collected Works of C. G. Jung*, paragraph 40). Both procedures can be seen as standard in contemporary works focusing on Jungian psychology.

SNZ Jung, C. G. (1988). *Nietzsche's Zarathustra: Notes of the Seminar Given in 1934–1939.* (J. L. Jarrett, Ed.). Princeton: Princeton University Press, 2 vols.

SVI Jung, C. G. (1997). *Visions: Notes of the Seminar Given in 1930–1934 by C. G. Jung.* Princeton: Princeton University Press, 2 vols.

Other Abbreviations

e.a. emphasis added. (When there already were emphases in the original, in order to distinguish them I have placed "[e.a.]" inside the quotation, immediately after the part emphasized by me).

ImCon, imaginary of consumption, or imaginary of consumerism (see Introduction and Glossary).

1

Introduction

This study is basically an exploration of what (night) dreams can express about aspects of contemporary *consumerism* and its social imaginary, being a subject in it, and how it conditions and institutes such being—from the perspective of C. G. Jung's analytical psychology, in terms of theoretical framework and hermeneutics. To introduce it, let me first tell the reader a bit about my trajectory, how the object of study, the problem, and the research focus were defined, their cultural context, and how and why I propose to investigate the problem through dreams.

1.1 Defining the Object of Study: A Trajectory

1.1.1 First Moment: Capitalism, Consumerism, and the Subject

One of the main reasons for my wanting to study such themes, or research subjects, was simply the initial context of my doctorate at the UAB: I was part of a research group called *coLABORando*, coordinated by my doctoral

M. Xavier, *Subjectivity, the Unconscious and Consumerism*,
https://doi.org/10.1007/978-3-319-96824-7_1

supervisor, that studied contemporary capitalism and its *colonization* of institutions, practices, and subjectivity, in an international research called Kofarips.[1] More specifically, the study centered on organizational capitalism[2] and sought to research how it conditions work and work-subjectivity (*subjetividad laboral*) (Blanch & Stecher, 2009). Although I struggled to collaborate and propose and do research in accordance with such focuses, my interest was at once much more general (the theme of subjectivity) and specific (the *unconscious* aspects of subjectivity). A broad perspective emphasized in Kofarips eventually became central for this work: its proposition that capitalism's logic of commodification and market ethos not merely affect and shape subjectivity, but represent a mode of production of "psychological life" in general (Blanch & Cantera, 2007b, p. 12).

In lieu of organizational capitalism, I gradually became more interested in defining *consumerism* as the general cultural context of this work, focusing on what Allott (2002) broadly called its *psychic ethos*, that is, its (socio)psychological dimensions. Consumerism represents the fundamental doctrine of contemporary capitalism: a cultural ideology founded on the idea and the imperative of consumption (in its common significance, but also and crucially in the sense of "using up entirely, disposing of, wasting, destroying": *consumere*[3]). As such, it seems to define more accurately the profound sociocultural changes effected by capitalism today. Indeed, consumption has arguably become the main definer of our culture, the chief basis of the social order (Baudrillard, 1968/1996; Poster, 2001); rather than being merely an aspect or part of our lives, of our milieu, we all become creatures defined by the "age of consumption" (Baudrillard, 1970/1998, p. 191). As a socioeconomic system, consumerism seeks to produce and shape its subjects according to its logic and needs. If industrialism was rooted in production (and its subject was thus defined by work or ownership of means of production), then such emphasis has been displaced and shifted toward consumption and

[1] *Kofarips* is the acronym in Spanish for "Organizational Capitalism as a psychosocial risk factor: An international research". IP: JM Blanch, UAB. See the website of the coLABORando group at http://psicologiasocial.uab.es/colaborando/es

[2] It refers to the progressive commodification of public institutions in the fields of health and education effected by contemporary capitalism.

[3] See Raymond Williams (1976, p. 68) and Mike Featherstone (2007, p. 21).

disposal, and, presently and most importantly, to the *production of consumers*.[4] The result is that, in our global culture, *being a consumer is what ultimately defines the subject* (Baudrillard, 1970/1998; Bauman, 2007a; Dufour, 2008; Gottdiener, 1996).

1.1.2 Logic of Colonization and Total Capitalism

What the Kofarips project studied as the capitalist logic of colonization interested me more under two of its facets: the tendency of capitalism (and consumerism) to *total* colonization, and its colonization of subjectivity. As regards the first, Marx (1858/1978), in the *Grundrisse*, had already pointed that a *totalizing imperative* is characteristic of capitalism: the "development to its totality consists precisely in subordinating *all elements of society* to itself" (p. 278; e.a.). For Lukács (1923/1971) and Castoriadis (1997), capitalism's orientation toward progressive conquest of the whole of society, effected through its logic of reification and commodification, is one of its most conspicuous specificities. Contemporarily, the actualization of such orientation appears as the relentless *colonization* of social and psychological forces, of life realms, or reality itself, by the capitalist ethos,[5] and the totalizing (or even totalitarian) aspects of capitalism have been pointed out by many scholars (e.g., Clarke, 2005; Fairclough & Graham, 2002; Gare, 2008; Graham, 2006; Jha, 2006; Lacher, 2005; Lebowitz, 2003; Leys, 2007; Liodakis, 2010; Radice, 2005).

Although such processes of colonization by capital obviously occur in multiple and complex forms and ways, under consumerism its colonizing force might be summarized (for the purposes of this work) under one principle or common denominator: *commodification*.[6] This new colonial

[4] A tendency that had already been noted in the primordia of consumerism (Strauss, 1924).

[5] Colonization by capitalism-consumerism of various life realms and cultural institutions, and their corresponding forms of subjectivity, has been studied by a number of authors: the commodification of *work* and workers (e.g., Huws & Herrman, 2008; Sennett, 1998, 2006); of *politics*, with political ideologies and positions consumed as commodities, and its monad, the citizen, becoming a consumer (Bauman, 2007a, 2007b; Bauman & Tester, 2001; Davis, 2008; Leys, 2007); of *health* (Blanch & Cantera, 2007a, 2011; Henderson & Petersen, 2002; Navarro, 1976, 1993; Waitzkin, 2003), and *education* (Blanch & Cantera, 2007b, 2011; Laval & Weber, 2002; Slaughter & Leslie, 1997, 2001; Slaughter & Rhoades, 2004), to mention a few.

[6] For Jameson (1991), this total process of expansion through "sheer commodification" (p. x) is what characterizes "late or multinational or consumer capitalism" (p. 36).

order whose fundamental drive is consumption strives to establish and impose the commodity as the *only referent*: the imperative is that *everything must become a commodity*, be represented, signified, and function as a commodity, and hence follow commodity logic and market logic, be governed by commodity exchange, have a certain market value, be consumed and disposed of, and so on. Such imperative is perhaps what best defines consumerism: "a culture of commodification" (Giroux & Pollock, 2011).

Therefore, the theoretical and political perspective on contemporary consumer capitalism (and its imaginary) that informs this work is that its *telos* is one of *total colonization* through total commodification: it represents a totalizing system. Such perspective can be summarized through the concept of *total capitalism* (Dufour, 2003, 2005, 2008; Leys, 2007). Dufour (2001) underlines two main aspects of this "last stage of capitalism" that are central for this work: a transformation of *minds* by the ideologies of neoliberalism and consumerism through education, mass media, and culture, and the collapse of transcendental values and the symbolic world. The transformation of minds means a psychological colonization of subjectivity, which, according to Dufour (2008), represents an anthropological mutation. Under consumerism, commodification is not restricted to labor power, as in capitalism; it aims at the total commodification of the whole *being*.[7] According to Bauman (2007a, p. 12), that has become "The most prominent feature of the society of consumers (…) the *transformation of consumers into commodities*"—the mass production of *commodity-subjects*.

1.1.3 Second Moment: Consumerist Colonization, Subject, and the Unconscious

It follows logically that, for such production of commodity-subjects, it is fundamental to command organization, configuration, and functioning of the subject's psyche.[8] At this point, my focuses of research became

[7] Under total capitalism "everything, *including our very being*, will be dragged into the orbit of the commodity" (Dufour, 2008, p. 168; e.a.).

[8] In fact, the power of capitalism-consumerism and its colonial force of commodification go beyond the conquest of world and mind (psyche); it reaches the biological being: "In the expanding vortex

centered on such psychological dimensions: on the one hand, the subject's mind or mentality, her/his psychic subjectivity (which is social by definition) assailed by commodification; on the other hand, the social world in its psychic dimension, its psychic ethos: consumerism as a totalizing ideology or regime of signification, what I would later call a totalizing imaginary. More specifically, I wanted to study the processes of psychic colonization by capitalism-consumerism, and how the subject is formed, affected, conditioned by them—but with a focus on the *irrational, imaginary, unconscious aspects* of such processes. Such desire was connected to my struggle to find a space for dialog in academia, endeavoring to discuss such themes (capitalism, consumerism) in the context of social psychology from the perspective of analytical psychology and its concept of unconscious, and to what I envisaged as a valuable contribution to social psychology resulting from such discussion. Then the dilemma I was faced with was, how to study the unconscious aspects of subjectivity under (total) consumerism? Influenced by the Jungian tradition of seeing dreams as a precious way of assessing the unconscious, and because of my relatively long experience working with dreams both clinically and theoretically, and of the possible originality that a research on dreams and capitalism promised, the idea of using night dreams as empirical material eventually became central for this research proposal.

1.1.4 Third and Final Moment: Consumption Dreams, or *sueños de consumo*

The reader can probably imagine that such proposal was beset with difficulties. After many different attempts and turns (some of which I discuss briefly in the chapter on Method), my supervisor came up with a suggestion that would define the theme and outlook of this work: to study "consumption dreams". The expression is very common in Portuguese (*sonhos de consumo*) and a bit less in Spanish (*sueños de consumo*), though fairly

of capitalism, we continue to see the process of commodification extending to the far corners of the earth and encroaching on the most intimate facets of life, with not only land, labor and resources commodified, but also public utilities, knowledge, education, friendship, the means to control people's minds, and even people's genes" (Gare, 2008, p. 9).

uncommon in English,[9] and can be defined as the desires, fantasies, and ideals about goods and experiences—and, in fact, life in general—that have *consumption* as their underlying idea or motif. The concept follows what seems to be a general transformation of the meaning or in fact of the very *idea* of *dream*: from night dream (an autonomous, mysterious, irrational experience that happens to us and can be fantastic but also terrible) to dream as personal *desire*, image of the future, main goal, the "good life", and so on.

Although I later decided not to take this concept or idea of "consumption dream" as an empirical object of study, it provided a form of looking at or approaching consumerism *theoretically*: through its relation with dream, fantasy, and imagination, it condenses the role of the *imaginary* in consumption and consumerism—that is, their psychic, and *unconscious*, irrational aspects. At the same time, it immediately reminded me of a *night dream* that I was told a long time ago, which would be a perfect prototype for the *empirical* research object of this thesis: I called it the *prototype dream*. I discuss briefly both themes in what follows.

1.1.5 Consumption as Imaginary: Consumption Dreams

Here "consumption as imaginary" is meant in a double sense: how consumption is based on *imagination* and imaginary things, and the crucial role that *images* play in it. The first sense refers to the notion that consumerism is founded on the consumption of the object[10] *not* for its materiality or use-value, nor for what it is or does in any concrete sense (Tomlison, 1990), but for what it *signifies*. And it signifies through an image or representation: what is consumed is the commodity-image. That is connected to the fundamental role of *image* for postmodernity and mass consumer society (Baudrillard, 1983a, 1983b; Jameson, 1984a,

[9] In the English-speaking world, some works (see the short review of literature below) use the expression "consumption dreams", although "consumer's dream" also appears. More generally, in common parlance people simply employ "dream" with the same meaning, without distinguishing it from night dreams.

[10] "Object" here can mean *anything*: a concrete object, an idea, a representation, a person.

1984b, 1991), whose *dynamis* consists essentially in the endless production, proliferation, and consumption of a liquid "surfeit of signs and images" (Featherstone, 2007, p. xiv). Such signs and images, as commodities, are endowed with socially perceived meanings, values, differences[11]: the irrational, immaterial, artificial *fetish* manufactured and attached to the commodity is what is most desired and dreamed about. Hence what is consumed is essentially the promise that a *dream* will be fulfilled by the commodity and/or the act of consuming. From this viewpoint, contemporary consumerism is largely sustained by the immaterial, the fictional, *the imaginary*: it consists fundamentally in "marketing dreams" (Ewen, 1990), *consumption dreams*; it depends on the consumption of dreams.

1.1.6 Imaginary of Consumerism: *ImCon*

As delineated above, the concept of *imaginary of consumerism* represents this study's theoretical outlook in relation to contemporary consumerism. To employ the concept of *imaginary* seemed the most adequate manner[12] of looking (*theoria*) at such cultural context, for it allowed for focusing on consumerism's imaginary *and* irrational aspects—its elements, forces, dynamics related to the unconscious and to image, symbol, and representation; to dream, fantasy, and imagination—all the aspects I yearned to study through the empirical object, night dreams (which are also imaginary and unconscious products). There were also some practical reasons for choosing such theoretical approach. As the themes of this work are considerably vast, a theory that was ample enough to cover them *and* their interrelationships was needed; and indeed, the concept of "imaginary" fulfills that need.[13] Moreover, its tradition of studies finds

[11] Images of exotica, beauty, transcendence, success, individuality, identity, social insertion, etc., which are manipulated and marketed as desirable and as social markers of distinction (Bourdieu, 1984; Douglas & Isherwood, 1980). The engineering of such "discourse of the commodity" through the manipulation of significations corresponds to the logic of advertisement.

[12] I wish to express my heartfelt thanks to Dr. André G. Vieira for suggesting the use of such concept and theory.

[13] Yves Durand's (1988) definition illustrates how ample the concept and its field of research are: "The imaginary covers the totality of the anthropological field of image, which is extended indis-

many of its origins in Jung's analytical psychology, and—especially in Michel Maffesoli and his school—includes a strong focus on key elements of consumer society (advertising, mass media, communication, etc.); in the work of Marc Augé (1999), it incorporates a focus on the *colonization* effected by imaginaries, and their relation with night dreams.

Henceforth the consumerist imaginary will be called ***ImCon***, for short—and to give it an Orwellian touch. "ImCon" can be read as both imaginary "of consumption" and "of consumerism", and that is on purpose: I think both meanings are important. "Consumerism" is broadly defined above as the social system and the ideology that define our present ethos. As for "consumption", it is seen as the supraordinate idea in the system that defines its ideology, the idea to which all the system's constituents are connected, refer, and function according: its main social categorical imperative, or *absolute principle* (Baudrillard, 1970/1998). It would correspond to the main *archetype* of such imaginary, were "consumption" an archetype. To sum up: the ImCon is fundamentally a *semiotic*[14] imaginary constituted of signs and consumption dreams, whose *idée fixe* is consumption.

1.1.7 The Prototype Dream

As mentioned, this night dream was recalled in connection with the idea of researching "consumption dreams". I saw it then as a prototypical empirical object for this study; in fact it later originated the study's research problem and further defined its theme. It illustrates its empirical object—*night dreams related to the ImCon*—and the approach used to understand them. The dreamer, a young female patient, told it to me more than ten years ago. In the dream, a *church*—old, menaced by the environment, falling into disrepair, yet still solid, functioning: inside, rites were being celebrated by serious, dignified elderly people—is about to be transformed (by the dreamer) into a McDonald's franchise.

---

tinctly from the unconscious to the conscious, from dream and fantasy to what is constructed and built, in sum, from the irrational to the rational" (p. 15). Some may say it is *too* ample (or ill-defined) a concept.

[14] From Greek σῆμα, *sema* = sign.

First of all, let me state clearly an important thing: a dream ought to be seen as a *possibility,* not as a deterministic decree; it usually shows a picture of the psychic situation, a *tendency*—and often in an exaggerated, dramatized way. But what can this dream possibly mean? Seen from the perspective of analytical psychology,[15] it is an illustration of how the unconscious, through dreams, autonomously portrays and criticizes the *colonization* of the very foundations of *both the individual and culture* by the ImCon. But what is colonized? If we read the dream on a subjective level (i.e., all the dream elements refer to the dreamer's psyche), it is *her* church, her (inner) *imaginary.* As a parcel of her psychic system, it represents her own symbolic, imaginary function (a religious function), the very source of imagination and representation. Broadly, it means what *in her and for her* (still) functions as mythic and *religious*, what she holds sacred: a regime of signification connected to a traditional (Catholic) social imaginary that shapes the way she imagines, signifies, and experiences the world. That is about to be transformed into a church of consumerism, that is, to be replaced by the ImCon in her psychic system: what becomes sacred then is consumption and commodity, and that defines her as a subject, her being and existence: she becomes a faithful devotee, a consumer.

Let us look at the dream on an objective level (i.e., the dream elements also represent concrete and social factors: the dream is seen *culturally*). Previous cultures and ages lived under and through myths, rites, religions, and their imagery—*imaginaries*, religious-symbolic systems that signified and organized experience, inserted the individual into community and social life, and distinctly characterized the culture in its specificity. The church was the symbol and edifice of the Christian imaginary that defined our Western culture. If we understand McDonald's as a symbol for *consumerism* and its imaginary, her dream hints at the possibility that the ImCon takes over the old religious imaginaries and comes to command our lives, to define existence, in the same way: it becomes the *new religion*, as totalizing as the symbolic imaginaries of old, aimed at

[15] It is important to note that the possible understandings (interpretations) of the dream that follow do not come from the dream taken alone; they depend on and stem from seeing the dream in the context of other dreams and the dreamer's life history, and in comparison with many other similar dreams by different people.

organizing and signifying—*colonizing*—the whole of experience and life. In that case, the dream would be revealing not merely a subjective mutation, but a historical and cultural one: the dreamer was following a *cultural tendency*, a trend that defines our contemporary imaginary.

It is not by chance that the dream (i.e., the unconscious) chose McDonald's as a symbol for such colonizing trend. In sociology, one can find a related concept in which McDonald's defines a form of global colonization by consumerism-capitalism: *McDonaldization*[16] (Ritzer, 1993, 1998, 2000, 2002), or, as Barber (1995) put radically, the *McWorld*. The prototype dream therefore hinted at the possibility of investigating such forms of colonization in dialog with sociological theories on them—but through night dreams. However, the dream introduces a novelty and a form of critique that go far beyond what Ritzer described as McDonaldization: on the one hand, it shows that the colonizing forces of consumerism and its icons encroach upon the deepest recesses of the psyche, in the subject's own dreams. On the other hand, if the "church" symbolized the old symbolic, sacred imaginary, what the dream expressed as McDonaldization was its (possible) complete substitution by the ImCon: the dream hints at a *mutation* or *colonization of imaginaries*.[17] Therefore, McDonald's appears in the dream as what Augé (1999) described as "the *new regime of the imaginary* which nowadays touches social life, *contaminating and penetrating* it [colonizing it!] to the point where we mistrust it, its reality, meaning and the categories (identity, otherness) which shape and define it" (pp. 2–3; e.a.). The result is that "We all have the feeling that we are being colonised but we don't exactly know who by; the enemy is not easily identifiable" (p. 6). However, the dream reveals and identifies *precisely* the "enemy" that colonizes us: the ImCon, a new colonial order of imagination.

That was the trajectory that led me to propose this study. In presenting it, together with the prototypic oneiric narrative that originated it, I hope to have elicited the reader's curiosity and interest for the dreams presented in this work. Before we delve into such oneiric worlds, however,

---

[16] It must be emphasized that neither the dreamer nor myself was acquainted with such theory then. See Bryman (2004b) for an excellent summary of the McDonaldization thesis.

[17] The expression is Gruzinski's (1988), *La colonization de l'imaginaire.*

given the general unfamiliarity with night dreams and lack of studies on them that characterize our scientific field, perhaps the reader would welcome a more detailed justification of their use as empirical material, of why certain specific dreams (dreams with *Dream-worlds of consumption*) were selected for such, and how the theoretical perspective chosen here considers them.

1.2 Justification

1.2.1 Why Dreams? Justification and Outlook

The way "dream" (as both concept and empirical material) is seen here is based on Jung's concept of *unconscious*, which will be discussed later on. For now, let it suffice to say that the dream, being an embodiment of the unconscious psyche, its natural product, carries all its qualities. It thus represents a *spontaneous, autonomous, objective fact*, neither created nor directed by the human will or intention (Bergson, 1919; Jung, CW11, CW18, SCD), which presents the unconscious discourse on, or reaction to, the individual's psychological situation, that is, the dreamer's *subjectivity*. As each individual is by definition a social being, thereby embedded in a cultural setting, dreams can also reveal the unconscious critical discourse and reactions in relation to the dreamer's *sociocultural* reality—which, in this work, is seen through a focus upon its social imaginary (ImCon). The night dream, however, is seen as a representation of the natural symbolic imaginary, the *nocturnal imaginary*: the unconscious.

Historically, such concepts of dream and imaginary stand in opposition to our modern and postmodern views. It might be affirmed that one of the defining traits of modernity—and its exaltation of science, instrumental rationality, and calculability: what defined old capitalism—was that it was founded upon the irreconcilable opposition between *dreams* (as the imaginary, the fantasy, the irrational: the suprasensory) and *reality*. Such idea is found in Descartes, who saw dreams and reality as antithetical. His philosophy, which arguably defined modernity and the modern *Weltanschauung*, originated from the fear, nay the *nightmare* that reality could be nothing but a dream-delusion produced by an evil genius.[18] Spectacularly enough, under postmodern consumerism reality progressively *becomes* a "dream-delusion"[19]: the hyperreal imaginary of a dream-world of consumption made of commodity-signs and simulacra. One of its main characteristics is the effacement of the distinction reality/dream, or reality/imaginary; everything becomes dreamy *images* to be consumed and discarded fast. Furthermore, the very *concept* of "dream" is colonized, as "dream" comes to mean "consumption dream". What was once seen as "dream" and "imaginary"—now produced artificially and circulated globally—come once more to define "reality". Descartes' nightmare has, to a large extent, become hyperreal.

However, prior to the advent of modernity, historically the dream had always been seen in a different way across cultures: as the representation or manifestation of irrational, transcendent, superior (or chthonic) forces and knowledge. Dreams were the symbolic bridges with the sacred, mythic world. As the "messengers of the gods", they were the foundation of the symbolic *imaginary*, the myths that defined culture and social and individual life.

What we have under contemporary consumerism, then, is a *mutation of dream*: from "messenger of the gods" to "consumption dreams"—which parallels and mirrors the mutation of the imaginary, from a symbolic, mythical, transcendental one, to the semiotic, hyperreal consumerist imaginary. If that represents an ontological cultural and anthropological mutation, then it must underlie all the processes of psychological colonization by consumerism.

Yet, the objectivity of *night dreams* can unveil and illuminate such colonizing power of the ImCon: they are its opposite. Moreover, they are possibly one of the most real, *convincing* means for such illumination—precisely

[18] Descartes' main arguments in his *Meditations* (1641/1996) can be seen as derived, to a significant extent, from his consideration of dreams. The other founder of modernity, Hobbes, commences his *Leviathan* (1651) with a philosophical anthropology in which dream plays a major part.

[19] The best example of such reversal of the opposition dream-reality in a contemporary cultural product is in the movie *Matrix* by the Wachowski Brothers (1999), in which reality has become a simulated hyperreality, an artificial *dream*. True reality is brought to Neo by a real dream, and later by Morpheus, the Lord of dreams, who asks: "Have you ever had a dream, Neo, that you were so sure was real? What if you were unable to wake from that dream? How would you know the difference between the dream world and the real world?"

because they are *objective*, emotionally engaging *facts*, obviously not produced by the person's consciousness, nor by "social agencies", nor much less by a "censor". In this age of consumption and radical alienation, Baudrillard (1970/1998) affirmed that the individual is no longer confronted with her own split image, with the contradiction within being—ever. As this work will show, dreams confront the dreamers precisely with that: their alienation, commodification, and contradictions—with themselves and with culture. Providing an objective perspective on both the individual and the social, night dreams can reveal the functioning and impact of the consumerist regimes of signification, their imaginaries, and their colonization of subjectivity. Furthermore, they reveal a confrontation, or sort of *clash*, of the consumerist imaginary with the natural, unconscious imaginary function. That clash, seen in the *symbolic* oneiric reactions, unveils the logic and dehumanizing effects of consumerism with almost incredible acumen, deep irony, and at times profound emotionality. To understand the origins of such knowledge implies rescuing the concept of dream as a "messenger of the gods", the purest expression and origin of the truly symbolic imaginary, buried by signs in our culture. Against the dissolution of all symbols into commodity-signs, in dreams the psyche still produces symbols, unimpeded by the colonialist ImCon; for dreams are the connecting channels to our lost symbolizing faculty,[20] expressions of the very *foundations* of the psyche. From Jung's viewpoint—based on an age-old, ubiquitous tradition—the dream theoretically allows one to know what Arendt (1958, p. ix) called the "subterranean stream", not of tradition, but of the psyche.

1.2.2 Why Night Dreams with McDonald's, Disney, and Shopping Malls?

The night dreams used as empirical data had to focus on certain scenarios, or what I called *dreamscapes* of consumerism. Based on the prototype dream, and also for a number of other reasons which are discussed at length in the chapter on Method, such scenarios were eventually reduced

[20] "Dreams are the commonest and universally accessible source for the investigation of man's symbolizing faculty" (Jung, CW18, §431).

to three types of dreamscapes: McDonald's, Disneyland and Disney parks,[21] and shopping malls and other iconic department stores. They appear in all the night dreams analyzed here.[22] The fundamental reason for such choice is that such scenarios represent and signify *dream-worlds of consumption*[23] (Benjamin, 1999; Buck-Morss, 1989, 2000; Williams, 1991) made of consumption dreams: they appear as *symbols of the ImCon* globally and, as in the prototype dream, also in night dreams spontaneously produced by the unconscious.

What characterizes them—to varying degrees, Disney and Disneyland probably being the apex, the most radical instance—in general is: they are producers, circulators, and embodiments of regimes of signification that form the ImCon; they represent the *signifying structures* of consumption society and its totalizing imaginary, its *temples of consumption.*[24] Disney and McDonald's being among the most influential and powerful global megacorporations, and shopping centers being the defining edifices of consumer society, they are seen worldwide as the great icons of consumerism, condensing its ideology, functioning, and logic—so much so as to have been studied sociologically as its typical forms of *colonization*: under McDonaldization, and also *Disneyization* (Bryman, 1999, 2003, 2004a; Cypher & Riggs, 2001; Ross, 2004; Wasko, 2001). Albeit seen as forms of *globalitarian* (Virilio, 2001) colonization, they are typically American in origin[25] (which is an important fact for, apart from

[21] Henceforth I employ "Disneyland" meaning Disney thematic parks in general.

[22] With the exception of one dream, a "special" dream in which the whole *city* seems to function as a shopping mall. Also, in two dreams (including the prototypical dream), they are not exactly the oneiric *scenarios*; rather they constitute one of the dream's main *themes*, even though the oneiric drama is not staged within them. Some other night dreams that do not have to do with the ImCon or such dreamscapes were also analyzed as comparative material; they present symbolic images that are similar, or analogous in meaning, to the night dreams of consumption, and therefore allowed for clarifying the interpretations of the latter.

[23] The concepts of "dream-world" and "temple of consumption" originated in Walter Benjamin's (1999) seminal work, *The Arcades Project*.

[24] "If the Gothic cathedral was the symbolic structure of the feudal era, and the factory [that] of the industrial [era], the distinct structures of today are cultural sites or theme parks like (…) Disneyland, and the carnivals of consumption—the shopping malls" (Langman, 1992, p. 41).

[25] In the case of shopping malls, which have arguably originated in European world fairs and arcades (see Rosalind H. Williams, 1991), they are *perceived* as, and have come to be, typically American. I employ the term "American" throughout this work with the sense of "from the USA"; because it is the standard English usage, and for being more convenient (as a simple and concise

the prototype dream's dreamer, a Brazilian, all the other dreams studied in this work came from American dreamers).

Most importantly for this work—and most radically in the case of Disneyland—such dreamscapes are cultural icons and embodiments of a *totalizing imaginary*: a hyperreality of consumption which progressively becomes the hegemonic form of imagination, apperception of world and self, and experience, and as such strives for hegemony in the production and control of subjectivity itself. They are the actualization (either concrete or virtual, imaginary) of a commodified culture within commodified, self-contained environments: commercial worlds made of consumption dreams, the dream-worlds of consumption. *And are so perceived by the unconscious, in the night dreams it produces.*

1.3 Research Question and Aims

The research problem, formulated as a question, would be:

How do the night dreams represent the colonization of subjectivity by the imaginary of consumerism?

Given the general panorama of the themes of study under consideration presented above, the peculiarities of this study's empirical object, and its exploratory character, thus its main objective consists in *exploring how night dreams represent the colonization of subjectivity by the imaginary of consumerism.*

Such general exploration is informed by, and aims at fulfilling, a set of *specific objectives* centered upon hermeneutic-interpretative procedures. Thus the specific aims consist in *identifying, interpreting, and understanding patterns in meaning* in the night dreams, regarding:

1. *which* psychological factors, domains, or realms are colonized;
2. *how* such colonization is effectuated; and
3. the *effects* brought about by such colonization.

---

form of referring to the US). Being South American myself, I am aware of the politically correct controversy regarding this.

These central aims, focused upon the empirical material, imply three further *specific objectives* of a more theoretical and epistemological character:

4. To advance theoretical propositions, informed by a theoretical framework, so as to understand the patterns in meaning identified;
5. To recover the importance of dreams for psychosocial analyses of reality and subjectivity;
6. To illustrate how the Jungian symbolic-hermeneutic method, applied to dreams, can be valuable for psychosocial analyses, and to indicate further possible research.

Meeting such objectives entailed the development of an eminently qualitative and exploratory methodological design, consisting in a *multiple-case study* whose empirical data were night dreams. The dreams were collected from various sources (but mainly volunteered on the internet, as dream series, to non-clinical settings) and selected according to their relevance, meaningfulness, and information-richness (Patton, 1990). Each dream was considered as a case study, or "critical case" (Putney, 2010), and interpreted through Jungian symbolic hermeneutics. The process of interpretation and theory-generation followed a hypothetico-deductive approach.

1.4 Risks, Brief Literature Review, and Relevance

The main fact underlying the discussion of possible risks, limitations, and relevance of this work is that, to my knowledge, there seems to be no other previous study like it in the literature. That makes this work *original*, yet also risky and necessarily preliminary and exploratory. Broadly speaking, perhaps the greatest risk derives from the fact that I could not possibly follow a *model* previously done, and so had to build new arguments, procedures, and structures for this work. In what follows I briefly discuss some other risks and present a very short literature review, discussing some studies that are close to this work in their thematic focuses of research but also dissimilar in important aspects (their theoretical and/or empirical approaches); the objective is to place this study in the context of other works and highlight its original features.

1.4.1 Risks

First of all, regarding the empirical procedures and data, researching night dreams with a deeply qualitative, hermeneutic approach involves many difficulties and risks. A discussion on this work's methodological and empirical (practical) difficulties and limitations can be found in the chapter on Method. Dreams, by their very nature,[26] can be exceedingly complex and ample in their themes and meanings, elusive and ambiguous in their discourse, and seem utterly alien to most readers. Understanding them in depth, or even proposing cogent interpretations, depends on a multiplicity of factors and often represents a quite difficult task. Due to their symbolic nature, it is often rather difficult to delimit very clearly, in terms of strictly defined concepts, what subjective factors and realms the dreams are alluding to. This is one of the main reasons for formulating the more empirical specific aims of this study with the expression "patterns in *meaning*"—because dreams usually do not refer directly to the dreamer's "unconscious psyche" or "personal identity", for instance; these are interpretations and translations of symbolic images (such as "the underground" or "what is hidden and buried", and "house", respectively) into psychological concepts, translations that, by definition (*traduttori traditori!*), should be viewed as somewhat forced and incomplete in relation to the original dream symbol, but which are necessary for discussing the dreams rationally. Furthermore, the interpretations proposed for the dreams are always hypothetical (though far from arbitrary) and *not exhaustive*. Although I have tried to select the dream-specimens that seemed most clear, meaningful, and representative of the phenomena studied here, and to interpret them in depth and in a clear manner, there remains the risk that such selection and interpretations could be problematic, or inappropriate, or incomplete. That risk also refers to

[26] As Meier (1987, p. x) asserts, "there is hardly a more complex feature of the human psyche than the dream".

another context: the majority of dreams analyzed here were selected because of their typical (at times archetypical) images, rather than due to their detailed portrayal of the dreamer's subjectivity. Quite the opposite: although "subjectivity" is one of the main themes of this work, the dreams that could be interpreted without mentioning many personal details from the dreamers were preferred. Thus the focus of analysis is the *dream* and what it represents (in terms of subjectivity, colonization, etc.), rather than the individual dreamer. Accordingly, some dreams were chosen because of their *cultural* critique on colonization (and consumerism); their main focus was not on subjectivity per se.

Regarding theory-building and theoretical discussions of subjectivity, clearly, the more theoretical themes of this work (consumerism, imaginary, and subjectivity) are exceedingly broad in scope and complexity, which makes it risky to interrelate them in a concise manner while at the same time connecting them to the other research subjects (dreams, night dreams, unconscious, symbol, etc.). Also, it is always difficult to discuss subjectivity, this all-encompassing, elusive and (in our postmodern mass society) contradictory, controversial, salable concept—and even more so if one attempts to discuss it from the perspective of night dreams. As mentioned above, as the focus of analysis is the *dream*, the reader will notice that often there are only a few mentions to personal, individual aspects of the dreamer's life and its subjective details. This was done on purpose; discussion in depth of such details would require clinical cases and long elaborations, which was not possible within the limits of this work. Moreover, this proposal is complicated further by the fact that, strictly speaking, the findings cannot be compared with previous studies (only with other studies that have utilized night dreams to research subjectivity, and more generally with theory and research on subjectivity under contemporary consumerism). Considering such difficulties, this work runs the risk of being considered simplistic or superficial, given the amplitude of its subjects, and controversial or debatable, given the concise and general way it discusses subjectivity.

Another problem is the *sociocultural context* of the dreamers, which is, of course, of the utmost importance regarding both their subjectivities *and* the dreams they produced. As mentioned, all empirical dreams studied in this work were reported by dreamers from the United States, with the exception of the prototype dream, by a Brazilian. Unfortunately, it was not possible to develop extensive theoretical discussions of specific American (or Brazilian) consumerist imaginaries due to the limits of this work. However, as this research proposes to study both subjectivity and the ImCon (in whatever forms it may assume) through *night dreams*, the theoretical discussion offered on both themes is indeed general and based on what *the dreams* presented. Furthermore, this work does not claim any kind of statistical generalizability; generalization is limited to the theoretical level.[27] Therefore, if it is probably true that the United States represents the most "consumer-oriented society in the world" (Schor, 2004, p. 9), the reader should bear in mind that the majority of the dreams presented here come from such society. Nevertheless, the reader should also consider the perspective that the ImCon—like (and through) globalized capital and media—is increasingly global and total, that is, whether American in origin or not, it represents a global sociocultural context that is increasingly homogeneous, and that the dreamscapes studied here (McDonald's, Disney, shopping malls) are obviously global. Moreover, some dreams from dreamers coming from (in principle) different sociocultural contexts (United States, Brazil, Finland, Italy) portrayed and criticized colonization by the ImCon with great similitude. That the colonizing force of consumerism appeared in more or less the same ways in the dreams (whatever the more specific sociocultural conditions of the dreamers) gives support to the view that consumerism and its imaginary are essentially a global and *increasingly homogeneous* force, and that, for the purposes of this work, particular sociocultural contexts can be disregarded.

1.4.2 Brief Literature Review

Consumption dreams: There is some volume of literature (e.g., Bryce & Olney, 1991; D'Astous & Deschênes, 2005; Fournier & Guiry, 1993; Gabriel & Lang, 2006; McCracken, 1988) that theorized on and/or investigated "consumption dreams", predominantly from the (uncritical)

[27] Questions of generalizability related to this are also discussed in Chap. 6, on Method.

perspective of consumer research.[28] In it, "consumption dreams" refer variously to fantasies, desires, daydreams, the "ideal life": the "dreams" consumers have about goods and experiences, and their relations with or foundation upon the imagination (Belk, Ger, & Askergaard, 1996, 2003; Christensen, 2002).

In Brazil, there seems to be a variety of studies on "sonhos de consumo" from diverse perspectives and scientific fields (probably because in Brazil such expression is very common—it is an important part of the imaginary, of collective consciousness). Particularly relevant for this work is a line of research on consumerism and its imaginary that is more critical and draws from the more contemporary French sociological tradition (Baudrillard, Maffesoli, etc.) and anthropology. For instance, Piedras (2006, 2007) and Rocha (1990, 1995, 2006) discussed the consumer imaginary focusing on its "consumption dreams", their mythic, mystic character, and their fabrication by the advertising industry and mass media—through concepts such as "dream society" (a concept analogous to what I call *ImCon*), "magic capitalism", "the mythology of consumption". However, *none* of these studies on "consumption dreams" researched night dreams.

Night dreams: Although there are some (relatively scarce) publications and studies on night dreams that employed hermeneutics[29] and/or the perspective of analytical psychology,[30] the vast majority of literature is dominated by neurobiological and psychiatric perspectives (which almost never employ symbolic-hermeneutic approaches), followed by psychoanalysis under its many schools and methods. For comprehensible reviews on the study of dreams in psychiatry, see Hebbrecht (2007) and Reiser (2001); for a review on the contemporary psychoanalytic approaches to dream, see Flanders (1993); for an extensive review on multiple contemporary approaches to dream, see Shafton (1995). However, as regards proximity in terms of method and approach toward night dreams, some

[28] I found very little literature in Spanish and Italian.

[29] See, e.g., *Dreaming: Journal for the Association of the Study of Dreams*, at http://www.asdreams.org/asdj03.htm (with full list of abstracts across 20 years of publications; only few articles employed hermeneutics, though).

[30] See, e.g., the *Journal of Analytical Psychology* (with more than 200 articles on dreams) at http://onlinelibrary.wiley.com/journal/10.1111/(ISSN)1468-5922

anthropological studies are more relevant for this work. Two of them seem indeed closer to what is proposed in this study. One work that deserves to be highlighted is the classic one by Duvignaud, Duvignaud, and Corbeau (1981), who proposed to revisit what they called the infinite world of the *imaginary* through dreams, trying to search for and give voice to such "lost languages" in an extensive research. In order to understand the dreams, they utilized a double focus that prioritized and converged in the majoritarian role of the *social*: how the social acts in the dream and gives meaning and logic to it; and how the dream is a (meaningful) part of the social imaginary. In Brazil, a similar approach appears in a number of studies on the oneiric imaginary organized by Martins (1996). Again, these studies did not employ symbolic interpretations, but rather a sociological approach focusing on the concepts of "daily life" and the city (which often did not really apply, empirically, to the dreams[31]). In my opinion, both works, albeit interesting and valuable, fall short in their task of deeply understanding the dreams, mainly because they do not employ a truly symbolic-hermeneutic approach in conjunction with a consistent theory on the unconscious; the result is that they often forcefully reduce the dreams to their presumable "social" aspects and meanings.

Night dreams and the imaginary: After searching for a long time, I found *one* doctoral dissertation that closely resembled the present one in its proposal: it researched the sociocultural imaginary, in relation to its religious aspects, through the night dreams of university students. Espinosa (2009) reached some results that were similar to the ones found in this work; for instance, "although now one would think that myth is no longer dreamed, on the contrary, it keeps manifesting itself in the nocturnal imagination under many guises, one of which seems to be totally approached by the media" (p. 89; i.e., by the ImCon through mass media). However, his analysis is limited to a content analysis of the dreams, restricted to describing their recurrent images in a non-symbolic way.

[31] To give one example of a dream discussed in such work: an upper-middle-class worker dreamed he was a medieval knight, fully clad with armor; he then kills his co-workers in a fit of rage. That the image of a medieval knight could be seen as pertaining to "daily life" (when it is obviously its very *opposite*) demonstrates the forceful, reductive character of such interpretations (i.e., at times they impose a theory upon the dream, thereby mutilating its image and hence its meaning).

Night dreams and colonization: Marc Augé's (1999) *The war of dreams* is without a doubt the work that is closest to this study, especially as regards to Augé's themes (the interrelations between night dreams, imaginary, colonization, and contemporaneity) and his critical view. Augé argues that, historically, processes of colonization have always involved and required struggles for the conquest and domination of the imaginary (of the colonized); through "cultural contact", anthropologists have observed

> how *confrontations of the imaginary* accompanied the clash of nations, conquests and colonisations, and how *resistances*, withdrawals and hopes took shape in the imagination of the vanquished for all that it was lastingly affected by, and in the strict sense imprinted with, that of the victors. (p. 5; e.a.)

In that, Augé draws from the work of Gruzinski (1990), who convincingly showed that, from the sixteenth century onwards, Catholic and European brutal colonizing efforts toward indigenous populations were inevitably accompanied by the *colonization of their imaginaries* (Gruzinski, 1988), a battle for the conquest of their mentalities in a *war of images*.

Augé (1999) demonstrates that, in our contemporaneity, what he calls a *war of dreams* is a crucial part of such battles for the colonization of imagination: through ethnographic materials, he shows how dreams revealed the people's colonization and domination by the foreign colonial power's imaginary. Dreams thereby signaled that the intermingled processes of colonization (of the people and of their dreams) represented the threat of effacement of the people's imaginary, which could actually mean their very *extinction* as a people. However, although he considers the dream as a form of individual imagination (p. 6), Augé deals with and speaks in terms of *peoples*, of collective imagination, and unfortunately does not employ a systematic, hermeneutic interpretation of dreams. My proposal here is to use such method to investigate essentially the same phenomena Augé describes anthropologically—but in the individual nocturnal imaginary, in the pure autonomous productions of the subject's unconscious psyche: the dream, and its resistances, its confrontation, its clashes with the overwhelming global colonization effected by the ImCon.

Apropos of historical colonization of peoples, of their imaginaries, and dreams, Jung (CW10) also mentioned phenomena similar to those related by Augé. Speaking of African primitives (the Elgonyi, ruled by British colonizers) who he had visited in the 1920s, Jung reported how the dominating power (the British) depended on *colonization* and conquest of the Elgonyi's culture and knowledge, and therefore of the *imaginary* that sustained both. In the case of the Elgonyi, such colonization was not merely of their dreams, but of their very *capability of dreaming*[32]: their unconscious psyche had been colonized.

Night dreams and consumerism: Empirical explorations of night dreams in relation to consumerism are noticeably lacking. I found only *one* academic work similar to what I propose here: Valtonen (2011) set out to study dreaming in consumer culture, but from a completely opposite viewpoint in relation to mine. He posits the existence of what is hereby called "colonization" of dreams (and subjectivity) by the ImCon as a fact, but *naturalizes* it altogether. In his view, market discourses and practices govern *also* the sleeping life of consumers, the world of dreams: "both the content of dreams and the way dreams are conceived are shaped and structured by the practices, values, and symbols offered by the globalized media and consumer culture" (p. 93). Although the dreams he studied clearly reveal the criticism of the unconscious,[33] he invariably overlooks it. Mirroring and affirming the ideology of consumerism, he inverts the relationship proposed here and takes total colonization (of subject, psyche, and dreams) for granted: it is not that consumption is sold as and through (artificial) dreams, but that the *dream itself is a form of consumption* (which he calls "dreamtertainment"): "a set of images, thoughts,

[32] "Our Elgonyi porters maintained in all seriousness that they never had dreams—only the medicine-man had them. When I questioned the medicine-man, he declared that he had stopped having dreams when the British entered the land. His father had still had 'big' dreams, he told me, and had known where the herds strayed (…) and when there was going to be a war or a pestilence. *It was now the District Commissioner who knew everything, and they knew nothing.* (…) God now speaks in dreams to the British, and not to the medicine-man of the Elgonyi, he told me, because it is the British who have the power. Dream activity has emigrated" (Jung, CW10, §128; e.a.).

[33] Not surprisingly, the first dream he presents, from a Finnish man, has McDonald's as its scenery (dreamscape). In the dream, *nothing works* in the McDonald's (which is actually a recurring theme in such dreams): "the *system* was not working, not at all" (p. 103), there is anger and perplexity, the price is abusive; but all of that is considered irrelevant: what matters is that the dreamer was being a regular consumer even while sleeping.

sounds, emotions, illusions, fantasies, memories, and irrational experiences pass through consumers' minds having the power to bewilder, frighten, enchant, and amuse them—*just like many other forms of consumption*" (p. 94, e.a.). In fact, the title of his study says it all: "*We dream as we live*—Consuming": we really ought to be consumers 24-7 in a "New Sleep Order".

1.4.3 Relevance

As delineated above, through the brief literature review, one of the main sources of relevance for this work is that it is probably *unique* (at least in some regards). Some main aspects related to the relevance of studying dreams were discussed above, together with the justifications for their study. It seems clear that studies on night dreams, and even on dreams in general (including consumption dreams), are lacking in social psychology. Therefore this work can also be relevant in that it calls attention to a rather unexplored subject (and field of studies). Also, this study combines an interdisciplinary theoretical approach with a symbolic-hermeneutic perspective and method, which seems uncommon in social psychology. All of such possible relevant features—dreams, interdisciplinarity, symbolic-hermeneutic approach—coalesce in the centrality of Jung's analytical psychology for this work; it is the common source for all of them. Its possible relevance is discussed in what follows.

Relevance of employing analytical psychology as theoretical framework: One reason for its relevance is that, in social psychology and in the social sciences in general, studies using the perspective of analytical psychology are rather rare. Another reason refers to the unique perspective it provides for the study of the imaginary, dreams, subjectivity, and consumer culture.

From such perspective, the "imaginary" is the condensation of forms—images, representations, symbols—through which we imagine, fantasize about, perceive, represent, make sense of, and signify ourselves and the world (i.e., both the inner and the outer world). It corresponds to our *psychic reality*. In Jung, the primordial forms of imagination configure *symbolic thought*, which is the imaginary function *par excellence*. It has its roots in the unconscious, which is the rhizome of everything psychological. Dreams are seen as the primordial and purest expressions of symbolic thought, and hence of the unconscious. Therefore, analyzing dreams means rescuing and trying to understand what such historical roots express symbolically about the subject's psyche in a contemporary consumerist world characterized by relentless *colonization* of everything that is symbolic and psychological—that is, by the colonization of the rhizome itself, in every individual. If such colonization characterizes a cultural and anthropological mutation—a new regime of the imaginary and a new subject—in order to illuminate it, we need a theoretical perspective that is founded on such rhizome; a psychology that is characterized by the consideration, import, and value it gives to the symbolic, oneiric, and religious factors—the imaginary—in understanding culture, psychic functioning, and subjectivity. Moreover, in order to interpret and understand the dreams, we need a hermeneutic-symbolic approach based precisely on a truly symbolic psychology. We find such perspective and approach in Jung's analytical psychology, its hermeneutics, and in the vast interdisciplinary dialogs that it offers.

Jungian theory on the unconscious and subjectivity therefore underlies the whole theoretical outlook of this work, and furnishes its hermeneutics. The main relevance of such proposal consists in an attempt at rescuing for (and applying in) social psychology an original depth psychology and a concept of unconscious that are truly humanistic and symbolic. Put very concisely, and to situate it within the tradition of social psychology, such depth psychology consists in a kind of complex *symbolic interactionism*—one that at once expands and integrates the two main paradigmatic tendencies of such perspective, the schools of Chicago and Iowa. Herbert Blumer, the main exponent of the Chicago school, represents a phenomenological approach that focuses more on the role of the *subject* as a symbolizing actor—on his/her interpretative processes and interaction with other social actors—and less on the social macrostructures. The Iowa school, whose main representative is Sheldon Stryker, represents a structural symbolic interactionism that privileges the more *objective* macrostructures of social reality and the *external* processes of signification within which the self, or subjectivity, is built (Álvaro & Garrido, 2003; Álvaro, Garrido, Schweiger, & Torregrosa, 2007; Blanch, 1982; Carvalho,

Borges, & Rêgo, 2010). Thus, Jungian depth psychology may be understood firstly as a reunion of such paradigmatic tendencies, in a dialectical perspective that gives equal importance to the structuring force of the social (viewed as collective consciousness) and to the subjective (and *individual*) interpretative and meaning-creating capabilities for the construction of subjectivity. Secondly, and most importantly, what differentiates such perspective is its humanist concept of unconscious: within the dialectics between the subject and the sociocultural realm is inserted an *objective* factor, the unconscious psyche, which is seen as the original foundation and common denominator of both. Moreover, such foundation is the very historical matrix that produces symbols—and thus signification—autonomously in each person. Therefore, and to use a Bakhtinian term, such depth psychology postulates that the psyche is *dialogical*: in relation to both the social, "external" relationships, *and* to the inner psychic world, to the relations with one's own unconscious contents—to the historical *Others*, as it were, within one's own psyche. It represents a radical symbolic interactionism in which the symbol is the very definer of what is human.

Finally, such depth psychology also represented one of the main basis and impulses for the development of the whole school of the *imaginary*—from the early beginnings, with G. Durand, reaching today, with Maffesoli and others. However, in my opinion, Jung's analytical psychology has been misunderstood and/or misrepresented to a large extent.[34] That is why I propose to discuss his contributions through his original works (and of close collaborators) and with extensive quotations, in order to convey his original thought and, whenever possible and convenient, to rescue theories and authors that formed his thought and have been forgotten by official, mainstream psychology.

To return to the import of dreams: this proposal to study night dreams in social psychology can also be seen as *subversive*—it means trying to study the social in a moment that is almost entirely personal, private, individual, when the person is "alone with herself" (and alone with her

[34] For example, today's hegemonic tendency of assessing and classifying Jung's analytical psychology as a school of psychoanalysis. It is not only very different from psychoanalysis, but its *antipode* in many aspects (starting with its paradigm).

self); it is a completely *imaginary* moment, when psychic life naturally flows unimpeded and *unmediated.* In fact, *the dream itself is by nature subversive* and opposed to any domination: "by definition it eludes the control of the dreamers and *a fortiori* the control of those who are officially responsible for their souls" (Augé, 1999, p. 59)—or of those who want to buy and sell our souls. Researching dreams also represents a much-needed complementation for the current hegemony of studies on "everyday life", which is increasingly organized and ruled by the consumerist ethos—a complementation reached through a shift to researching what we may call the every *night, unconscious* life, the "nocturnal depth of our being" (Von Schubert, 1814).[35]

In uniting the perspective of a deep psychology of the unconscious with a psychosociological critique of capitalism, this work attempts to deepen our understanding of the relationship between consumer capitalism and psychology—though not in the sense of criticizing psychology as a dispositive of power (as in Parker, 2007; Roberts, 2015) or "psychological governance" (Pykett, Jones, & Whitehead, 2017). Rather, it strives to illuminate the profound colonization of our (unconscious) psyches effected by consumerism and to reveal that such colonization is simply the basis upon which the latter is founded. In that regard, this work also tries to revitalize and see anew that old bridge between sociology and psychology—notably in considering how relationships between the unconscious, the symbolic realm, and social and economic structures and institutions are constituted under consumerism.

But perhaps all the possibly relevant aspects of this work and their relation with our society can be summarized through a comparison with a quote. In it, Mark Featherstone (2010) expressed perfectly the context of contemporary consumerism and one of the main challenges it poses us:

> [W]e must seek out the fragments of human significance able to escape from the logic of commodification, and the black hole of the market, and try to save them for some future reconstruction project that, similar to Walter Benjamin (1999), who engaged in the construction of what the Frankfurt critical theorists called a thought-image of modern consumer

---

[35] As quoted in English by Meier (1987, p. 79).

> capitalism, may enable us to piece together a serious critical theory of post-modern global capitalism and the horrendous post-political situation we currently occupy. (…) The problem of critical theory today, then, revolves around the problem of the totalitarian or globalitarian nature of neoliberal capitalism and the omnipotence of the logic of commodification which has effectively colonized the space of critique and critical thought. (p. 141)

What I propose is that such "fragments of human significance" can be found in the dreams. In our present dream-world of consumption, where everything seems to be unreal or more-than-real and devoid of value, the night dream is precisely *the living element that presents real significance and value*. Dreams not only escape but *denounce* such "omnipotent logic of commodification", *reveal* how its colonization is effected, and therefore constitute the expression of a psychic domain that *refuses* to be colonized—and for such reasons they must be rescued and understood. For that, I have attempted to present a modest composite of *dream-images* (*Traumbilder*) of total consumer capitalism, a small *anthropology* of the dreams and "nightmares that haunt *Homo consumens*" (Bauman, 2007a, p. 99). So let us look at what the subterranean stream of these persons' psyches has to tell us….

1.5 Book Overview

The structure of this work reflects the theoretical expectation, derived from what the night dreams revealed, that the imaginary of consumerism represents a historical mutation and a colonizing force (in relation to other imaginaries, subjectivity, and dreams); therefore it conflates and compares two imaginaries and two concepts of dream. The argument is: if there is colonization—or a mutation—then we need two distinct historical and cultural perspectives, so as to distinguish or point at differences, at what is/has been colonized. Or, in more simple terms, how it is "without", or before, colonization, and after, under colonization.

Thus the Part I of this study, presenting its theoretical framework, consists of two blocks. The first block, comprising the first two chapters, offers a general theoretical basis for the whole dissertation, which is grounded on C. G. Jung's analytical psychology. It explores the idea of social imaginaries (Durand, 1963, 1994, 1996, 2004; Taylor, 2004) as being historically and culturally *symbolic*, originally founded upon the unconscious psyche, and naturally connected to the world of dreams. The discussion aims at situating the reader in relation to analytical psychology and its concepts, yet it also draws upon anthropological, sociological, and ethnological arguments and literature. Chapter 2 explores the concept of symbolic imaginaries, a psychology of the unconscious and its symbolic and imaginative function, and their relations with subjectivity. Chapter 3 provides a general theoretical discussion on dreams and their relations with the symbolic imaginary, and on how both dreams and imaginary are related to and configure subjectivity.

The second block consists of Chaps. 4–6 and provides theoretical reflections on the concepts of imaginary of consumption (ImCon) and consumption dreams and their relations with subjectivity and its colonization. It shall clarify the ethico-political stance assumed by this work. While drawing from a broad array of authors from distinct fields of academia, its main theoretical reference is Jean Baudrillard's work on consumer society and consumption. Thus this block is aimed at presenting these authors' main contributions on such themes, but seen from and adapted to the viewpoint of the concept of social imaginary, and in dialog with the psychological perspective outlined in the first block. An important warning for the reader is that this whole second block (but especially Chap. 5) should be viewed in the tradition of *ideal type*[36] theoretical discussions: as ideal models that describe not only facts, but also possibilities and tendencies.

Chapter 4 focuses on the discussion of the ImCon as a semiotic imaginary, its logic and characteristics, and its difference in relation to symbolic imaginaries. Consumption logic and a theory on the commodity-sign as the main concepts for the understanding of consumerism are presented. Consumerism and its social imaginary are analyzed through the concept of *dream*, focusing on the idea of consumption dreams. Finally, the chapter

[36] Todorov (2002) presents a concise definition of the concept: "El tipo ideal: así se designa, desde Max Weber, la construcción de un modelo destinado a hacer más inteligible lo real, sin que por ello sea necesario poder observar su encarnación perfecta en la Historia. El tipo ideal indica un horizonte, una perspectiva, una tendencia. Los hechos empíricamente observables lo ilustran en un grado más o menos alto, todos sus rasgos constitutivos se encuentran en él, o sólo algunos, a lo largo de todo un período histórico o sólo en una de sus partes, y así sucesivamente" (p. 18).

discusses how the ImCon and its dreams define and colonize subjectivity, and the possible effects of such processes.

Chapter 5 discusses the idea that the ImCon may function as a simulacrum of symbolico-religious imaginary, a totalizing ideology. Walter Benjamin's concept of dream-world of consumption is employed to discuss the ImCon as a hyperreality. The chapter closes with the discussion of a possible colonization of the unconscious psyche by the imaginary, and how it seeks to institute the subject as a commodity.

Finally, Chap. 6 explores the *dreamscapes*—the scenarios of the night dreams interpreted in this research—as dream-worlds of consumption, discussing how they symbolize particular aspects of the ImCon and its typical forms of colonization of culture and subjectivity, in a dialog with the sociological theories of McDonaldization and Disneyization.

Part II is dedicated to the empirical section of this work and comprises Chaps. 7–11. Chapter 7, on Method, describes the qualitative design and methodology employed in this research, and offers a general discussion on Jungian symbolic hermeneutics, which grounded its processes of interpretation and theory-generation. Chapters 8–11 are dedicated to presenting the findings of this study through the interpretation and discussion of its empirical material: the night dreams, focusing on how subjectivity appears colonized in them, how consumer culture seems to be criticized by them, and the general implications that they seem to show in relation to both subjects and culture.

Finally, the book closes with the Conclusions of this study, which present a condensation and articulation of its major findings in relation to the main research aims proposed and discuss some of their main implications. The chapter is concluded with a discussion of the limitations of this work and offers brief recommendations and suggestions for future research.

References

Allott, P. (2002). *The health of nations: Society and law beyond the state*. Cambridge: Cambridge University Press.

Álvaro, J. L., & Garrido, A. (2003). *Psicología social: perspectivas psicológicas y sociológicas*. Madrid: McGraw Hill.

Álvaro, J. L., Garrido, A., Schweiger, I., & Torregrosa, J. R. (2007). *Introducción a la psicología social sociológica*. Barcelona: Editorial UOC.

Arendt, H. (1958). *The origins of totalitarianism* (2nd ed.). New York: Meridian Books.

Augé, M. (1999). *The war of dreams: exercises in ethno-fiction* (L. Heron, Trans.). London: Pluto Press.

Barber, B. (1995). *Jihad vs McWorld*. New York: Crown.

Baudrillard, J. (1983a). *Simulations*. New York: Semiotext(e).

Baudrillard, J. (1983b). *In the shadow of the silent majorities*. New York: Semiotext(e).

Baudrillard, J. (1996). *The system of objects* (J. Benedict, Trans.). London: Verso. (Original work published 1968).

Baudrillard, J. (1998). *The consumer society: Myths and structures*. London: Sage. (Original work published 1970).

Bauman, Z. (2007a). *Consuming life*. Cambridge: Polity Press.

Bauman, Z. (2007b). Exit *Homo Politicus*, enter *Homo Consumens*. In K. Soper & F. Trentmann (Eds.), *Citizenship and consumption* (pp. 139–153). Hampshire, UK: Palgrave Macmillan.

Bauman, Z., & Tester, K. (2001). *Conversations with Zygmunt Bauman*. Cambridge: Polity.

Belk, R. W., Ger, G., & Askergaard, S. (1996). Metaphors of consumer desire. *Advances in Consumer Research, 23*, 368–373.

Belk, R. W., Ger, G., & Askegaard, S. (2003). The fire of desire: A multisited inquiry into consumer passion. *Journal of Consumer Research, 30*, 326–351.

Benjamin, W. (1999). *The arcades project* (H. Eiland & K. McLaughlin, Trans.). Cambridge: The Belknap Press of Harvard University Press.

Bergson, H. (1919). *L'enérgie spirituelle. Essais et conférences*. Retrieved from http://classiques.uqac.ca/classiques/bergson_henri/energie_spirituelle/energie_spirituelle.html

Blanch, J. M. (1982). *Psicologías sociales: Aproximación histórica*. Barcelona: Hora.

Blanch, J. M., & Cantera, L. (2007a). El *capitalismo sanitario* como factor de riesgo psicosocial. In C. Guillén & R. Guil (Orgs.), *Psicología social: un encuentro de perspectivas* (Vol. 1, pp. 1075–1080). Cádiz: APPS.

Blanch, J. M., & Cantera, L. (2007b). Efectos colaterales del capitalismo académico. In FES (Org.), *IX Congreso Español de Sociología: Poder, Cultura y Civilización*. Comunicaciones orales sobre sociopsicología del trabajo y de la organización (pp. 12–29). Barcelona: FES.

Blanch, J. M., & Cantera, L. (2011). La nueva gestión pública de universidades y hospitales. Aplicaciones e implicaciones. In E. Agulló, J. L. Álvaro, A. Garrido, R. Medina, & I. Schweiger (Eds.), *Nuevas formas de organización del trabajo y la empleabilidad* (pp. 515–534). Oviedo: Ediuno.

Blanch, J. M., & Stecher, A. (2009). La empresarización de servicios públicos y sus efectos colaterales. Implicaciones psicosociales de la colonización de universidades y hospitales por la cultura del nuevo capitalismo. In T. Wittke & P. Melogno (Eds.), *Psicología y organización del Trabajo: Producción de subjetividad en la organización del trabajo* (pp. 191–209). Montevideo: Psicolibros.

Bourdieu, P. (1984). *Distinction: A social critique of the judgment of taste* (R. Nice, Trans.). London: Routledge & Kegan Paul.

Bryce, W., & Olney, T. (1991). Gender differences in consumption aspirations: A cross-cultural appraisal. *Social Behavior and Personality, 19*(4), 237–254.

Bryman, A. (1999). The Disneyization of society. *Sociological Review, 47*, 25–47.

Bryman, A. (2003). McDonald's as a Disneyized institution: Global implications. *American Behavioral Scientist, 47*(2), 154–167.

Bryman, A. (2004a). Disneyization. *Encyclopedia of social theory*. London: Sage. Retrieved from http://www.sageereference.com/socialtheory/Article_n81.html

Bryman, A. (2004b). McDonaldization. *Encyclopedia of social theory*. London: Sage. Retrieved from http://www.sage-ereference.com/socialtheory/Article_n187.html

Buck-Morss, S. (1989). *The dialectics of seeing: Walter Benjamin and the Arcades Project*. Cambridge, MA: MIT.

Buck-Morss, S. (2000). *Dreamworld and catastrophe: The passing of mass utopia in East and West*. Cambridge, MA: MIT.

Carvalho, V. D., Borges, L. O., & Rêgo, D. P. (2010). Interacionismo simbólico: origens, pressupostos e contribuições aos estudos em Psicologia Social. *Psicologia ciência e profissão, 30*(1), 146–161.

Castoriadis, C. (1997). The "rationality" of capitalism. In *Figures of the unthinkable* (pp. 81–122). Stanford, CA: Stanford University Press. Retrieved from http://www.costis.org/x/castoriadis/Castoriadis-Figures_of_the_Thinkable.pdf

Christensen, G. (2002). *Mental simulations, anticipations, and dreams: Toward a theory of consumption visions in consumer behaviour*. Unpublished doctoral dissertation, Pennsylvania State University, State College, US.

Clarke, S. (2005). The neoliberal theory of society. In A. Saad-Filho & D. Johnston (Eds.), *Neoliberalism: A critical reader* (pp. 50–59). London: Pluto Press.

Cypher, J., & Riggs, E. (2001). Colonizing the imagination: Disney's wilderness lodge. *Critical Studies, 21*, 403–423.

D'Astous, A., & Deschênes, J. (2005). Consuming in one's mind: An exploration. *Psychology and Marketing, 2*(1), 1–30.

Davis, M. (2008). *Freedom and consumerism: A critique of Zygmunt Bauman's sociology*. Hampshire, UK: Ashgate.

Descartes, R. (1996). *Meditations on first philosophy* (J. Cottingham, Trans, Ed). Cambridge: Cambridge University Press. (Original work published 1641).

Douglas, M., & Isherwood, B. (1980). *The world of goods*. Harmondsworth: Penguin.

Dufour, D.-R. (2001, November 1). Rumo ao "capitalismo total"? *Le Monde Diplomatique*. Retrieved from http://diplo.uol.com.br/2001-11,a121

Dufour, D.-R. (2003, October 1). A arte de reduzir as mentes. *Le Monde Diplomatique*. Retrieved from http://diplo.uol.com.br/2003-10,a763

Dufour, D.-R. (2005, April 1). O homem neoliberal: da redução das cabeças à mudança dos corpos. *Le Monde Diplomatique*. Retrieved from http://diplo.uol.com.br/2005-04,a1098

Dufour, D.-R. (2008). *The art of shrinking heads: The new servitude of the liberated in the era of total capitalism*. Cambridge and Oxford: Polity.

Durand, G. (1963). *Les structures anthropologiques de l'imaginaire*. Paris: Dunod.

Durand, G. (1994). *L'imaginaire: Essai sur les sciences et la philosophie de l'image*. Paris: Hatier.

Durand, G. (1996). *Introduction à la mythodologie. Mythes et sociétés*. Paris: Albin Michel.

Durand, G. (2004). *Las estructuras antropologicas del imaginario: Introducción a la arquetipología general*. Mexico: FSE.

Durand, Y. (1988). *L'Exploration de l'imaginaire: Introduction à la modélisation des univers mythiques*. Paris: L'Espace Bleu.

Duvignaud, J., Duvignaud, F., & Corbeau, J. P. (1981). *El banco de los sueños: ensayo antropológico del soñador contemporáneo*. Mexico: Fondo de Cultura Económica.

Espinosa, O. N. (2009). *El imaginario sociocultural a través del sueño en jóvenes universitarios*. Unpublished doctoral dissertation, UNAM, Ciudad de México, Mexico.

Ewen, S. (1990). Marketing dreams: The political elements of style. In A. Tomlinson (Ed.), *Consumption, identity and style: Marketing, meanings, and the packaging of pleasure* (pp. 29–39). London: Routledge.

Fairclough, N., & Graham, P. (2002). Marx as critical discourse analyst: The genesis of a critical method and its relevance to the critique of global capital. *Estudios de Sociolingüística, 3*(1), 185–229.

Featherstone, M. (2007). *Consumer culture and postmodernism* (2nd ed.). London: Sage.

Featherstone, M. (2010). Event horizon: Utopia–dystopia in Bauman's thought. In M. Davis & K. Tester (Eds.), *Bauman's challenge: Sociological issues for the 21st century* (pp. 127–147). Hampshire, UK: Palgrave Macmillan.

Flanders, S. (Ed.). (1993). *The dream discourse today, The new library of psychoanalysis, 17*. London: Routledge.

Fournier, S., & Guiry, M. (1993). An emerald green Jaguar, a house on Nantucket, and an African safari: Wish lists and consumption dreams in materialist society. *Advances in Consumer Research, 20*, 352–358.

Gabriel, Y., & Lang, T. (2006). *The unmanageable consumer* (2nd ed.). London: Sage.

Gare, A. (2008). Marxism and the problem of creating an environmentally sustainable civilization in China. *Capitalism, Nature, Socialism, 19*(1), 5–26.

Giroux, H. A., & Pollock, G. (2011). *How Disney magic and the corporate media shape youth identity in the digital age*. Retrieved from http://truth-out.org/index.php?option=com_k2&view=item&id=2808:how-disney-magic-and-the-corporat e-media-shape-youth-identity-in-the-digital-age

Gottdiener, M. (1996). *The theming of America: Dreams, visions, and commercial spaces*. Boulder, CO: Westview Press.

Graham, P. (2006). 'Capitalism' as false consciousness. *Studies in Language & Capitalism, 1*, 57–76.

Gruzinski, S. (1988). *La colonization de l'imaginaire*. Paris: Gallimard.

Gruzinski, S. (1990). *La guerre des images*. Paris: Fayard.

Hebbrecht, M. (2007). The dream, anno 2007. *Tijdschrift voor Psychiatrie, 49*(12), 877–886.

Henderson, S., & Petersen, A. R. (Eds.). (2002). *Consuming health: The commodification of health care*. London: Routledge.

Hobbes, T. (1651). *Leviathan, or the matter, forme, & power of a common-wealth ecclesiasticall and civill*. London: Yale University Press.

Huws, U., & Herrman, C. (Eds.). (2008). *The new gold rush: The new multinationals and the commodification of public sector work*. London: Work Organisation, Labour and Globalisation.

Jameson, F. (1984a). Postmodernism: Or the cultural logic of late capitalism. *New Left Review, 146*, 53–92.

Jameson, F. (1984b). Postmodernism and the consumer society. In H. Foster (Ed.), *Postmodern culture* (pp. 111–125). London: Pluto Press.

Jameson, F. (1991). *Postmodernism, or the cultural logic of late capitalism*. Durham, NC: Duke University Press.

Jha, P. S. (2006). *The twilight of the nation state: Globalisation, chaos and war.* London: Pluto Press.
Lacher, H. (2005). International transformation and the persistence of territoriality: Toward a new political geography of capitalism. *Review of International Political Economy, 12*(1), 26–52.
Langman, L. (1992). Neon cages: Shopping for subjectivity. In R. Shields (Ed.), *Lifestyle shopping: The subject of consumption* (pp. 40–82). New York: Routledge.
Laval, C., & Weber, L. (Orgs.). (2002). *Le nouvel ordre éducatif mondial.* Paris: OMC, Banque Mondiale, OCDE, Commission Européenne.
Lebowitz, M. (2003). *Beyond 'Capital': Marx's political economy of the working class* (2nd ed.). Basingstoke: Palgrave Macmillan.
Leys, C. (2007). *Total capitalism: Market politics, market state.* London: Merlin Press.
Liodakis, G. (2010). *Totalitarian capitalism and beyond.* Surrey, UK: Ashgate.
Lukács, G. (1971). *History and class consciousness* (R. Livingstone, Trans.). London: Merlin Press. (Original work published 1923).
Martins, J. S. (Org.). (1996). *(Des)figurações: a vida cotidiana no imaginário onírico da metrópole.* Hucitec: São Paulo.
Marx, K. (1978). Grundrisse. In R. C. Tucker (Ed.), *The Marx-Engels reader* (2nd ed., pp. 222–293). New York: WW Norton. (Original work published 1858).
McCracken, G. (1988). *Culture and consumption: New approaches to the symbolic character of consumer goods and activities.* Bloomington: Indiana University Press.
Meier, C. A. (1987). *The meaning and significance of dreams.* Boston: Sigo Press.
Navarro, V. (1976). *Medicine under Capitalism.* New York: Prodist.
Navarro, V. (1993). *Dangerous to your health: Capitalism in health care.* New York: Monthly Review.
Parker, I. (2007). *Revolution in psychology: Alienation to emancipation.* London: Pluto Press.
Patton, M. Q. (1990). *Qualitative research and evaluation methods.* Newbury Park: Sage.
Piedras, E. R. (2006). *Sonho de consumo: a publicidade na intersecção entre o consumo material e o simbólico, pelo olhar do receptor.* Anais do XV Encontro da Compós. Bauru, SP, Brazil.
Piedras, E. R. (2007). *Publicidade, imaginário e consumo: Anúncios no cotidiano feminino.* Unpublished doctoral dissertation, PUCRS, Porto Alegre, Brazil.

Poster, M. (2001). Introduction. In M. Poster (Ed.), *Jean Baudrillard: Selected writings* (2nd ed., pp. 1–9). Cambridge: Polity.

Putney, L. G. (2010). Case study. In *Encyclopedia of research design*. London: Sage. Retrieved from http://www.sage-ereference.com/researchdesign/Article_n39.html

Pykett, J., Jones, R., & Whitehead, M. (Eds.). (2017). *Psychological governance and public policy: Governing the mind, brain and behaviour*. London: Routledge.

Radice, H. (2005). Neoliberal globalization: Imperialism without empires? In A. Saad-Filho & D. Johnston (Eds.), *Neoliberalism: A critical reader* (pp. 91–98). London: Pluto Press.

Reiser, M. F. (2001). The dream in contemporary psychiatry. *The American Journal of Psychiatry, 158*(3), 351–359.

Ritzer, G. (1993). *The McDonaldization of society*. Thousand Oaks, CA: Pine Forge.

Ritzer, G. (1998). *The McDonaldization thesis*. London: Sage.

Ritzer, G. (2000). *The McDonaldization of society* (New Century ed.). Thousand Oaks, CA: Pine Forge.

Ritzer, G. (2002). *McDonaldization: The reader*. London: Sage.

Roberts, R. (2015). *Psychology and capitalism: The manipulation of mind.* Washington: Zero Books.

Rocha, E. P. G. (1990). *Magia e capitalismo: Um estudo antropológico da publicidade* (2nd ed.). São Paulo: Brasiliense.

Rocha, E. P. G. (1995). *A sociedade do sonho: comunicação, cultura e consumo*. Rio de Janeiro: Mauad. Retrieved from http://books.google.es/books?id=vYVf_ll8jX4C

Rocha, E. P. G. (2006). *Representações do consumo: estudos sobre a narrativa publicitária*. Rio de Janeiro: PUCRio/Mauad.

Ross, D. (2004). Escape from Wonderland: Disney and the female imagination. *Marvels & Tales: Journal of Fairy-Tale Studies, 18*(1), 53–66.

Schor, J. (2004). *Born to buy: The commercialized child and the new consumer culture*. New York: Scribner.

Sennet, R. (1998). *The corrosion of character: The personal consequences of work in the new capitalism*. New York: W. W. Norton.

Sennet, R. (2006). *The culture of the new capitalism*. Yale: Yale University Press.

Shafton, A. (1995). *Dream reader: Contemporary approaches to the understanding of dreams*. Albany, NY: State University of New York Press.

Slaughter, S., & Leslie, L. L. (1997). *Academic capitalism: Politics, policies and the entrepreneurial university*. Baltimore: Johns Hopkins University Press.

Slaughter, S., & Leslie, L. L. (2001). Expanding and elaborating the concept of *Academic capitalism. Organization, 8*(2), 154–161.

Slaughter, S., & Rhoades, G. (2004). *Academic capitalism and the new economy: Markets, state and higher education.* Baltimore: Johns Hopkins University Press.

Strauss, S. (1924). Things are in the saddle. *Atlantic Monthly, 134*(5), 577–588.

Taylor, C. (2004). *Modern social imaginaries.* Durham and London: Duke University Press.

Todorov, T. (2002). *Memoria del mal, tentación del bien* (M. S. Crespo, Trans.). Barcelona: Península.

Tomlinson, A. (1990). Introduction: Consumer culture and the aura of the commodity. In A. Tomlinson (Ed.), *Consumption, identity and style: Marketing, meanings, and the packaging of pleasure* (pp. 1–27). London: Routledge.

Valtonen, A. (2011). We dream as we live – Consuming. In R. W. Belk, K. Grayson, A. M. Muñiz, & H. J. Schau (Eds.), *Research in consumer behavior* (Vol. 13, pp. 93–110). Bradford, UK: Emerald.

Virilio, P. (2001). From modernism to hypermodernism and beyond: An interview with Paul Virilio. In J. Armitage (Ed.), *Paul Virilio: From modernism to Hypermodernism and beyond* (pp. 25–57). London: Sage.

Von Schubert, G. H. (1814). *Die Symbolik des Traumes.* Leipzig: Brockhaus.

Wachowski Brothers (Directors). (1999). *The matrix* [Motion picture]. US: Warner Bros. Pictures.

Waitzkin, H. (2003). *At the front lines of medicine: How the health care system alienates doctors & mistreats patients … & what we can do about it.* New York: Rowman & Littlefield.

Wasko, J. (2001). *Understanding Disney: The manufacture of fantasy.* Cambridge: Polity.

Williams, R. (1976). *Keywords.* London: Fontana.

Williams, R. H. (1991). *Dream worlds: Mass consumption in late nineteenth-century France.* Berkeley: University of California Press.

Part I

Theoretical Framework

2

Symbolic Imaginaries and the Subject

The key to an understanding of the nature of the conscious life of the soul lies in the sphere of the unconscious.

C. G. Carus, *Psyche* (1846)[1]

Overview
This chapter explores theoretically the imaginary and its relations with subjectivity through the outlook of analytical psychology. The view that the imaginary is essentially symbolic is discussed with the help of Jung's theoretical concepts, and anthropological arguments and examples. In this framework, social imaginaries and subjective imagination are seen as having the same basic origins: the unconscious psyche, its archetypes, and especially its symbolic function—which is the typical mode of unconscious functioning, called symbolic-, dream-, or fantasy-thinking, responsible for imagination, dream, and fantasy. Subjectivity is understood as being constructed in the dialectics between social imaginaries, the subject's own historical and individual context and actions, and the unconscious psyche.

[1] Carus (1846, p. 1).

M. Xavier, *Subjectivity, the Unconscious and Consumerism*,
https://doi.org/10.1007/978-3-319-96824-7_2

2.1 The Concept of Imaginary

The concept of (social or collective) *imaginary* has been studied in depth by a number of authors from the social sciences and psychology (Bachelard, 1942; Castoriadis, 1975/1987; Corbin, 1964; Durand, 1963, 1994, 1996; Jameson, 1981; Maffesoli, 1988; Taylor, 2004; Wunenburger, 1997). To offer a definition intentionally broad, the concept of imaginary refers to the world of *images* and *representations* and its relations with *imagination* (both collective and individual): how human beings imagine, organize, and represent *meaning* through images, representations, symbols, and myths.

Collectively or culturally, we have *social imaginaries*: the ensemble of typical symbolic forms that are shared socially. These symbolic regimes or templates articulate collective mentalities and their typical forms of representing and signifying experience: distinctive social imaginary configurations that shape social structure, action, and processes, give social bonding and provide social cohesion, and generate social identity and inclusiveness. Anthropologically, they correspond to the social group's mythic narratives, its symbolic or imaginary wealth: the imaginary forms that *define* that given culture, that prefigure and express its *collective reality*, and therefore ground, shape, or condition how the *individual* is socially inserted, her/his identity, and how she/he imagines, organizes, understands, and assigns meaning to her/his life, experience, and world.

In this sense, Xiberras (2002) provides a succinct definition when she affirms that the imaginary represents the typical psychological forms through which we construct *reality*: "The imaginary is at the same time an individual and collective creation and representation. Reality is constructed in, through and with images, symbols, and myths. (…) we cannot distinguish reality from the imaginary anymore" (p. 11). Such typical forms are based on "un dynamisme organisateur des images" (Thomas, 1998, p. 15) that is also typical, or universal (Durand, 1994, 1996).

2.2 The Symbolic Imaginary and the Collective Psyche

In Jung, such dynamism that originally underlies both cultural and individual imaginary creations is essentially *symbolic* and rests on the same psychological foundations: the *unconscious psyche* and its characteristic symbolic function. In cultural form, its imaginary productions will appear as myths, religious narratives, fairy tales, legends, and so on. In the individual, it appears chiefly in creative fantasy and imagination, in visions and delirium, in the child's psychological functioning—and in dreams.

The unconscious psyche is formed by two realms: the collective unconscious and the personal unconscious. Let us explore the concept of collective unconscious first.

2.2.1 The Unconscious Psyche: The Collective Unconscious

The collective unconscious is formed by instincts and archetypes: collective or suprapersonal psychic elements that are common to all human beings. Instincts and archetypes correspond to two sides of the same dynamic, the somatic and mental poles of the psyche, indissolubly connected (Jung, CW16, §185), and as such represent an a priori factor in all human activities.

Instincts are defined as collective *patterns of behavior.* They represent psychic factors, more connected to our biological foundations, that function as a compulsion or impulse to act or react in determinate ways: they are typical, "uniform and regularly recurring modes of action and reaction" (Jung, CW8, §273). As such they correspond to the *drives* for certain basic forms of human behavior: self-preservation and hunger, sex, knowledge, creativity, activity, religion, reflection, and so on. As impulses, they can be understood as the unconscious *vis motrix*, blind and compulsive, that expresses a specific energetic quantum, or libido.

Libido is the concept of psychic energy in Jung. Returning to the original sense of the word, it means energy conceived as *desire*, or *appetite* (Jung, CW4, §567). However, the libido does not have a dominant quality (such as sexuality, in Freud); it is analogous to the concept of energy in physics: energy can assume different qualities and does not have a preponderant one. In the same way that the instinct is irrepresentable in itself and can only be perceived through its manifestation (as typical forms of behavior), libido, as *psychic* energy, can only be perceived as images, as *representations*. "Libido can never be apprehended except in a definite form; that is to say, it is identical with *fantasy-images*" (Jung, CW7, §345; e.a.).

2.2.2 Instinct and Archetype

Such representations of libido are the primary constituents of our psyche. While the instinct is the typical manifestation of libido as action or reaction, the archetype corresponds to the typical forms through which libido is represented as images. Hence, the archetype corresponds to the psychic aspect of instinct, or to its image: an equally transpersonal and unconscious factor that represents, apperceives, organizes, and gives meaning to instinct. As such, it represents a *formal* factor of psychic life: it organizes and arranges the psychic elements into certain images, representations, and later ideas, according to characteristic types, or motifs, which Jung called archetypal (CW11, §222). While the instincts are typical modes of action and reaction, archetypes are uniform and regularly recurring modes of apprehension, perception, and representation of reality (Jung, CW8, §280). Both are collective regularities, or *universals*, that characterize our psychic constituency as *human*:

> (…) the way in which man inwardly pictures the world is still, despite all differences of detail, as uniform and as regular as his instinctive actions. Just as we have been compelled to postulate the concept of an instinct determining or regulating our conscious actions, so, in order to account for the uniformity and regularity of our perceptions, we must have recourse to the correlated concept of a factor determining the mode of apprehension. It is this factor which I call the archetype (…) the *instinct's perception of itself*, or as the self-portrait of the instinct. (Jung, CW8, §277)

As a perception or representation of the instinct, the archetype provides it with a *telos*, a direction manifested as *meaning*. Being a nucleus of meaning (Jung, CW9i, §155)—which appears as a *motif*, for example, "mother", "marriage", "spirit"—it organizes the material of experience, its images, according to a specific meaningful configuration. Therefore, in relation to behavior, whereas the instinct corresponds to compulsion or impulse, the archetype represents intention, goal, and meaning. Being images of the instincts, archetypes signify and evoke them (Jung, CW8). As such they represent the bridge, the necessary *connection* with the primitive, instinctual psyche—with Nature itself. "They are thus, essentially, the chthonic portion of the psyche (…) that portion through which the psyche is attached to nature" (Jung, CW 10, §53).

2.2.3 The Archetype as Image and Idea

In one of his first definitions of the concept of archetype, Jung proposes it as both idea and image:

> They are ideas *ante rem*, determinants of form, a kind of pre-existent ground-plan that gives the stuff of experience a specific configuration, so that we may think of them, as Plato did, as *images*, as schemata, or as inherited functional possibilities. (CW6, §512)

As an autochthonous, a priori structure of apperception that defines cognition and that, in shaping knowledge and perception of world and subject, conditions all experience, the archetypes correspond to Kantian categories. However, two particularities should be borne in mind. Differing from Kant, whose categories are essentially static and immutable, Jung confers the archetypes a *historical* value: they represent the whole history of humankind in us, but as a possibility, a *virtuality*. That is because the archetypes are *not* inherited ideas, which is an impossibility, but "innate *possibilities* of ideas, *a priori* conditions for fantasy-production" (Jung, CW10, §14; e.a.), "an inherited mode of psychic functioning" (Jung, CW18, §1128). As a *facultas praeformandi*, an empty form of apperception (Jung, CW9i, §155), the archetype itself is transcendental; it determines the (typical) *form*, not the content of the representations, and as such must be distinguished from its apprehensible manifestation, the archetypal image or *primordial image*. The primordial image is the synthesis of the a priori archetypal form (type) with the individual's experience, that is, the empty form filled by subjective, experienced content. The archetypal image is, therefore, historical—like the psyche and the body.

With such distinction, Jung avoided a mystical Neoplatonism and at the same time asserted the cultural and historic configuration of our psyche. Through it, he accomplished a dialectical reunion of two schools of thought whose schism permeated Western thought and who represent the typical (archetypal!) ways we have seen reality: Plato and Aristotle.

> [M]en have always talked about two kinds of reality: one that we see with our eyes and touch with our hands, and one that cannot be experienced with our senses. Here two different principles show. The Aristotelian will say: the archetypes are ideas derived from the experience with real fathers and mothers. The Platonist will say: fathers and mothers have only come into existence out of the archetypes, as those are the primal images, the pre-images of the manifestations, stored in a heavenly place, and it is from them that all forms come from. That is the origin of the term archetypos. (Jung, SCD, p. 72)

In Jung, our psyche is *both*: a dialectics between sensory and individual experience (which is historic and sociocultural) and the a priori conditions for image formation (which are also historic and represent the condensations of human culture across time as a virtual scheme), the suprasensory.

2.2.4 The Archetype as Image: The Primordial Image

The manifestations of the archetype as image are called primordial images. An archaic character is what defines them, that is, they appear in accord with definite *mythological motifs*. (In fact, they are the "stuff" of which myths are made.) As such, the primordial image expresses typical psychic occurrences related to ever-recurring natural human experiences. However, the important element here is the mythological and imaginary aspect that—in contradistinction to mere sensuous perception—the primordial image imprints onto our natural experiences. Jung provides the example of solar myths. Albeit the daily setting and rising of the sun has obviously been a primary experience for humans since time immemorial, such motions do not appear in their simplicity or concreteness for the primitives.[2] For them the environmental conditions, and all other typical natural occurrences, are always seen in a mythical, symbolical way. The sun is seen as the hero, the great father, the god, the origin of all life, and so on and as such must be adored, worshipped, so that it can fulfill its daily battle against darkness and death. That means that the psyche adopts a standpoint *outside* of mere sense perception; it apperceives and gives form to such natural processes and conditions through a *creative* capacity that defines it just as much as the outside occurrences and the senses do. It is that psychic *imaginative* faculty that perceives the solar phenomenon not as a mere sensory experience, but as a meaningful, mythical one.

> The organism confronts light with a new structure, the eye, and the psyche confronts the natural process with a symbolic image, which apprehends it in the same way as the eye catches the light. And just as the eye bears witness to the peculiar and spontaneous creative activity of living matter, the primordial image expresses the unique and unconditioned creative power of the psyche. (Jung, CW6, §748)

The primordial image thus orders and organizes sensory perception and inner perception, in what one could call a creative (and unconscious) act of comprehension, through a determined meaning that will govern and direct action. Seen from an opposite and complementary viewpoint, the psyche *projects*[3] the primordial image (and all its characteristics) upon the environment. Because it is connected to the instinct (it is an expression, as image, of the instinct), it will give definite *emotional* color and affective *value* to the exterior perception—which correspond to the libido expressed by and contained in the representation. As a mythic image, it is

---

[2] Jung (CW8) employs the term "primitive" in the sense of "primordial", not implying value judgment (§218), and I follow his usage in this work.

[3] The phenomenon of projection will be dealt with in more detail later on.

naturally and typically fascinating, enchanting, tremendous, and so on. That is due to an essential characteristic of the archetypal image in its empirical manifestation: its *numinosity* and fascinating power (Jung, CW8, §414).

Numinosity refers to the concept of *numen*, elaborated by Rudolf Otto (1917). In his phenomenological studies, Otto proposed the numen as the essential element that underlies all religious experience, all the "states of the soul" related to the experience of the sacred, the holy. The numinosum, or *numen innefabile*, is characterized as a *mysterium tremendum et fascinans*, wherein the *mysterium* represents *das ganz Andere* (the totally Other), what is qualitatively different, and presents two possible elements: the *tremendum*, which causes fear or terror, and the *fascinans*, which attracts and fascinates. According to Jung, the numinosity characteristic of the primordial image corresponds to the specific *value* of an archetypal event; it is its libidinal charge, derived from its connection to instinct. Being *numinous* is therefore a distinguishing feature of the archetype: it is felt as something extremely significant that attracts, fascinates, convinces, and overpowers (Jung, CW9, §11); at the same time it can be perceived as *tremendum*, originating fear, dread, and reverence, or as something *suprapersonal*, transcendent, spiritual (or daemonic), irresistible, immediate, ineluctable, and autonomous. In this sense, if every primordial image refers to a transcendental, mythical reality, then the experience of the world will be painted with such enchanted colors—as it has been for millennia, and still is in the natural products of our imagination.

2.2.5 The Archetype as (Precondition for the) Idea

As a category of apperception, an organizer of all experience, the primordial image represents the matrix, or the previous phase, of the idea. It is its substratum, connected to instinct, and therefore to emotion, affect, and numinosity—to the original libido, the energies that underlie the idea. In comparison with Plato, here what is given a priori is not the idea itself, but "its affective-representative mold, its archetypal motif" (G. Durand, 2004, p. 63). It is reason that will transform the primordial image into a concept,

> an idea which differs from all other concepts in that it is not a datum of experience but is actually the underlying principle of all experience. The idea derives this quality from the primordial image, which, as an expression of the specific structure of the brain, gives every experience a definite form. (Jung, CW6, §750)

In contrast with the immediacy, emotionality, and mythic character of the primordial image, the idea is an abstraction, a rational formulation. Here Jung follows Kant. In dealing with the primordial image, reason moves from representation to abstraction: from its symbolic image (its representability) and concrete reality to a pure abstraction (idea). "It is this pure 'abstract' which I term an idea" (Jung, CW6, §680). The ideas will then form the material of reason. If we return to Jung's definition of the archetypes as "ideas *ante rem*" or a priori, we may qualify it by stating that the ideas are a priori only in the sense that they derive from the a priori psychic structure; and that they find their roots in the primordial image, the archetype. "[The idea] derives this quality [of being a priori] from its precursor—the primordial, symbolic image" (Jung, CW6, §736). Jung then ascertains his Kantian heritage by quoting him:

> In this sense Plato sees the idea as a prototype of things, while Kant defines it as the "archetype [*Urbild*] of all practical employment of reason," a transcendental concept which as such exceeds the bounds of the experienceable—"a rational concept whose object is not to be found in experience[4]". (CW6, §733)

And Vieira (2003, p. 54) summarizes the articulation with Kant and his categories:

> In the same way that Kant interposes a *subject* of knowledge between the empirical world and the formulation of knowledge itself—a way in which the role of distancing and orienting the subject vis-à-vis empirical reality is assigned to the ideas—, Jung [in CW6] revisits the same subject, adding, as archetypes (or primordial images), a linkage with instinct, feeling, and sentiment.

---

[4] Kant's quotes are respectively from: *Critique of Pure Reason* (trans. Kemp Smith), p. 319; and *Logik I*, sec. I. par. 3 (*Werke*, ed. Cassirer. VIII. p. 400). *Urbild* literally means "archaic image".

Against cold, purely abstract reason, such proposition rejoins the ideas with their imagistic and emotional origins. For Jung, beyond being mere components of reason, as *archaic* ideas they come to shape philosophical ideas "that influence and set their stamp on whole nations and epochs" (CW18, §547); their origins in primordial images explain, or at least help us understand, the emotional (and at times religious) attraction of certain ideas.

Therefore, with the theory on archetypes and the collective unconscious, Jung proposes a common archaic basis for all mental activities and phenomena—for all that is *imaginary*: from fantasy and dream to fairy tales, religions, and myths, to ideas and science.[5] Next, we will see that such psychic foundations are symbolic: their natural expression is the symbol.

2.2.6 Archetypal Image as Symbolic Rite

Anthropologically, a rite represents one of the primary formations of a social imaginary. As such, it illustrates some of the main theoretical premises related to our discussion of imaginary and symbol: how the primordial image (archetype) manifests itself as a symbolic product; how such symbol transforms the instinctual libido and is translated into a symbolic narrative, the rite, which organizes and mediates action and perception (i.e., experience); and how what is imaginary (the symbolic rite) institutes culture.

As an example of rite, Jung offers a fertility spring ceremony of the Wachandis, an Australian aboriginal people. Before cultivating the soil, the men perform a ritual:

> They dig a hole in the ground, so shaping it and setting it about with bushes that it looks like a woman's genitals. Then they dance round this hole all night, holding their spears in front of them in imitation of an erect

[5] "This [the theory of archetypes] explains why even fantasy, the freest activity of the mind, can never roam into the infinite (although it seems that way to the poet) but remains anchored to these preformed patterns, these primordial images. The fairytales of the most widely separated races show, by the similarity of their motifs, the same tie. Even the images that underlie certain scientific theories—ether, energy, its transformations and constancy, the atomic theory, affinity, and so on—are proof of this restriction" (Jung, CW6, §512).

penis. As they dance round, they thrust their spears into the hole, shouting: "Pulli nira, pulli nira wataka!" (Not a pit, not a pit, but a cunt!) (...) Before and during the whole ceremony, none of them may look at a woman. (CW5, §214–216)

We can easily see that the instinct would be naturally directed to sexuality and procreation, to its original object: the female (in fact, to the female genitals). In a natural state, the primitive merely follows the instinctive current and does not produce "work" proper, but simply fulfills his animal needs (sex, food, shelter, etc.). What transforms and canalizes libido into an *analogue* of the object of instinct is the *symbol.* In this case, an archetypal symbol, the expression of the primordial image: the earth as woman, and the whole act or rite as a sacramental mating, the *hieros gamos* or holy marriage, between the earth (woman) and the spear (*phallus*, the men's procreative masculine energy). Typically, the symbolic images[6] offer a wealth of meanings and cannot be reduced to any single one.

The rite occurs in a very emotionally charged atmosphere, the dancing representing a mating-play: through the ecstatic atmosphere created by shouting, dancing, and branding the spears, the men are immersed in the *imaginary* view of the hole as vulva (and earth as woman). In order to guarantee that the libido will not be disturbed and "flow back" to its original object, they cannot look at women. In perceiving the field through the symbol (or, by *projecting* the psychic symbol, the primordial image, upon the field—which is the same), the earth is endowed with a special psychic value, an expectation analogous to the primary object (the woman and the sexual act).

Our example is a very simple one; it is a basic form that will eventually develop into more elaborated religious practices and narratives. In them, Nature and earth will be symbolized as goddesses, with their specific fertility rites and forms of worship: they will be seen as numinous, or *sacred*, as feminine deities related to cultivation and fertility.[7] That corresponds

[6] In fact, the whole ritual imagery is symbolic. Namely, the spears symbolize the erect phallus—not mere sexuality, but masculine procreative force; the dance symbolizes the mating-dance, effort, preparation, courtship (of the earth); the hole in the ground symbolizes the female genitals; and, finally, the earth symbolizes the woman, the feminine.

[7] For example, Gaia, Cybele, and Demeter (Greek); Parjati (Hindu); Freyja (Norse); Pachamama (Quechua).

to the motif of the "Great Mother" or mother-goddess, the *mother archetype*.

If one generalizes from this simple rite to more elaborated imaginary constructions, it can be affirmed that the symbolic is what gives meaning and value (and *sacredness*) to the world and the human action in it: what becomes numinous and sacred is not merely the earth (and thus Nature), but also the *role* of men as cultivators, as active participants in a sacred rite (in communion with the sacred earth), and later their activity in the field, their *work*—in fact themselves, their existence, and the world share in sacredness, and therefore in dignity.

Such numinosity is an expression of the *libido* contained in the archetype and expressed symbolically. As such, it will appear in every imaginary form connected to an archetypal symbol; it represents an archaic concept of psychic *energy*. In physics, the concept of energy comes from the idea of ἐνέργεια, which has its ancient roots in the primitive notion of "extremely powerful or efficient", which underlies all religious forms. The numinosity characteristic of the archetypal symbol is what Mauss, Marett, and a generation of anthropologists saw as *mana*. Hubert and Mauss, in *Mélanges d'histoire des religions* (1909), had already affirmed—*avant la lettre*—that the idea of mana corresponded to what Jung would call an archetype: mana represents an "unconscious a priori category of understanding" that directs "habits of consciousness" (Shamdasani, 2003, p. 295).

To return to our example, the rite illustrated how the symbol, as archetypal representation charged with mana, is what channels and transforms merely instinctual libido toward cultural constructions, giving birth to religious processes of an essentially symbolic nature.

> In abstract form, symbols are religious ideas; in the form of action, they are rites or ceremonies. They are (…) stepping-stones to new activities, which must be called cultural in order to distinguish them from the instinctual functions that run their regular course according to natural law. (Jung, CW8, §91)

In our example, the symbol, as pure representation (a symbolic image), is an expression of a primordial image (earth as procreative woman, or feminine); as a complete rite or myth, it is the symbol as narrative (a symbolic narrative). Those are the two forms of perception, of cognitive organization of experience and act, that are typical of the archetype: as image *and* narrative, through the symbol.

2.2.7 Symbol, Imaginary, and Culture

Therefore, it is a symbolic and *religious* act, through a rite, that founds and is the foundation of culture. Indeed, myth and rite are omnipresent occurrences across cultures and history; culture, symbol, and myth seem to be inseparable phenomena. From the primitives to the Middle Ages, all existence was mediated by rites: for hunting, agriculture, birth, death, marriage, and so on. Instinctual life functioned through symbolic systems, or symbolic *imaginaries*, that defined, limited, and signified both individual and sociocultural life.

In this view, culture thus stems from *nature*—for the collective unconscious, as instincts and archetypes, is Nature in us—and at the same time is *opposed* and autonomous in relation to nature as mere instinctuality—for the natural instinctual impulse, and its inertia, are transformed and redirected through the symbol.[8]

The symbol is therefore what renders possible the transcendence of our mere animality, mere nature (what the Roman and Renaissance humanists[9] called *feritas*, or *barbaritas*—brutality), and its refinement (*cultivation*) into culture. Thus, it defines what is *human* (*humanitas*). Jung associates such capacity to a self-regulatory, developmental *telos* in the psyche, the regulating principle of individuation. "Multiplicity and inner

[8] As the old alchemist Pseudo-Democritus wrote in the fourth century BC, *Nature rejoices in Nature, Nature conquers Nature, Nature restrains (or masters) Nature.* This conception of non-enmity, indeed of complementarity and *dialectics* between nature and culture, is at the same time archetypal and the foundation of humanism: "Ecco il più importante principio che attraversa l'umanesimo: (…) la natura costituisce il fondamento iniziale (…) della cultura, intendendo questa come elaborazione, educazione ed. emancipazione della natura" (Batkin, 1990, p. 83). It stands in opposition to the modern conception, in which nature and culture are enemies and therefore nature must be dominated, colonized, conquered, as in Hobbes and Freud (and capitalism).

[9] Among the great authors of this humanism, with which Jung becomes a *symbolic humanism*, were Cicero, Seneca, Bruno, Llull, Ficino, Petrarca, Pico della Mirandola, and Espinosa (see Batkin, 1990; Garin, 1973; Stephens, 1990; Yates, 1996).

division are opposed by an integrative unity whose power is as great as that of the instincts. Together they form a pair of opposites necessary for self-regulation, often spoken of as nature and spirit" (Jung, CW8, §96). The human child is never born as *tabula rasa*; a newly born is already endowed with a whole instinctive disposition, but also with all the ancestral differentiations, which are historical and hereditary. "Thus every child is born with an *immense split* in his make-up: on one side he is more or less like an animal, on the other side he is the final embodiment of an age-old and endlessly complicated sum of hereditary factors" (§98). That means that we are all born with the split nature-culture (and history) as our mental configurations; such conflict, or contradiction, is the tension that expresses our psychic energy. Again, in Jung, the psychic element that expresses such energy by uniting and whereby transcending the conflicting opposites through a synthesis is the symbol.

2.2.8 Symbol: Definition and Difference

As a representation, and therefore a psychic content, the symbol is seen in analytical psychology as the natural product and expression of the unconscious psyche. "As a plant produces its flower, so the psyche creates its symbols. Every dream is evidence of this process" (Jung, MHS, p. 64). However, in Jung such process is vital: the *symbol-creating function* represents the most important function of the unconscious (CW10, §25).

Jung provides a synthetic definition: "a symbol is the best possible expression for an unconscious content whose nature can only be guessed, because it is still unknown" (CW9i, §7, 10n). That means that a symbol *always* expresses an unconscious (unknown) quantum, and, being an unconscious product, is autonomous. Another characteristic is that it unites opposites: "*symbolum*, a bringing together of heterogeneous natures" (CW11, §648). Jung is referring to the Greek etymon: *sym bollom*, from *syn-* "together" + *ballé* "to throw", hence "to throw together" the *opposites*, into *one* image. As such, the symbol represents *synthesis*, the very possibility of dialectics. It is the psychic mechanism that brings together two (or more) heterogeneous natures into one homogeneous image, a whole, according to a determinate *meaning*. It can be said that it is the prime expression of *meaning* by the unconscious. As noted by Schelling, the word in German cannot be clearer: symbol is *Sinnbild*, the *image of meaning* (or meaning-image). Another form of understanding the symbol is that it is the union of the sensory (appearance) with the suprasensory (the transcendental, i.e., the archetypal). Gadamer (1975) expresses it almost poetically: in the symbol "the idea itself gives itself existence. (…) A symbol is the coincidence of sensible appearance and suprasensible meaning, and this coincidence is (…) the union of two things that belong to each other" (p. 67).

The symbol as a totality, a *whole* in itself, is perhaps the most important idea here; Jung inherited it from the tradition of Kant, Goethe, and Schelling (see Vieira, 2003). Its manifold meanings—which, being (at least in part) *unknown or unconscious*, are not given a priori—are contained in its image; the image is its own meaning. "Image and meaning are identical and as the first takes shape, so the latter becomes clear. Actually the pattern needs no interpretation; it portrays its own meaning" (Jung, CW8, §402). Being a whole, in the symbol both image and meaning, signifier and signified, are inextricably united. G. Durand (1963, p. 20) put it simply: "le symbole présuppose *homogénéité du signifiant et du signifié au sens d'un dynamisme organisateur*". And so did Gadamer (1975, p. 67): "the concept of symbol implies the inner unity of symbol and what is symbolized". As a dynamism, the symbol is precisely the motor and expression of such (re)union of signifier and signified—its unknown unconscious content, an invitation to knowledge, a call to consciousness.

2.2.9 Distinction from Allegory and Sign

Considered in this way, the symbol is what defines the human unconscious psyche, and—as consciousness springs from the unconscious—therefore the whole psyche, which is the source of social imaginaries and culture. Ergo the symbol defines what is human: *homo symbolicus* (Cassirer). It is therefore necessary to distinguish the symbol from the other forms of representation, *especially in relation to the sign*; for in this crucial difference rests the mutation of imaginaries, and ultimately the anthropological and cultural mutation that this work studies.

Jung finds proximity with contemporary semiotics when he distinguishes between symbol, sign, and allegory. As forms of representation and signification, they constitute the forms of *imagination*: of representing and signifying realities through images.

> The concept of a *symbol* should in my view be strictly distinguished from that of a *sign*. Symbolic and *semiotic* meanings are entirely different things. (…) Every view which interprets the symbolic expression as an analogue or an abbreviated designation for a *known* thing is *semiotic*. A view which interprets the symbolic expression as the best possible formulation of a relatively *unknown* thing, which for that reason cannot be more clearly or characteristically represented, is *symbolic*. A view which interprets the symbolic expression as an intentional paraphrase or transmogrification of a known thing is *allegoric*. (Jung, CW6, §815)

As we have seen, the symbol is the representational form that *naturally* expresses the unconscious; its image and its meanings (its signifying force) are *one* unconscious construction, through which it expresses its idea. In comparison, both sign and allegory are conventional, a priori constructions, whose significance is already given before the image is built. Allegory, by definition, refers to another thing, to something *extrinsic* to itself (from *allos* "other" + *agoria* "speaking", to speak or signify something *other* than itself). They are *fabricated significations*.

> The symbol is not a sign that disguises something generally known. Its meaning resides in the fact that it is an attempt to elucidate, by a more or less apt analogy, something that is still entirely unknown or still in the process of formation. If we reduce this by analysis to something that is generally known, we destroy the true value of the symbol. (Jung, CW7, §492)

Whereas the symbol is always *more* than what can be understood at first, for it is a totality that *includes* the unconscious, irrational element (and is created by it), the sign is always conventional and *less* than what it refers to—it is a *reduction*, by definition, and something artificial and not spontaneous. If the symbol is a unity, a (re)union of differences into a totality that simply *is what it is*, the sign represents a split, a *schism* between signifier and signified. As G. Durand (1963) defines it: "signe: convention arbitraire qui laisse étrangers l'un à l'autre le signifiant et le signifié" (p. 21).

Although signs and allegories are common forms of representation, they are not the only ones. As we have seen, the symbol is the primary, vital form of psychic representation and must be taken and understood in its specificity: as a psychic form of irrational and autonomous nature (i.e., *unconscious*) that contains a wealth of meaning indistinguishable from its own image—not as something whose meaning is given a priori and intentionally constructed. In this definition, it is impossible to *consciously* build or create a symbol, for then it would be an allegory or sign. "A symbol is never an invention. It *happens* to man" (Jung, SNZ, p. 1251).

The opposite is to propose or even *engineer* a sign as if it were a symbol, or else to always, by definition and a priori, construe the symbol as a sign. In fact, *that is precisely what characterizes postmodernity and consumerism: the Reign of Signs, which nevertheless considers everything "symbolic"*. Producing a sign as if it were a symbol requires and means to "disguise it [the sign] as a 'symbolic' *phantasmagoria.* No matter how *fantastic* the trappings may look, it would still be a sign hinting at a conscious thought, and not a symbol" (Jung, CW18, §482; e.a.). As the sign is by definition a designation of a thing *known* a priori, "destroying the true value of the symbol" means destroying what is unconscious, the unconscious expression and its signification, and substituting a phantasmagoria for the unconscious discourse—or superimposing a given discourse (an ideology) upon the original symbolic discourse. It means a denial of the reality and creativity of the unconscious, and therefore a *denial of psychic reality*.

If we return to the example of the rite, to see it semiotically—as a sign—would simply obliterate its sociocultural aspect, its value: the whole rite, and therefore the whole of culture, would be nothing but an epiphenomenon—or worse still, a perversion, a symptom—of the sexual instinct, of primitive, animal *desire*. A debasement into crass *feritas*: no possible dialectics. In other words, what is typically *human*—the cultural, spiritual element—is destroyed when the symbol is erased or substituted artificially by the sign.

2.2.10 Imaginary Function in the Subject: Symbol and Fantasy

As the example of rite discussed above demonstrated, such social imaginaries—as rites, myths, religions, and so on—are genuinely *symbolic* and have a collective nature; they are formed by *collective symbols*.

In his works and practice, Jung discovered that certain *individual* symbolic products, such as dreams, fantasies, imaginations, delirium, and so on, also presented certain common symbolic patterns (motifs) that were similar to the mythic symbols; they were isomorphic between themselves or else had the same *patterns in meaning*.[10] As in many cases the hypothesis of cultural transmission would not hold (as, e.g., in European children's dreams, or deliriums of psychiatric patients, that presented cosmogonic motifs found in ancient pagan and Eastern religions), Jung proposed that their similitude was due to their stemming from the same source: the collective unconscious and its typical symbolic function.

That is the origin of the theory of the collective unconscious as a symbolic matrix for humanity and the subject. If the individual imaginary product, a symbol, derives from such source, it follows that one will have to compare it with the historical symbolic production of humanity, in myths, rites, fairy tales, religions, and art—with the manners in which the symbol appeared culturally—in order to establish parallels and understand it. That corresponds to the hermeneutic method of *amplification*: it presupposes that the symbol—like its source, the unconscious—is historical.

However, in such individual imaginary products, the symbol can also assume an *individual*, more *subjective* character (as opposed to a collective and archetypal one). Dreams and fantasies can have impersonal, collective contents and narratives; yet, more commonly, they have a more personal character, referring to the subject's individual psyche, his particular trajectory, problems, and psychological configuration.

[10] In Cassirer (1946, p. 37), we find the same idea: "the motives of mythical thought and mythical imagination are in a sense always the same. In all human activities and in all forms of human culture we find a 'unity in the manifold'".

The symbolic image as a product of the individual's psyche, whether it has a collective or personal character, corresponds to the image of *fantasy*: as an inner image, it is a homogeneous product, with its own wealth of meaning, appearing autonomously and spontaneously. Its relation to the exterior object is indirect; its significance cannot be reduced to the exterior object. It expresses primarily the situation, at a given moment, of the *unconscious psyche*: its autonomous portrayal of itself, of its energies (libido) and their dynamics—in relation and possible *union* with the conscious situation—represented as symbolic images. Such autonomous functioning of the unconscious psyche appears in every individual as *symbolic imagination*: as fantasy.

2.2.11 Imagination as Symbolic Fantasy: Symbolic Thinking, Dream-Thinking

For Jung, fantasy corresponds to the natural *imaginative activity* of the psyche. As imagination, it represents the reproductive or *creative* activity of the mind in general. "Fantasy as imaginative activity is, in my view, simply the direct expression of psychic life (…) it is identical with the flow of psychic energy" (Jung, CW6, §722).

The natural flow of libido corresponds to the autonomous functioning of the unconscious. Indeed, already in 1912, Jung (CW5) proposed fantasy as our unconscious natural form of *thinking*, which he termed fantasy-thinking, or dreaming-thinking. It is complementary to another general type of psychic functioning, more familiar to us, which he called logical or directed thinking. Both can be seen as modes of cognitive functioning: of ordering experience, assigning meaning, and constructing reality.[11]

Logical, directed thinking is directed at outward reality, has an objective character, is productive as regards adaptation, and depends on consciousness and effort (and hence is not continuous but intermittent). As it functions through language and verbal concepts, it is also called *linguistic*

[11] Vieira (2003) pointed the analogy with Jerome Bruner's (1986) two modes of thought: paradigmatic or logico-scientific thought, and narrative thought (Bruner, 1986, pp. 11–14). The latter is connected to the imagination, in that building narratives is an imaginary activity.

thought. Being directed by an idea or principium, it aims at communication, differentiation, and empirical reality; as such, it is the instrument of culture.

Symbolic thinking, the function of imagination or imaginary function, is continuously happening underneath directed thinking. It is the archaic mode of thinking typified by fantasy: it is directed inwardly, has a subjective and associative character, is spontaneous, effortless, and imagistic; it works through emotionally charged images. Being the characteristic form of unconscious thinking, it appears in all those situations in which there is an *abaissement*[12] of consciousness (in dreams, reverie, intoxication, certain psychopathologies; or even when one gets very tired) or when consciousness is still incipient (in primitive peoples and children), that is, when what we consider as our regular state of focused consciousness gives way to a more or less unconscious state. Then the unconscious foundation once again conduces the process of thinking through *fantasy*, which becomes the primary form of perception. Guided by the unconscious imagery, as bundles or trains of images and sensations associated by contiguity, fantasy leads away from empirical reality, for the apperception of the external object is then defined by the inner unconscious form of representation, which is characteristically *symbolic*: it associates typical images with their correspondent emotions and sensations. Moreover, there will be the characteristic *projection* of unconscious contents upon the environment, which becomes animated and characterized by them (i.e., it is *perceived* or imagined as such). In sum, it perceives reality according to subjective unconscious motives; it is a dream-like perception, hence *dream-thinking* (Jung, CW5, §25).

If we recall what was discussed above in relation to symbol and archetype, we shall conclude that fantasies and imagination speak a typical language, symbolic and pictorial, "the emotionally charged picture-language of dreams" (Jung, CW18, §464), a *dream-language*, to which we shall return in the next chapter. Again, the psychic roots of such language are to be found in the archetypes. That is why such language (and

[12] Lowering of the level of consciousness. That refers to Pierre Janet's (1890) concept of *abaissement du niveau mental* (or *de la tension psychologique*) often employed by Jung (see, e.g., CW3 and CW10). It also happens whenever an *emotional* condition exists (Meier, 1986), i.e., when the subject is seized by a strong emotion (which makes him or her correspondingly more *unconscious*).

functioning) is universal: it is the language of the unconscious, the language of the instincts, which is the basis or origin for all languages (a view found also in Cassirer) and thought (for fantasy-thinking precedes logical thinking). As Wolfgang Pauli once wrote to Jung,[13] "the archetypal concepts (or, as you once said, the '*instinct of imagination*')" (Meier, 2001, p. 33) are what conceive such imaginary products. While its cultural expressions—myths, religious narratives, and so on—unveil the unconscious dispositions and typical characteristics of a *culture*, its individual expressions—fantasies, dreams, imagination—will reveal the unconscious *subjective* dispositions, the individual inner reality, in symbolic form.

Because the archetype is numinous by definition, such expressions of symbolic thought are always ultimately connected to a magical-religious thinking. Anthropologically, such fact can be seen both culturally and individually. If symbolic thinking naturally and autonomously produces numinous symbols, which originate religious practices and systems, then the psyche must be naturally religious. Jung referred to such dynamism as the autochthonous religious function of the psyche (CW12, §12; see also Xavier, 2006).

For the individual, the vital importance of such thinking and its language consists in the fact that, as the symbol connects consciousness to its instinctive foundation, "through fantasy-thinking, directed thinking is brought into contact with the oldest layers of the human mind, long buried beneath the threshold of consciousness" (Jung, CW5, §39). It is the connection of individual ego consciousness (the *I*, the subject) with its psychic roots in the archetype and instinct. To summarize and conclude, both cultural and individual forms of imagination have its roots in the imaginary symbolic function inherent to the unconscious psyche. Its foundation corresponds to the archetypes and its typical symbols.[14]

---

[13] Letter from Pauli to Jung, December 23, 1947.

[14] To reiterate: that can be seen through a historical comparison of unconscious individual products (dreams, fantasies, etc.) with products from cultural imaginaries, such as those presented by folklore, mythology, and history of religions: they always present certain analogous patterns or motifs, organized around a central symbolic meaning.

2.2.12 The Transition from Natural Symbols to Cultural Symbols

As we have seen, symbolic thinking represents both the foundation of psychological functioning and the radix of the cultural imaginary. In its cultural forms, its symbolic expressions go through a number of transformations and elaborations, eventually reaching high levels of sophistication and specificity. Whereas the agricultural rite mentioned above represents a somewhat basic, primitive symbolic form, in Roman religion, prior to the Greek influence, one could see astounding symbolic differentiation.

> In the life of a Roman farmer every act, however specialized, had its specific religious meaning. There was one class of deities—of *Di Indigites*—that watched over the act of sowing, another that watched over the act of harrowing, of manuring (...). In all agricultural work there was not a single act that was not under guidance and protection of functional deities, and each class had its own rites and observances. (Cassirer, 1944, p. 97)

In such example, every facet of the cultural activity (in our example, agriculture), and the ways in which it was *thought and understood*, was inextricably connected to and organized by a religious system and its rites; therefore, one could say that every major aspect of life was connected to symbolic thinking and functioned through it.

Such typical images, narratives, and rituals, through endless historical differentiation and conscious elaboration, come to constitute a culture's imaginary wealth, its typical psychological functioning: the original primordial images (or *natural* symbols) turn into collective representations, and these, in their differentiated and elaborated forms, become *cultural* symbols (Jung, CW18, §579). In analytical psychology, that represents the other part of the collective psyche, which Jung called *collective consciousness*, and its collective representations.

2.2.13 The Collective Consciousness: *Représentations Collectives*

Jung took the concepts of collective representations and collective consciousness from Durkheim, via his studies of Lévy-Bruhl and Mauss (Shamdasani, 2003). For Durkheim (1912/1995), collective consciousness was made up of collective representations of a social and historical nature: the typical ways in which the collective aggregation, the social group, shared symbolic forms such as myths, legends, rites, and religious narratives and practices. Meaning, social bonding and structure, thought, and action were predicated upon such collective mentality, which presented a specific "psychical individuality" (Durkheim, 1895/1982, p. 129)—the particular imaginary configuration that instituted and characterized a society in its specificity.

In his *Les formes élémentaires de la vie religieuse*, Durkheim (1912/1995) inaugurates the study of the role of imagination and symbolic forms in the constitution of social life among primitives. He finds such role inextricably connected to religious forms. "Religion is an eminently social thing. Religious representations are collective representations that express collective realities; rites are ways of acting that are born only in the midst of assembled groups and whose purpose is to evoke, maintain, or recreate certain mental states of these groups" (p. 9).

Lévy-Bruhl (1910/1985) clarifies Durkheim's concept of collective representations. He agreed with Durkheim in many regards: *représentations collectives* conform the mentality of a certain social group and are common to all the group members, appearing as rites, beliefs, mythical narratives, and so on, shared by the group; they are socially determined and historical and function as collective categories. However, Lévy-Bruhl focused more on their specific *functioning*: their feeling-tone, their emotional and affective character. For him, what defined collective representations was that they are contaminated or permeated by emotional and motor elements. As categories, they are interposed between the subject and the object or empirical reality. Then the resulting image (the representation as primitive "idea") of the object is never "objective", but always mingled with sensations and emotions. Therefore, the representations and their accompanying emotions are what configure "reality", and they can be impervious to experience, to the point of openly contradicting it (Vieira, 2003). However, the affective elements are not subjective in the sense that they pertain to the individual. The contamination of the representations follows a *collective* pattern, shared by the whole social group or people (Lévy-Bruhl, 1910/1985), and is in fact what defines the group's mentality, the way the whole group experiences reality. As such, the *représentations* constitute an object of faith which is not reflexively considered; they are taken for granted—for the primitives, they *are* their reality; their existence and their world are predicated upon them.

Like Durkheim, Lévy-Bruhl found that such primitive imaginary was essentially religious. For the primitive, the representations always commanded respect, fear, and adoration (Lévy-Bruhl, 1910/1985). That is why he called them *mystical*: they constitute a mentality founded on imaginary, invisible, immaterial forces and influences. As mentioned before, Marcel Mauss (1903) found in the concept of *mana* the archaic idea that underlay all such magic, mystical representations, and was their form and condition—the element common to all primitive symbolic imaginaries. In other words, the "contamination" expressed by Lévy-Bruhl corresponds to the representations' *mana*, their mystical character and general functioning. As a category, *mana* functions as a psychic quality[15] that conditions knowledge and representation and thus configures collective and *unconscious* "*habitudes directrices de la conscience*"—the group's mentality and behavior, its categories of identity and otherness. Indeed, it represents an archaic form of all other mental categories, that is, a primordial image or archetype: "But mana isn't only a special category of primitive thought, and today, by way of reduction, it is again the first form assumed by other categories always functioning in our mind, those of substance and of cause" (Hubert & Mauss, 1909, p. xxx).

Jung affirmed that all such "mystical" collective representations originally spring from religious forms, the archetypes. They are projections of the unconscious psychic structure—its archetypes—upon reality and symbolic systems. Their *mana* corresponds empirically to their *numinosity*:

[15] "Le *mana* n'est. pas simplement une force, un être, c'est. encore une action, une qualité et un état" (Mauss, 1903, p. 77): it is at once a *symbol*, a primordial image, an archetype.

the ability to command "respect, fear, and adoration" is the very definition of *numen*. As *numina*, they are emotionally charged and hence embody collective forms of *feeling* and *valuing*.[16] Such collective forms—collective feeling-values—are not restricted to the primitive mentality; they somehow reach our modern mentalities and underlie collective psychic contents.

2.2.14 Collective Consciousness as a Social Imaginary

Jung called collective consciousness the ensemble of such collective contents that configure collective mentalities, or *cultures*. Broadly speaking, these correspond to "common sense", cultural worldviews, *Weltanschauungen*. More specifically, collective consciousness refers to "universally recognized ideals or feeling toned collective ideas" (Jung, CW9ii, §54), general beliefs, values, and so on. We can see that, as a concept, it corresponds to our modern *social imaginaries*[17]: the common collective representations that underlie culture and tradition and as such are historical, that is, have been transformed and evolved socially and collectively into *collective formulae*—collective ideas, beliefs, and values bound with collective feeling. Such formulae function and configure our identity and psychical dynamics analogously to *représentations collectives* in primitive mentality. To recall, the latter are

> general ideas and value-categories which have their origin in the primordial motifs of mythology, and they govern the psychic and social life of the primitive in much the same way as our lives are governed and moulded by

[16] "It is not only concepts and ways of looking at things, however, that must be termed collective, but also *feelings*. Among primitives, the *representations collectives* are at the same time collective feelings, as Lévy-Bruhl has shown. Because of this collective feeling-value he calls the *representations collectives* 'mystical,' since they are not merely intellectual but emotional" (Jung, CW6, §692).

[17] Some other authors also revisited and reworked Durkheim's concept of collective consciousness, but approximating it to the concept of *imaginary*, as I have attempted to do in this work. Among them are Castoriadis (1975/1987), Taylor (1989, 2002, 2004), Maffesoli (1993a, 1993b), and Appadurai (1996). Another didactic—albeit rather limited—way of looking at the concept of collective consciousness in Jung would be to consider it as the ensemble of *social representations* (e.g., Farr, 1987; Farr & Moscovici, 1984; Jodelet, 1991; Jovchelovitch & Gervais, 1998; Moscovici, 1988) that are particular to a culture or social group.

> the general beliefs, views, and ethical values in accordance with which we are brought up and by which we make our way in the world. They intervene almost automatically in all our acts of choice and decision, as well as being operative in the formation of concepts. (Jung, CW16, §247)

That means that the contents of collective consciousness are also interposed between the subjects and empirical reality; they function as *typical and collective* mental categories for seeing and experiencing reality, and thus shape how the world and oneself are imagined, represented, sensed, signified, *felt*.

Of course, in comparison with the primitive, in us all of that supposedly happens in a much more differentiated, rationalized, secularized, modern, and *civilized* way. Nonetheless, what is important for this work is the archaic modes of psychic functioning, and its needs, do not simply disappear, no matter how secularized, a-symbolic, and rationalized a culture and its subject are. As Lévy-Bruhl affirmed, opposing Durkheim, such primitive ways are not "phases" that simply go away, superseded by reason and logical thinking; prelogical thought and collective feeling continue to live in modern (and even postmodern) women and men. If we follow Jung's theory, we must acknowledge that the unconscious psyche, as the depository of such archaic ways, is our very psychic foundation, and therefore never disappears; its instinctual necessities and primeval emotionality have always needed expression through symbols, primordial images, and myths.

In the contemporary social imaginaries, certain systems of ideas and values seem to fulfill such deep-seated needs. For this work, it is necessary to highlight those elements that, *though being neither truly symbolic nor religious*, still function as *représentations collectives* and correspond, in one way or another, to the old forms of symbolic thinking—to mythic, religious imaginaries (and as such are best understood through their comparison with anthropological material, as argued in this chapter).

Speaking about and from the perspective of the last century, Jung saw such secularized imaginaries in *mass ideologies*: the "political and social isms of our day" (CW9i, §617). They operate as ersatz mythological imaginaries: "Our fearsome gods have only changed their names: they now rhyme with -ism" (CW10, §469), and, just like religions, they have an equal fascinating force and totalizing claim.

> Now religious ideas, as history shows, are charged with an extremely suggestive, emotional power. Among them I naturally reckon all *representations collectives*: everything that we learn from the history of religion, *anything that has an "-ism" attached to it*. The latter is only a modern variant of the denominational religions. A man may be convinced in all good faith that he has no religious ideas, but no one can fall so far away from humanity that he no longer has any dominating *representation collective*. His very materialism, atheism, communism, socialism, liberalism, intellectualism, existentialism, or what not, testifies against his innocence. Somewhere or other, overtly or covertly, he is possessed by *a supraordinate idea*. (Jung, CW9i, § 125; e.a.)

As supraordinate ideas, such ideological systems function like the collective representations did for the primitive: as cultural "categories of the imagination" (Jung, CW8, §254), they condition how reality—both inner and outer reality—is experienced and represented; as mass phenomena, they are commonly taken for granted as self-evident truths; they exude a "mystical" aura, a somewhat magical power or enchantment, derived from the feeling-value of their ideas and images, which elicit collective feelings and emotions.[18] "These are the magical *representations collectives* which underlie the slogan, the catchword" (Jung, CW7, 231)—and the *propaganda*, the advertisement. Such fascination originates *identification*, for it touches the primal, collective roots in each subject. Accordingly, such collective ideas will govern the prescribed modes of behavior and shape the *habitudes directrices de la conscience*. Therefore, these social imaginaries, as with the primitives, will be typified by a characteristic *mass psychology*, *a mass mentality*.

In our present century, the *ism*, the ideology that characterizes our social imaginary is the one studied in this work: that of total capitalism and total *consumerism*.

[18]To advance one contemporary example: the general postmodern enthusiasm, fascination, and blind faith in *technology* (and the commodities that represent it, of course), a prime embodiment of consumerism's *numen*. Among its divine prerogatives would be to concede us *eternal* progress and *transcendence* of the human condition; we can be anything, everything is possible (virtually). Such ideologies reach their apex in the image of the *cyborg*, a sign for the *posthuman* condition. In such postmodern mythologies, the creed is that we can become technological *Übermenschen*, genderless, malleable, performing like demigods (see, e.g., Braidotti, 2006; Butler, 2003; Gane, 2006; Haraway, 1991; Warwick, 2000). The hubris is obvious, even obscene; its numen sells, though.

"Each culture or epoch produces a new interpretation of archetypal motifs, trying thereby to establish a link with those structural elements that are the roots of consciousness in human nature" (Vieira, 2003, p. 57). This new interpretation, as the mythological aspect of collective consciousness, corresponds to the specific imaginary of each culture. As stressed before, the archetypes of the collective unconscious represent the connection of the psyche with Nature, and at the same time the foundations of what is human, for they characterize the specifically human modes of *perceiving, acting, fantasizing, and imagining*. Therefore, the way the imaginaries articulate expressions of such fundamental basis is crucial, for they will represent the connections to our foundations and at the same time shape and configure the individual psyche and subjectivity.

In this section, the *collective* realms of the psyche—collective unconscious and collective consciousness—were discussed in their relations with the imaginary. The next section will discuss the personal realm: how *subjectivity* is shaped through and in such symbolic imaginaries, in (possible) dialectics with the individual's own will, agency, history, and imaginative-symbolic function.

2.3 Subjectivity and the Imaginary: The Personal Psyche

In analytical psychology, the concept of *subjectivity* corresponds to the *personal* part of the psyche: the personal unconscious and its complexes, and ego consciousness.

2.3.1 Ego Consciousness

The ego, or in fact *Ich*, the *I*, corresponds to a psychic *complex* that is the center of consciousness. As such, it is the subject of all personal acts of consciousness (Jung, CW9, §1). As the center of the conscious personality, the "I" is equal to our conscious *subjectivity*, our continuous sense of identity: to what and how we think, sense, feel, and imagine we are consciously; it represents "the subjective factor" (Jung, CW8, §77). What distinguishes the ego—in relation to the other complexes—is consciousness. In a manner similar to William James's, consciousness is defined as a quality, not as a substance (Vieira, 2003); it is the quality that characterizes the contents that are in relation to the ego. In opposition to unconsciousness, which means undifferentiation, consciousness means precisely differentiation, discrimination, distinction—"the ability to distinguish between the *objects of the imagination* and especially to distinguish between them and the subject" (Meier, 1989, pp. 21–22; e.a.)—and subsequent *assimilation* (into a relationship with conscious contents, whose center is the ego).[19] As such, it is related to decision, choice, and thus to *freedom*: the more conscious one is, the more one has free will, at least theoretically; if one behaves unconsciously, that implies no decision and hence has no ethical value. That means that only ego consciousness is capable of agency proper, of acting ethically (cf. Hannah Arendt's concept of *action*, as opposed to mere behavior).

The process of formation of consciousness is an immensely complicated one. In this work I shall be content with pointing out some of its basic elements. Ego consciousness is constituted partly by the inherited disposition (the character constituents) and partly by unconsciously acquired impressions and their attendant phenomena (Jung, CW17, §169). Starting from such basis, consciousness is enlarged by the gradual assimilation of materials from experience—as contents and representations—in a historical process, that is, during the subject's lifetime. Such assimilation refers to experiences of the external world as well as of the inner world; ego consciousness mediates their dialectical relationships, acting as a "*connecting system* both for them and between them" (Meier, 1989, p. 18). To return to our themes of image, representation, and imaginary, ego consciousness is at once the mediator for, the result of, and what gives meaning to the dialectics between the unconscious psyche and collective consciousness, or the social imaginaries. This idea is formulated in Kant's definition: the ego is the "transcendental synthesis of apperception" (ibid., p. 29).

[19] Meier (1989, p. 22) quotes Rosenkrantz, a disciple of Schelling's, for his clarity: "We only come to know it when we can distinguish between ourselves and the thing (outside us), that is with our discrimination, and can look upon the thing as it is presented to us. We must separate ourselves and the thing and then link them up again in our consciousness (our assimilation)". That was written in 1868.

However, ego consciousness is intermittent: underneath it, there flows continually the unconscious psyche. Consciousness arises out of such depths, in the child, but also in us every morning.[20] As discussed, such unconscious depths function as fantasy- or dream-thinking, whose dynamics can happen every time we are in a more or less unconscious state, or (put differently) unconscious of something. In the child, however, ontogeny recapitulates phylogeny: ego consciousness and subjectivity emerge gradually out of such primitive, primary state of unconsciousness, just as they did in the primitive.

2.3.2 *Participation Mystique* and Unconscious Identity

According to Jung, what typifies subjectivity and its relation to the outer world in such primeval unconscious state is what Lévy-Bruhl called *participation mystique*, a psychical functioning characterized by *identity with the object* and *projection*. Unconscious identity, in fact, is equal to participation mystique:

> It denotes a peculiar kind of psychological connection with objects, and consists in the fact that the subject cannot clearly distinguish himself from the object but is bound to it by a direct relationship which amounts to partial identity. This identity is founded on an a priori oneness of object and subject (…) [on] the original non-differentiation of subject and object, (…) the *primordial* unconscious state. (Jung, CW6, §781, 741)

Such state is archaic in the sense that it is prior to the formation of a distinct subject: whereas consciousness means differentiation, what characterizes the primitive unconscious mentality is undifferentiation, indistinctness from the object. The object here can be concrete, or a person, but also an image or an idea: "an identification with a thing or the idea of a thing" (Jung, CW 6, §781), that is, with something imaginary. It means

[20] "In childhood it awakens gradually, and all through life it wakes each morning out of the depths of sleep from an unconscious condition. It is like a child that is born daily out of the primordial womb of the unconscious" (Jung, CW11, §935).

that both object and subject are perceived through the *imagination*. Such dynamics can happen to us whenever we are in a more or less unconscious state. "Unconscious identity is a well-known psychological and psychopathological phenomenon (identity with persons, things, functions, roles, positions, creeds, etc.), which is only a shade more characteristic of the primitive than of the civilized mind" (Jung, CW11, §817, note 28).

Identity implies that the subject becomes bound to the object; it is as if the object, or its *idea*, became part of the subject. The key point here is the idea, or representation. The subject identifies with the idea, the meaning, and the value seen in the object: because this is a perception conditioned by the unconscious, the subject sees the object as a *symbol*. That is why participation mystique as original identity involves projection: in identifying with the object, the subject projects some part of her psyche upon the object, as a *symbol*—it is the projected symbol that constitutes the bondage. "It is an irrational, unconscious identity, arising from the fact that anything that comes into contact with me is not only itself, but also a symbol" (Jung, CW11, §389). Therefore, what are projected are psychic (unconscious) contents, as symbols, through which the object is perceived. As we have seen, that is characteristic of symbolic thinking, of imagination and fantasy. "Participation mystique is a characteristic of symbols in general. The symbol always includes the unconscious, hence man too is contained in it" (CW11, §337, note 32). The symbol projected is an expression, a representation, of an unconscious content and its corresponding *meaning* and affective *value* (its quantum of libido). With projection, the object will carry the symbol, will be its depositary; inasmuch as the unconscious content symbolized is emotionally toned, or charged with libido, the object will therefore be perceived as fascinating, or numinous; it will be charged with "mana". Again, that is why it is *mystique*; the object acquires a mystical, numinous character. Its objective reality is contaminated by the subjective content: its image or representation is endowed with an archaic imaginary quality. Being symbolic, the object is always more than what it is concretely; it has acquired layers of meaning, symbolic meaning. Jung agrees with Lévy-Bruhl (Segal, 2007) in that such primitive thinking is indifferent to contradiction, both as regards identity and projection: the primitive can believe he is a parrot or other sacred bird, and yet he knows he cannot fly; the object can be absolutely banal and yet be perceived as mana, sacred, numinous.

This archaic identity or indistinction means that the primitive psyche, being unconscious, is always *projected*, remaining in a state of fusion with the outside world: "the psychic and the objective coalesce in the external world" (Jung, CW10, §128), the inner world and the exterior world are one. In this state there is no individual subjectivity proper, for the "subject" here is still collective, or indistinct from the object. One cannot speak of individuality, or an *I*: ego consciousness is still nascent, and the unconscious psyche is projected and mingled with the environment.[21]

Therefore, in *participation mystique*, one only finds collective relationship (Jung, CW6, §12). Moreover, if the psyche of the primitive and the child is projected, their relationship to the world, and to themselves, will be completely imaginary. Their psychic functioning corresponds to a fusion with the *imaginary*.

Here we can recall the other concept of Lévy-Bruhl that characterizes primitive mentality. Such symbolic projections and corresponding contaminations of the object are not arbitrary. They are collective and specific to the social group: as a symbolic system, they correspond to the *représentations collectives*, the ways the collective psyche has been projected into symbolic productions. As mythical narratives, rites, religious forms, and so on, they condition the specific forms of projection and identity for the whole social group and each of its members. It is through such imaginary and its primordial images that the primitive's unconscious psyche will be projected; if the symbols are the channels for libido, then their specific cultural configurations will direct her/his libido and therefore her/his life and the way she/he perceives the world. The primitive's psyche will correspond to such collective system, *projected*, with which she/he *identifies* at the same time.

For the primitive and infants, whose psyches are projected upon people and things, the world and life will be enchanted, impregnated with a mysterious, fascinating, terrible, sacred character, derived from the symbols that express the archetypal foundation. They both live a symbolic life

[21] In the small child, such state corresponds to an archaic identity with the parents (especially with the mother).

in a primeval symbolic world, in archaic *union* with both world and instinct—but undifferentiated from them, without individuality, without conscious reflection: unconscious. They live in and through affects and emotions, and their corresponding images—the symbolic images of fantasy and imagination. *They live in a dream.*

This description corresponds to our archaic functioning, which underlies all conscious life. On the other hand, the more the person is *dissociated* from such symbolic life, from the *symbol* and hence from instinct, from nature—the more she/he will dream of returning to such state of wholeness, of primal unity. This form of existence—as *whole*, but unconscious, united to affects and symbol—will then correspond to the "paradise of childhood" (Jung, MDR, p. 272).

2.3.3 Personal Unconscious and the Complexes

With the progressive formation of ego consciousness, the child's (or the primitive's) psyche is gradually differentiated from collectivity, and subjectivity or personhood begins to form. Such differentiation from the collective psyche (both the collective unconscious and collective consciousness) also implies the formation of a *personal unconscious*. The personal unconscious is constituted by the contents derived from the individual's personal experience and therefore depends on his/her particular history, attitudes, and decisions. Such contents can become conscious, that is, they are incompatible or infantile individual factors that ego consciousness has either repressed or simply never acknowledged. As such, they correspond to an *unconscious subjectivity*.

As distinct from the contents of the collective unconscious (the archetypes), the contents of the personal unconscious are called *complexes*. A complex can be defined as an image (representation) of a specific psychic situation imbued with strong emotional content. Such image is charged with libido, that is, with a strong emotional tone (feeling), and functions as a nucleus of *meaning*, around which an ensemble of other feeling-toned ideas is organized. The most important complexes—for example, the mother and father complexes—are based on archetypes. The complex has inner coherence, is a "whole" in itself, and is relatively autonomous in relation to consciousness. Empirically, complexes appear projected as *partial personalities*: in the child, as imaginary beings; in the primitive or in schizophrenics, as spirits, magical or terrible beings, and so on; but also in the normal products of our imagination—in fantasies and dreams, our psychic contents appear as personalities, as people, or voices. They correspond to the different *voices* within us. Following Duarte (2000), who put this theory of Jung's in dialog with Bakhtin (1929/1984), we might affirm that our *subjectivity is polyphonic*. Together with the conscious subjectivity (i.e., the ego's identity), the complexes represent our "many subjectivities". As complexes are unconscious by definition, they also attest to the dissociability of the psyche. In Jung, the subject is *relatively* dissociated.

As distinct from the archetypes, which are collective forms given a priori, the complexes are personal: they are formed in the dialectical relations between the individual's life history and conscious choices, his cultural context—the social imaginaries that inform him—and the archetypal foundation. That means that complexes and the personal unconscious are *sociocultural*—and at the same time individual and subjective, given that they depend on the individual's unique life history and context, and his (possible) agency.

2.3.4 Two Typical Complexes: Shadow and Persona

Let me illustrate such theoretical propositions with two examples of complexes that are important and will be useful later: shadow and persona.

The shadow complex corresponds to the aspects of the personality that are opposite to ego consciousness (the I): the neglected, inferior, non-developed unconscious contents of subjectivity. As a complex, it usually appears personified (e.g., Mr. Hyde, the primitive barbaric shadow of the one-sided rational scientist Dr. Jekyll) and is projected upon people or things or ideas.[22]

The persona corresponds to the *social mask* we put on; it serves as a function for relating to others and to the world. It represents the collective role, the *ideal social identity*, a representation of subjectivity given by

[22] In dreams, it usually appears as a figure of the same sex, the *bête noire* (Meier, 1989).

the social imaginary, which the subject adopts and more or less identifies with. However, being a mask, it merely denotes an appearance that represents *collective* consciousness; as such, it is partial and superficial, or two-dimensional. By definition, it only feigns and simulates individuality (Jung, CW7); it refers to what one (the individual) *is not*, but that oneself and others think or believe one is (Jung, CW9i, §221).

The persona as such is necessary for social relationships; the problem is the extent to which the subject identifies with it. The more identified the subject is, that is, the more she/he thinks or believes she/he really *is* the persona, that it is her/his identity or subjectivity, the more she/he becomes collective and artificial, that is, not individual: *massified*, identical with a parcel of the collective imaginary (e.g., the ruthless lawyer, the coveted celebrity and the lifestyle, the sex symbol, etc.). Correspondingly, the more the *shadow*—the repressed and neglected individuality, which is left unconscious—will compensate. Against such superficial or one-sided identity, the inner world (the hidden unconscious depths) usually reacts, with the shadow-figure becoming more primitive and activated[23] (Mr. Hyde). This produces a schism in the personality, a split subject. As a complex, the shadow will be projected upon the environment: whereas certain people, or places, or ideas are seen in a terrible light, the ideal imaginary embodiments of the persona (celebrities, etc.) are seen as Olympian gods or sacred creatures. Of course, none of such perceptions correspond to objective reality: here we are dealing with the dynamics of unconscious projection and identification.

2.3.5 Complexes and Projection: *Participation Mystique*

One can readily see that, as unconscious factors, the complexes follow the dynamics of *participation mystique*: they tend to be projected, and the subject to be bound to them emotionally by partial identity. To recall the dynamics: part of one's psyche (subjectivity) is projected; the subject

[23] Seen from an energetic standpoint, the unconscious gets activated with the surplus of libido from all the contents of individuality that, being opposed to the persona, have been excluded from conscious life.

becomes attached to the object upon which the psychic content (through a symbol) was projected, that is, the subject identifies with it; being unconscious, the projection acquires a compulsive and repetitive character; objective reality is "contaminated" by the projection, by the emotional value that was projected; and, instead of experiencing empirical reality, the subject perceives his/her own unconscious contents projected.

Therefore, the complexes function as *categories*. As our *personal* unconscious foundations, they define, in an analogous manner to archetypes, the unconscious ways one sees, feels, and acts in the world—but in a historical, cultural, and familiar way, that is, in accordance with the individual's specific life history and context. Hence, the complexes are the personal equivalent to the *représentations collectives*; they are the expression of how the cultural imaginary "fills up", shapes, or conditions the subjective psyche. The analogy is rendered explicit by Jung:

> One can perceive the specific energy of the archetypes when one experiences the peculiar feeling of numinosity that accompanies them—the fascination or spell that emanates from them. This is also characteristic of the personal complexes, whose behaviour may be compared with the role played by the archetypal representations collectives in the social life of all times. As personal complexes have their individual history, so do social complexes of an archetypal character. (CW18, §547)

2.3.6 Complexes and Archetypes: An Unconscious System of Projections

Jung's theory establishes that the unconscious psyche precedes consciousness and is by definition limitless and inexhaustible: consciousness can never assimilate the whole of the unconscious psyche. That implies that we *always* have unconscious factors (as complexes and archetypes), that is, we are always unconscious to some extent. If we follow the axiom that everything that is unconscious will be projected (for there is no differentiation between unconscious contents and the environment, by definition), a second conclusion is that the complexes and archetypes will form and function as a *system of projections*, in which what one perceives is not the object or objective reality, but one's own projected contents as images. Such system, in a manner that is analogous to the primitives', is partially and collectively shaped by the culture's collective representations, its *imaginary* forms. In other words, our psyches always function through such categorical filters. However, the difference lies in the possible attainment of consciousness. The more the subject is unconscious, the more her apperception, experience, and so on will be conditioned-mediated by both her culture's collective representations and her own projected psychic contents. And, the more unconscious the subject is, the more such dynamics resemble *primitive psychology*: as participation mystique is the opposite of consciousness and individuality, the more her (unconscious) psyche is projected, the more the subject remains *collective*, immersed in and indistinguishable from the outside world (which is not experienced objectively either, but as a reality contaminated by unconscious contents).

The implication is that such unconscious state always means *alienation*: from oneself, and from the world. An alienation that incurs in a fault, an ethical blemish, for one is not being oneself in the world. If the complexes represent substantial parts of the subject's individuality, or her subjectivity, when projected they produce an *emptiness*, an inferiority: a portion of the subject's psyche—meaning, value, emotion: a complex part of subjectivity—is severed from her, and she, alienated from herself, becomes unconsciously bound to the object onto which it was projected. The Narcissus myth expresses such fundamental psychological dynamics in a radical way: what is projected in the myth is the whole personality (as self-image).

If we all have complexes, such dynamics are bound to appear continuously during our whole life. Again, in Jung's theory, the subject is dissociated, consisting of multiple subjectivities; the personality is a disjointed agglomerate, not a whole. However, *contra* the postmodern creed, for Jung such state (of unconsciousness) represents an ethical fault, and therefore an *ethical task*. That is due to the empirical fact that the personality has a tendency to differentiate itself, a tendency toward consciousness and individuality, with which we must reckon. Against the unconscious inertial tendency—to projection, partial identity, and non-differentiation—Jung ascertains an opposite inner tendency to differentiate what is individual from what is collective; to recognize in the projection a subjective content and synthesize it with the conscious personality—a synthetic process mediated by the *symbol*. Such tendency, as a lifelong process, he called the process of individuation.

2.3.7 Individuation and Subjectivity: The Desires of Social and Individual

Individuation is defined as "the development of the psychological individual as a being distinct from the general, collective psychology" (Jung, CW6, §757). It represents the progressive psychic differentiation (from the collective) into a wholeness, a totality: the formation of a dialogical unity out of the multiple voices, personalities, and collective contents that constitute us. A unity that composes an *in-dividuum*: an indivisible, non-atomizable subject.

Against the inertial, natural unconscious functioning, individuation is based on an opposite *telos* of the psychic system: it corresponds to what was mentioned before regarding the collectivity as the "principle of individuation" (*principium individuationis*), the spiritual principle of differentiation that seeks development and cultivation, through the symbol, in opposition to mere instinctuality—but functioning *in the individual*. The progressive actualization of such principle in the individual—which is never completed: it is a lifelong process—is the meaning of individuation,[24] the "legitimate realization of the individual entelechy" (Jung, 2002, p. 191).

Seen from a collective or social standpoint, such *telos* is contained in archetype and symbol: the striving to form *culture* through differentiation from mere animality-instinctuality (*feritas*). Seen from the standpoint of the individual, the spiritual *telos* corresponds to individuation, the impulse toward differentiation from what is collective and unconscious.

[24] The relation between individuation and Self is summarized by Jung thusly: "Individuation means becoming a single, homogenous being, and, in so far as 'in-dividuality' embraces our innermost, last, and incomparable uniqueness, it also implies becoming one's own self. We could therefore translate individuation as 'coming to selfhood' or 'self-realisation'" (CW 7, §171).

It can be said that it is the *telos* of what Jung called *Self*[25]: the center of the unconscious and at the same time the (virtual) center of the whole personality. Both sides of the spiritual *telos* (the cultural and the individual ones) depend on the ego, on individual consciousness, for their complete actualization. Only the individual consciousness is capable of autonomy, ethical effort, and agency, and—through them—of differentiation in relation to the unconscious and to what is collective.

Seen from an energetic standpoint, such principle implies that libido, or *desire*, has two possible finalities. One is the natural inertia: to remain instinctive, close to animality, unconscious, undifferentiated. The other finality, mediated and directed by archetype and symbol, is a desire for *differentiation and synthesis: the desire for individuality and culture.* Miriam Freitas (1991) rescues in this dual face of desire a plea for the consideration of the virtual *uniqueness* and singularity of each human being. In her work, such inherent *telos* of the personality, of its libido, is seen in an analogous way to Espinosa's *conatus*, and translates into a subjectivity based on an unalienable dialectics between the desire for the *social* and the desire for the *individual*,[26] and their strict interdependence (Freitas, 1991, pp. 149–151). The desire for individuality corresponds to a *telos* for being unique, for a singular identity, for being *whole*. The other face of such desire corresponds to the fact that we humans are social, *plural* beings (or, as Hannah Arendt put it, based on Kant: the human condition is that of *plurality*). That is the desire for the social, the collective: not merely for social insertion and relationship, but for *acknowledging, and relating to, the other as also unique*; for one's uniqueness is perceived in the (necessarily different) uniqueness of the other. The interdependence of the desires means that the subject's *humanity* is a virtuality: it represents the life task of *realizing socially* her or his individuality. Hence, a truly human society, the *plurality*, corresponds to *the social actualization of equality among uniques* (p. 94).[27]

[25] Henceforth, I employ "Self", with a capital S, whenever there appears the need to sharply distinguish Jung's concept from the common usage. This is not without its problems, for in quotations from Jung's Collected Works, for instance, the concept appears as "self" (not capitalized).

[26] "Desejos do social e do individual", in the original.

[27] In the original, "realização social da igualdade entre únicos". In her *Diaries*, Hannah Arendt (2006) affirms the same idea through the Greek *agonal* principle, which she opposes to the *aris-*

Jung posits that the actualization of such desires requires an ethical effort, against a natural gradient or inertial force. That represents first an *opus contra naturam*: socially, there has to be an endeavor, mediated by the symbol, to constitute culture against the natural instinct. Analogously, the individual has to stand against the natural tendency to project and identify with the object, and to remain unconscious, in an infantile, primitive state.

However, it is the opposite, or in fact the *perversion* of such desires that characterizes our contemporary ethos: instead of individuality—the *mass man*, standardized, identified with individualism, selfish egotism, and private interest; in lieu of a social world—a *mass society*, collapse of plurality. Therefore, Freitas (1991) will stress that, for the actualization of the desires for the social and the individual, an act *contra culturam* that institutes a different human relation with both nature and culture is required.

> If it is possible to say that culture emerges from an *opus contra naturam*, today we may add that the establishment of a healthy relation with men's nature will inevitably require an opus *contra culturam*. (…) It is only going against the grain [or in the opposite direction] of the capitalist logic's desires that we will find the realization of the desire for the social. (p. 138)

As we have seen, the primordial expression of the relation (and possible unity and synthesis) between nature and culture appears as a *symbol*. Without the symbol to give it direction and meaning, instinct (nature) remains a blind compulsion; without the symbol, there is no refinement and no cultivation toward culture and consciousness, and no connection to our archetypal foundations. Confrontation with and integration of the unconscious can only happen through the latter's symbolic productions. Such process engenders consciousness and individuality, and a symbolic life.

Those are some of the reasons why this work proposes a study of the nocturnal, natural source of symbols in us: the *dream*.

---

teuein principle: "the agonal principle, which is not about the best or the worst, but rather 'to come into one's own' together with the other" (p. 402). Her translator notices the difficulty of translating "to come into one's own" (in "Notas y apendices", p. 999): it means "'Llegar a lo proprio de uno mismo', literalmente; para Arendt, 'Llegar a lo suyo proprio (a su distinción)'—que un hombre consigue 'su forma' o llega a su 'esencia'" ('To reach one's own proprium', literally; for Arendt, 'To become what one really is (his distinction)'—[through] that a man actualizes 'his form' or reaches his 'essence'). This is only actualized socially, in plurality, *inter homini*: *junto con el otro*.

References

Appadurai, A. (1996). *Modernity at large: Cultural dimensions of globalization*. Minneapolis: University of Minnesota Press.

Arendt, H. (2006). *Diario filosófico 1950–1973* (R. Gabás, Trans.). Barcelona: Herder.

Bachelard, G. (1942). *L'eau et les rêves: Essai sur l'imagination de la matière*. Paris: Corti.

Bakhtin, M. M. (1984). *Problems of Dostoevsky's poetics* (C. Emerson, Trans.). Minneapolis: University of Minnesota Press. (Original work published 1929).

Batkin, L. M. (1990). *Gli umanisti italiani: Stile de vita e di pensiero*. Roma: Laterzi.

Braidotti, R. (2006). Posthuman. All too human: Towards a new process ontology. *Theory, Culture & Society Annual Review, 23*(7–8), 197–208.

Bruner, J. (1986). *Actual minds, possible worlds*. Cambridge: Harvard University Press.

Butler, J. (2003). *Gender trouble. Continental feminist reader*. London: Routledge.

Carus, C. G. (1846). *Psyche*. Pforzheim, Germany: Flammer und Hoffmann.

Cassirer, E. (1944). *An essay on man: An introduction to a philosophy of human culture*. New Haven: Yale University Press.

Cassirer, E. (1946). *The myth of the state*. New Haven: Yale University Press.

Castoriadis, C. (1987). *The imaginary institution of society* (K. Blamey, Trans.). Cambridge: MIT Press. (Original work published 1975).

Corbin, H. (1964). *Mundus imaginalis or the imaginary and the imaginal* (R. Horine, Trans). Zürich/New York: Spring.

Duarte, L. F. B. (2000). Bakhtin e Jung: Relações dialógicas. *Boletim do Centro de Estudos Junguianos C. A. Meier, 5*(1), 6–9.

Durand, G. (1963). *Les structures anthropologiques de l'imaginaire*. Paris: Dunod.

Durand, G. (1994). *L'imaginaire: Essai sur les sciences et la philosophie de l'image*. Paris: Hatier.

Durand, G. (1996). *Introduction à la mythodologie. Mythes et sociétés*. Paris: Albin Michel.

Durand, G. (2004). *Las estructuras antropologicas del imaginario: Introducción a la arquetipología general*. Mexico: FSE.

Durkheim, É. (1982). *The rules of sociological method* (W. Halls, Trans.). New York: Free Press. (Original work published 1895).

Durkheim, É. (1995). *The elementary forms of religious life* (K. E. Fields, Trans.). New York: Simon & Schuster. (Original work published 1912).

Farr, R. M. (1987). Social representations: A French tradition of research. *Journal for the Theory of Social Behavior, 17*(4), 343–370.
Farr, R. M., & Moscovici, S. (Eds.). (1984). *Social representations*. Cambridge: Cambridge University Press.
Freitas, M. G. (1991). *Taipas e toupeiras*. Porto Alegre: Fonte Phi.
Gadamer, H. G. (1975). *Truth and method*. London: Continuum.
Gane, N. (2006). When we have never been human, what is to be done: An interview with Donna Haraway. *Theory, Culture & Society Annual Review, 23*(7–8), 135–158.
Garin, E. (1973). *L'umanesimo italiano: Filosofia e vita civile nel Rinascimento*. Roma: Laterzi.
Haraway, D. (1991). *Simians, cyborgs and women: The reinvention of nature*. New York: Routledge.
Hubert, H., & Mauss, M. (1909). *Mélanges d'histoire des religions*. Paris: Alcan.
Jameson, F. (1981). *Narrative as a socially symbolic act*. New York: Cornell University Press.
Janet, P. (1890). *L'automatisme psychologique*. Paris: Alcon.
Jodelet, D. (1991). *Madness and social representations*. London: Harvester/Wheatsheaf.
Jovchelovitch, S., & Gervais, M. (1998). *The health beliefs of the Chinese community in England: A qualitative research study*. London: Health Education Authority.
Jung, C. G. (2002). *Cartas de C. G. Jung* (Vol. II). Petrópolis: Vozes.
Lévy-Bruhl, L. (1985). *How natives think* (L. Clare, Trans.). Princeton: Princeton University Press. (Original work published 1910).
Maffesoli, M. (1988). *Le Temps des tribus. Le déclin de l'individualisme dans les sociétés de masse*. Paris: Méridiens Klincksieck.
Maffesoli, M. (1993a). *El conocimiento ordinario: Compendio de sociología*. Mexico: FCE.
Maffesoli, M. (1993b). *La contemplation du monde: Figures du style communautaire*. Paris: Grasset.
Mauss, M. (1903). *Esquisse d'une théorie générale de la magie* (l'Année Sociologique, 1902–1903). Retrieved from http://classiques.uqac.ca/classiques/mauss_marcel/socio_et_anthropo/1_esquisse_magie/esquisse_magie.html
Meier, C. A. (1986). *Soul and body: Essays on the theories of C. G. Jung*. Santa Monica: Lapis Press.
Meier, C. A. (1989). *Consciousness*. Boston: Sigo Press.

Meier, C. A. (Ed.). (2001). *Atom and archetype: The Pauli/Jung letters, 1932–1958*. Princeton: Princeton University Press.

Moscovici, S. (1988). Notes towards a description of social representations. *European Journal of Social Psychology, 18*, 211–250.

Otto, R. (1917). *Das Heilige: Über das Irrationale in der Idee des Göttlichen und sein Verhältnis zum Rationalen*. Breslau: Trewendt und Granier.

Segal, R. A. (2007). Jung and Lévy-Bruhl. *Journal of Analytical Psychology, 52*(5), 635–658.

Shamdasani, S. (2003). *Jung and the making of modern psychology: The dream of a science*. Cambridge: Cambridge University Press.

Stephens, J. (1990). *The Italian renaissance: The origins of intellectual and artistic change before the reformation*. New York: Longman.

Taylor, C. (1989). *Sources of the self: The making of modern identity*. Cambridge, MA: Harvard University Press.

Taylor, C. (2002). *Varieties of religion today: William James revisited*. Cambridge, MA: Harvard University Press.

Taylor, C. (2004). *Modern social imaginaries*. Durham and London: Duke University Press.

Thomas, J. (Ed.). (1998). *Introduction aux méthodologies de l'imaginaire*. Paris: Ellipses.

Vieira, A. G. (2003). *Imagem, símbolo e narrativa na Psicologia Analítica de C. G. Jung*. Unpublished doctoral dissertation, Universidade Federal do Rio Grande do Sul, Porto Alegre, Brazil.

Warwick, K. (2000). *I, Cyborg*. London: Century.

Wunenburger, J.-J. (1997). *Philosophie des images*. Paris: PUF.

Xavier, M. (2006). O conceito de religiosidade em C. G. Jung. *Psico, 37*(2), 183–189.

Xiberras, M. (2002). *Pratique de l'imaginaire: lecture de Gilbert Durand*. Quebec: Les Presses de l'Université Laval.

Yates, F. (1996). *Lulio y Bruno: Ensayos reunidos I*. Mexico: FCE.

3

Symbolic Imaginaries: The World of Dreams

Overview
This chapter introduces a general theoretical framework on the subject of dreams in relation to the other research subjects. Dreams as important origins of symbolic imaginaries and cultures, and their specific significance, roles, and functions in the latter, are presented. Next the main theoretical fundaments regarding the concept of dream are discussed. The dream is conceptualized as a natural product of the unconscious and its symbolic function. Dynamics and functioning of the unconscious are explained through the dream as its embodiment. Possible relations between dream and subjectivity—the ways dreams can express or reveal subjectivity and social reality—depend on interpretative and hermeneutic outlooks, which are presented.

M. Xavier, *Subjectivity, the Unconscious and Consumerism*,
https://doi.org/10.1007/978-3-319-96824-7_3

3.1 Dream, Culture, and Symbolic Imaginaries: Historical Import

In stark contrast to our modern Western view on the dream, historical and anthropological studies[1] have evinced the vast importance dreams always had across prior cultures and ages. Like its brother myth, the dream was usually connected to the very foundations of a culture and society—their particular cosmology, anthropology, religion and cult, language, medicine, ideas of individuality, and social roles—and was seen and understood through such specific cultural traits, forming distinct dream cultures. If seen anthropologically, therefore, dreams are always bound to the culture in which they originate, and cannot be completely dissociated from it[2] (Shamdasani, 2003). As a vital cultural factor, the dream had many-sided social functions in important decisions and prophecy, in institutions such as initiatory and passage rites, in dynamic cultural changes, in art and other creative acts: it was a fundamental factor of the symbolic imaginary and its corresponding practices.

A distinguishing characteristic of such prior societies was that their main symbolic formations and narratives—their mythical and religious imaginaries, which sustained and shaped the whole of culture—were indissociably intermingled with dream. Indeed, some societies do not even make clear distinctions between dream and myth (Kracke, 1987). The similarities between dream and myth seem quite clear: both are imaginary narratives, consisting of symbolic images that are full of meaning for both the collective and the subject. As Jung put it, myths are dreamlike structures (CW5, §28), and so have been seen as *collective or social dreams* since the beginnings of psychoanalysis. Freud wrote that myths were the "age-long dreams of young humanity" (1908/1925, p. 182), and for Karl Abraham (1913), myths were the dreams of a culture, and dreams were the myths of the individual.

[1] See Kilborne (1981), with extensive bibliography; Shulman and Stroumsa (1999), Tedlock (1992a), Von Grunebaum and Caillois (1996).

[2] The ancient dream theories of Artemidorus, Synesius, and Macrobius, for instance, were more holistic and respected historical and cultural context (of dream and dreamers) in their interpretations.

3.1.1 Dream as Origin of Symbolic Imaginaries

The dream's vitality and importance for cultural life were consistent with its mythic character, and related to its being seen as of divine origin, as a form of communication with the heavens, the netherworld, or the spiritual world.[3] To use a symbolic image, the dream was the *messenger of gods* (and of *daimons*, spirits, etc.): as the premier expression of the symbolic function, it conveyed the "messages" of the archetypes, the primordial images—which, projected, were seen as gods, demons, or spirits.

However, the role of dream goes beyond that of a mere messenger: it can be said that the "gods" themselves—and therefore the whole symbolic imaginaries they were part of—originated in dreams. As collective representations, gods can be understood as *cultural symbols*, as we have seen. Yet their primordial origin is to be found in the raw, original *natural symbols* that appeared spontaneously and involuntarily in *individual* dreams and fantasies.[4]

> Symbols were never devised consciously, but were always produced out of the unconscious by way of revelation or intuition. In view of the close connection between mythological symbols and dream-symbols, and of the fact that the dream is "le dieu des sauvages," it is more than probable that most of the historical symbols derive directly from dreams or are at least influenced by them. (Jung, CW8, §92)

If the *représentations collectives* that made up social imaginaries were at first symbolic images originating in dreams and creative fantasies (Jung,

[3] Here are a few examples from our Western historical roots. In Greek antiquity: in Plato, the dream still had divine origin. As demonstrated by Meier (1983/2003), the origins of modern Western medicine and therapy lie in the ancient Greek practices of dream incubation and the cult of Asklepius; Hippocrates and Galen diagnosed through dreams. In Homer, *oneiros* was either a winged, divine messenger of the gods, or the gods themselves (Meier, 1986). The Stoics made prognostics through dreams, which were seen as objective facts that happened to (or befell) the dreamer. As for Judeo-Christian tradition: as is well known, Talmud, Kabbalah, and Bible ascribe great import to the dream. In the Jewish tradition, the dream is seen as a conversation with God, source of transformation, guidance, and development. In the Zohar, the dream is a step in the journey toward God.

[4] Of course the natural symbolic function could also appear in a more collective or social fashion, such as in collective visions, fantasies, and so on, which probably played an important role too in the origin of cultural symbols.

CW18, §579), then dreams were part of the very foundation of culture. As the most natural, spontaneous, and primeval expression of symbolic thought, dreams were the main source of natural symbols (CW18, §497), which, through continuous development and refinement, became the cultural symbols that constituted sophisticated imaginaries.

That is the reason why cultural imaginary forms (myths, religions, etc.) were always intermingled with dreams: they all spring from the same source, our "inner pantheon", the symbolic function of the unconscious psyche, which shaped all experience of reality.[5] The dream, however, is naturally the more subjective or direct experience of such primeval substratum of life: it is its nocturnal half (Bastide, 1966).

However, the expression "nocturnal *half*" is a bit misleading. From the so-called primitive cultures up to early Greek antiquity, the dream was not seen as completely separate or even essentially different from "reality", nor as a mere "imaginary experience" or illusion. There was no sharp distinction between reality and dream. For the ancient Greeks, for instance, the dream was an objective datum, not something one *had*[6] but that rather *happened* to one, as real as the lightning and the stars.[7] In sum, there was no schism between the everyday, "outside" or waking world, and the dream world. The dream itself was chiefly a nocturnal experience—the *nocturnal imagination*; yet its world permeated the waking state as well, for imagination and symbolic thinking were integral to psychic reality.

Such view is characteristic of societies in which the symbol lived and was paramount; societies in which nature and culture were united and shone with numen and awe; societies in which the symbolic imaginary permeated all life, in a fundamental union of the inner, oneiric, and symbolic world of the unconscious with the "outside" world. If the psyche is

[5] I am referring to Jung's idea of *psychic reality*—namely, that all our immediate experience of reality is by definition mediated by the psyche (it is *represented* as image); hence all reality is psychic, or imaginary.

[6] Or worse still, *made*—"I've made a dream", as the French and the Italians say, an expression Jung considered to be the zenith of European rational hubris.

[7] Augé (1999) mentions that such notion is common to all the original African cultures (or imaginaries): "What *all the African systems of representation* stage (…) is the reality of the dream (to be more precise, the continuity between waking life and the life of the dream)" (p. 27; e.a.).

naturally and originally symbolic, and our experience of reality is always psychic (psychic reality), then reality is symbolic: *symbolic life*.

Symbolic life means a life in which the symbolic function in each one lives and is united to and expressed by the social symbolic imaginary. As we have seen, with the primitive the archetypal realm was projected upon people and things, upon the *world*, impregnating it with a mysterious, fascinating, numinous, sacred character. In symbolic cultures, such mythic, imaginary worldview not merely persists with, but can be considered as *foundational* for the development of rational, logical culture and individuals. For the ancient Greeks, our utmost example of the cultural and human wealth that derives from the union of symbol and reason, it produced a characteristic passion, an "admiring wonder" (Arendt, 1978, p. 148): Plato's and Aristotle's *thaumadzein*, wonder at and reverence for the enchantment of the world.[8] The Greeks still lived in an enchanted world, the world of sacredness, symbol, and imagination: the world of dreams.

3.2 A Concept of Dream: Jungian Theory

Let us begin with a synthetic conceptualization of dream. For Jung (CW8, §505), the dream is the spontaneous self-portrayal or representation, in symbolic form, of the actual situation in the *unconscious*. Being the most natural product of the unconscious psyche, the dream reflects its characteristics and functions.

3.2.1 Dream and Its Imagistic Symbolic Language

The first and most important characteristic for us is that its form of expression is symbolic: it speaks the *symbolic language* of the unconscious

[8] Pier Paolo Pasolini (1969) expressed the wonder and sacredness of such dream-life with the beautiful words he placed on the lips of the centaur—the symbolic integration of human, animal (instinctual principle), and divine (spiritual principle)—in his film *Medea*: "All is sacred! There is nothing natural in Nature (…). Wherever your eye roams a god is hidden. And if he be not there, the signs of his presence are there—in silence, or the smell of the grass, or the freshness of water. Yes, everything is holy!"

psyche. As the concept of symbolic language (and symbol) has already been discussed, let me just remind the reader of some of its general characteristics: it is an imagistic language, poetic, fantastic, and metaphoric, that engenders creative, imaginative narratives through flows (trains) of images, associated through analogy and contiguity. Oftentimes its representations and narratives are sensed as being full of meaning and value, which is a reflection of its symbolic character: the symbol represents meaningful ideas of an irrational nature, charged with emotion and value (which are equivalent to its libido-charge). Jung calls such symbolic language "the emotionally charged picture-language of dreams" (CW18, §464).

These notions of an imagistic symbolic language and its fundamental connection with the oneiric were already in G. H. von Schubert (1780–1860), influential author from the *Naturphilosophie* movement of German Romanticism:

> In (…) *The Symbolism of Dreams* [1814], Von Schubert declared that when man has fallen asleep, his mind starts thinking in a 'picture language', in contrast to the verbal language of waking life. For a while both languages may flow parallel or mingle, but in dreams proper only the picture language (*Traumbildsprache*) remains. It is a hieroglyphic language in the sense that it can combine many images or concepts into one picture. Dreams use a universal language of symbols, which is the same for men throughout the world. (Ellenberger, 1970, p. 205)

Traumbildsprache means literally "dream-image language" (or "speech"). Such "universal language of symbols" corresponds to Jung's concept of an *archetypal* symbolic language, which is the language of instincts, the language of imagination. As we have seen, Jung (CW5) relates such language to an archaic mode of thinking, the dream- or fantasy-thinking, which thinks through the symbolic language: in such psychic functioning, everything is connected and touched by the same emotional colors and sensations. A corollary is that, when we dream, we return to the kind of thinking—mythological, magic, symbolic—of ancient mankind and children, the historical psychological roots[9] from which consciousness

[9] Such view had already been advanced by Nietzsche (1880/1984, pp. 20–21): "in our sleep and dreams, we go through the work of earlier mankind once more (…) man still draws conclusions in

and logical thinking spring. In dreaming we are still *symbolic*, connected to our foundations, to the primeval imaginary; we are *whole* and function as humans have functioned for millennia.

> (…) in dreams we put on the likeness of that more universal, truer, more eternal man dwelling in the darkness of primordial night. There it is still the whole, and the whole is in him, indistinguishable from nature and bare from all egohood. Out of these all-uniting depths arises the dream. (Jung, CW10, §304)

In relation to the conscious psyche, which represents the "surface", as it were, symbolic thinking expressed as dream and fantasy is a continuous process that flows in such depths, underneath conscious, logical, or rational processes. As the expression of the non-stop unconscious psyche, it represents the basal psychic functioning underground. In other words, *we are always dreaming* (or fantasizing), even while fully awake, but only perceive it when there is an *abaissement* or a voluntary concentration on the objective fantasy. Dream-thinking, the symbolic function of imagination, therefore defines our very psychic functioning.[10] Jung expressed such continuous flow of the unconscious process as "the dream that is going on all the time in your unconscious" (Jung, SVI, p. 25).

3.2.2 Dream as Nature: A Symbolic Expression

Such concepts of *natural* unconscious language and thinking underlie Jung's stress on the natural and spontaneous character of dreams. Having its own language and form of thinking, there is no reason to imagine that the unconscious distorts or dissimulates anything. Nature is not

his dreams as mankind once did *in a waking state*, through many thousands of years (…). This old aspect of humanity lives on in us in our dreams, for it is the basis upon which higher reason developed, and is still developing, in every human: the dream gives us a means by which to understand them better". And: "in me ancient humanity and the animal world, even the entire primeval age and past of all sentient being continues to mediate, love, hate, and reason in me—I have suddenly awakened in the midst of this dream" (1882/1974, section 54).

[10] In fact, long before Freud and Jung, the pioneers Frederick Myers and Théodore Flournoy, influenced by German Romanticism, had already proposed the *psyche as a continuous dream*, and hence the dream "as the paradigm for a general psychology of the unconscious" (Shamdasani, 2003, p. 129).

deceitful—quite the opposite: it is often crudely direct and blunt. As the unconscious psyche is by definition autonomous in relation to consciousness, the dream represents the *autonomous* voice of Nature in us, our daily experience of the "nocturnal realm of the psyche" (Jung, CW16, §325).

Vieira (2003) points that the language of symbols and dreams thus resembles the parable, which does not dissimulate but *teaches*, a concept that connects Jung to Jewish hermeneutics: Jung (CW12, §41) takes from the Talmud the idea that "the dream is its own interpretation'. In other words *I take the dream for what it is*" (CW12, §41). Seeing the dream as a natural symbolic expression implies that its image and meaning (signified and signifier) are one and the same thing, are a unit in the symbol: *the dream is its own meaning.*

Such hermeneutical and symbolic view represents the antithesis of the Freudian theory on dreams, which has become a hegemonic part of collective consciousness. For Freud, the dream-image (manifest content) always represented *something else* (latent content), which was already known a priori (the wish or desire: the instincts or drives, *distorted* by repression). Through seeing repression as inescapable, Freud split apart the dream-image: then signifier and signified are alienated from each other by definition. In defining the dream-image as a distorted product, Freud proposes a *semiotic* consideration of dream (and by extension of any unconscious product) in which the dream itself is rendered useless: one can dream about a hat, or a key, or stairs, or any other image—the images will always refer to the (sexual) theory given a priori. In other words, the dream and its meaning are replaced by *ideology* (Freitas, 1991).

By contrast, for Jung the unconscious images of fantasy, seen as symbols, are found *pure* in the dream—not distorted, not repressed, not as symptoms, *not as signs*: pure. Walter Benjamin (1916/1982) expressed it very lyrically and imaginatively: "Fantasy is also the soul of the dream. To dream means to pluck/catch/harvest the images in their purity[11]" (p. 157). If we recall that the symbol always expresses something unknown, thus being of unconscious origin, we reach one of the most important conclusions for us: it means that *the dream is an objective datum, an objective fact*

[11] "La fantasia è anche l'anima del sogno. Sognare vuol dire cogliere le immagini nella loro purezza".

that carries an irrational quantum, something *unknown* that wants and needs to be known. Such unknown factor is the discourse of the unconscious, its *objective perspective* on the dreamer and the world, expressed autonomously and symbolically. "The dream presents an impartial truth. It shows the situation which by law of nature is" (Jung, DAS, p. 204)—no matter how terrible, or beautiful, or vitriolic, or tender, or grotesque, or sacred its dream-portrayal is. J. V. Foix (1953/2004) expressed an age-old truth when he wrote "*It's when I sleep that I see clearly*[12]".

3.2.3 Dream as Drama or Narrative: The Oneiric Structure

Common to all the expressions of such symbolic language—symbolic imagination, fantasy, myths, rituals, and dream—is their archetypal tendency to have a *narrative* character and appear structurally as a *drama*,[13] in the classical Aristotelian sense (Jung, CW8; Meier, 1977; Vieira, 2003). Whereas myths, rites, and so on are social imaginary dramas, the dream can be analyzed as a *drama intérieur*[14] (Meier, 1986), our psychic drama in the unconscious. It usually presents the following typical structure:

1. *Exposition*: The narrative begins with the *dramatis personae*, time and place of the action, and a presentation of the problem or *theme* with which the dream will deal.

---

[12] "És quan dormo que hi veig clar".

[13] Which is another datum endorsing the view that the origin of symbolic imaginaries lies in the dream: "The dramatic tendency of the unconscious also shows in the primitives: here, possibly everything undergoes a dramatic illustration. Here lies the basis from which the mystery dramas developed. The whole complicated ritual of later religions goes back to these origins" (Jung, SCD, p. 30).

[14] Jorge L. Borges comments: "Si el hecho de soñar fuera una suerte de creación dramática, resultaría que el sueño es el más antiguo de los géneros literarios; y aun anterior a la humanidad, porque los animales sueñan también. Y vendría a ser un hecho de índole dramática; como una pieza en la cual uno es autor, es actor, es el edificio también—es el teatro. Es decir, que, de noche, todos somos dramaturgos de algún modo" (Borges & Ferrari, 2005, p. 110). This idea was already in Schopenhauer (in *Parerga and Paralipomena*), who said that every dreamer is a Shakespeare and the director of his own oneiric dramas (cf. Meier, 1987, pp. 77, 87).

2. *Development*: There happens a complication of the drama's theme, some tension in the initial situation; "the problem stated at the beginning starts to have an effect, it gets complicated, the plot thickens" (Jung, SCD, p. 380), which leads to a
3. *Culmination or* peripeteia: There is a conflict or crisis, "a certain escalation, a climax, a turn of events" (ibid.); something decisive must occur.
4. *Solution* (*lysis*): Reasonable and meaningful ending for the crisis and the initial problem (in ancient drama, the solution usually came deus ex machina). Sometimes the solution is lacking in the dream (i.e., it ends with an unsolved situation), which is also meaningful. The end of the dream usually presents a new problem (ibid.).

For dream interpretation, it is also important to notice that, for Aristotle and Jung, "drama" means action (Meier, 1986; Vieira, 2003). Hence it is essential to perceive how the dreamer *acts* in the dream, that is, his/her positioning regarding the problem posed by the dream, and how the drama changes because of it. That is called *ego attitude*, for ego consciousness is represented by the dreamer himself or herself in the dream narrative: it is his or her conscious subjectivity.

3.3 Subjectivity and Interpretation: Subjective and Social Dimensions in the Dream

The ways the dream reflects, expresses, and represents subjectivity are contingent on the way one looks at and tries to understand the dream: they depend on its *interpretation*. Interpretation will necessarily reflect the *theoria* (Greek: to look attentively at), the specific ways one looks at the object. In what follows I present possible interpretative strategies, how they are embedded theoretically, and how they may unveil subjectivity and social-collective dimensions in the dream.

3.3.1 Two Levels of Interpretation

Jung (CW7) proposes two different *levels* of interpretation: on the objective level, and on the subjective level.

In the *interpretation on the objective level* the oneiric images and contents are seen concretely, that is, as objects. Here the dream expresses something about the persons, figures, and situations that appear in it "as they exist objectively", in "outer reality" (Meier, 1986, p. 111). It refers the oneiric contents concretely to *external situations*. For instance, if someone dreams with "a friend from work", in this interpretative level one would see the dream as referring to the friend concretely. This interpretation is justified as long as the conditions that exist in the dream are a known part of the dreamer's external world (Meier, 1986). On this level the dream shows its view on the dreamer's subjectivity presenting the way the external world has influenced it—and how the subject reacts to, experiences, and assesses external reality.

In the *interpretation on the subjective level*, "all the contents of the dream are treated as symbols for subjective contents" (Jung, CW7, §130). This means that we should take everything that happens in the dream as psychological, symbolic personifications of elements in the dreamer's own psychic system or personality (Meier, 1986): that is, as parts of the dreamer's subjectivity, or subjectivities. Here the oneiric contents are not taken concretely, but *symbolically*: the dream is seen as an expression of the symbolic function of the unconscious, through its symbolic language. This level thus corresponds to a symbolic interpretation, the hermeneutic method (Jung, CW7, §131).

The personifications of subjectivities in the dream correspond to the *complexes.*[15] As we have seen, complexes are partial personalities that tend to appear personified; in dreams, they also tend to be acted out as dramatic narratives. In the same way that they tend to be projected upon the environment (and especially on other people), in dreams they appear *projected* upon the oneiric objects (other people, animals, things, etc.). Seen this way, all the *dramatis personae* in the oneiric drama are parts of the dreamer's *subjectivity* as it is seen from the standpoint of the unconscious. The energy with which such subjective contents are charged appears as the *emotional tone* they elicit or carry in the dream (their libido-charge corresponds to the affect, the emotional value of their representation).

[15] Archetypes can also appear: in which case, the oneiric content will not present a "subjective" character but rather a definite collective and mythological one (analogous to a myth motif), and an accompanying strong emotional tone (for the archetypes are numinous). As the main complexes are rooted in archetypes, they can also appear with an archetypal character.

Accordingly, important dreams will appear very vivid, dramatic, cathartic, and affective; their drama usually fills the dreamer with a seemingly alien, autonomous emotion.

In analytical psychology, both levels of interpretation can be seen as complementary. Furthermore, the proposal that characterizes the empirical part of this research consists in (tentatively) applying both levels of interpretation to the dreams studied. The symbolic interpretation (on the subjective level) will reveal the unconscious discourse on the dreamer's *subjectivity*, seen as ego (conscious subjectivity) and the complexes (unconscious subjectivities). The more concrete interpretation (on the objective level) will refer to the "external conditions" of subjectivity, to the "outside world" which the subject inhabits. An important part of such external conditions is the specific cultural configuration (collective consciousness) in which the subject lives. In this work, the *imaginary of consumerism* (ImCon) is seen as the specific form of such cultural configuration. As seen, the psychic contents and forms that one calls subjectivity are sociocultural in origin; one must consider them in relation to both individuality and their collective aspects, for there is always interplay between them in every psyche (i.e., we are social subjectivities).

> As individuals we are not completely unique, but are like all other men. Hence a dream with a collective meaning is valid in the first place for the dreamer, but it expresses at the same time the fact that his momentary problem is also the problem of other people. (…) Moreover, every individual problem is somehow connected with the problem of the age, so that practically every subjective difficulty has to be viewed from the standpoint of the human situation as a whole. (Jung, CW 10, §323)

If we take the expression "problem of the age" as signifying the main forms of influence that the cultural ethos has on each of its subjects' psychic configuration, then presently we have much more reason to take the cultural factor into consideration: our age is characterized by massification, that is, "subjective" problems and forms tend to be more and more of a collective nature.

When one tries to apply both levels of interpretation, the dream can offer the possibility of seeing the relationships between the social (social imaginary, collective consciousness) and the subject from the standpoint of the unconscious. This view assumes that dreams have both cultural and individual significance, which lies in their capacity for furnishing an objective (or *transcendental*) discourse on both culture and subject. In fact, this view on dreaming is historical and traditional: it seems to be the most commonly found notion of dreams across cultures and ages (Lincoln & Seligman, 1935). In fact, it is this methodological proposition of applying simultaneously the interpretations on the subjective level and on the objective level (Jung, CW7) to the empirical night dream that situates the dream as object of study of the dialectical relationship between individual and culture, and reflects the idea of *psychological dialogism* put forward by cultural psychology (Valsiner, 1989, 2002).

Based on such view, in this proposal the oneiric image is seen and interpreted *both* in its subjective and objective significance: it is meaningful as a symbol of a subjective psychic process, but also as depicting the social aspects that shape and form the latter—the collective consciousness, the imaginary of consumerism.

As the reader might have guessed, the example I have in mind is that of McDonald's and McDonaldization, seen in the prototype dream. In it, "McDonald's", seen subjectively, represents the dreamer's *subjective identity* with the meanings, values, significations that McDonald's embodies for her, and the effects it has in her psychic system; seen objectively, it represents such meanings, values, and so on, in culture, in our consumerist imaginary, and all their concrete, objective, and psychic effects (i.e., McDonaldization, the world as *McWorld*).

Looked at in this way, the oneiric appears as the interface between the collective (the social imaginaries), the unconscious psyche, and subjectivity—having the subject as mediator, a participative, and (possibly) active actor in the symbolic drama. However, as the dream is orchestrated and directed by the unconscious, it will inevitably feature *clashes* with collective consciousness—and especially with the dreamer's perception or view of the latter. This work is especially interested in such clashes between the nocturnal, natural imaginary and the social imaginaries of consumption and how the subject is positioned, or positions her-/himself, in relation to them in the dream—for that defines her/his *subjectivity*.

3.3.2 Interpretation: Causal and Final Viewpoints and Functions of the Dream

In analytical psychology, every psychic phenomenon must be tackled via two complementary viewpoints: causality and finality. If the dream is seen strictly from a causal standpoint, it will be regarded as a mere result of some previous factor (day remnants, instinct, or even biological phenomena). This implies a semiotic interpretation: if the dream was merely *caused* by a factor, and there is nothing else to see in it, therefore it is seen as a *sign*, whose meaning is already known a priori: its value is that of a *symptom* of something that already happened. This is a causal-reductive approach[16] and is useful in itself, that is, it represents a possible and at times valuable way of looking at the dream-image.

Nonetheless, for Jung the psyche as a whole has a *telos*, a finalist character, which is expressed by the autonomous unconscious psyche: this idea implies that the dream has a meaning, a direction and reach of its own, and its own value. This is a *symbolic* standpoint: being symbolic, the dream always has some hidden (unknown, unconscious) meaning, of which it intends to be the best expression. Such hidden meaning, and in fact the whole dream, expresses the finality of the unconscious psyche: as self-regulation, but also as creative activity.

Self-regulation refers to the axiom that the psyche, like the body, constitutes a self-regulatory system, whose finality will therefore be homeostasis. Again in analogy to the body, the processes by which the psyche seeks equilibrium are essentially unconscious (autonomous, involuntary) in nature; and dreams are its expression and tool: "Dreams are the natural reaction of the self-regulating psychic system" (Jung, CW18, §248). Through them, the unconscious—as an autonomous *organ*—seeks psychic balance, which is an adequate and parallel relation between the ego (system of consciousness) and the unconscious system. Such finality will appear as certain qualities or *functions* of dreams. With the *compensatory function*, the dream attempts to compensate for some one-sidedness in the conscious attitude with the opposite material or attitude (i.e., the

[16] As the reader can see, such approach parallels Freudian interpretation: the difference is that in the latter the "cause" is a wish, a manifestation of desire, of the unconscious drives.

oneiric image stands more or less in opposition to the conscious attitude). The *complementing function* means that the unconscious content complements (i.e., attempts to make *complete*) the conscious picture of the dreamer's situation with something that was left out of it (i.e., that was repressed, judged wrongly, etc.). The *reductive function* is also compensatory but in a negative way: it works through a reduction or depreciation of a conscious attitude. Its expression, the reductive dream, tends "rather to disintegrate, to dissolve, to devalue, even to destroy and demolish" (Jung, CW8, §496). This function appears mainly in individuals whose internal reality is rather different from the one presented outwardly, the persona with whom the ego identifies.[17] The creative function of dreams appears under many guises; one of them is revealed in its *prospective function*: a dream's "symbolic content sometimes outlines the solution of a conflict" (Jung, CW8, §493); it anticipates future events through combinations of possibilities.[18] Besides these functions, it must be borne in mind that the dream is a fruit of unconscious *imagination*: the source of all creativity and inspiration.

If we assume that the unconscious tries to rectify or modify the conscious configuration through the dream, as a general rule the dream and its possible meanings (its possible interpretations) will have to be seen in light of the conscious attitude (Meier, 1977), the *conscious situation of life* that constellated or elicited that particular dream (or answer) from the unconscious. However, as further discussed in the chapter on Method, this requisite can be waived when one uses *series* of dreams.

One important point that is repeatedly stressed in this work is that the dream ought to be seen as a *possibility*, rather than a determinist decree; it usually shows a picture of the psychic situation and its *tendencies*. In fact, one can affirm that one of its main virtues is its "aptitude for revealing different points of view" (Jung, 1933/1994, p. 39). If we see this

---

[17] I mention this function and its tendency because many of the dreams analyzed in this work fit such category.

[18] It "is an anticipation in the unconscious of future conscious achievements, something like a preliminary exercise or sketch, or a plan roughed out in advance" (Jung, CW8, §493). It can appear as a positive guiding idea, or an aim, that transcends conscious knowledge. This is in line with the ancient belief that dreams are oracles; as the reader will see next, such "guiding idea", seen broadly, corresponds to the goal of individuation.

process dialectically, the tendencies, viewpoints, compensations, and so on—as expressions of the unconscious brought by the dream—stand as *antitheses* to ego consciousness. The synthesis at which they aim is *creative*, a third term which unites conscious and unconscious, and is expressed as a symbol. The oneiric symbol is therefore an expression of the hitherto unknown, a synthetic and paradoxical formation that tends to unite the opposites, creating a new situation. It is the bridge uniting the psychic poles; the basis and way of expression of what Jung called the transcendent function of the psyche.[19]

3.3.3 Dreams, Projection, and Ethical Trial: Subjectivity as Individuation

Positing the possible integration of the psyche through the oneiric symbol requires that we see the dream through a synthetic approach: the interpretation on the subjective level. Here the unconscious contents of the personality, the complexes as subjectivity, will appear personified and *projected* unto persons and objects. Seeing them on the subjective level implies that the dreamer has to *confront his/her projections* and acknowledge that they are parts of his/her subjectivity; they are aspects of and in him-/herself, in his/her psychic system. What is usually projected unconsciously on the environment (in participation mystique, which "empties" the subject) here appears as dream symbols, which need to be integrated into consciousness. That requires conscious *differentiation*: the dreamer has to distinguish between what is part of her/his subjectivity (or individuality) and what is not (what is the Other, the collective); it involves a moral and value judgment (is this tendency good or evil, creative or destructive, mine or alien?).

Through confronting the projections, the dreamer can be reunited with the unconscious parts of the personality that also make up subjectivity: ego consciousness then *assimilates* the qualities and contents that were projected and is thereby enhanced. The process of differentiation also involves recognizing what is *not* subjective: the collective in his/her

[19] "[I]t represents a function based on real and 'imaginary,' or rational and irrational, data, thus bridging the yawning gulf between conscious and unconscious" (Jung, CW7, §121).

psyche (i.e., archetypes and collective consciousness). It might be said that the process of acknowledging and reconciling with the Other in oneself is the condition for recognizing and reconciling with the Other exteriorly.

Therefore each meaningful dream represents an ethical trial, a plea for self-knowledge through self-examination: a moral task. As Meier (1987, p. 137) wrote, "Jung's interpretation of the dream 'on the subjective level' means that there is no more evading implacable self-awareness": the dream *demands* responsibility for acknowledging and assuming a critical positioning regarding oneself (one's unconscious tendencies and contents) *and* the objective world, the collective consciousness and the Other. Yeats (1914) expressed this idea poetically: "In dreams begin responsibility".

That can represent a dialectical process through which the unconscious becomes progressively conscious, that is, is assimilated by consciousness, and the personality thereby becomes more *whole*: the subject becomes more *individual*. This process of integration of the personality is the *telos* underlying each dream: the process of *individuation*.

3.3.4 Self and the Dream as Ethical Trial

One important question remains from such theoretical discussion on the dream. In and through the dream, what (or *who*) confronts us with such ethical task? What expresses our contradictions, criticizes us with acumen, and aims at a wholeness that by definition transcends our conscious knowledge?

Meier (1987) answers it concisely: "The phrase 'Dreams come from the self' would be very consistent with Jung's ideas" (p. 137). As mentioned, the Self (*Selbst*) is an *ethical center* in the unconscious, the actualization of which corresponds to the entelechy of individuation. Again, the historical origin of such idea, and in fact of the concept of *self*,[20] is to be found in the pioneer theoreticians of the imaginary, the unconscious, and dreams: the German Romantics. The closest forebear of Jung's concept is found in

[20] Modern and postmodern ideas of self usually bear little resemblance to both this original idea of self and Jung's concept.

Von Schubert. In his *Symbolik des Traumes* (1814), he postulated the existence of a second center in the psyche (*Seele*), which gradually emerged from the unconscious: he called it *Selbstbewusstein*,[21] the *inner poet* in us who, in dreams, speaks the poetic, oneiric, imagistic language of nature—*Traumbildsprache*—and calculates, by a superior algebra or knowledge, the relations between the past and the future, today and tomorrow (Béguin, 1954; Vieira, 2003).

Therefore the Self is what criticizes the dreamer, and provides him with an objective view on himself and the world through the dream. Anthropologically, Augé (1999) expresses in a beautiful way that *all* the "African systems of representation" (imaginaries) hold the same idea:

> The dreamer is the author of his dream but the dream imposes an image of himself and of his relation to others which he might reject in his waking state. *The dream introduces a problematic relation between oneself and one's self.* (p. 28, e.a.)

According to this tradition, dreams are expressions of the Self, through which such superior knowledge can be conveyed to us. The dreams interpreted in this work attest to that.

3.4 Final Remarks

If the dream is the most natural expression of the unconscious and its symbolic imaginary function, then to apprehend the dream means to apprehend the unconscious psyche. And, as C. G. Carus asserts in the epigraph above, if the unconscious psyche is the foundation of the whole psyche (*soul*), in order to understand the psyche—the subject, the psychological human being—one needs to understand the dream.

If, however, the objective is not to understand, but its opposite: to conquer, colonize, and commandeer the psyche, then one will necessarily

[21] The same concept is found in other Romantics under different names: e.g., Heinroth's *Über-Uns*; or Troxler's *Gewissen,* which represented, in his words, "The true individuality of Man, by means of which he is in himself most authentically, the hearth of his selfhood, the most alive centrepoint of his existence" (as cited in Ellenberger, 1970, p. 206).

seek to colonize the unconscious, the roots of the psyche and the imaginary, and the symbolic function that defines us as humans: one will attempt to colonize our dreams. In the next chapter, it will be argued that the colonization of subjectivity by the imaginary of consumerism attempts to consummate precisely that, through its artificial dreams: *consumption dreams*.

References

Abraham, K. (1913). *Dreams and myths*. New York: Journal of Nervous and Mental Disease.

Arendt, H. (1978). *The life of the mind*. New York: Harvest.

Augé, M. (1999). *The war of dreams: exercises in ethno-fiction* (L. Heron, Trans.). London: Pluto Press.

Bastide, R. (1966). The sociology of dream. In G. E. von Grunebaum & R. Caillois (Eds.), *The dream and human societies* (pp. 199–211). Berkeley: University of California Press.

Béguin, A. (1954). *El alma romántica y el sueño*. Mexico: Fondo de Cultura Económica.

Benjamin, W. (1982). L'arcobaleno (1915–1916). In G. Agamben (Ed.), *Metafisica della gioventù: Scritti 1910–1918* (D. Regenbogen, Trans., pp. 151–158). Torino, IT: Einaudi. (Original work written 1916).

Borges, J. L., & Ferrari, O. (2005). *En diálogo/I* (Edición definitiva). Madrid: Siglo XXI.

Ellenberger, H. (1970). *The discovery of the unconscious*. New York: Basic Books.

Foix, J. V. (2004). *És quan dormo que hi veig clar*. Barcelona: Edicions 62. (Original work published 1953).

Freitas, M. G. (1991). *Taipas e toupeiras*. Porto Alegre: Fonte Phi.

Freud, S. (1925). The relation of the poet to day-dreaming. In *Collected Papers, IV*. London: Hogarth Press. (Original work published 1908).

Jung, C. G. (1994). *Los complejos y el inconsciente* (J. L. Pacheco, Trans.). Madrid: Altaya. (Original work published 1933).

Kilborne, B. (1981). Pattern, structure, and style in anthropological studies of dreams. *Ethos, 9*(2), 165–185.

Kracke, W. (1987). Myths in dreams, thought in images: An Amazonian contribution to the psychoanalytic theory of primary process. In B. Tedlock (Ed.), *Dreaming: Anthropological and psychological interpretations* (pp. 31–54). Cambridge: Cambridge University Press.

Lincoln, J., & Seligman, C. G. (1935). *The dream in primitive cultures*. Retrieved from http://books.google.es/books?id=wH9qj79iU00C&printsec=frontcover&hl=es
Meier, C. A. (1977). *Jung's analytical psychology and religion*. Carbondale, IL: Southern Illinois University Press.
Meier, C. A. (1986). *Soul and body: Essays on the theories of C. G. Jung*. Santa Monica: Lapis Press.
Meier, C. A. (1987). *The meaning and significance of dreams*. Boston: Sigo Press.
Meier, C. A. (2003). *Healing dream and ritual: Ancient incubation and modern psychotherapy*. Switzerland: Daimon Verlag. (Original work published 1983).
Nietzsche, F. (1974). *The gay science* (W. Kaufmann, Trans.). New York: Vintage Books. (Original work published 1882).
Nietzsche, F. (1984). *Human, all too human: A book for free spirits* (M. Faber & S. Lehmann, Trans.). Lincoln: University of Nebraska Press. (Original work published 1880).
Pasolini, P. P. (Director). (1969). *Medea* [Motion picture]. Italy: San Marco SpA.
Shamdasani, S. (2003). *Jung and the making of modern psychology: The dream of a science*. Cambridge: Cambridge University Press.
Shulman, D., & Stroumsa, G. (Eds.). (1999). *Dream cultures: Explorations in the comparative history of dreaming*. New York: Oxford University Press.
Tedlock, B. (Ed.). (1992a). *Dreaming: Anthropological and psychological interpretations*. Santa Fe: School of American Research Press.
Valsiner, J. (1989). *Human development and culture: The social nature of personality and its study*. Massachusetts: Lexington Books.
Valsiner, J. (2002). Forms of dialogical relations and semiotic autoregulation within the self. *Theory and Psychology, 12*(2), 251–265.
Von Grunebaum, G. E., & Caillois, R. (Eds.). (1996). *The dream and human societies*. Berkeley: University of California Press.
Vieira, A. G. (2003). *Imagem, símbolo e narrativa na Psicologia Analítica de C. G. Jung*. Unpublished doctoral dissertation, Universidade Federal do Rio Grande do Sul, Porto Alegre, Brazil.
Von Schubert, G. H. (1814). *Die Symbolik des Traumes*. Leipzig: Brockhaus.
Yeats, W. B. (1914). *Responsibilities*. Retrieved from http://www.sacred-texts.com/neu/yeats/lpy/lpy080.htm

4

The ImCon as a Semiotic Imaginary: Consumption Dreams and the Subject as Consumer

The man with the proper imagination is able to conceive of any commodity in such a way that it becomes an object of emotion to him and to those to whom he imparts his picture, and hence creates desire rather than a mere feeling of ought.
W. D. Scott, *Influencing Men in Business* (1911)[1]

Overview
This chapter discusses the imaginary of consumption (ImCon) as a semiotic and semiological imaginary: a regime of signification composed of signs as social signifiers, which, like symbolic imaginaries, is also based on imagery and the irrational. Its logics of consumption, founded on consumption of social signification through commodity-signs, and of commodification, as the production of sign-values, are discussed. Consumption dreams, as fundamental constituents of the ImCon, are presented as the imaginary social representations that, being mass-produced following the logic and practices of advertising, determine and colonize desires and irrational factors, and signify and institute the social subject as a consumer.

[1] W. D. Scott quoted in Ewen (1976, p. 31).

M. Xavier, *Subjectivity, the Unconscious and Consumerism*,
https://doi.org/10.1007/978-3-319-96824-7_4

4.1 The ImCon as a Social System of Images and Signs

The social imaginary of consumption—the *ImCon*—refers essentially to three elements that are fundamental for contemporary consumerism: the *image*, the *irrational*, and *signs*.

Indeed, our culture can be defined by the epochal role that the image has for it. As Fine (2002) correctly notices, such role is perhaps its most conspicuous and obvious characteristic: "But what precisely is it that makes up consumer society? A flood of images immediately suggests itself" (p. 155). Expressing the same idea differently, Jameson (1991) called our postmodern, late capitalist society the "image society", the age of "media capitalism" (p. xviii). In many senses, the image has become the main product of our society. Contemporary global consumerism seems to be inexorably and fully engaged in what is one of its central activities: to turn everything into an image. It might be said that the economy itself becomes an economy of images. "Symbolic capital"—a truly eerie neologism that, in my opinion, summarizes our age—in fact means essentially this: how one's *images* are valued in the markets. Thus we can affirm with Debord (1967), "the image has become the final form of commodity reification" (quoted in Jameson, 1991, p. 17). Image, accompanied by appearance and signification, thus determines production, reproduction, and exchange. Accordingly, some contemporary social theorists have asserted that the fantastic and important role played by imagery today configures consumerism as a new, unprecedented social reality. Discussing Baudrillard, one of such theorists, Mike Featherstone (2007) notes that "it is the build-up, density and seamless, all-encompassing extent of the production of images in contemporary society which has pushed us towards a qualitatively new society in which the distinction between reality and image becomes effaced and everyday life becomes aestheticized" (p. 67). As noted, Jameson (1991) identifies in the full aestheticization of postmodern culture one of its marking characteristics; consumer society as "a new culture of images" is defined not merely by superficiality, but by "depthlessness" (p. 5). De Zengotita (2005) called it a "society of surfaces" (p. 100).

Somehow incongruously, what has traditionally been considered as the *depths* of the psyche—the realm of the unconscious—also plays a fundamental role in consumer society: consumption is essentially based on irrational and imaginary forces and elements, such as desires, emotions, affects, and impulses. Bauman (2007), for instance, ascribes to such elements a central import: "'consumerism' is a type of social arrangement that results from recycling mundane, permanent and so to speak 'regime-neutral' human wants, desires and longings into the *principal propelling and operating force* of society" (p. 28). Such "wants and desires" are of an irrational nature; to paraphrase Bell (1976), the axial principle for consumption is *functional irrationality*.[2] Bauman (2007) concludes that ultimately consumerism relies "on the *irrationality* of consumers, not on their thoroughly informed and sober calculations; on arousing consumerist *emotions*, not on cultivating *reason*" (p. 48).

From this point of view, the system of consumption is founded on what is intangible, immaterial, and essentially psychic: emotions are aroused and felt as psychological experiences; desires are ultimately based on our all-too-human longings and needs for meaning, value, and signification, or, more specifically, for a sense of individuality and of belonging socially (the desires for individuality and sociality already mentioned)—that is, for things or experiences that are thought, imagined, pictured. This idea constitutes the proper psychological side of the system: it depends on *imagination*.

If we now recall that everything psychic is by definition an image (a representation); that the basic functioning of the psyche rests on its capacity for imagining, for creating a flow of images (as imagination, fantasy, dream); and that such capacity is extensively *sociocultural*, then we can imagine the tremendous importance and power the social imaginary will have for consumption: the power to deploy, create, and fashion the "proper imagination", and thus "impart pictures", as the epigraph above goes, will be central for the system and will impact everything *psychic*, starting with the subject.

The ImCon therefore refers primarily to this cultural imagination, the social order of image, representation, and signification. What underlies

[2] Bell (1976) wrote that "In modern society, the axial principle is *functional rationality*" (p. 11).

and defines such order, under the social logic of consumerism, is the *sign*: it is a semiotic, semiological social imaginary. Whereas in previous eras the *symbol* represented the transition from nature to culture—transition which originated and was made possible by symbolic imaginaries that defined both culture and the human being—our age of consumption is marked and defined by a system of signs:

> What is sociologically significant for us, and what marks our era under the sign of consumption, is precisely the generalized reorganization of this primary level [the natural and biological order: nature] in a system of signs which appears to be a particular mode of transition from nature to culture, perhaps *the* specific mode of our era. (Baudrillard, 2001, pp. 47–48)

Such system of signs, together with the overwhelming imagery that accompanies it, corresponds to the ImCon as a semiotic imaginary.

4.1.1 The Social Logic of Consumption and the Sign

According to Baudrillard's (1970/1998) semiological theory on consumption, which grounds this chapter, it can be affirmed that the key principle of the social logic of consumption is: consumption is never based on the object per se—on its functionality, materiality, instrumentality, its use-value—but on *signification and difference*. What is fundamentally consumed (through the object) is social *meaning*. Hence what defines our consumer culture now is not the Marxian mode of production but the mode of signification (Baudrillard, 1975): the systematic production, consumption, and manipulation of social signifiers. The form these social signifiers assume under consumerism, and which is the central determinant of the system, is the form of *signs*.

Hence the radical assertion: "If it has any meaning at all, consumption means *an activity consisting of the systematic manipulation of signs*" (Baudrillard, 1968/1996, p. 200). Positing such fundamental role of the sign reflects the fact that there is a structural *homology* between sign and commodity: as the commodity functions as a sign, and the sign follows commodity-logic, the unit of analysis and elemental form of consumerism consists in the commodity-sign; it defines and summarizes the whole social system of consumption.[3]

To recall the previous discussion, what primarily characterizes the sign is that it is the form of representation in which *signifier and signified are split*; there is a fundamental schism between them, which is only united as an artificial (conventional) construction. Put differently, the relationship between them is always arbitrary. To simplify the argument, let us say that signifier and signified correspond to *image* and *meaning*. If seen as a sign, the meaning of the representation is by definition *exterior* and relatively *arbitrary* in relation to the image. The meaning is only united to the image through (1) convention and (2) fabrication. An example for (1) is a common social convention: a red cross represents a hospital. There is nothing in the image of the cross that naturally signifies "hospital". (Though the cross can have a wealth of meaning *if seen as a symbol*). In (2), meaning and value (signified) can be artificially attached to, or grafted into, the image: for instance, a logo for a brand, the Nike swoosh sign. There is absolutely nothing in that sign (well, maybe something resembling a wave) that signifies *anything*; the meanings and values (victory, sportsmanship, transcendence, success, etc.) that are crafted into it are completely arbitrary and external to it.

The sign here is the opposite of the symbol: whereas the symbol naturally unites, the sign splits and unites *arbitrarily and artificially* signifier and signified. While the symbolic image is its own reality, the sign substitutes for the *reality* of image an artificial (differential) meaning or convention, a significance that is by definition *external* to the image (if not completely, at least to some extent). Therefore the sign allows for non-reference to reality, for a certain *emancipation* from the real; this corresponds to its (possible) ideological character.

4.1.2 Commodity-Sign and Commodification

Let us return to the theme of consumption. From a semiological perspective, what is consumed is the sign, as the object or good that it signifies:

---

[3] Accordingly, Caro (1993/2002, p. 9) named such system as "neocapitalism of the commodity/sign".

the *commodity-sign*. This is a basic principle of consumption and its process of *commodification*—the fabrication of commodities as signs, through the systematic manipulation of signs. Baudrillard (1968/1996) explains such process referring to objects. First and foremost, "*To become an object of consumption, an object must first become a sign*. That is to say: it must become external, in a sense, to a relationship that it now merely signifies" (p. 200). This reflects the external character of signification in relation to the image, in the sign. Here the object cannot be taken in its concrete, objective functionality (for then it would not be *consumed*). In a way, it has to lose its real character and become external to a living, real, symbolic relationship with human beings and with other human artifacts—as, for example, a tool for the primitive: it remains at once material, concrete, and symbolic, and mediates symbolically the relationships with work, self, and others; it is thus not arbitrary.

In contrast, like the signified in a sign, the object *has* to become arbitrary: "only thus can it be consumed, never in its materiality, but in its *difference*" (Baudrillard, 1968/1996, p. 200). To sum up, in becoming a sign, an (arbitrary) object is consumed because of its (arbitrary) difference and signification (social meaning), which are external to the object itself. For example, a table (or a toothpaste, or cars, etc.) is consumed not for anything intrinsic or material about it, but because it represents "family life", signifies a certain taste, confers status, and so on. That is, the process of commodification is based on the social assignment of sign exchange value, or *sign-value*, to the object. Its arbitrary difference, meaning, and value are signified in relation to all other *sign-objects* within the social system of differences and signification: sign-value is always and by definition established in relation to *the code*, which personalizes the sign-object, the commodity-sign.

4.1.3 The Code as a System of Social Signification

An important concept in Baudrillard's theory, the system of exchange, or its abstract model, consists in what is known in semiotics as the *code* (*le code, la grille*: Baudrillard, 1968/1996, 1970/1998, 1973/1981; Gottdiener, 1996): the signifying system of "differences", of social values, a key to sociocultural interpretative frameworks, the ways we interpret signs and hence ascribe meaning. "A code is the overarching mode of sign organization that provides the social and cultural context for the 'correct' or widely accepted interpretation of specific symbols. Sometimes we also use 'semantic field' or 'the universe of meaning' for the concept of code" (Gottdiener, 1996, p. 10). To put it simply, under consumerism, such cultural codes become subsumed under *one* general code of sign exchange value, which reflects sign logic and commodity-logic and determines the political economy of the sign prevalent in consumerism. The code functions (including, and especially, in its acculturative role) as a grammar, or a language[4] without a syntax: it "is undoubtedly the most impoverished of languages: full of signification and empty of meaning. It is a language of signals" (Baudrillard, 2001, p. 20). It is in this sense that Baudrillard (1968/1996) says that consumption is a *system of meaning*, like a language; its code is equivalent to consumer society's "signifying fabric" (p. 200), its regime of signification.

Therefore, being a system of *social signification*, the code determines consumption through its logic of *social differentiation and personalization*—applied not merely to the commodities but to the consumers. The fundamental idea here is that commodities are consumed because their sign-value, their signification, and difference (as social meaning, and as social classification: status values in a social hierarchy) are magically transferred to the consumer. By consuming the sign (as a commodity), the consumer is personalized and differentiated: she is (*imaginarily*) *socially signified*, acquires social meaning, is assigned a place in the social order, and so on. By positioning herself in relation to the sign (her choice of a product), and therefore to the code (partaking of the code), she is integrated into consumer society, and positioned within it in relation to the other consumers and to herself: the meaning, significance, and difference that constitute the relationship with world, others, and self are instituted by the sign-value and its consumption. It must be noted that the code (and therefore consumerism as a totalizing social system) is inescapable.

[4] A language in the Saussurean sense: it consists of a system of arbitrary signs that derive their meaning from their position in relation to other terms in the system, never by absolute, intrinsic, or essential value (Pawlett, 2008).

Even if one does *not* consume—for instance, by making one's own clothes—such political attitude and its *image* are viewed (i.e., socially signified in their difference) as a sign in terms of the code: as "rebellious", "green", "environmentally responsible", "creative", or whatever; thus it can—and in fact *has*—become a commodity as well, indeed a whole market niche. Of course, the same is valid for any other practice, stance, or value.

Thereby what becomes crucial for consumerism is that its systematic fabrication or conversion of objects (here meaning *any* object) to the status of signs "implies the simultaneous transformation of the *human relationship* into a relationship of consumption—of consuming and being consumed" (Baudrillard, 1968/1996, p. 201). This logic will eventually apply to *all* human relationships: with objects, society, and self. The object as sign becomes the inescapable mediation of such relationships—"and, before long, the sign that replaces it altogether". The result is that the "relationship is no longer directly experienced: it has become abstract, been abolished, been transformed into a sign-object, and thus consumed" (ibid.).

To summarize and conclude, ultimately what is consumed is never the material object but the imaginary and artificially signified *social relationship*—between consumer and object, and between consumer and society; the social relationship is consumed as a *sign*—as sign-value, which replaces both use-value and exchange value, and determines the political economy; in consuming it, one consumes the code, the system of imaginary differences and significations, the system that signifies relationships (of consumption).

4.2 The ImCon and Consumption Dreams

4.2.1 The Fabrication of the ImCon: Advertising Logic

From this viewpoint, consumption society is marked by a shift from the production and consumption of objects to the production and proliferation of *signs* (and sign-values); from the importance of the means of production to the central role of the means of consumption as *means of signification*. The whole process of production, reproduction, and proliferation of signs, as commodity-signs, and their articulation with the irrational (desires, emotions, fantasies, etc.) and imagery (images and accompanying narratives), corresponds to the fabrication of the ImCon as an artificial semiotic imaginary; this process follows the logic of advertising and marketing.

Let me first briefly note that "advertising" (and also "advertisement") here means: the *main* engineers of the ImCon and its dreams, which are fabricated, circulated, and so on according to its social *logic*.[5] That is, here I employ that term more or less in the same sense that, for instance, Fairclough (1989) does, in order to explain a social logic, for which it serves as a metonym. Such logic, however, is seen in marketing, mass media, information, communications, fashion, and entertainment industries: broadly, it corresponds to the logic of our present-day culture industry (or at least an essential part of it). It can be argued that, in contemporary consumer societies, all these cultural fields largely depend on advertising for their existence, and they function socially mostly through advertising; advertising is what *moves* them today. Another argument is that, as all these fields are more and more dominated by the *same* giant corporations, these distinctions—advertising, entertainment, and so on—are imploding and fading away. But the overall logic remains the same.

Advertising embodies the cultural mechanics for constructing sign-value and commodity-signs (Goldman & Papson, 1996). Such mechanics are based on a systematic manipulation of signs, and can be briefly defined thusly: "The commodity sign is formed at the intersection between a brand name [or any commodity] and a meaning system *summarized in an image*" (Goldman & Papson, 1996, p. 3; e.a.). Images and narratives are manipulated and arbitrarily attached to other images and products (brands, commodities); the resulting commodity-sign thereby functions as a social signifier of particular relations and experiences; that is, it is socially endowed with a certain value, meaning, and difference, always in relation to the code.

[5] Or, as Goldman (1992, p. i) put it: "advertisements are an ideal site for observing how the logic of the commodity form expresses itself culturally and socially".

For example, some image of a signifier—a representation of "manliness"—is detached from its context (from its "system of meaning") and arbitrarily attached to some brand or product (e.g., a car, or cigarettes, or a politician). The product is suffused with such semiotic content, wherefore becoming endowed with, and functioning as equivalent to, the original image, as its sign—that is, cigarette (brand) = manliness, manliness = cigarette (brand).

The same logic applies to any other "object" of consumption (ideas, people, experiences, one's own body, etc.). It is a requisite that both the object and the signification and difference attached to it be relatively arbitrary. As the signifiers are unchained, that is, they become autonomous in relation to referents or underlying reality, they can be hinged onto anything. Put differently, different systems of meaning can be combined arbitrarily, so that a wide range of differential significations (success, failure, happiness, love, affluence, sex appeal, manliness, etc.) can be attached to any commodity, and the same commodity can signify anything.[6]

This process corresponds to the fabrication of *sign-value*, which is generally equal to *desire*: desire and emotion are elicited by the sign-value (its capacity for signifying meaning, value, difference, etc., socially) and attached to the commodity by the arbitrary restructuring of the relation between word, image or meaning, and referent (Poster, 2001, p. 1). What we have here is a dynamics of *fetishization*, of producing and educing desire and emotion for commodities—the *irrational* ingredient of consumption—through the deployment of systematically manipulated sign-images, the ingredient of *imagery* and *signs*. The articulation of these elements with that other fundamental ingredient of consumption—fantasy, or *imagination*—defines both consumerism and its imaginary. Illouz (2009) summarizes this idea, quoting Slater: consumerism is a *culture* in which "emotions are stimulated, incited, made into obsession through the use of imagination, the production of 'longing' and imaginative dissatisfaction, *along the model of day-dream*" (Slater, 1997, p. 96; e.a.). This daydream form, this model—what McLuhan (1964/1994, p. 291) called "the most magical of consumer commodities"—is what is referred to as *consumption dream* in this work.

[6] For example, in the famed beginning of such ethics and logic (of both consumption and advertising), cigarettes were sold as "torches of *freedom*" for women (see Curtis, 2002; Ewen, 1976), as phallic signs; and Marlboro, long before the association with manliness (the Marlboro Man in the "world of Marlboro"), was initially sold as a woman's cigarette that was "mild as May".

4.2.2 Consumption Dreams

Consumption dreams can be defined as:

(a) The matter of *ads*: elaborations of sign-value as fetishized narratives and imagery that articulate cultural fantasies and desires, and determine the commodity-forms that promise to satisfy such desire-fantasy (or are at least connected to it);

(b) The fantasies of *consumers*: the desires, fantasies, and ideals about goods and experiences—and, in fact, life in general—that have *consumption* as their underlying idea or motif. Here the dream is seen as a more or less *personal* desire or object of desire, image of the future, main goal, the "good life", and so on—all of which are *imagined* to be reachable, fulfilled, or attainable through consumption.

The whole point, however, is that, far from being personal, the consumption dream *(b)* merely reproduces the discourses elaborated as *(a)*: it reflects the logic of advertising, the code, the system of sign-values; as a "commodity-narrative" (Goldman & Papson, 1996, p. 3) morphed into a dream, in fact it represents an *atom* of the code. Through the social manipulation of imagination and fantasy, advertisements function as seductive, persuasive consumption dreams, industrialized so as to elicit, arouse, and ultimately engineer desire and longing; to provoke and promise pleasure, passion, emotions, and sensations (Hirschman & Stern, 1999; Illouz, 2009); and to inculcate (and profit from) imaginary, arbitrary ideas and ideals, reified social relations and subjectivities. However, they can also work through the opposite message: frightening subtly or not so subtly, menacing, inducing envy and discomfort, some "consumption bad dreams" are designed to induce fear, displeasure, disquiet, dissatisfaction.[7] Together with continuous, omnipresent social scrutiny (which, ideally, is introjected), the point is to keep the consumer in a permanent state of self-conscious discontent, "constant uneasiness and chronic anxiety" (Lasch, 1984, p. 28), with a feeling of lack and emptiness, so as that desire (for consuming) peaks and the promise (embodied by a commodity or the act of consuming) seems more enticing. Therefore consumption dreams and consumption "bad dreams" are expressions of the dual role of advertising as both "merchants of discontent" (Packard,

[7] A combination of both forms (promise and fright) is indeed common.

1961, p. 269) and "merchants of mystique" (Belk, Ger, & Askegaard, 2003, p. 327).

It is easy to see that the aim of both types of consumption dream is the same, however: to center all such *irrational* factors on consumption, that is, on the basic *imaginary* promise that consuming the commodity-sign will instantaneously fulfill such desires, cause the appropriate and coveted emotions, alleviate the pains and fears, and so on, and that failing to consume it will turn the consumer's life into a bad dream or nightmare. Thus, consumption dreams are based on irrational elements that manipulate, control, and ultimately produce more irrational psychic contents. The whole system therefore is contingent upon *functional irrationality*, geared through stylized hollow images toward the consumption of more hollow images: to create, control, and direct functional irrationality is the objective of the "dream-images which speak to desires, and aestheticize and de-realize reality" (Haug, 1987, p. 123).

4.2.3 Consumption Dreams and Desire

Such functional irrationality is commandeered through *desire*, which is elevated to and exalted as the motor of social consumption (Ewen, 1976, 1988; Ewen & Ewen, 1982; Forty, 1986; Williamson, 1986), the motivational structure of consumerism (Belk, Ger, & Askegaard, 2003; Illouz, 2009; Slater, 1997). This development is only logical. If mass production required capitalism to produce a mass society of consumers, under total consumerism the functioning and reproduction of the system will depend on the (re)production of desires as a function of *unlimited* mass production and mass consumption: engineering mass desires represents the control over production not merely of consumers, but of their *unlimited demand*. To attain that kind of control, the system of consumption had to tap into the irrational and the imaginary sides of existence, to dominate and engineer not mere needs or wants—which are finite and limited, of a more rational nature, and related to use-value—but *desires*, which are *unlimited* and related to sign-value and sumptuary value. That is, as desires are by definition connected to imaginary, intangible, *irrational* things, the objects of desires become unrestricted: anything can be the object of desire.

Needs and wants refer to more logical, rational processes, which are more easily subjected to individual control and will. "Desires, on the other hand, are overpowering; something we give in to; something that takes control of us and totally dominates our thoughts, feelings, and actions" (Belk, Ger, & Askegaard, 2003, p. 99). The objective, therefore, will be to create and program desire as an unlimited, objectless *passion that consumes*—an *all-consuming* desire as the central mode of psychic functioning of a mass society. As Marcuse (1955/1966) noted, this process is equivalent to a form of social control that does not aim at reason and mind—it aims at managing and dominating the gut feelings, the emotional, the irrational, the very foundations of our psychological being: the instincts, the irrational libido. To colonize and control desire means to determine the directions and forms of psychic energy: it is tantamount to controlling the functioning of psyche. As the contemporary British artist Lily Allen (2008) sings, "And I am *a weapon of massive consumption*. It's not my fault, *it's how I'm programmed to function*."

To retain that control and keep the system moving, desire must be both unlimited and never satisfied: both its object and source must be imaginary. "Desire does not desire satisfaction. To the contrary, desire desires desire. The reason images are so desirable is that they never satisfy" (Taylor & Saarinen, 1994, p. 34). However, Baudrillard (1968/1996, 1970/1998) went further: the reason why desire is irrepressible and insatiable is because it is founded on a *lack*. If what is desired is ultimately *social meaning*, such lack is a dearth of meaning and difference, a lack of *social signification*—which is consumed as images. The whole system is therefore based on a fundamental *emptiness*; "I can't get no satisfaction" (The Rolling Stones) and the more contemporary "I just can't get enough" (Depeche Mode) become mass mantras.

The logical conclusion is that consumerism, the ImCon, and its subject are all intrinsically founded on hypocrisy and outright deception (Bauman, 2005). The sacred promise of consumerism—the consumption dream—is that our desires for value, meaning, and identity will be satisfied through the commodity (i.e., through its sign-value). However, the continuous functioning of the whole system relies precisely on the unfulfillment of such promise; it depends on eternal dissatisfaction. The instant gratification reached through consumption must be ephemeral, vanishing immediately after the act of consuming, so that dissatisfied consumers not only consume more, but *keep consuming*. Bauman (2007) called this phenomenon "economics of deception". Dissatisfaction is guaranteed because the whole system functions based on the opposite of what it promises (one could say that it is fundamentally based on a Big Lie, or, in more technical terms, its logic is absolutely ideological): instead of differentiation and personalization, it works based on dedifferentiation and mass production; instead of individuality and uniqueness, it engenders and delivers massification (everyone is a consumer, no matter what). Therefore, if the consumption dream is empty, not only is the lack behind desire never solved: it is actively fed by the dynamics of the system. Restless dissatisfaction and everlasting desire generate and accelerate the relentless cycle of waste, consumption, and disposal, or, as Ewen and Ewen (1982) put it, "continual waste and spending would be elevated as a social good, driven by a cycle of continuous dissatisfaction" (p. 73).

The characteristics of desire will therefore mirror and sustain system reproduction: the continuous and accelerated process of production, consumption, and waste is met by continuous and unlimited desire, instantaneous gratification and dissatisfaction, and more desire. The consumer, in this sense, turns into a sort of addict—for the goal of consumerism is to industrialize desire as analogous to a craving for potent drugs and their vanishing effects, to engineer a psychic "objectless craving" (Baudrillard, 2001, p. 47), a boundless voracity for meaning. "Consumerist society thus proves to have become, today, (…) toxic, not only for the physical environment, but also for mental structures and psychic apparatuses: as drive-based, it has become massively *addictogenic*" (Ars Industrialis, 2010).

Baudrillard (1977/2007, p. 25) had already written that, within consumer society, desire (as libido) replicates commodity-logic:

> This compulsion towards liquidity, flow, and an accelerated circulation of what is psychic, sexual, or pertaining to the body is the exact replica of the force which rules market value: capital must circulate; gravity and any fixed point must disappear; the chain of investments and reinvestments must never stop; value must radiate endlessly and in every direction.

For all that to happen and keep happening, the imagined object of desire must be fickle, transient, transitory, volatile, elusive. It must be like a dream: a consumption dream.

4.2.4 The ImCon as a System of Cultural Consumption Dreams

Seen from the viewpoint of social imaginaries, contemporary consumerism thus becomes centered on the consumption of dreams and their celebration of desires, imaginary fulfillment, escape, freedom, autonomy, fun, entertainment, and hedonism. A society defined by the mass consumption of the image (Taylor & Saarinen, 1994), of the illusion (Debord, 1967)—of the dream.[8]

Taking all the above into consideration, the expression *consumption dream* (*sonho de consumo, sueño de consumo*) seems perfect for the description of consumer society and the ImCon: it defines a society based on what is immaterial, intangible, *fictional* (Augé, 1999)—on what is imaginary. It evokes an irrational, magic world—the oneiric world of advertising, marketing, and mass media—in which nothing is impossible, animals and things speak, everything can appear undifferentiated and contiguous, fragmented, connected: success and cigarettes, toothpaste and sparkling happiness, bubble gum and god-like transcendence. It conjures up a fantastic imaginary world, a dreamworld that defines social fantasies and imagination: the imaginary of consumption.

Although such description resembles quite closely the world of the *unconscious* and its night dreams, under consumerism the nocturnal imaginary has other masters and products. Advertising and marketing—as the factories of commodity-narratives (Goldman & Papson, 1996), the industries of image-production (Mitchell, 1986)—are the kings of this magic world of dreams ruled by capital and globally circulated across mass mediascapes. As the makers of the ImCon, these prime-magicians of sign combinatorics function as social architects of desire, as the society's designers of dreams—in fact, as the *dream industry* (Biocca, 1991; Fournier & Guiry, 1993). By fashioning this semiotic imaginary, they also fashion its subjects: the consumers.

---

[8] Put differently, the advertising imaginary comes to constitute "the core of the *established social imaginary* in force in the consumerist capitalist societies we live in" (Caro, 2007, p. 133).

4.2.5 The Mass Production of Consumers

As discussed above, the primary objective of the ImCon is manipulation, colonization, and configuration of desires (and fears) through images and narratives (Zayas, 2001), through dreams; such colonization aims at rendering desires—*libido*—mimetic with the code, with the ImCon. However, consumerism goes beyond that. Ewen (1976) has showed that, since the very beginning of advertising, publicity, marketing, and PR, the objective of the dream industry was *social production*: social management through the mass production of consumers. For that, it sought actively to "mobilize the instincts" (p. 31) and engender *identity* with models of what kind of person the subject should be, what kind of life s/he should lead, and so on—all models, of course, being variations of a single homogeneous form: the *consumer*.

In that sense, the advertisement industry has always been more a machine of production of consumers, rather than an attempt at selling products. Its core social function has been summarized by Fairclough (1989): "Advertising has made people into consumers, i.e. has brought about a change in the way people are, in the sense that it has provided the most coherent and persistent models for consumer needs, values, tastes and behaviour" (p. 207).

If advertising began by developing a highly effective strategy—identifying the product with an "imaginary state of being" (Lears, 1983, p. 19), the consumption dream—it moved on to producing imaginary *forms* of being, and finally to defining what being *is* and means: an imaginary existence, an imaginary life, an imaginary *self*. How to be an individual, a subject, was to be expressed and defined through the consumption of *identities* formed by commodity-signs: identikits.

4.2.6 Subjective Identities: Identikits

An identikit can be defined as a purchasable, prepackaged narrative-visual-psychological identity.[9] The commodity here is subjectivity, a *self*:

[9] As the Webster Dictionary tells us, identikit is "a *set of images* containing a wide variety of facial features, such as noses, hairlines, chins, etc. on transparencies which can be overlayed in *combinations* to build up *a picture of a person*".

a prefabricated personality, which is not necessarily coherent but provides a sense of *social identity*. It corresponds to the social significations conferred by the consumption of commodity-signs, which, combined and articulated in the form of a self-image, personalize and differentiate the consumer socially.

Indeed, the whole process of creating commodities as social signifiers is centered on and directed at identity, at the promise of identity-formation:

> contemporary ads operate on the premise that signifiers and signifieds that have been removed from context can be rejoined to other similarly abstracted signifiers and signifieds to build *new signs of identity*. This is the heart of the commodity sign machine. (Goldman & Papson, 1996, p. 5; e.a.)

Therefore an identikit would correspond to an ensemble of such signs, consumed as images of a social self: *self-images*, social imaginary *models* of being. As a mass-produced sign, or combination of signs, the identikit is arbitrary, and only derives its signification and difference from the code. If seen from the viewpoint of the desires for individuality and for the social, the identikit offers fulfillment of both, and at the same time feeds them and channels them to commodity-signs. The desired subjectivity (individuality) is bought and consumed in the *personality of the product* (its "distinctive" sign-value). This represents a reversal: what has personality, discourse, uniqueness, and so on is the commodity, not the human being. The desired social insertion, sociability, is bestowed in the same way: the consumer is socially signified through the sign, and thus inserted and differentiated socially.

If the whole ImCon functions through such mechanics (i.e., social identity and individuality are its main products), it can be said that its identikits become the cultural definitions of personhood, of self, of *who one is*—which, despite the panoply of different self-imagery it can assume, in the end is reduced to: a consumer. In her seminal work, Judith Williamson (1978) summarizes this process and mentions one of the ideologies that underlie it, the romantic dream of the consumer-as-an-artist:

> This is one of the most alienating aspects of advertisement and consumerism. (…) We are both the product and the consumer; we consume, buy the product, yet we *are* the product. Thus our lives become our own creations

> through *buying*; an identi-kit of different images of ourselves, created by different products. We *become* the artist who creates the face, the eyes, the life-style. (p. 70)

"We are the product": when identity and self are solely defined by (consumed) social signs (i.e., one is what one consumes), a process of thorough reification and commodification of the consumer is made possible. Only through identity with the product (in fact, with the imaginary *dream*—of personhood and social insertion—behind the product) the consumer *is*: that defines his reality, the "reality" of the ImCon, imaginary, fabricated, and arbitrary. As Lasch (1979, p. 91) contends, for the consumer "the only reality is the identity he can construct out of materials furnished by advertising and mass culture, themes of popular film and fiction, and fragments torn from a vast range of cultural traditions"—that is, a reality and an identity mimetic with the reified images of the ImCon.

If that is so, it means that consumption becomes fundamentally enshrined upon dreams and fantasies about who one can and should be: upon *consumption dreams of identity*. All such dreams are based on some main underlying (ideological) dreams that sustain the ImCon. One refers to the promise of social mobility and deep personal transformation (Featherstone, 2007, p. xv) through consumption. The consumer can be socially mobile and cultivate refined identities through the continuous expression of a *lifestyle* through the consumption of signs: "carefully choose, arrange, adapt, and display goods—whether furnishings, house, car, clothing, the body or leisure pursuits" (Lyon, 2001, p. 82) to make a personal statement. This series of personal statements defines the consumer's self, and can change (and thus appear more upwardly mobile) according to his will and means of consumption. The related dream (and imperative) here is the creative expression of a "true" self, of individuality, through mass-produced signs. However, perhaps the main basic dream is that, ultimately, any form of subjectivity (identity, self) is possible, or purchasable, consumable: by manipulating signs of identity, consumers can become any of their "possible selves" (Markus & Nurius, 1986), and be *whatever* they want (De Zangotita, 2005)—the way one changes clothes[10] or, to use a more appropriate image, the way one changes *avatars* in cyberspace. The omnipotent dream of the consumer as a demiurge of himself.

Fulfillment of these dreams is to happen by consumption of commodities (and their respective identities) and identification with them. Therefore, what defines the subject here is their identification with the sign as a social signifier, and through it with the social imaginary that confers signification: their identity with the ImCon.

4.2.7 The ImCon as an Artificial Semiotic Imaginary: Final Remarks

Before further discussing the subject and colonization, here are some final summarizing and concluding remarks on the imaginary of consumption. Based on the arguments above, the ImCon can be described as a form of social imaginary that is semiotic and semiological, that is, it is characterized by the hegemony of *sign* as its form of representation. As commodities are produced as signs, and every sign (every representation) can be commodified, it follows that *the commodity-sign is the primal form of representation within the ImCon*. As a massive system of sign-values, an ensemble of social signifiers, a semiotic template, *the ImCon strives to mediate all social signification, and hence all social relationships* under the regime of consumerism. Its representations are signified and stem from the code, following the logic of advertising (i.e., of sign-value production). The signifying *code*, therefore, corresponds to the framework of the ImCon as a social system of signification: "The object/advertising system constitutes a system of signification, but not language, for it lacks an active syntax: it has the simplicity and effectiveness of a code" (Baudrillard, 2001, p. 22). This code of signification is empty of meaning, arbitrary, and by definition "external" to reality. Its discourse, the discourse of the commodity—the discourse-form of advertising—corresponds to the *discourse of consumption*: the commodity-narratives, their imagery (and their dreams) that represent and proliferate the code as typical forms of *seeing*

[10] "As a 1991 cover of Cosmopolitan declared: 'By changing the way you look … you can create a new you!'" (Goodman, 2004).

the world and self, of ascribing meaning to, understanding, and experiencing both of them, and their interrelationships. It thus corresponds to a cultural imagination that signifies (and thus institutes) society and subjects, and interpellates[11] its subject as a consumer through typical imaginary forms: "the images through which society sees itself and makes us see ourselves, an imaginary that defines how to work and desire" (Martín-Barbero, 1987, p. 61)—and, in fact, largely defines experience and how to *live*.

In comparison with the symbolic imaginaries studied in the previous chapter, the ImCon represents an *artificial, fabricated social imaginary*: it is *not* symbolic[12] but semiotic, made of *signs* that are, by definition, artificial constructions. Although it is also founded on the *irrational* and the *image*, instead of *dreams* (the origin and foundation of symbolic imaginaries) what defines the ImCon are synthetic dreams: its fundamental societal factors, its mythic monads, are the *consumption dreams*. They too are social imaginary narratives, yet fashioned as *semiotic* images that are full of meaning for both the collective and the subject. They also speak an emotionally charged, pictorial language; they too seem unreal, or more than real; they are fantastic, magic, mesmerizing, even numinous. They are *not* symbolic unconscious products, however: the main difference is that these dreams (and the whole ImCon) are *ideological*. Each commodity-sign with its sign-value, each industrialized dream of consumption, stems from the code, and therefore carries the social logic, the ideology of consumerism.

Such ideology is circulated as an (global) imaginary, shaping minds and bodies, especially through the socially situated deployment of cultural fantasies (Illouz, 2009, p. 377): through what Walter Benjamin saw as "the mass marketing of dreams within a class system" (Buck-Morss, 1989, p. 284)—now a system in which the classes are progressively

[11] "The 'society of consumers' is a kind of society which (to recall the (…) term coined by Louis Althusser) 'interpellates' its members (that is, addresses them, hails, calls out to, appeals to, questions, but also interrupts and 'breaks in upon' them) *primarily in their capacity of consumers*" (Bauman, 2007, p. 52).

[12] I will return to this point in the next chapter.

reduced to sellers and buyers, that is, consumers. Writing about the beginnings of the last century, Benjamin saw the primordia of what now arguably defines our culture, our imaginary—an imaginary *made* of mass marketing dreams.

Nordström and Riddestråle (2000) illustrate this point: "Power exists—as it always has—in providing people with dreams. Dreams that touch people, excite and arouse them. (...) The question must be how you can provide relevant and potent dreams for the tribes of the world" (p. 245). In their works, these "business gurus" inadvertently describe perfectly the dynamics of capitalism-consumerism, the ImCon, and consumption dreams: a system in which the markets (i.e., capital) seek to become the *vis motrix* of life—especially psychic life—through the *economies of the soul* and the *management of dreams* (Nordström & Riddestråle, 2000). The objective is to turn desires, emotions, and fantasies into commodities (which, strangely enough, would convert capitalism into a "humanism"). The power for that is "in providing people with dreams"; and "shopping and fucking shape the dreams of our times" (Nordström & Riddestråle, 2000, p. 210). And who engenders, provides, and promises to fulfill those dreams? Great corporations and leaders of business (Nordström & Riddestråle, 2005), engaged in a struggle for the total colonization of bodies, minds, and dreams, in a sort of Hobbesian nightmare-society: "dream against dream, organizations around the world in a total global battle for a share of customers' money *and minds*" (p. 243, e.a.). This *war of dreams* (Augé, 1999) pictures the ImCon and its colonizing power over the subject: the consumer's mind becomes the greatest commodity.

4.3 The ImCon and the Production of Subjectivity

This section concludes the chapter by summarizing how the semiotic ImCon institutes psychological subjectivity, a social subject: how it conditions *being* under its regime of signification.

4.3.1 The Subject as Consumer: Identity

The ImCon, at this level of analysis (i.e., seen as a *semiotic* imaginary), produces the subject as a *consumer* defined by *partial identity* with commodity-signs and sign-values, congealed as *identikits*. "Identity" here refers to two distinct phenomena, both of which, however, coalesce into the idea of "subject". First, as discussed in Chap. 1, identity refers to the meaning ascribed to it in analytical psychology: the subject's (unconscious) *identification* with something. Second, it denotes the more common meaning: a self-definition, a "singular" personality, a sense of identity or individuality.

Therefore, the consumer's social identity is equivalent to his identification with identikits: as cultural and imaginary roles, models, lifestyles that are socially recognized in a hierarchy of values and involve a continuous "personal" combination and recombination of commodity-signs. In sum, social identity here derives essentially from the consumer's patterns or *styles* of consumption, which personalize and signify him socially within the code.

Such self-definition or sense of identity is defined in relation to *others*: in relation to the imagined relationships with the collective, the social field. As mentioned, social insertion and inclusiveness are signified within and through the code. Instead of social class—and profession, work, religious affiliation, and so on—what is determinant here is the consumption, manipulation, and disposal of commodity-signs, which inscribe the consumer in a certain group and (imaginarily) differentiate him within the group and from all other consumers. By consuming consumer-identikits and identifying with them, the subject gains inscription within the system of social exchange: personal identity requires conformity with the code, with the ImCon.

As the ImCon is a social regime, all such consumer relationships—relations with others, but also one's relation with oneself—become mediated by signs, by the code: they are thus reified and consumed. The consumer sees himself and is seen by others through the models (identikits) he consumes and identifies with; he relates to others, and they relate to him, in terms of commodified models. That implies that sociabilities resemble processes of consumption: the ImCon institutes a "reorganization of our personal lives and relationships on the model of market relations" (Davis, 2003, p. 41). The conclusion is that market relations and commodity exchange progressively determine and colonize both our personal self-definitions and our social relationships. Bauman (2007) described well such phenomenon:

> The existential setting that came to be known as the "society of consumers" is distinguished by a remaking of interhuman relations on the pattern, and in the likeness, of the relations between consumers and the objects of their consumption. This remarkable feat has been achieved through the annexation and colonization by consumer markets of the space stretching between human individuals; that space in which the strings that tie humans together are plaited, and the fences that separate them are built. (p. 11)

There are some logical requisites for such processes, requisites that characterize the ImCon in its subjectivation force. One is that such identity, or sense of self, is both *exteriorized* and *mediated by signs*. The traditional *inner* sense of identity and subjectivity—a self which is anchored in, and derives its substance from, inner (psychic) life and its wealth of contents, feelings, thoughts, and so on, which provide a sense of inner integrity, character, and individuality—is denied and replaced: the locus of self becomes thoroughly "other-directed" (Riesman, 1950/1969; Thomson, 2000), or extrinsic (Ewen, 1990). J. E. Davis (2003) summarizes this point:

> We identify our real selves by the choices we make from the images, fashions, and lifestyles available in the market, and these in turn become the vehicles by which we perceive others and they us. In this way, (…) self-formation is in fact exteriorized, since the locus is not on an inner self but on an outer world of objects and images valorized by commodity culture. (p. 44)

4.3.2 Logic and Effects of Consumer-Subject Production

As the reader can see, such process is analogous (and parallel) to the fabrication of signs, or commodification: the sense of identity must become *external* and more or less *arbitrary* in relation to the individual subject and their inner psychic reality; thus it can be consumed as models (identikits). Individual difference, value, and meaning—which define individuality—simply cannot originate in inner experiences, substances, or essence. They must be abstracted, so that "difference" only exists as defined through the code, through the (consumed) commodity-sign—as defined by social perception, in complete exteriorization of value and difference. As my favorite purveyors of illustrations Nordström and Riddestråle (2005) express so tenderly, "Basically, there are only two ways in which you can be different—either you are perceived as *cheaper* or you are perceived as better" (p. 251; e.a.).[13]

Two other requisites, as typical dynamics, appear to be inherent to such subject-formation: *projection* and *emptying*. If the sense of identity, or self, is always to be found in the outer world, in the images and signification provided by the ImCon, and in the perception of others, then subjectivity is by definition projected unto the environment: it is an imaginary construction entirely dependent on the latter. This is related to the fundamental sense of *lack*, of inner emptiness, upon which the whole mechanics of desire is founded: simply put, signification cannot be found inside, in the inner world, for then the consumer would not crave for it outside (as social signs).

However, what seems to underlie all the processes of fabrication of the subject-as-consumer is that his sense of identity depends vitally on an identity with the fabricated desires, with the consumption dreams—and through them with the whole ideology of consumerism. Again, "identity" here refers to *irrational identification*: an emotional, imaginary, *unconscious* identity that bonds the subject to something external to his psyche.[14] This identity with consumption dreams represents the basic foundation for the whole process: on the primary colonization of desires and fantasies—of the irrational, emotional, imaginary, unconscious foundation of the subject's psyche—rests the identity with the whole consumption system, which institutes a self-definition as a consumer. To put differently the same idea, "desire" means *libido*, psychic energy. Therefore, to the

[13] According to them, that is how the consumer-subject "dares to be different" in a "copycat world".

[14] In this (Jungian) sense, identity is by definition an unconscious process, for it requires unconscious non-differentiation between the subject and the object with which he identifies.

extent that the consumer identifies with consumption dreams, the ImCon colonizes his libido, and thus directs and forms his psychic functioning, working mostly through its irrational—unconscious—aspect.

In this logic, the consumer-subject's identity is fashioned with fragments of the imaginary—as consumption dreams, and their respective assemblage of commodity-signs. Thus oneiric identikits become the grand purveyors of identity, the cultural ideas of personhood as distinct *images* of what *being* a consumer means. Under this semiotic imaginary, you are made of what signs you consume, how you consume them, and, most importantly, what *images* this whole process conveys: the all-important thing here is *appearance*, the images we project through consumption. Being a consumer-subject means being defined by management and marketing of self-images, exchanged at the market of social identities—a pastiche personality, as Gergen (1991) called it.

4.3.3 Commodification of Self: The *Homo Commoditas*

Such description corresponds to the apotheosis of "Homo consumens" (Bauman, 2007, p. 99), a new subject whose identity amounts to near-complete identification with the *persona*. However, this is also a new, postmodern persona. Jung's concept referred to an idealized (imaginary) and stereotyped social role (the doctor, actor, bohemian, etc.) that, though collectively fabricated, was fairly fixed and had some *concreteness* about it. The new ImCon personae are not merely imaginary but *arbitrary*, *artificial*, and *superficial*: they are composites of image-signs of identity industrially produced and socially recognized. Maffesoli (1989) writes that such personae have replaced the notion of modern individual, and describes them: they are fluid, deindividualized, directionless identities, peripheral and performative. Each consists in an "amalgam of roles" (Tester, 1993, p. 77); as the consumer-subject is supposed to consume and change them according to the logic of the markets, constantly *upgrading* his self-image, his mutating identity will be defined by "perpetually playing roles (…) in a pointless theatre of the world" (ibid.). Maffesoli (1988) affirms that, in opposition to individuation, this is a subject characterized by almost complete *dedifferentiation* and deindividualization, by "the 'losing' of self into a collective subject" (p. 145)—or, in fact, its dissolution into a social imaginary of signs.

From this point of view, what defines the consumer-subject is the salability of the persona(e) chosen and consumed. That means that identity is formed according to these questions: Are you, your identity, marketable? How is it positioned in the "personality market" (Fromm, 1955)? What is your sign-value? All answers to these questions are relatively arbitrary and change all the time by definition, in accord with market demands.

If this is so, it signs a further anthropological mutation. If, as argued in the previous chapter, the human being under symbolic imaginaries was defined as *homo symbolicum*, and under a semiotic imaginary we have the *homo consumens*, defined by the consumption of signs, here there appears a transition from *homo consumens* to *homo commodity* (or *commoditas*). If consumer society and the ImCon establish and impose a process of subjectivation, or identity-formation, that becomes essentially identical to commodification, then they will engender a subject whose identity is defined by being a commodity. The logic and practice of this process of *commodification of self* (Davis, 2003) appear clearly in the contemporary movement of "personal branding"[15] (Hearn, 2008; Lair, Sullivan, & Cheney, 2005; Wee, 2010), which consists in manipulating signs and images of oneself in order to become a brand—a process of self-commodification, of turning oneself into a commodity-sign. "Sell your soul" here is not merely metaphoric. Again, Nordström and Riddestråle (2000) innocently instantiate this imperative: "We must brand, package and market ourselves so that we are desirable. Under what slogan will you be sold?" (p. 242).

The imperative for the consumer-subject is thus to become a carefully crafted *image*, a successful brand, a good working package that makes him more sellable—the perfect persona for that specific moment, for that specific market. In a mass society characterized by the implosion of differences, the ultimate need and desire is to be different somehow, to stand

[15] "Within the personal branding movement, people and their careers are marketed as brands complete with promises of performance, specialized designs, and tag lines for success" (Lair et al., 2005, p. 307). That is, people commodify and sell *themselves* as consumption dreams....

out in a sea of commodities and consumers; and the promise of difference is conveyed through images, fashioned into consumption dreams. As Bauman (2007) puts it, "In a society of consumers, turning into a desirable and desired commodity is the stuff of which dreams, and fairy tales, are made" (p. 13).

To summarize and conclude, the ImCon thus manufactures the subject as both consumer and commodity: a subject in identity with its consumption dreams, and *turning into a consumption dream.* Inasmuch as the consumer identifies with such dreams (i.e., makes his personal identity dependable on commodity-signs, on consuming-buying-displaying-disposing them), he follows the social logic of consumption and is signified and differentiated like a commodity: he progressively becomes a commodity too, part of the capital of consumption society. Thus the ImCon institutes and colonizes subjectivity: "I come to view my 'self' as a project—as my own bit of capital, to be developed, marketed, packaged and sold" (Knights & Wilmot, 2006, p. 68).

References

Allen, L. (2008). *The Fear* [CD single]. London: Regal Recordings.

Ars Industrialis. (2010). *Manifesto 2010.* Retrieved from http://arsindustrialis.org/manifesto-2010

Augé, M. (1999). *The war of dreams: exercises in ethno-fiction* (L. Heron, Trans.). London: Pluto Press.

Baudrillard, J. (1975). *The mirror of production.* St. Louis, MO: Telos Press.

Baudrillard, J. (1981). *For a critique of the political economy of the sign.* St. Louis, MO: Telos Press. (Original work published 1973).

Baudrillard, J. (1996). *The system of objects* (J. Benedict, Trans.). London: Verso. (Original work published 1968).

Baudrillard, J. (1998). *The consumer society: Myths and structures.* London: Sage. (Original work published 1970).

Baudrillard, J. (2001). *Selected writings* (M. Poster, Ed., 2nd ed.). Cambridge: Polity.

Baudrillard, J. (2007). *Forget Foucault.* New York: Semiotext(e). (Original work published 1977).

Bauman, Z. (2005). *Liquid life.* Cambridge, UK: Polity.

Bauman, Z. (2007). *Consuming life*. Cambridge: Polity Press.

Belk, R. W., Ger, G., & Askegaard, S. (2003). The fire of desire: A multisited inquiry into consumer passion. *Journal of Consumer Research, 30*, 326–351.

Bell, D. (1976). *The cultural contradictions of capitalism*. New York: Basic Books.

Biocca, F. (Ed.). (1991). *Television and political advertising (Vol. 2): Signs, codes, and images*. Hillsdale, NJ: Lawrence Erlbaum.

Buck-Morss, S. (1989). *The dialectics of seeing: Walter Benjamin and the Arcades Project*. Cambridge, MA: MIT.

Caro, A. (2002). *La publicidad de la significación: Marco, concepto y taxonomía*. Madrid: E-prints UCM. (Original work published 1993).

Caro, A. (2007). Jean Baudrillard y la publicidad. *Pensar la Publicidad: Revista Internacional de Investigaciones Publicitarias, I*(2), 131–146.

Curtis, A. (Director). (2002). *The century of the self [Motion picture]*. London: BBC Series.

Davis, J. E. (2003). The commodification of self. *Hedgehog Review, 5*(2), 41–49.

De Zengotita, T. (2005). *Mediated: How the media shapes your world and the way you live in it*. New York: Bloomsbury.

Debord, G. (1967). *La sociètè du spectacle*. Paris: Champ Libre.

Ewen, S. (1976). *Captains of consciousness: Advertising and the social roots of the consumer culture*. New York: McGraw-Hill.

Ewen, S. (1988). *All consuming images*. New York: Basic Books.

Ewen, S. (1990). Marketing dreams: The political elements of style. In A. Tomlinson (Ed.), *Consumption, identity and style: Marketing, meanings, and the packaging of pleasure* (pp. 29–39). London: Routledge.

Ewen, S., & Ewen, E. (1982). *Channels of desire*. New York: McGraw-Hill.

Fairclough, N. (1989). *Language and power*. London: Longman.

Featherstone, M. (2007). *Consumer culture and postmodernism* (2nd ed.). London: Sage.

Fine, B. (2002). *The world of consumption: The material and cultural revisited* (2nd ed.). London: Routledge.

Forty, A. (1986). *Objects of desire*. London: Thames and Hudson.

Fournier, S., & Guiry, M. (1993). An emerald green Jaguar, a house on Nantucket, and an African safari: Wish lists and consumption dreams in materialist society. *Advances in Consumer Research, 20*, 352–358.

Fromm, E. (1955). *The sane society*. New York: Rinehart & Company.

Gergen, K. J. (1991). *The saturated self*. New York: Basic Books.

Goldman, R. (1992). *Reading ads socially*. London: Routledge.

Goldman, R., & Papson, S. (1996). *Sign wars: The cluttered landscape of advertising*. New York: The Guilford Press.

Goodman, D. (2004). Consumption as a social problem. In G. Ritzer (Ed.), *Handbook of social problems*. London: Sage. Retrieved from http://www.sage-ereference.com/hdbk_socproblems/Article_n14.html

Gottdiener, M. (1996). *The theming of America: Dreams, visions, and commercial spaces*. Boulder, CO: Westview Press.

Haug, W. F. (1987). *Commodity aesthetics, ideology and culture*. New York: International General.

Hearn, A. (2008). 'Meat, Mask, Burden': Probing the contours of the branded 'self'. *Journal of Consumer Culture, 8*, 197–217.

Hirschman, E. C., & Stern, B. B. (1999). The roles of emotion in consumer research. *Advances in Consumer Research, 26*(1), 4–11.

Illouz, E. (2009). Emotions, imagination and consumption: A new research agenda. *Journal of Consumer Culture, 9*(3), 377–413.

Jameson, F. (1991). *Postmodernism, or the cultural logic of late capitalism*. Durham, NC: Duke University Press.

Knights, D., & Wilmot, H. (2006). *Introducing organizational behaviour & management*. London: Thomson Learning.

Lair, D. J., Sullivan, K., & Cheney, G. (2005). Marketization and the recasting of the professional self: The rhetoric and ethics of personal branding. *Management Communication Quarterly, 18*(3), 307–343.

Lasch, C. (1979). *The culture of narcissism*. New York: W.W. Norton.

Lasch, C. (1984). *The minimal self: Psychic survival in troubled times*. New York: W.W. Norton.

Lears, T. (1983). From salvation to self-realization: Advertising and the therapeutic roots of the consumer culture, 1880–1930. In R. Fox & T. Lears (Eds.), *The culture of consumption: Critical essays in American history, 1880–1980* (pp. 1–38). New York: Pantheon Books.

Lyon, D. (2001). *Jesus in Disneyland: Religion in postmodern times*. Malden: Blackwell.

Maffesoli, M. (Ed.). (1988). *The sociology of everyday life*. London: Sage.

Maffesoli, M. (1989). Jeux de masques: Postmodern tribalism. *Design Issues, IV*(1–2), 141–151.

Marcuse, H. (1966). *Eros and civilization*. Boston: Beacon. (Original work published 1955).

Markus, H., & Nurius, P. (1986). Possible selves. *American Psychologist, 41*, 954–969.

Martín-Barbero, J. (1987). *De los medios a las mediaciones: comunicación, cultura y hegemonía*. Barcelona: Ediciones Gili.

McLuhan, M. (1994). *Understanding media: The extensions of man*. Cambridge, MA: MIT Press. (Original work published 1964).
Mitchell, W. J. T. (1986). *Iconology: Image, text, ideology*. Chicago: University of Chicago Press.
Nordström, J., & Riddestråle, K. (2000). *Funky business: Talent makes capital dance*. Harlow, UK: Pearson.
Nordström, J., & Riddestråle, K. (2005). *Karaoke capitalism: Daring to be different in a copycat world*. Westport: Praeger.
Packard, V. (1961). *The status seekers: An exploration of class behaviour in America*. Middlesex: Penguin.
Pawlett, W. (2008). Against banality: The object system, the sign system and the consumption system. *International Journal of Baudrillard Studies, 5*(1). Retrieved from http://www.ubishops.ca/baudrillardstudies/vol5_1/v5-1-article13-Pawlett.html
Poster, M. (2001). Introduction. In M. Poster (Ed.), *Jean Baudrillard: Selected writings* (2nd ed., pp. 1–9). Cambridge: Polity.
Riesman, D. (1969). *The lonely crowd: A study of the changing American character*. New Haven: Yale University Press. (Original work published 1950).
Slater, D. (1997). *Consumer culture and modernity*. Cambridge: Polity.
Taylor, M., & Saarinen, E. (1994). *Imagologies: Media philosophy*. London: Routledge.
Tester, K. (1993). *The life and times of post-modernity*. London: Routledge.
Thomson, I. T. (2000). *In conflict no longer: Self and society in contemporary America*. Lanham: Rowman & Littlefield.
Wee, L. (2010). Personal branding and the commodification of reflexivity. *Cultural Sociology, 4*(1), 45–62.
Williamson, J. (1978). *Decoding advertisements*. London: Boyars.
Williamson, J. (1986). *Consuming passions*. London: Boyars.
Zayas, E. C. (2001). *Publicidad y hegemonía: matrices discursivas*. Buenos Aires: Norma.

5

The ImCon as Simulacrum of Symbolic Imaginary: Dream-Worlds of Consumption and the Subject as Commodity

La vida es sueño.
Calderón de la Barca[1]

Overview
This chapter discusses the ImCon as a simulacrum of symbolic imaginary: as a myth or desacralized religion based on a transcendental ideology. Following the logics of total consumerism-capitalism, its colonization and fabrication of signification, imagination, fantasy, and dream imply the fabrication of an ideological hyperreality, which is discussed through the concept of dream-world. The concepts of fetish, phantasmagoria, and collective dream are then introduced to discuss the mythic-ideological character of the ImCon and some of its effects. The chapter concludes by exploring the possibility that, by simulating a symbolic imaginary, the ImCon colonizes the unconscious psyche and, through archaic identity and mimesis, institutes its subject as a consumer-commodity.

[1] Calderón de la Barca (1635/2009).

M. Xavier, *Subjectivity, the Unconscious and Consumerism*,
https://doi.org/10.1007/978-3-319-96824-7_5

5.1 The ImCon as a Totalizing System of Signification

In this chapter, it will be argued that the imaginary of consumerism, more than being merely semiotic and semiological, functions as a simulacrum[2] of symbolic imaginary: like the old symbolic systems, it is a totalizing social system of signification. As mentioned previously, this proposal should be seen as an ideal type, in Weberian tradition; it is a more radical and possibly exaggerated view, a theoretical elaboration of some possibilities, tendencies, and developments that were in fact pointed by the night dreams studied. As such, it may be situated in what Eco (1964) called "apocalyptic" theorization on culture industry—in this case, on its correspondent social imaginary.

5.1.1 Total Capitalism Logic and a Totalizing Imaginary

Such proposal complements the previous chapter[3] and is derived from the perspective delineated by the concept of *total capitalism*, discussed in the Introduction: the characteristic totalizing imperative of consumer capitalism as a social order. Following its logic of unlimited expansion and colonization, the ImCon, as its regime of signification, exhibits a definite tendency to become *total*, to absorb and subordinate all other imaginaries (symbolic or otherwise) and imaginary forms under its logic. (Some contemporary authors, e.g., Jean Baudrillard, Félix Guattari, Arthur Kroker, Paul Virilio, claim that this tendency has in fact been *actualized*). Differing from a mere semiotic imaginary, however, which colonizes and manipulates systems of meaning, here we should consider that the logic does not stop at colonizing but proceeds to manufacture

[2] Here I use simulacrum more in the original Latin sense (*simulare*): "to make like", simulate, an *artificial* construction that superficially resembles something original, presupposing (*contra* Baudrillard and postmodernists in general) that it *does* substitute for something truer and factual, i.e., for *reality*—in this case, *psychic reality*, the unconscious and its autonomous production of symbols—and the old symbolic imaginaries.

[3] Which made the repetition of some arguments unavoidable, for which I apologize.

and *simulate* social signification, seeking *monopoly* over it, and hence over *reality*: here we move from the order of signs (the semiotic and semiological) to the order of simulacra and hyperreality.

Seen as a totalizing social system, consumerism's main logic and colonizing force remains the principle of commodification, but as a total imperative: *everything must become a commodity*. If we recall that what is consumed within consumerism is social signification, the objective and *telos* of a total semiotic economy is to institute globally this logic: signification is a commodity, and the commodity is signification; every signification is a sign, and every sign can and has to be exchanged and marketed as a commodity-sign. In order to control totally and retain monopoly over this semiotic capital (and thus over reality, through its representational form), everything must turn into an image; and every image must become a commodity-sign. The main difference in relation to semiotic imaginaries, however, is that here images and signs are not only colonized as commodities, and not merely industrialized en masse, but also fabricated without reference to any underlying reality, or original. That is the ultimate total character of the ImCon: unlimited production, reproduction, and consumption of images and signs, the possible totalization of commodity-logic. Indeed, already in the 1970s, Baudrillard (1970/1998) affirmed that as a *fact*, rather than as a possibility:

> Commodity logic has become generalized and today governs not only labour processes and material products, but the whole of culture, sexuality, and human relations, including even fantasies and individual drives. Everything is taken over by that logic, not only in the sense that all functions and needs are objectivized and manipulated in terms of profit, but in the deeper sense in which everything is *spectacularized* or, in other words, evoked, provoked and orchestrated into images, signs, consumable models. (p. 191)

The outcome was, as mentioned, a society defined by the image. Twenty years ago, Jameson (1992) claimed that "no society has ever been saturated with signs and messages like this" (consumer) society, and, following Debord, pointed out "the omnipresence and omnipotence of the image in consumer capitalism today" (p. 22): a logic of total expansion gradually accomplished through the endless proliferation of images, attesting to "the fundamental character of consumption, its *unlimited* character" (Baudrillard, 1968/1996a, p. 61).

Put simply, the unlimited fabrication of imagery and representations, which becomes progressively emancipated from any referents or reality, will ensure monopoly over signification. To recall the definition, the social imaginary corresponds to the order of signification: the social way of organizing and instituting meaning. This process of unlimited reproduction (coupled with unlimited consumption) of signification will engineer an unlimited, *unreal*, artificial imaginary, which simulates and replaces reality: a totalizing imaginary whose production follows the logic of the *simulacrum*. It completes the mutation of imaginaries delineated in this thesis: from the order of symbols, we have moved to the order of signs, and toward the order of simulacra. Next I briefly discuss the logics of the orders of sign and simulacrum, and their relations with the symbolic.

5.1.2 Order of Signs: Its Logics of Colonization and Fabrication

The logics behind the appearance of the ImCon as a semiotic order were seen in the previous chapter through the mechanics of advertising. First, it follows the logic of total *colonization*: sign-production entails manipulating meaning systems and colonizing symbolic images and narratives. As the sign will necessarily function as a commodity-sign, colonization here means the commodification of representation; the sign replaces the symbol with commodity-discourse. This process of semiotic formation demands colonizing progressively the whole of culture and history, manipulating and transforming every component of every system of meaning—narratives, images, representations, symbols—into commodity-signs.

Together with this process of colonization, there is a logic of *fabrication* of signification, which means that culture itself is mass-produced as (commodity-)signs. Thus the whole system of production comes to mean the production of signs: the commodity is now "immediately produced as a sign, as sign value, and (...) signs (culture) are produced as commodities" (Baudrillard, 1973/1981, p. 147). In other words, what was/is *not* produced as a (commodity-)sign is colonized; all the rest of culture is henceforth fabricated following commodity-logic. Here the logic of commodification is inescapable—it is total.

The result of both colonization and fabrication is that the semiotic imaginary gradually dissolves and incorporates all existing cultural, historical, social imaginary narratives and representations, including symbolic ones; or, in other words, culture, political economy, and the social are subsumed under the logic of the commodity-sign. This is related to the much-discussed process of declension, destabilization, and commodification of traditional institutions for identity-formation: family, school, work, education, class, and so on; or, as Bauman (2007) said, every (social) space is invaded. Such process, in fact, is extended to the whole of culture: there is a general volatilization, liquefaction, and commodification of values, referents, and culture (Jameson, 1992), which has been called the postmodern condition. From this viewpoint, postmodernity essentially means that both culture and history are debased into images and signs, thus becoming commodity-signs.

The implication for the symbolic orders is vast. Basically, everything eventually becomes mediated by signs, rather than symbols: the hegemony of semiotic imaginaries implies the loss of the symbolic. Due to its very nature, the order of signs not merely colonizes but *effaces* the symbolic: whereas the symbol unites realities, is dialectics itself, and signifies naturally and irrationally, the sign splits, reduces, and allows for emancipation from reality, for signifying artificially through the manipulation of disconnected signifiers and signifieds. With the sign, irrational signification (which, as we have seen, is founded upon the unconscious cultural, spiritual principle) is replaced by *ideology*: the political economy of the sign, summarized as consumption- and commodity-logic, defining all meaning a priori. As Baudrillard[4] (1973/1981) put it, "It is the semiological organization itself, the entrenchment in a system of signs, that has the goal of reducing the symbolic function. *This semiological reduction of*

[4] Although Baudrillard's concept of "symbolic" differs considerably from the Jungian one employed in this work, in the quotes used here both theories agree.

the symbolic properly constitutes the ideological process" (p. 98). Later Baudrillard qualifies this statement: beyond mere reduction, "the absolute condition for its ideological functioning is the *loss* of the symbolic and the passing over to the semiological" (ibid.; e.a.).

Ultimately this represents the collapse of transcendental values and the symbolic world, mentioned by Dufour (2001) as an important aspect of total capitalism; it is the breakdown and disappearance of the symbolic order. This assessment stands in sharp contrast to the hegemonic view maintained by social sciences today, which speaks of "symbolic consumption" and its "symbolic means of identity-formation", "symbolic narratives and products", and the like—as if anything that is somehow *signified* could be considered "symbolic", including, and especially, the social system of consumption. The term "symbolic consumption" is an oxymoron. None of these things are truly and strictly symbolic, for they are fundamentally based on ideology and signs, not on symbols. Furthermore, they depend precisely on the absorption and abolishment of the symbolic order. That they are all called "symbolic" merely reflects the phenomenon of colonization (of language and signification), through which *the very idea of symbol disappears.*

However, for the system of signs to fulfill its inherent logic and become *total*, it cannot halt at eradicating the symbolic order and taking its place; it needs to emancipate itself from any reality, replacing reality. This part of the process represents the passing over to the order of simulacrum.

5.1.3 Order of Simulacra: Simulation, Simulacrum, and Hyperreality

There are subtle differences between the concepts of simulation and simulacrum. First, there is a passage of the semiotic to the *simulation*: whereas the sign presumably represents some reality—its signifier is connected in some way to the signified or referent, which represents its "real" basis—the simulation is a form of semiotic representation in which the sign does not refer back to any signified or referent; it merely *simulates* the real through its semblance or appearance, eventually colonizing and replacing the real. The simulation "not only presents an absence as a presence, the imaginary as the real, it also undermines any contrast to the real, absorbing the real within itself" (Poster, 2001, p. 6). The logic here can be summarized as the fabrication of signs but without referent, without representative equivalence or any necessary connection to any reality: logic of emancipated, combinatorial *reproduction*.

According to Baudrillard (1976/1993, 1981/1994), the simulation thus refers to the autonomization of signification, achieved through the autonomization of the signifier: signs become absolutely emancipated from any signified or referent (reality, essence, substance), that is, they become completely unchained signifiers. Here the sign is not exchanged for meaning and value: it is exchanged against other empty signs, in a circular self-referentiality; that is the definition of simulation.

> [S]imulation, in the sense that, from now on, signs are exchanged against each other rather than against the real (it is not that they just happen to be exchanged against each other, they do so *on condition* that they are no longer exchanged against the real). The emancipation of the sign: remove this "archaic" obligation to designate something and it finally becomes free, indifferent and totally indeterminate. (Baudrillard, 1976/1993, p. 7)

At the level of simulation, signs no longer stand for anything; they no longer represent anything that is real—they are *empty*. There is a *short circuit* of reality, of the connections between signifier and signified, between reality and representation. We reach the level of simulacrum and hyperreality when the empty signs take *precedence* over reality, that is, when the automatic reproduction of signs according to the code engenders a *precessional semiurgy*—of images, signs, information, and so on—that precedes any "reality". Such semiurgy is hyperreal, that is, its semblance is more real than any real, and, preceding reality, it replaces it[5] and finally erases it.

[5] To provide a very simple illustration: a mass-produced strawberry yogurt. Through the image of a giant blood-red strawberry, it promises to deliver (and might actually do) a super, explosive, bubbly taste of strawberries, yet there is not a single trace of actual strawberries in it, only a concoction of chemical substances that simulates the taste of strawberries, enhancing it, making it hyper, more tasty, more "strawberry-like" than any real strawberry. This becomes a simulacrum when it is taken as the "real" taste of strawberries, and the actual strawberry (whatever its real taste or image was) is

Table 5.1 Simplified comparative between the orders of sign and of simulacra

	Logic	Practice	Consequence
Order of sign	Colonization and commodification	Colonize and commodify symbol (and imagery)	Loss of symbolic
	Fabrication, production	Culture is produced as signs; signs are produced as commodities	Commodification of culture and history
Order of simulacra	Fabrication without reference to reality, reproduction	Emancipation of representation from reality	Effacement of symbolic Hyperreality replaces reality

Reality is imploded and disappears: first by the substitution of the referent, the essence or substance, by a model of simulation, and then the destruction of the difference between simulation and reality, that is, the model engenders "reality" absolutely: it precedes and thus *becomes* "reality". Put differently, the endless and unlimited reproduction of copies effaces the real original; the copy becomes the original, only to be duplicated and disappear. According to Baudrillard, this process goes beyond *ideology*: "Ideology only corresponds to a betrayal of reality by signs; simulation corresponds to a short-circuit of reality and to its reduplication by signs" (2001, p. 182). Under the order of simulacrum, the distinctions between true and false, real and imaginary, copy and original all collapse, and the very ideas—the original ideas, *primordial ideas*—of truth, real, original, and so on wane and vanish. *The symbolic disappears*—and, with it, *meaning* (Table 5.1).

5.1.4 Hyperreality of Consumerism and Total Colonization

Having commodified away the symbolic, total consumerism can proceed and substitute reality by its hyperreal dream-world: an all-enveloping semiurgy of consumption where hyperreal appearances, images, and illusions

erased. Substitute "strawberry" for "social relations" and "subject" and you have the goal of total consumerism and its imaginary.

flow free and reign supreme, where it becomes impossible to distinguish simulations from reality—"reality" converts into the surface of images and their arbitrary, meaningless significations. That is the *murder of reality*, the "perfect crime", the most important event of modern history (Baudrillard, 1996b, 2000). Such hyperreal dream-world represents the most insidious form of colonization under consumerism: *a totalizing colonization of representation, and through it a colonization of the real.*

However, my argument is that this goes beyond colonizing; it implies the *fabrication* of a synthetic imaginary and a synthetic reality: more than colonizing, this is the equivalent of *fashioning reality* as (and through) an imaginary. By monopolizing the power to *manufacture* the real, a real that is more real than real, consumerism actualizes its totalizing character. Baudrillard (1968/1996a) expressed this idea thusly: "consumption may be defined as a *total idealist practice* of a systematic kind which goes way beyond relations to objects and interpersonal relations and extends to every level of history, communication and culture" (pp. 221–222). As argued, behind such practice are the totalizing code of signification, the omnipresence of commodity-narratives, and the ethereal spectacle of their imagery. As a semiotic order passing over to the simulacra, consumerism thus attempts to define all signification *and* reality, an *imaginary reality*, the ImCon: a fiction, a faux imaginary construction, a gigantic artificial "dream" that replaces and effaces reality. Therefore what will essentially move the consumption machinery is the fabrication and circulation of such imaginary, which mediates every experience: an *industry of unreality* comes to define it.[6]

---

[6] It must be emphasized that this industry is by no means limited to advertisement, mass media, and so on; as a social imaginary, its logic extends to every social domain, and to any remaining interstices between them. Perhaps an example can clarify this point. In the movie *Inside Job* (Ferguson, 2010), about the global economic and financial system and its corruption, Andrew Sheng (then the chief advisor of the China Banking Regulatory Commission) asks: "Why should a financial engineer be paid four to a hundred times more than a real engineer? A real engineer builds bridges; *a financial engineer builds dreams.*" My points are: finance (and economy, political economy, etc.) also becomes based on *building dreams* (i.e., the financial engineer is another *imagineer*); and this phenomenon is not restricted to the financial system; it defines global society.

5.1.5 The Industry of Unreality and the Fabrication of Imagination

The social system of present consumerism thus becomes characterized by the apotheosis of the *image*, as its main commodity and product, as the element that signifies everything. Thus, as Retort (2004) put it, "control over the image is now the key to social power"—not only social but economic, political, and cultural power depend on the control of the means "to systematize and disseminate appearances, and to subject the texture of day-to-day living to a constant barrage of images, instructions, slogans, logos, false promises, virtual realities, miniature happiness-motifs". Reiterating, control of the image-world, the imaginaries, and the *imaginary function*—imagination, fantasy, and creativity—becomes the vital factor: it determines the fabrication of reality and subjects, and the functioning of the entire system.[7] It signals "how important capitalism deems its monopoly of the imagination to be" (Jhally, 2006, p. 107).

This radical shift of consumerism can be illustrated with the concept of *imagineering:* it explicitly states and instantiates concisely the logic, goal, and practice of fabricating imaginaries and imagination. "Imagineering" is a portmanteau word that fuses "imagination" and "engineering", that is, it refers to the *engineering of imagination*. According to Wikipedia,[8] the term "was popularized in the 1940s by Alcoa to describe its blending of imagination and engineering, and adopted by Walt Disney a decade later". Appropriated by Disney, it came to mean *Walt Disney Imagineering* (or simply *Imagineering*), the design, building, and development arm of the Walt Disney Empire. Although it refers mainly to the fabrication of theme parks and other entertainment venues, it can be seen as representing the logic of fabricating synthetic imaginaries of consumption: the Disneyization of the cultural imaginary, "the process of capturing all the real world to integrate it into its synthetic universe, in the form of a vast 'reality show' where reality itself becomes a spectacle" (Baudrillard, 1996c).

[7] Appadurai (1996), although holding a quite different stance in relation to what I call "fabrication of subjects", seems to concur: "The imagination is now central to all forms of agency, is itself a social fact, and is *the key component of the new global order*" (p. 36; e.a.).

[8] See http://en.wikipedia.org/wiki/Walt_Disney_Imagineering.

Juxtaposing Alcoa and Disney illustrates clearly the mutation of the system: from a capitalism based on the industrial production of concrete objects (and a logic of factory, Fordism, etc.), the exploitation of labor power, and the harnessing of desires, to a consumerism based on the industrial production or engineering of images and imaginaries, and through them, of imagination and minds. As Lash and Lury (2007, p. 3) comment, while discussing Adorno and Horkheimer, "Now the logic of the factory colonized the dream factories of the culture industry"; or was it rather that the dream factories absorbed the logic of production and reproduction of factories so as to industrially manufacture imaginaries, hyperreal dream-worlds, and became the main factories of consumer capitalism.

Disney was the model and pioneer of this capitalist revolution. As Baudrillard (1996c) wrote, Disney was "the precursor, the grand initiator of the imaginary as virtual reality". Today his name and empire stand as a metonym for the mass production of dreams; yet the logic for such seems to be extending to globalized mass media, to all kinds of visual and imaginary products and narratives that use technologies of *image* (including games, movies, animation, ads, etc.), mass-produced by synergistic corporations. Although it follows the overwhelming logic of colonization through commodification, this giant process of cultural phagocytosis is clearly not restricted to advertising and marketing: this is the capitalist signification machinery.

Disney's imagineering thus illustrates such logic, moving from the semiological to the simulacra, behind the advent of synthetic imaginaries. If, following a marketing logic, "producing marketable commodity signs depends on how effectively advertisers are able to *colonize and appropriate referent systems*" (Goldman & Papson, 1996, p. 9; e.a.), implying that all forms of discourse and image are liable to absorption and commodification, to becoming part of the code, the logic of imagineering is to effectively colonize *all the historical forms of human imagination and creativity*—all natural products of symbolic- and fantasy-thinking—and fabricate and reduplicate them as hyperreal imaginary narratives, under an ethos of marketed entertainment and leisure: as commodified imaginary worlds. This process crucially includes the wholesale colonization of the symbolic, archetypal, mythological wealth of humanity: fairy tales, myths, religious narratives, and so on—the fundaments of cultural imaginaries that used to signify the whole array of psychological functioning and human experience.

As mentioned, the tendency is for this process to follow a logic of simulation and simulacra: to colonize diverse elements from symbolic imaginaries and replicate them by recombining images, narratives, and motifs, in a typical process of technological bricolage, while erasing the referents, the original narratives, and symbols (which thus run the risk of disappearing). For instance, the countless mythic narratives about the *hero* and his quest are appropriated, simulated, and reduplicated by news, movies, videogames, and a myriad of other prepackaged images and narratives, and commercialized as a pastiche of mythic images, whose underlying ethics is that of profit, of unlimited accumulation of capital. Two factors are important here. One is that, with the effacement of the referents, the cultural *image* of the hero—what used to be a *primordial image*, a symbolic *représentation collective* derived from an archetype, inserted in a mythic system—is henceforth solely purveyed by the imagineers as a commodity, that is, it is fabricated as a simulacrum. The second factor is that such products usually leave no space for creative imagination—the narrative and imagery are already given (it is the merchandise itself), with all its significations readily presented in simplified, easily absorbed, transparent, spectacularized ways; thus fantasy-thinking is appropriated and presented as a synthesized, ready product to be consumed fast—as a manufactured *experience*.

If this is so, then *imagineering* becomes the main form of production and source of cultural and individual *imagination*. It produces not only consumption dreams but imaginary dream-worlds whose stuff is consumability: it creates *simulacra worlds*. This process of cultural dissolution and replication can be viewed as what Augé (1999) called a "systematic 'fictionalisation' to which the world is subjected" (p. 7)—a cultural mutation. "We have arrived at the 'all-fictional'—in the same sense as we use the term 'all-electric'. All the old collective imaginaries now have the status of fiction" (p. 103)—and, I would add, of commodities.

The implication is that such processes are indeed "imagineering", in the full sense of the word: they accomplish the logic of colonizing and manufacturing (engineering) human imagination and fantasy. Other authors have pointed out the same idea. Giroux and Pollock (2010) speak about colonizing and harnessing the imagination "to forces of unfettered consumerism" (p. 4; see also Thussu, 1998). Cypher and Riggs (2001) write about the colonization of the imagination as "the pattern that connects all of the diverse attempts to manufacture experience": "By shaping people's experiences and interpretations of popular cultural events and symbols, Disney and other thematic engineers are not merely regulating impressions of those things, they are reconfiguring people's imaginative capacities" (p. 404). With an interesting metaphor, Zukin (1991) speaks of the colonization of fantasy effected by mass media corporations:

> The domestication of fantasy in visual consumption is inseparable from centralized structures of economic power. Just as the earlier power of the state illuminated public space—the streets—by artificial lamplight, so the economic power of CBS, Sony, and the Disney Company illuminates private space at home by electronic images. With the means of production so concentrated and the means of consumption so diffused, communication of these images becomes a way of controlling both knowledge and imagination. (p. 221)

My argument is that this phenomenon is not restricted to the home: as a social imaginary of a society in which every experience is mediated, it is virtually *everywhere*, omnipresent in private and public spaces—*including the consumers' dreams, their psyche*. The verb she uses is also interesting, "to illuminate": it is the necessary requisite for perception, *seeing*, imagining—that is, it determines psychic functioning. Therefore imagineering, meaning the industrial production of synthetic imaginaries, can be viewed as representing a global effort "to alter the dreams and re-fashion the imagination" (Augé, 1999, p. 6): to manufacture minds.

5.1.6 Hyperreal Imaginary as Cultural Discourse

The idea that such hyperreal imaginary is "everywhere" has been voiced by different authors. Indeed, one can say that it represents a radicalization and totalization of the logic of commodification of representation embodied by advertisement, marketing, and publicity; by turning to the imagineers' logic of simulation, it gradually replaces and erases previous social imaginaries, and simply becomes the cultural discourse. Thus Norris (2006) affirms that "Advertising and marketing become the signs and language and entire communicative structure within our society, which come to dominate all other forms of discourse and signification." And Jhally (2006) says that advertising has taken over our public and private landscapes (p. 29), becoming an all-pervading imaginary-narrative force: "This commercial discourse is the *ground* on which we live, the *space* in which we learn to think, and the *lens* through which we come to understand the world that surrounds us" (p. 102). These authors echo what Baudrillard (1981/1994) had already announced more than 30 years ago—the era of *absolute advertising*:

> Today what we are experiencing is the absorption of all virtual *modes of expression* into that of advertising. All original cultural forms, all determined languages are absorbed in advertising because it has no depth, it is instantaneous and instantaneously forgotten. Triumph of superficial form, of the smallest common denominator of all signification, degree zero of meaning, triumph of entropy over all possible tropes. (p. 87; e.a.)

Facing the prospect of what seems to be a total "colonization of imaginaries" (Gruzinski, 1988), Augé (1999) asked, "What is now our imaginary universe and are we still capable of imagination?" (p. 81). The answer may condense what has been argued so far: our imaginary universe is becoming a totalizing semiotic imaginary; as a self-reproductive system of signification, its logic is to imagineer a world of images into existence, a hyperreal world of surfaces that turns into an absolute, shaping and actually *fabricating* all cultural imagination and dreams.

Thus, if Morpheus was the "shaper", the god that gave form (morphē) to the world through oneiric images, in contemporary consumerism this role has been hijacked by mass media, advertising, and imagineering. Under the ImCon, consumption dreams become the "messengers" of the market gods: by setting the mediatic gospels, it fashions the new cultural "gods", the icons, idols, and models to be adored and followed through mass consumption. These commercial divinities guarantee the main product of such imaginary, the almighty commodity: "the consumable life, the buyable fantasy" (Ewen, 1989, p. 85), a life lived and purchased in a consumerist dream-world.

5.2 The ImCon as a Dream-World of Consumption Dreams

If dreams and symbol were the origins and stuff of previous symbolic imaginaries, and consumption dreams represent a semiotic ersatz dream-stuff... here we enter a dream-world of consumption—a simulacrum of imaginary, or imaginary made of simulacra and signs—a fantastic imaginary world in which reality becomes a dream-delusion.

Here I use "dream-world" in *four* possible senses. The first refers to what Langman (1992, p. 48) called "a new dream-like order of commercial reality": a reality made up by the ImCon. It serves to describe how everyday postmodern life, fully mediatized by representational technological apparatuses, becomes flooded by a barrage, indeed a deluge of dreamy commodity-signs, imagery, and information. Through a massive deployment of a semiurgy of images, narratives, and messages circulated fast through global mediascapes, the ImCon intertwines and proliferates emotions, desires, affects, representations, and fantasies. Permeating and pervading all reality, it creates a sort of dream-world made of consumption dreams, which amplifies the latter's characteristics: an endless and unavoidable flow of emotionally charged, desirable images, with a neon aura, a fantastic magic, even hypnotic power that seems "unreal", more than real, hyperreal, and embrangles, mesmerizes, enchants. It is a "dream-world" also because, through saturating the senses with a white noise of information, it produces an effacement of the distinction reality/dream, or reality/imaginary; everything becomes dreamy *images* to be consumed and discarded at growing speed. It means a hyperreality of consumption fully dominated by the surface of images—what Baudrillard (1983) called an aesthetic hallucination of the real. Or, as Mike Featherstone (2007) has described it, a "surfeit of images and information which threatens our sense of reality. The triumph of signifying culture leads to a simulational world in which the proliferation of signs and images has effaced the distinction between the real and the imaginary" (p. 83). To illustrate the point with a movie, as *The Truman Show* (Weir, 1998) depicted, here the imaginary approaches a saturation in which the difference between reality and mass-marketed fantasies and imagery blurs and implodes: everything becomes an ad, reality becomes a *reality show*. Or, as Marcuse (1964, p. 14) put it, "There is only one dimension, and it is everywhere and in all forms."

The *second* sense is the one mentioned in the Introduction: it refers to shopping malls, giant department stores, McDonald's, and Disneyland as *dream-worlds of consumption* (Benjamin, 1999; Buck-Morss, 1989, 2000; Williams, 1991), that is, as global symbols of the ImCon *and* the concretization of its dream-worlds. As the scenarios or "dreamscapes" of the night dreams analyzed in this work, they will be discussed in the next chapter.

The *third* sense refers to an analogy with the idea of consumption dreams. If the latter can be described as fragments of the ImCon, its atoms, as it were, that promise experiences, meanings, difference, lifestyle, and so on, the dream-worlds of consumption mean the promised imaginary world, or life, that is *behind* all consumption dreams as their ideological, hyperreal foundation. Rolnik (2006) mentions more or less the same idea:

> financial capital does not fabricate commodities like the industrial capital does: it fabricates *worlds*. But what worlds are those? Worlds of signs through advertisement and mass culture. Now it is known that more than half of the earnings of transnational companies is dedicated to advertisement, an activity that precedes the fabrication of products and commodities. In the advertisement campaigns *images of worlds* [e.a.] are created, with which the consumer will identify themselves and then will desire.

These "images of worlds"—dream-worlds—can be seen as the illusory, imaginary worlds that underlie the mentality of consumerism: they represent the collective emotional expectations that are central for all consumption dreams; they summarize the ImCon's ideology, its metaphysics and transcendental promises, indeed its set of central beliefs, or gospel. Here I mention a few of them.

- The first refers to what I called the "paradise of childhood" in Chap. 2: a sort of dreamy unconscious world in which *everything is available*, abundantly and immediately: a cornucopia-world of fantastic and unlimited goods and experiences that are ready for grabs, which is interrelated to a dream of immediate and never-ending gratification. Ritzer (2001) has described it thusly: "The dream here, and one that is played to by most of the new means of consumption, is to be immersed in a world filled with everything one could ever imagine, with all of these things there for the taking. It is akin to the childhood dream of finding oneself in a land in which everything is made of candy and all of it is within reach" (p. 121).

- The second is similar, or related: the dream-world of a "Land Without Evil"—without poverty, lack, difference, or even bad weather—a total capitalist "society of divine happiness" (Clastres, 1974/1989, p. 215) and unfettered hedonism, without conflicts or contradictions. A sort of commercial, ethereal *paradis artificiel*—a paradise of consumption.
- The third relates more to the subject: a dream-world of *unlimited freedom* in which personal responsibility is erased—every judgment and every opinion can be consumed, politics is either non-existent or equated with sign exchange, ethics means consuming and expressing whatever is deemed politically correct, and so on, that is, a world in which every choice is viewed as a consumer choice (and thus implies no real choice at all). A bit like a postmodern dream.
- The fourth can be called a *dream of omnipotence*, a dream-world in which everything is possible, every way of being is reachable—through consumption, and only through consumption. This is related to what I called the dream of "deep and instantaneous personal transformation", "the omnipotent dream of the consumer as a demiurge of himself", in the previous chapter. Jhally (2006) mentions it as a magical world of consumption in which people can be magically and instantaneously transformed (by objects, by images and signs).

Probably more dream-worlds could be added to this list (e.g., a dream-world of an *eternal present*, effacement of time and history and mortality; a dream-world in which *progress* through consumable technology is certain, inevitable, and independent of human action: like an almighty divinity, technology guides and transforms mankind, with all its misery, into posthumans; and so on). However, it can be perceived that all such dreams and dream-worlds are related; they may be seen as central to the

ImCon, its main constituents as a hyperreal world, the supernatural "commodity-world" (Jhally, 1989, p. 217). In fact, as central metaphysical beliefs, as *archaic ideas*, they work like *myths*: they inform *transcendent*, ideal, imaginary worlds, which condense the social utopias, litanies, and liturgies of total consumerism. As such, they are behind the fact that, under global consumerism, the *imaginary itself is the fundamental commodity*; the myth is what is essentially sold and consumed, what moves the whole social system. As Juremir Machado puts it, "What needs to be sold is an imaginary, i.e., a reservoir of images and sensations and an engine that impulses the actions of every consumer" (Silva, 2007, p. 161); these dream-worlds can be seen as the main ideological motors for such.

And, finally, the *fourth* and perhaps most disturbing sense, it is indeed a dream-*world*, for, with globalization, the fantasy world of consumption, the ImCon, goes global: it progressively colonizes all imaginaries, absorbing their elements and replicating them, relentlessly homogenizing and commodifying all cultures. In 1983, Hamelink had already pointed to this process: "the impressive variety of the world's cultural systems is waning due to a process of 'cultural synchronization' that is without historical precedent" (p. 3). Such "synchronization" I call colonization: the logical conclusion of a totalizing pan-consumerism, global colonization corresponds to the extension of commodity-discourse and imagery through mass media, everywhere—produced and reproduced globally as a *techno-imaginary* (Balandier, 1985, p. 222).

Although this is a controversial subject (*pace* the advocates of glocalization, hybridization, etc.), some authors have affirmed the same idea: that the culture industry, dominated by advertisement and marketing logic (i.e., by commodity- and sign-logic), is going global. Lash and Lury (2007), for instance, analyze extensively such idea in their book *The Global Culture Industry*. That means that the ImCon is turning, or has already turned, into *a global collective consciousness*. If that is so, it represents an unprecedented cultural and anthropological mutation, and corresponds to what Hannerz (1989, 1992) called a "global ecumene", a world culture defined by the ImCon. Cultural critic Naomi Klein (2000) expressed it brilliantly as a "monoculture" that is redolent of a "global mall" (p. 117). If that is so, it means that all cultures and all imaginaries—all the historical wealth of mankind—are going through a behemoth process of commodification and simulation; the end result might be the total deconstruction of reality and its reconstruction as a total imaginary of consumption.

5.3 ImCon as Simulacrum of Symbolic Imaginary

Here we re-approach the central theme of this chapter: how the ImCon seems to function as a totalizing imaginary. The basic proposition is that it represents a simulacrum of symbolic imaginary that, by colonizing, replacing, and eventually effacing the old symbolic systems, simulates and functions like them: as a totalizing social system of signification, a myth or desacralized religion. In what follows I attempt to develop such proposition.[9]

The first idea is that the ImCon constitutes a globalitarian *collective consciousness*, in the same sense of the concept developed by Durkheim: at its most basic level, it functions as an archaic, primitive, "mythic" collective mentality, founded on a specific form of imagery and imagination (its order of signs and simulacra), and based not on rationality, but on irrational factors: on emotions, desires, fear, the instinctual—the unconscious psyche. Through its code, it monopolizes how meaning, value, signification, and difference are ascribed and consumed socially; thus it institutes social and individual life. However, it does *not* provide social cohesion—as one of its central beliefs is crass individualism, it can only foster weak and volatile bonds—but rather social homogeneity.

The second related idea is that the ImCon operates as an ensemble of *représentations collectives*, with more or less the same dynamics and consequences that they have in relation to so-called primitive societies. However, the main difference is that its *représentations* are *not* symbolic, mythic narratives that are natural and direct expressions of the unconscious psyche. They do not correspond to a *natural* "new interpretation of

[9] The reader should bear in mind that the arguments below are all based on what was presented in Chap. 2 regarding collective consciousness, *représentations collectives*, and *participation mystique*.

archetypal motifs[10]" (Vieira, 2003, p. 57), but rather to the absorption of all narratives and imagery that have a mystical, archetypal, "transcendent", and metaphysical character, and their fabrication and reduplication as a fetishized system of signs that functions as an ersatz symbolic order. This is perhaps the central idea of this thesis: under the ImCon, the symbolic is erased and substituted by a mass ideology. The political economy of the sign and its code and the logics of capital, consumption of signification, commodification, market, unlimited accumulation, and so on *are erected into a transcendental ideology.*

Accordingly, the constitutive elements of such ideology function as *supraordinate ideas.* Tentatively, one could say that the kernel ideas are commodity, capital (and money), market, and consumption. However, *consumption* seems to represent the dominant, the highest supraordinate, idea in the system that defines its ideology, to which all the system's constituents are connected, refer, and function according to the social system's fundamental drive, main categorical imperative, or *absolute principle* (Baudrillard, 1970/1998). It would correspond to the main *archetype* of such imaginary, were "consumption" an archetype.

However, and to recall Jung's (CW16, §247) expressions, all such ideas can be seen as subsumed under one "collective formula" or hegemonic representation: the *commodity-sign*, as "general idea" and "value-category". In comparison with symbolic imaginaries, within the ImCon its *atom*, the commodity-sign, replaces the symbol as its radix, origin, and primal form of representation. Indeed, if for Marx the commodity-form was the central form of representation within capitalism, under total consumerism the commodity-sign becomes the *only* form. Like a primordial image, it functions as an "idea *ante rem*",[11] defining production and reproduction—commodities are produced as signs, signs (culture) are produced as

[10] In fact, there *are* archetypal motifs behind the advent of the ImCon and mass consumerism. For example, unlimited accumulation and production, the objective of fashioning a world and a new human being, and so on correspond to a Luciferian hubris, an identification with the divinity that turns into a demonic principle of destruction (*consumption* as destruction, ruin, waste—*consumere*). The dream of becoming this demiurge, "posthuman" semi-divine being, for whom everything is possible, corresponds to the *Übermensch* dream, which is central for *capitalism as a religion*, according to Walter Benjamin (1921/1996) (and, crucially, was central for Nazism): the *Übermensch* is simply its *Deus absconditus*. However, I cannot go further into this discussion here; it will be appearing again at the end of the empirical part of this work.

[11] Baudrillard (1981/1994) affirmed something similar: "the only great and veritable idea-force of this competing society, the commodity and the mark" (p. 88).

commodities (Baudrillard)—and apperception—things, social relations, persons are perceived as and through commodity-signs. If we take the analogy with the primordial image to an extreme, the commodity-sign also orders experience and directs action (consumption) through a determined *meaning* (signification, difference: social signification given by the code); thus it can be seen (with some exaggeration) as *the archetypal image* of the ImCon.

If commodity-signs function as the primary particles of the ImCon as collective consciousness, it is chiefly by their formulation and agglutination into consumption dreams and dream-worlds that they operate as its *représentations collectives.* Consumption dreams and their dream-worlds articulate and communicate the ImCon's ideology; they carry and convey its metaphysics, collective formulae, its code and gospel. Just like a religious narrative, each consumption dream carries the sum total of collective practices and social ideology of consumerism[12]; the whole structure of consumption society and its logic are condensed in it. Just like *myth*, consumption dreams function as the *dynamis*, the prime mover that mobilizes and directs social and individual energies and affects (*desire*: libido) toward *rituals of consumption* (Belk, Wallendorf, & Sherry, 1989), the fundamental, monadic social act that constitutes consumer society.

Thus, as *représentations collectives*, the ideology of consumerism functions as typical and collective *mental categories*, except categories based on irrational, primitive thought, which is associative, pre-logical, magical: they are categories founded on fantasy- and dream-thinking. As categories of imagination (Jung, CW8, §254) and understanding that are interposed between the subject and reality, they condition how reality—both inner and outer—is experienced and represented. They are not merely "impervious to experience" and "indifferent to contradiction", like *représentations collectives*; as argued, the system of signs is a priori based on denial of reality, and eventually effaces reality, taking its place. That is, such semiotic representations define reality itself as hyperreality. As mental categories, they condition experience: approaching a totalizing functioning, every

[12] As McLuhan (1959, p. 340) put it, speaking of the "myth-making" function of Hollywood and Madison Avenue: such function strives to comprise "*in a single image* the total social action or process that is imagined as desirable" (e.a.). That corresponds *exactly* to the functioning of an archetypal image, translated into a mythological motif.

experience will bear the mark of consumption- and commodity-logic, that is, the world and its subjects are *seen* as functioning according to such logics; just like an archaic collective consciousness, such perception and functioning are taken for granted, naturalized (*das Fraglos-gegeben*): the hyperreal becomes the real.

Finally, the ImCon's *représentations collectives* also function based on the irrational, archaic psychic substratum (instincts, emotions, desires, etc.): they engender functional irrationality through their emotional, fascinating, magical power—their *mystical* character, to use Lévy-Bruhl's expression. To recall, the *représentations* are collective because they embody powerful collective feelings, emotions, and values; they are "contaminated" emotionally, and their contamination follows a collective pattern, shared by the whole of culture: their typical *mana*, expression of the numinosity of the collective unconscious. However, here the representations' fascination and spell do not come from archetypal images (projected as symbolic systems) but from the manufactured *sign-value*, the *aura* of the commodity (Tomlinson, 1990, p. 15). It is the sign-value, arbitrarily and artificially manipulated as a dream narrative, that gives the representations (and the objects) their emotional color and affective value, their dreamy, magical semblance. The emotional and affective value (*libido*, as numen), which the primitive projected upon the object, here is given a priori, inducing and *forcing* projection. Like *mana*, it channels the subject's affective value, emotions, feelings (desire, irrational elements) to the commodity-sign, to consumption as the great *habitude directrice de la conscience*.

Therefore, here numinosity is fabricated through manipulation of image and signification; thus it systematizes, directs, and ultimately engineers the irrational substratum in the subject that was the original source of such numinosity—unconscious substratum that is inevitably moved and caught by the aura of the commodity, which is extended till reaching omnipresence as a global regime of the image. That is the fundamental origin of the ImCon's *mana*, of its fascinating and mysterious character, its sacred aura, "the sanctification of the system as such, of the commodity as system" (Baudrillard, 1973/1981, p. 92): its *fetish*.

5.3.1 Fetish and Phantasmagoria as the ImCon's Numen

Indeed, if social signification defines consumerism, the commodity fetish (sign-value) is the key element for its imaginary as a surrogate symbolic-mythic system: instead of symbols and numen, the ImCon is defined by signs (and simulacra) and *ideology congealed as fetish* (or phantasmagoria). In what follows I discuss the concepts of fetish, phantasmagoria, and ideology based on the works of Baudrillard, Marx, and Walter Benjamin.

Baudrillard (1973/1981) at first adopted Marx's concept of commodity fetish as "the lived ideology of capitalist society—the mode of sanctification, fascination and psychological subjection by which individuals *internalize the generalized system* of exchange value" (p. 88). However, following his semiological perspective, he moved beyond Marx and proposed that the fundamental fetish corresponds neither to use-value, nor to the labor alienated from the subject and appropriated by the commodity, and even less so to the object itself in its materiality: consumerism institutes a *fetishism of the signifier*, of the manipulated, abstract sign-value that simulates and functions like a manufactured *mana*, or artificial numen. In fact, Baudrillard points that the very etymology of the word "fetish" originally signifies that sense:

> a *fabrication*, an artifact, a labor of appearances and signs. It appeared in France in the 17th century, coming from the Portuguese *feitiço*, meaning "artificial", which itself derives from the Latin *factitius*. The primary sense is "to do" ("to make", *faire*), the sense of "to imitate by signs". (p. 91)

To sum up, as "feitiço", fetish connotes an enchantment (numen) obtained by (artificial) sorcery: a fakery, a *semiotic simulation that fascinates and deludes*.

Marx's theory of capitalist fetishism is still valuable to us, however, for its articulation of fetish with the religious and sacred, and with the phenomenon of projection. Indeed, the original Enlightenment concept appropriated by Marx referred to *religious fetishism*, the "primitive, natural and irrational African practice of attributing material things with supernatural powers and therefore a special social value, or animism"

(Osborne, 2005, p. 17). As we have seen, that describes the basic functioning of symbolic thinking: the "supernatural powers" correspond to *mana*, the primordial religious form that informed symbolico-religious imaginaries. Naturally, Marx employed the concept of fetish to discuss the religious-like aspects of the commodity and capitalism. In the *Capital*, fetish is the illusory *mythic* force that animates the commodity, and thus the world made in its image; it establishes mystical (*geheimnisvolle*) and mysterious (*raetselhafte*) forms of relation between *things*—hegemony of commodified, reified relations—forming a capitalist world that abounds in "metaphysical subtleties and theological niceties" (Marx, 1867/1990, p. 163), derived from a fetishist worldview. Marx then speculates that the source of such worldview can only be found in the "nebulous realm of the religious world[13]" (*Nebelregion der religiösen Welt*) (Marx, 1867/1993, p. 86), which, psychologically, corresponds to the archetypes, the collective unconscious, and their numen.

The archetypal numen is what used to be "attributed" by the primitives to material things: a *projection* of the *sacred* upon the environment. However, what was a "natural and irrational" practice, which sustained an organic connection with the sacred and the world, is artificially engineered and reified under capitalism. This process will result in colonization, desecration, and volatilization of *both* the sacred and the world—including the human world, or reality—which sublimate into an ethereal "nebulous realm".

Such result was concisely expressed as the famous phrase in *The Communist Manifesto* (1848), "All that is solid melts into air, all that is sacred is profaned". The original German, "Alles Ständische und Stehende verdampft", signifies a process of *sublimation*; while "*melts* into air" still denotes something solid becoming liquid and then gaseous, *verdampft* means to *volatilize*, to *vaporize*.[14] This process of volatilization refers not

---

[13] However, Marx can only see the religious world as an *analogy* to capitalist ideology.

[14] Renditions into other languages preserve this meaning: "si volatilizza tutto"; "todo se esfuma"; "s'en va en fumée"; "se volatiliza" (see www.marxists.org/xlang/marx.htm for translations). I mention this point having Bauman's *liquid* metaphor (for postmodernity and consumerism) in mind; I think we are rather living under an *ethereal*, volatile social order—the *ethereality* of consumerism. Nonetheless, it is meaningful that the English translation "solid melts into air" comes from a text that has everything to do with this thesis: it alludes to Shakespeare's *Tempest* (Act IV, scene 1), which speaks of the volatilization of the human world, towers, temples, the whole globe, all dis-

only to the gargantuan process of dematerialization of the world (Ward, 2009) inherent to the process of producing commodities, as "not an atom of matter enters into the objectivity of commodities as values" (Marx, 1867/1990, p. 138), and of consuming them, as "eventually no object of the world will be safe from consumption and annihilation through consumption" (Arendt, 1958/1998, p. 115), or to the generalized monetization of all social values. This process is indeed equivalent to a dissolution of all *sense* of solidity—a dissolution *of reality itself.* My argument is that the second part of the sentence, "alles Heilige wird entweiht", all that is sacred is desecrated, points not merely to a phenomenon parallel to the volatilization but *to its central genealogy*. The profaned *sacred* here is not limited to the past, tradition, beliefs, and loyalties, as Bauman (2000, p. 3) contended; it fatefully refers to what has always been their very *foundation*—the mythic, religious, irrational realm: the symbolic-archetypal.

The central event of modernity: Nietzsche expressed it not as the mere profanation of such realm but as the "*murder* of the gods", slaughter of the symbolic. The symbolic—expression of the gods, of the transcendental—was what provided society with a stable, hierarchic system of meaning that underlay all social life; it gave it *solidity*, as origin and foundation of *culture* itself (in fact, as *principium*, beginning and principle: *arché*[15]), through the guarantee of absolutes (as symbolic manifestations of archetypes, the *archai*).[16] Without the symbolic, culture and reality are volatilized (and commodified); Nietzsche's "murder of the gods" in the marketplace is followed by Baudrillard's "murder of reality".

"Heilige" and the English "holy" have the same etymological source: "whole", integral, healthy, indicating an original wholeness—the *totality* of the sacred, symbolic domain, the transcendental or suprasensory, with

solve, and ends with "We are such stuff as *dreams* are made on; and our little life is rounded with a sleep", *a dissolution of life into dream*, now the nebulous, volatilized dream of consumption, the ImCon, and its narcotic illusions.

[15] See Arendt (1963, pp. 179ff).

[16] Bauman (2001, p. 239) concurs: "We call 'culture' the kind of human activity which in the last account consists in making the *volatile* solid, linking the finite to the infinite, and otherwise building bridges connecting mortal life to *values* immune to the eroding impact of time". Those bridges, as argued, are *symbols*.

the human realm of senses and experiences, the sensory. A totality that functioned through and was embodied in symbolic imaginaries: the symbol is what naturally represents and unifies the sensory and the suprasensory, the irrational-transcendental and the rational-physical, into a totality, a wholeness.

Such wholeness is fragmented, and the suprasensory, alienated from the human world ("murdered"), is then volatilized and projected upon the commodity-form, which contrives and mesmerizes the sensory through its empty appearance. The commodity becomes imbued with both: *ein sinnlich übersinnliches Ding* (Marx, 1867/1993, p. 85), a sensible suprasensible thing; it acquires a numinous ("sacred") character, its *fetish*, but in a perverted, both supernatural and unnatural, inhuman form: Marx calls it the "ghostly objectivity" (*gespenstige Gegenständlichkeit*) (Marx, 1867/1993, p. 52), the autonomous *phantasmagoria* of the commodity-form.

5.3.2 Phantasmagoria: A Technological Dream-Delusion

The concept of phantasmagoria—*die phantasmagorische Form*—appears in Marx's *Das Kapital* as a metaphor for the capitalist ideology of fetishism: it connotes how the volatilization and commodification of what was once both *human* and *transcendental*, when projected upon the commodities, endue social relations and the world with a *dreamy*, illusory, mystical character, as a sort of ghostly vapor that pervades everything. What was once a *living* human substance then animates the commodity-world—"Things [commodities] have gained autonomy, and they take on human features", as Benjamin (1999, p. 181) quotes Marx—and social relations become reified and sort of *undead*, not quite living, immaterial, a mere appearance: "There is a definite social relation between men, that assumes, in their eyes, the fantastic [phantasmagoric] form of a relation between things" (Marx, 1867/1993[17]).

[17] This is Sect. 2.4, Chap. 2 of *Capital*; I use this translation for it conveys the meaning I sought ("in their *eyes*", emphasizing perception and appearance; however, "fantastic" does not capture "phantasmagorische" well).

However, beyond articulating fetish and ideology with the resulting mystical, dream-like life that they fashion, what makes the concept of phantasmagoria even more appropriate to describe the ImCon is that—differing from the concept of "fetish"—it connotes the *technological* character of fetishization, the fundamental *artificial* character of the projection, and its logic of illusion, spectacle, and entertainment. That is, the concept simply condenses the ontology of the ImCon as a techno-imaginary. Such connotations can be seen in the origins of the term.

Originally, the phantasmagoria was a mechanical apparatus, a lantern or *projector*, used in magical illusionist spectacles to "conjure up" the ghosts of the past.[18] By concealing the back projection of ghostly images, it *simulated* their apparition, creating an autonomous, fascinating, and artificial reality. "The images were intended to appear as if they just emerged and had a life of their own" (Hetherington, 2005, p. 193). Marx used this trope to illustrate how labor is concealed in the production of value, which, as commodity fetish, is emancipated from labor and projected upon the world, thus producing a false, misty, *ideological* reality redolent of myth, dream, and primitive religion.

The analogy with the dynamics of the ImCon and the functioning of *représentations collectives* for the primitives is clear. The ImCon: projection *by technology* of magic images onto a smoke screen of empty commodities—creating a phantasmagoria with the spectral semblance of a mythical reality. What was "attributed" *naturally* by the primitives—that is, through the unconscious autonomous mechanism of projection of *symbols*, the operations of symbolic fantasy, imagination, and dream—here is artificially conjured up as disconnected images through an automated, technological artifact. Yet, if we connect this trope with my

[18] "The original phantasmagoria was a form of popular spectacle that emphasized the principle of deception or concealment, particularly associated with the presentation of the figure of the ghost" (Hetherington, 2005, p. 192). "Such phantasmagorical performances were enacted in late 18th and early 19th century Europe, relying upon a sophisticated deployment of the older magic lantern device, which projected the images from painted slides (although later using advances in photographic technology to project the performance of real, hidden actors) onto a secretly deployed [concealed!] gauze screen or literal smoke screen. The spectral effect was enhanced through technological and theatrical means" (Charles, 2009, p. 133).

previous argument, it can be used in a more radical way: under the ImCon, what is "conjured up" and projected, the "ghosts of the past", ultimately represents what was named before as "all that is solid and sacred"—history, culture, and *fundamentally* the archetypal, the mythical, symbolical, transcendental realms. That is, what was the domain of the *unconscious*—of nature, symbol, and dream—is colonized, volatilized, *manufactured*, and mechanically projected onto a commodity-world: that is its fetish, its phantasmagoria. Another form of saying the same, etymologically, phantasmagoria can be read as *phantasma agoreuein* (Cohen, 2006, p. 209), the ghosts of the agora, *the ghosts of the marketplace*. And who were murdered in the marketplace of capitalism? The gods. Hence, the commodity-world is imbued with the *ghosts of the gods* (i.e., of the archetypes as symbols), their supernatural, spectral numen what fascinates and haunts us.

In fact, the etymon of phantasmagoria does point to a connection with a god. In Greek mythology, *Phantasos* was one of the *Oneiroi*, the gods of dreams, sons of Hypnos. Whereas Morpheus and Ikelos, his brothers, sent people dreams in human and animal forms, Phantasos was the one responsible for sending dreams of inanimate objects, of *lifeless* things, in fact, according to Ovid,[19] *vacant anima*: things devoid of soul—and in *deceptive* shapes—in opposition to Morpheus, he *never* announced the truth.

Phantasos would then correspond to the god of *semiotic consumption dreams*, which "never tell the truth" (are artificial, unreal, and deny reality); the god who endows inanimate things with a dreamy character, and replaces true human dreams (sent by Morpheus) and imagination with deception, a phantasmatic, hypnotic illusion or phantasy. As Hetherington (2005, p. 191) commented, "His is the figural message (…) of a modern bourgeois civilization dreaming itself into existence through the commodity. In a capitalist society Phantasos has become the god of the commodity fetish." Indeed, Phantasos would be the apposite god of the ImCon dream-world and its surrogate religion—if it had any real, historical gods….

[19] "Il occupe tous les objets qui sont privés de vie" (Ovid, 1806, Book XI, p. 641).

5.3.3 Consumerist Phantasmagoria as Collective Dream

Walter Benjamin, in his *Passagen-Werk*, published in English as *Arcades Project* (1999), reinterpreted such Marxian insights while focusing more on the transition from capitalism to consumerism; he articulated capitalism-consumerism's mythic, religious traits with the concepts of dream and phantasmagoria.

Benjamin (1999) first proposed seeing life and psychic functioning under capitalist ideology and its commodity fetishism as *dream*, a "dreaming collective"—a concept that allowed for illuminating all the oneiric and irrational elements of capitalism. He emphasized the central role played by the irrational aspects in the modern apotheosis of the commodity: through new technologies, images, and spectacles, high capitalism sought to conjure the supernatural dimension, the mystique, the powers of "the visceral unconscious" (p. 396), in order to manufacture a *dream life* in a "primordial landscape of consumption" (p. 827) governed by the commodity-fetish as "wish-image" (p. 46) (i.e., what I called a consumption dream, a *desire image*). Its signifying edifices were the Parisian arcades, galleries, and world fairs—predecessors of shopping malls, department stores, and Disneyland-like thematic parks. They embodied the first *dream-worlds of consumption*, as the "dream houses of the collective" (p. 405), the producers of the "dream- and wish-image of the collective" (p. 905), that is, the factories of an artificial *irrational*, emanating exclusively from the commodity fetish, which mystified and acted as a fermenter "of intoxication in the collective consciousness" (ibid.). Benjamin expressed the religious character of such inebriating, enchanted dream-worlds calling them "temples of commodity capitalism" (p. 36).

Following Marx, Benjamin later exchanges fetish and ideology for the concept of commodity *phantasmagoria*, which condenses the commodity's spectacular, hypnotizing power, its "ghostly objectivity". For Benjamin, it was as if all the dissolved cultural and irrational elements—history, value, meaning, dream, desire, organic social relations—projected upon the commodity returned and, as a spectral presence, saturated and conditioned all *experience* as ghost-like, immaterial, illusory, and unreal, and yet forceful and moving, supernatural, *mythic*.

The arcades embodied socially such uncanny, mystical experience—a phantasmagorical dream. However, such form of collective consciousness was not limited to the arcades. In a society defined by the production and consumption of commodities, their properties, and specifically their fetish character, come to define how society "represents itself and thinks to understand itself" (Benjamin, 1999, p. 669). Hence ultimately the whole of culture and modernity become defined by their phantasmagoria: Benjamin saw "the culture of the commodity-producing society as phantasmagoria[20]" (Benjamin, 1991, p. 1172), and technological modernity as the world dominated by its phantasmagorias (Benjamin, 1999, p. 26).[21]

For Benjamin, mass culture—in fact the whole of modernity—was overtaken by the ideological superstructure of consumer capitalism, which has the phantasmagorical appearance of a *collective dream*: the "collective dream of the commodity phantasmagoria" (Buck-Morss, 1989, p. 271), whereby the "collective consciousness sinks ever into deeper sleep" (Benjamin, 1999, p. 389). For Benjamin, the masses of commodity society live in a somnambular dream state, a dream-world: the phantasmagoric dream of capitalist ideology, raised to the role of a Hegelian *Geist* (or a phantasmal *imaginary*) that animates, and at the same time anesthetizes, consumer society.

The politico-psychological consequences of such society are condensed in another quote: "capitalism is a natural phenomenon with which a new dream-filled sleep [*Traumschlaf*] came over Europe, and, through it, a *reactivation of mythic forces*" (Benjamin, 1999, p. 391; e.a.). *Traumschlaf* represents the cultural lethargy, alienation, and unreality that compose the phantasmagorical collective dream. Its accompanying mythic reactivation, the return of the alienated, colonized irrational aspects, was fatefully actualized as Nazism: underneath the illusory, "mythical" dream-world of consumption lurked destructive, indeed devastating,

[20] Letter to Gretel Adorno, March 1939. I tried to affirm essentially the same when I wrote that the ImCon becomes a global collective consciousness.

[21] In fact, Benjamin's monumental (and unfinished) *Arcades Project* can be seen as an archaeology of the phantasmagoria that was modernity.

irrational elements. In the same way that the phantasmagoria represents the eerie, dark aspect of the appropriation of irrational forces by the commodity, ultimately the whole system, the capitalist machine, sits upon primeval, alienated unconscious factors: for Benjamin, capitalism is a cultic, nihilistic religion "which offers not the reform of existence but its complete destruction" (Benjamin, 1921/1996, p. 289). That is, the *Traumschlaf* hid the reappearance not only of relatively harmless "barbaric" elements such as the treadmill, poor laws, and so on, as pointed by Marx,[22] but of sheer destructive, nihilistic barbarism, an atavistic nightmare skulking in the subterranean stream of capitalism: masses marching like somnambulant ghosts not in the arcades, but inside a "mythic", techno-mechanical totalitarianism. The modern dream-worlds of consumption became death factories.

5.3.4 ImCon as a Mythic Dream-World: The Myth of the Cave

After this historical digression, let us return to the contemporary ImCon. The reader can infer that the idea of phantasmagoria as a technological *projector* advanced the theme of mass media, communications industries, and the massive circulation of (fetishized) images they promote. The argument delineated above is that, through their global extension and all-pervasiveness, these forms of technological proliferation of images constitute a "global projector", which institutes collective consciousness as a mythical imaginary (a simulacrum of symbolic reality). Perhaps this idea of a mythical ImCon, as a sort of all-abiding dream-delusion within which we live relatively unawares, might be best illustrated with an analogy to Plato's myth of the cave, found in his *Republic*, a sort of mythic fairy tale.[23]

[22] I am referring to another famous phrase of Marx's (1847): "Barbarism reappears, but created in the lap of civilisation itself and belonging to it; hence leprous barbarism, barbarism as leprosy of civilisation".

[23] Months after writing this, I found a very similar idea in Ward (2009, p. 98): "In a world where content disappears and brand names (…) float free and ethereally on electronic waves of advertising, we enter a parody of Plato's world of pure forms". My point is that it is not merely a parody: it

It is as if the modern Platonic man, feeling like a prisoner and terrified by the light, transcendence, and ethical imperative of the images that used to be seen in the world-cave (images that came from his "back": from the unconscious, the world of Ideas and Forms, *eidos*, the *archetypal ideas*), decided not to believe in them, and to build a projector instead.... Concealed from view, the *projector* is henceforth what manufactures the ideas and their images, and confers them veracity and reality—artificial *eidolon* that shapes the world through technology. The projection is made upon the ethereal canvas of empty commodity-signs; capturing and dazing all the senses, the cave becomes a consumption world of fantasy and dream. The phantasmagoria referred to such apparatus: the projection of icons of desire, endowed with a mystical (numinous, phantasmagorical) character, that conduce to a ghostly unreality. The fascinating nebulous power of the projection occupies all the Platonic caveman's mental and spatial fields; mesmerized and giddy by the artificial enchantment of such disfigured world, he never leaves the cave, for the cave *becomes* his world: inner and outer world dissolved into a dream-world.

If this image correctly portrays the ImCon as a mythic world, the essence of its worship may be seen as precisely this promise: that the consumer will never *have* to leave the "cave", the dream-world where metaphysical dreams proliferate. Such dreams, the transcendental *dream-worlds* mentioned before, constitute the *passion* of consumption, its "religious" essence. Nordström and Riddestråle (2005) offer a somewhat different (and more crude and concise) formulation of them; in the ImCon's advertising worldview, they can be summarized as "the five perpetual dreams of mankind: eternal life, eternal youth, eternal richness, eternal virility, eternal happiness" (p. 229). These "eternal" dreams represent "the basic urges of people" (ibid.) in metaphysical mode. The ImCon, therefore, is based on the promise of their satisfaction through consumption. But more than that, the central and metaphysical idea underlying such imaginary is that it promises a fusion, a religious immersion with a sort of paradise, the mythic world of commodity-dreams, in which eternal happiness, progress, transcendence, richness, and immortality can be bought. *That underlies all consumption.*

---

is a simulacrum. And Berry (2010) discusses at length the myth of the cave as a metaphor for mass media (i.e., my idea of using the cave metaphor was not as original as I thought at first...).

Therefore, what ultimately defines consumerism as a simulacrum of mythic system is that, through "the exaltation and worship of signs *on the basis of a denial of things and the real*" (Baudrillard, 1970/1998, p. 99), it offers a mystical symbiosis, a *communion* with the utopic collective imaginary, a state of synthetic wholeness in which all consumers partake of the same phantasmagoria coagulated in different images. A simulacrum of religion defined by full *participation mystique* with the ImCon: the dystopic epiphany of the *consumystic*.

5.3.5 ImCon as a Myth, or Desacralized Religion

Those were some reflections on how consumerism functions as a mythological system, or a simulacrum of religion: through its imaginary. However, what I argued above has also been expressed in different forms by other authors; here I mention some of them in order to substantiate my reflections. Quoted by Debord (1967, p. 9)[24] in the beginning of his *Sociètè du Spectacle*, Feuerbach, for instance, perfectly encapsulates many of my arguments:

> But certainly for the present age, which prefers the sign to the thing signified, the copy to the original, representation to reality, the appearance to the essence (…) illusion only is *sacred*, truth profane. Nay, sacredness is held to be enhanced in proportion as truth decreases and illusion increases, so that the highest degree of illusion comes to be the highest degree of sacredness.

Illusion, imagery, and ideology as a sacred system: According to Baudrillard (1970/1998), thus, consumption becomes "our new tribal mythology—the morality of modernity" (p. 194). A global mythology dreamt into being through the relentless absorption of all other myths and their re-fabrication as myths of consumption—ultimately, by the colonization of the very myth-making, symbolic function of imagination: the ImCon as a myth represents the epochal *effacement of myth*. "If

[24] Here I quote from the English translation found in http://www.marxists.org/reference/archive/debord/society.htm

the consumer society no longer produces myth, this is because *it is itself its own myth*. (…) That is to say, it is a statement of contemporary society about itself, the way our society speaks itself. And, in a sense, the only objective reality of consumption is the idea of consumption" (p. 193).

The "idea of consumption": Elemental religious form, archetypal *idée force* of its imaginary, revelation of its First Commandment. If for Baudrillard (1976/1993) the power of capital is "based in the imaginary", consumerism as a religion[25] announces itself as the parousia of its "fantastic secularisation" (p. 129)—a mythic religion of hierophanous signs in which the sign-value remains the only mystical or transcendental signifier, instituting society and consumers. As Maffesoli (2008) reminds us, myths are the "crystallization of collective dreams, [which] make a society what it is" (p. 11). Analogously, the ImCon as a dreaming collective is the crystallization—or rather the permanent flow—of collective *consumption dreams*. It institutes a social order defined by the idolatrous cult of *image*—omnipresent, all-signifying, transcendent—as a new Eucharistic sacrament of contemporary religiosity (Maffesoli, 1990, p. 112; 1993, p. 179).

Image and idea, omnipresent: Through them the social *ideology* of consumption works like a mythic imaginary, totalizing its consumer-subject—the ImCon as "a structurating force (like myth for Lévi-Strauss) that socialises, informs and, in fact, *produces* the individual of contemporary consumer society" (Baudrillard, 1973/1981, p. 147). My contention is that it is by becoming a *global simulacrum of myth* that "consumption can on its own substitute for all ideologies and, in the long run, take over alone the role of integrating the whole of society, as hierarchical or religious rituals did in primitive societies" (Baudrillard, 1970/1998, p. 94).

5.3.6 ImCon as a Totalitarian Ideology

Therefore, if the ImCon functions like a simulacrum of symbolic imaginary—like a myth or desacralized religion—it constitutes a signifying template through which world, self, and life are perceived. Like some

[25] Rolnik (2006) puts it in an interesting way: "the western idea of a promised paradise corresponds to a repudiation of life in its immanent nature of a continuous creative impulse. In its earthly version, the capital replaced God in its function of guarantor of the promise, and the virtue that makes us worthy of it came to be consumption: that is the fundamental myth of advanced capitalism".

religions (e.g., like colonial pan-Christianity) that allow for nothing outside themselves, it is an all-encompassing, total worldview, but an *ideological* one. Like a total religious system, thereby it governs every aspect of social and psychic life, becoming a totalizing force in fabricating, shaping, and controlling subjectivities.

Such process would thus constitute a globalitarian colonization of mentalities, corresponding to the same totalizing capitalist logic of unlimited expansion and colonization—but inner-directed, turned inward: directed to the subject's psyche. In this sense, total consumerism and its imaginary do indeed have many similarities with totalitarian ideologies and their propaganda methods (starting with the common origin of both). An excellent presentation of this theme can be found in Curtis (2002). Jhally (2006) also touches on the subject when he states plainly that "Twentieth century advertising is the most powerful and sustained system of propaganda in human history" (p. 99). Three ideas seem crucial for this work. The first regards the analogy between the ImCon and totalitarian ideology. If we see the ImCon as a semiotic order, then it corresponds to a totalizing ideology in Arendt's sense: a coherent and all-embracing fictitious explanation of reality, the logic of a system of ideas that provides reality with a "fantastically fictitious consistency" (Arendt, 1958, p. 352). However, if seen as a simulacrum of imaginary, it is not even a "fictitious explanation": as Baudrillard contended, it *fabricates* reality itself based on its ideological premises, in fact abolishing the difference between reality and fiction (or dream). Much like the totalitarian "phony world of propaganda" that, in order to be believed, had to be fabricated as reality (Arendt, 1946/2005, p. 199). Indeed, as argued throughout this work, the ImCon *is* such phony (dream) world.

The second idea is that, like totalitarian ideology and propaganda, the imaginary of consumption exploits and leads the masses fundamentally through manipulating, conditioning, and indeed engineering the *irrational, unconscious* psyche. In this sense, the ImCon's fashioning of consumers' mentalities closely resembles the indoctrination of "Nazi militants who, according to Goebbels, *obey a law they are not even consciously aware of but which they could recite in their dreams*" (Virilio, 1994, p. 11).

The third idea is that such totalization of subjectivities, of the psyche, is engineered from birth—indeed, even *before* the subject is born. Such phenomenon has been referred to as the colonization and commodification of *childhood* (Molnar, 1996; Gunter & Furnham, 1998; Schor, 2004), a process whose quintessence was pointed by Bauman (2005), quoting Adatto (2003): "'the *soul* of the child is under siege' ... Childhood turns into 'a preparation for the selling of the self' as children are trained 'to see all relationships in market terms' and to view other human beings ... through the prism of market-generated perceptions and evaluations" (Bauman, 2005, pp. 114–115; e.a.)—that is, trained to see through the "prism" of the ImCon, in which relationships, human beings, and in fact the whole of life are ultimately viewed as *commodities*. Bauman (2007) is quite right when he writes that "the battles waged over and around children's consumer culture are no less than battles over the nature of the person and the scope of personhood" (p. 55).

To finish this section, we can return to what Jung wrote about secularized imaginaries. This chapter presented arguments for considering the ImCon as the contemporary *-ism* that functions socially as an ersatz mythological imaginary: it replaces symbolic systems and religion, yet has an equal fascinating force and totalizing claim—it has a totalitarian *telos*. Such assessment has also been voiced by some classical authors, in different manners. Marcuse (1964), for instance, considered that within capitalism-consumerism "The products indoctrinate and manipulate (...) the indoctrination they carry ceases to be publicity; it becomes a way of life". This represents "domination—in the guise of affluence and liberty", "creating a *truly totalitarian universe*" (p. 14; e.a.). For Baudrillard (1968/1996a) it is the *code*—as consumerism's social system of signification, its ideological structure—that is totalitarian: "The code is totalitarian; no one escapes it: our individual flights do not negate the fact that each day we participate in its collective elaboration" (p. 22). And for Adorno and Horkheimer (1944/2002), the capitalist culture industry resembles a mythic system of totalization (p. 108). Finally, considering that the ImCon is a manufactured, artificial myth, what Cassirer (1946) wrote regarding political myths and totalitarianisms fully applies to it:

> Myth has always been described as the result of an unconscious activity and as free product of the imagination. But here we find *myth made according to plan*. The new political myths do not grow up freely; they are not wild fruits of an exuberant imagination. They are artificial things fabricated by

very skilful and cunning artisans. It has been reserved for the twentieth century, our own great technical age, to develop a new technique of myth. Henceforth myths can be manufactured in the same sense and according to the same methods as any other modern weapon (...). That is a new thing—and a thing of crucial importance. It has changed the whole form of our social life. (p. 282; e.a.)

5.4 The ImCon and the Fabrication of a Commodity-Subject

This section concludes the chapter by summarizing how the ImCon institutes psychological subjectivity—now from the perspective that it functions like a simulacrum of symbolic imaginary. It consists in a more schematic and speculative discussion, essentially based on what the empirical material, *night dreams*, brought to light, and intends to function as a theoretical framework to understand how subjectivity (and its colonization) is represented in them, in very broad terms. Such discussion will be brief, as it repeats many arguments already presented above. As in the previous chapter, its focus is on irrational psychic elements; although the imaginary also molds ego consciousness (and rationality), its subjectivation force is fundamentally based on the unconscious psyche—on a *functional irrationality* grounded in primitive, archaic functioning. As with symbolic imaginaries, the formation of subjectivity here may be described through two main ideas: how the ImCon's *représentations collectives* shape or "fill up" the subject's psyche, and how the subject's identity is instituted in *participation mystique* with the commodity fetish (with consumption dreams), and on a deeper level with the whole system of *représentations collectives*, with the ImCon as (hyper)reality itself.

5.4.1 *Représentations Collectives* and the Fabrication of the Irrational

The basic idea here is that the totalizing ideology of consumerism—translated as general beliefs, values, rites, models, codes, and so on—functions as archaic collective representations: a totalizing worldview that is simply taken for granted as reality. Within such reality the subject's psyche is molded, or unconsciously conditioned: the semiotic representations operate as social categories—of apperception, imagination, understanding—and aim at totalizing perception, experience, and behavior. (On the level of the simulacra and hyperreality, the representations do totalize perception and experience, for they totalize *reality*.)

To recall the classical expression, they thus institute collective and unconscious *habitudes directrices de la conscience*, as a sort of unconscious conditioning since birth: the subject simply functions in near-complete accordance with the ideological mass mentality. As such, the ImCon shapes the consumer's psyche on two levels. The first was discussed in the previous chapter: personal identity is equalized with multiple personae, or identikits, with which the ego identifies; thus the subject becomes more or less identical with segments of the collective consciousness. The second level corresponds to the feeling-toned complexes. To the extent that the collective representations determine all reality and experience, they will mold and form the *personal unconscious*: the subjects' complexes, their unconscious subjectivity, are "filled up" by the *représentations collectives*. Indeed, if the *représentations* are seen as *consumption dreams*, they function very much like complexes.[26] Theoretically, the ideology of the ImCon thus becomes the main content of the personal unconscious psyche, that is, of unconscious subjectivity.

Reiterating, the main difference in relation to symbolic representations is that the ImCon's representations are not projections of the unconscious psychic structure, of archetypes, but artificial, ideological constructions. Yet, they coordinate and direct libido, fantasy, imagination—the whole unconscious functioning—in much the same way. The argument delineated before is that imagination—the *imaginative activity*, as embodiment of what Castoriadis called the *poietic* function of the psyche, its capacity to creatively engender forms (*morphē*)—is annexed and conditioned by

---

[26] A definition of complex: an image (representation) of a specific psychic situation, which functions as a nucleus of meaning, imbued with strong emotional (feeling) content. In a consumption dream, the emotional feeling is given by the fetish, the sign-value designed to elicit emotion and desire; the nucleus of meaning is the signification and difference given by the code; the psychic situation can be any one (e.g., motherhood, happiness, good parenting, etc.), but it will by definition follow the imperative and logic of consumption.

the ImCon. Its semiurgy progressively replaces all symbols, and thus all symbolic thinking; symbols as "emotionally charged images" here are supplanted by commodity-signs. Thus, the *imaginary function*—symbolic-, dream-, and fantasy-thinking, the pre-logical, archaic mode of thinking of the unconscious mind—is taken over by ideological *représentations collectives* as categories of imagination.

If we remember that the imaginative activity represents the "direct expression of psychic life", this means that the very *functioning* of the psyche is colonized and conditioned via *the unconscious psyche*—via the very roots of consciousness, and their connection with archetype and instinct. Furthermore, this functioning represents the "flow of psychic energy" (Jung, CW6, §722), the manifestation of *libido* as fantasy-images. We have seen how libido, abstracted and reduced to *desire*, is industrialized and generated by the ImCon, replicating commodity-logic. Indeed, as consumer society's very existence depends on the extent that it manufactures desires, the goal is to render desires—*libido*—co-extensive with its imaginary, a function not only of mass production of commodities but of the production, reproduction, and proliferation of signs. In other words, its logic is of total configuration and commodification of desires and libido, of psychic energy together with psychic life. I turn once again to Baudrillard (1968/1996a) to describe such logic:

> Here we rediscover, in its most extreme expression, the formal logic of the commodity as analysed by Marx: just as needs, feelings, culture, knowledge—in short, all the properly human faculties—are integrated as commodities into the order of production, and take on material form as productive forces so that they can be sold, so likewise all desires, projects and demands, all passions and all relationships, are now abstracted (or materialized) as signs and as objects to be bought and consumed. (p. 202)

However, we must not forget that libido is fundamentally an expression of instinct. By fabricating and directing desire and fantasy, the imaginary also coordinates the *instincts*—just like archaic *représentations collectives* did. If the symbol expressed, directed, signified, and transformed the primitive's instinctual libido according to a cultural and spiritual *principium*, such role is seized by the sign and its fetish: the semiotic system thus defines all patterns of behavior (or *habitudes directrices de la conscience*), whose categorical imperative turns into *consumption*, as supraordinated and primordial idea, as totalizing *principium* or *arché*.

This process of colonization and fabrication of desire, fantasy, libido, and instinct is equivalent to a generalized mass production of functional irrationality. Indeed, if, as argued, consumerism is fundamentally based on irrational elements, to the extent that it determines the contents and functioning of the subject's irrational, instinctual foundation, the ImCon manufactures and totalizes the subject by commandeering his archaic functioning—the depths of his psyche.

5.4.2 *Participation Mystique*: Archaic Identity with the ImCon

If the ImCon functions as a surrogate symbolic system, then what characterizes its consumer-subject is *participation mystique*—an archaic and unconscious *identity* as particular mode of psychic functioning and form of subjectivity instituted by the imaginary.[27] In fact, Castoriadis (1975/1987) affirmed a similar idea in relation to modernity, although he did not elaborate on it: "[T]he life of the modern world is just as dependent on the imaginary as any archaic or historical culture. (…) In both cases [in archaic societies and modern society] we see at work *that particular form of the imaginary, the subject's identification with an object*" (p. 101; e.a.). However, there are crucial differences between archaic imaginaries and the ImCon. While the primitives identified with the symbolic image projected upon the object (with all its numen), the consumer's identification is *not* with the object (which would correspond to a non-semiotic, "normal" identification, the object or commodity in its materiality) but with the *idea* attached to it: the sign, and specifically the sign-value, the mystical signifier, the ideology congealed as *fetish*.

Participation mystique can thus be seen on two levels:

---

[27] Baudrillard (1970/1998) put it this way: "consumption is governed by a form of *magical thinking* (…) a primitive mentality (…) based on a belief in the omnipotence of signs" (p. 31).

1. *Partial* identity with sign-values, with consumption dreams and the artificial identities they confer. This corresponds to the ego's identity with personae (as identikits): personal identity seen as identification with the semiotic dreams of a social status, social positioning, ways of being and expressing oneself, and so on, all defined by the consumption of signs. The subject here is unconsciously bound (by identity) to consumption dreams.
2. *Archaic* identity with the *system* of consumption dreams, or dreamworld—with the *représentations collectives* and the whole ImCon. To produce this archaic identity is the ImCon's objective; at this level it fully operates as a mythic imaginary. Full identity with the imaginary means that the subject's psyche is practically indistinct from the semiotic system and its ideology; it is another form of describing the full colonization or "filling-up" of the unconscious psyche by the *représentations collectives.* Here the subject is not merely "bound" to the imaginary—the imaginary defines his psyche, and thus his reality and existence.

The other crucial difference regards *projection.* Primitives naturally project their own unconscious contents upon the environment as symbols, and according to collective patterns, the *représentations* (the culturally elaborated forms of unconscious archetypes, i.e., of the psychic structure). The ImCon's representations are not projections of the unconscious psychic structure, of archetypes or complexes, but artificial, ideological constructions; and everything that is socially recognized as subjective or individual contents—value, meaning, difference, signification—is already "projected" as semiotic products. The reader will recall the trope of the phantasmagoric *projector*: the environment already carries all the "symbols" (as semiotic signification and imagery), what was supposed to be projected, a priori.

That means that psyche and subjectivity are *already outside*, before any subjective projection. If we connect this idea with the notion that the ImCon ideology, as *représentations collectives*, fills up the subject's psyche, the conclusion will be that the unconscious subjectivity will *always* and by definition be outside, in a state of fusion with the imaginary. In other words, in a radical inversion, *what in fact projects "subjectivity"* (as semiotic contents) *is the imaginary upon the consumer.*

Perhaps this idea can be better explained with an illustration. As we have seen, the Narcissus myth expressed the dynamics of *participation mystique*: projection of the psyche as self-image, and radical and deadly alienation due to non-recognition of the projection. Under the imaginary of consumption there is a total inversion: it is not the Narcissus-consumer who projects anything; all self-images are already projected a priori and only available as identikits, with which he has to identify (consume) in order to have any sort of identity. Thus the Narcissus-consumer is condemned to *Echo* the ideological imaginary, compulsorily *replicating* it, and hence remaining bonded to, fascinated by, and indistinguishable from its dream-world. This idea is suggested by Miriam Freitas (1999), for whom the contemporary subject is:

> No longer the Narcissist subject who allegorizes the reflex of the same as an other; who falls ill from phantasmagoria is the subject as a mere reflex of the projection composed in society's mirror. Primacy of reflex, of the play of nexuses of consumption and capital, of images fabricated on a global level. (p. 5)

The state of full *participation mystique* induced and fabricated by the imaginary implies a number of other effects upon the subject. Narcissus, as some authors (Baudrillard, 1970/1998, p. 166; Lasch, 1984, p. 19; McLuhan, 1964/1994, pp. 42–51) have pointed out, means *narcosis*, narcotic: *participation* means remaining in a *dreamy*, lethargic state, the "primordial unconscious state", as Jung (CW6, §741) mentioned. That is, identity with the imaginary keeps the subject functioning in a dream-thinking mode, in a state of *abaissement* or unconsciousness, both of which are typical of primitives and children. This idea corresponds to what Walter Benjamin called *Traumschlaf*, a "dream-filled sleep", the collective dream characteristic of consumer society and its dream-worlds. Some other authors have connected such unconscious dream state with consumerism and its imaginary. For instance, Marcel Gauchet (2009) says we are living under an *anesthésie collective*, and Berry (2010) speaks of a "collective trance state". While Adorno and Horkheimer (1944/2002) had already diagnosed a sort of mass trance typical of industrial consumer society, Rosalind Williams (1991, p. 67) mentions the "numbed hypnosis" of consumers. Thus, if *participation* for the primitive and the child means living in an unconscious symbolic world, in a *dream*—for the consumer-subject it means living in full unconscious identity with a dream-world of consumption, enchanted, mesmerized by its phantasmagoria.

Other logical effects of forceful *participation* include dependency and inferiority. Indeed, if the psyche is "outside", if subjectivity is by definition exteriorized, that will engender an unconscious sense of *emptiness* and inferiority, a sort of "lack" of psyche, of individuality, which the primitives call "loss of soul", and an unconscious *bond* (dependency) to the signs that socially signify subjectivity, that is, to the whole ImCon. Both effects are connected to a central characteristic of unconscious identity: *alienation* from subjectivity and individuality. The subject remains massified, undifferentiated from the imaginary, always in need of guaranteeing a state of fusion with it. Indeed, one can say that *consumerism is founded* precisely on this state of *utter alienation*, which corresponds to the perpetual "lack" behind the dynamics of desire: lack of personhood and complete alienation from oneself. Baudrillard (1970/1998) advanced this idea: "Alienation cannot be overcome: it is the very structure (…) of market society", such structure referring to "the generalized pattern of individual and social life governed by commodity logic" (p. 190). And I mention Kellner (2009), who, commenting upon Baudrillard, connected utter alienation to what I have termed *total consumerism*: "in a society where everything is a commodity that can be bought and sold, alienation is total. Indeed, the term 'alienation' originally signified 'to sale', and in a totally commodified society where everything is a commodity, alienation is ubiquitous".

From the standpoint of Jung's psychology, it is important to consider that such alienation refers not only to alienation from subjectivity but also from the unconscious *foundations* in instinct and archetype, what Jung (CW18, §474) called "the world of instinct". It presupposes that, even if the ideological *représentations* shape the personal unconscious, thus directing and coordinating desire and instincts, the depths of the unconscious psyche can be manipulated but cannot be totally colonized, for they are autonomous and transcend both individual and culture. I am referring to the dynamics between shadow and persona, mentioned previously, but in a more radical context: the more alienated, superficial, or *emptied* the ego-persona subject is, the more one can expect the unconscious depths to return in the form of psychic disturbances; dissociated, they can remain as an archaic shadow, activated, primitive, and *destructive*. These dynamics are essentially related to the replacement of the symbol by the ideological sign. As mentioned, the instincts are blind compulsions without the symbol, without the symbolic image that naturally expresses their meaning and direction. Moreover, the symbol is the natural, irrational connection between consciousness and the instinctual foundations. Replacing the symbol, the semiotic ideology may organize, direct, and force instinctual expression; however, without the symbol, the instinctual foundation remains alienated from consciousness, and thus primitive, compulsive, unrefined—as *barbaritas*. These dynamics correspond to the psychological formulation of what Marx termed "leprous barbarism"—hidden in the consumer's psyche as an atavistic force.

Such force can be related to a characteristic psychological functioning that the ImCon, as a mass ideology, induces and produces in its subjects: a typical crowd psychology, or *mass mentality*. Indeed, if consumerism functions based on the manipulation of irrational, unconscious forces, the control of pre-logical thought (of dream-thinking, symbolic thinking, etc.), and the fostering and commercialization of mass feelings, emotions, and dreams, then the unconscious functioning that it engenders can only be seen as that of the horde: unstable, irrational, suggestible, easily carried away. Actually, it is characteristic of archaic identity, or *participation*, to engender psychic contagion and collective hypnosis. As Jung (CW6, §742) wrote, unconscious identity "forms the basis of suggestion and psychic infection". Therefore we may expect that, underneath consumer society's astounding rational and technological development, in the psychic depths of its anesthetized, anodyne masses, a mob mentality[28] may be prowling.

[28] As I was writing this work, violent riots were being waged in London by "excluded consumers" (Bauman, 2011)—excluded from *highly conspicuous consumption*, in fact, deprived from full, enchanted immersion in the global ImCon. In my opinion, such episodes rendered explicit the mob mentality that underlies even rich, developed, democratic consumption societies, and which can appear in full when certain social barriers collapse (as, e.g., in the event of a deep economic crisis).

5.4.3 Colonization of the Unconscious

A central idea that arises from all the arguments above is that consumerism depends on the colonization of the unconscious psyche: alongside its obvious manipulation of emotions, desires, and so on; by instituting a global semiotic imaginary that seizes dream, imagination, and fantasy, consumerism seeks to control and manufacture the entire unconscious, and, through it, the whole psyche. Perhaps this idea can be seen as the fulcrum of the ImCon's *telos*: to fashion the unconscious as a mere replication of its ideology.

Strangely enough, to my knowledge such an important hypothesis appears only in very few contemporary authors.[29] One is Fredric Jameson (1991), who mentions it in ways that are analogous to what has been argued here, as the "new and historically original penetration and colonization of Nature and the unconscious" by capitalism and "the rise of media and the advertisement" (p. 36); and in a later work, he alerts to "diagnoses of the colonization of the Unconscious by commodity reification, consumerism and advertising"—colonization that becomes known as postmodernism (Jameson, 1992, p. 202). In a passage, he actually coincides with my hypothesis (albeit he does not use the concept of imaginary): postmodern capitalism and the processes instituted by its new reproductive technology (including media) "constitute a system, a worldwide disembodied yet increasingly total system of relationships and networks hidden beneath the appearance of daily life, whose 'logic' is sensed in the process of *programming our outer and inner worlds*, even to the point of *colonizing our former 'unconscious'*" (p. 61; e.a.). And, of course, Gilles Deleuze and Félix Guattari wrote profusely about the production of the unconscious by capitalism, calling it the "machinic unconscious" (Guattari, 1979/2010), the basis for the hegemonic fabrication of subjects as "desiring-machines" (Deleuze & Guattari, 1972/2004).

---

[29] However, I have not used such authors' works extensively in this book as regards to the theme of colonization of the unconscious, and for two reasons: one is that I am not sufficiently familiar with Deleuze's and Guattari's works; and the other is my impression that these authors (including Jameson), in dealing with the concept of the unconscious, remain too attached to the Freudian legacy, even when they criticize it—and thus run counter, in important aspects, to the Jungian conception I have proposed here.

Nevertheless, such idea (or hypothesis) appeared in two important cultural products.[30] One has already been mentioned: the movie *Matrix* (Wachowski Brothers, 1999), in which Morpheus, the Lord of Dreams, reappears and wakes Neo from a world that has been manufactured as a dream (a computer-generated dream-world): colonization of dream and colonization of mankind, inseparable, engineering a completely unconscious and machinic existence inside a virtual dream. The other is *Sandman* (Gaiman, 1989), a series of graphic novels whose main character is Morpheus (as the Sandman, Oneiros, or Shaper): an incarnation of the archetypal human imagination, of Dream.[31] In the first story of the first volume of the series, *Sleep of the Just* (which was interpreted in depth by Duarte, 1998, 1999; my commentary here is based on his works), Morpheus, the Dream, is captured and held prisoner by Roderick Burgess: by the *bourgeois* ethos, capitalism-turning-consumerism and its imperative of total expansion and domination. An unknown syndrome ensues *globally*, the "sleepy sickness": "people fell *asleep*, and did not wake up … they lived their lives like sleepwalkers; eating if fed, sometimes talking *nonsense, dream-stuff*…" (Gaiman, 1989, p. 14). A situation that resembles quite closely what Benjamin called the *Traumschlaf* of commodity capitalism; both depictions of "collective dreaming" are preludes for the world wars. At the end of the story, Dream frees himself—only to find out that dream and the imaginary had been conquered by mass culture and the capital (Duarte, 1998).

Both art products depict critically the central theme of this work: a global process of colonization and domination of Dream. Here I argue that such process is being actualized, under total consumerism, through its artificial techno-imaginary: its phantasmagoria replaces dream and imagination. Controlling Dream signifies the power to expropriate the imagination and the irrational, the symbols and the gods: thus consciousness is colonized, instinct is guided and shaped, the unconscious is

[30] Such idea is also the theme of Terry Gilliam's magnificent *The Imaginarium of Doctor Parnassus* (2009), in which the imaginary (*imaginarium*) is sold to the devil (Nick), and ends up being commercialized as *replicas*; Parnassus's fables, tales, and imagination are replaced by Nick's addictions and feeble desires.

[31] McConnell (2002, p. 2) describes Sandman-Morpheus poetically: "He is not a god; he is older than all gods, and is their cause. He is the human capacity to imagine meaning, to tell stories: an anthropomorphic projection of our thirst for mythology".

controlled; from *homo symbolicum*, capable of creatively giving shape (imagining!) to the world and to himself, the human being then can be transformed into a thing, an automaton, or the *homo commoditas*. Capturing dream means capturing the imaginary; and capturing the imaginary means subjugating the psyche—the human *soul*.

5.4.4 Mimesis with the ImCon: The Commodified Subject, or Commodity-Self

The final conclusion of all such arguments is that, to the extent that the ImCon becomes and operates as a totalizing imaginary, its institution of a social subject can be seen as a process of total colonization and fabrication of psychological subjectivity, or of the psyche itself. It thus works like an archaic symbolic imaginary does with primitives: the imaginary simply constitutes their psyches; they are almost indistinguishable from the imaginary. The tendency of the ImCon is therefore to produce a *fusion* of the psychological subject with the imaginary: unconscious psyche, instincts, identity, cognitive apparatus, all formatted by its ideology, since birth. The prospect of such total colonization is equivalent to a *mimesis* with the imaginary, with its logic and contents, with its machinic phantasmagoria: mimesis in the sense of homoousia and homology, of *reproduction and replication*. In fact, Marcuse (1964) had already hinted at this very idea in *One-Dimensional Man*:

> Today this private space [the psyche] has been invaded and whittled down by technological reality. Mass production and mass distribution claim the entire individual, and industrial psychology has long since ceased to be confined to the factory. The manifold processes of introjection seem to be ossified in almost mechanical reactions. The result is, not adjustment but mimesis: an immediate identification of the individual with his society and, through it, with the society as a whole. This immediate, automatic identification (which may have been characteristic of *primitive forms of association*) reappears in high industrial civilization. (p. 14)

My argument is that, under total consumerism, this "primitive form of association" corresponds to a state of *participation mystique* with its entire techno-imaginary. What founds it and makes it possible is a fundamental *inversion*: it is not the subject's or the collectivity's *unconscious* that, through dreams, fantasies, and so on, produces and institutes the (symbolic) imaginary; rather, the artificial simulacrum of imaginary, a fabricated ImCon, produces subject, collectivity, *and* the unconscious psyche.

The possibility of mimesis and *participation mystique* with an imaginary made of commodity-signs logically represents the total commodification of the subject: the subject is thus manufactured as both consumer and commodity, and remains inseparable from the imaginary, which becomes his sole reality. Therefore, this process would be equivalent to the mass production of commodity-selves: accomplishment of a totalizing imperative, realization of total consumerism.

5.4.5 Consumption as Definer of Existence and the *Homo Simulacrum*

Thus, more than mere sources of identity and definers of social relations, under a totalizing ImCon, the commodity-sign and the act of consumption become the only foundations of *being*. As Benson (2000) claims, mutating Descartes's cogito, *I shop therefore I am*: shopping (consuming) thus becomes "the basic certainty" (C. Campbell, 2004, p. 33), guarantee, and guarantor of *existence*, its immanent principle. The commodity-subject, or commodified self, is thus instituted as *the* subject of contemporary consumption societies.

Logically, the commodity-subject will mirror the characteristics of the commodity: transient, disposable, superficial, artificial, and so on. But more than that, as argued in the previous chapter, inasmuch as the subject is formed in identity with the imaginary and becomes identical with its consumption dreams (an idea illustrated by phantasmagoric personae), s/he will resemble an assemblage of unchained signs, disconnected from reality, exchangeable against other signs or commodities. Theoretically, this idea reveals how a cultural mutation (total capitalism-consumerism) is connected to a mutation of imaginaries (from symbolic to semiotic to simulacric); both mutations thus shape a corresponding anthropological mutation: the *subject as a (commodity-)sign, turning into a simulacrum.*

A parallel process: As *culture* is dissolved and volatilized into signs to be consumed—and the signs are emancipated from any reality—so is its subject. Baudrillard (1973/1981) mentioned this phenomenon of consumerism in an important passage that in fact summarizes the whole argument of "total colonization" by the ImCon of both reality *and* subject: "Homology, simultaneity of the ideological operation [of commodification] on the level of psychic structure and social structure" (p. 100).

Here we have homology between commodity-logic and subjectivation: the subject becomes a (commodity-)sign and, as referents disappear (signs become unchained simulacra), the subject turns progressively into a simulacrum. After the advent of *homo commoditas*, the consumer-commodity, and in line with the process of mimesis with consumption society and its imaginary, this daunting prospective signs a total anthropological mutation: the epiphany of the *homo simulacrum*.

Under such homology, the prospect is for the subject to be produced, reproduced, exchanged, and circulated as a hyperreal sign, or, put differently, a surface, a one-dimensional persona that is not even a mask but a mere screen for the projections of commodity-imagery. The model more illustrative for such subject is not even the replaceable identikit, but a radicalization of the "personal branding" model: the online *avatars*, virtual subjectivities instantaneously exchangeable and replaceable, through which the omnipotent dream of being anything and everything (by in fact being *nothing*) is experienced and consumed. The consumer-commodity thus "becomes a pure screen, a pure absorption and re-absorption surface of the influent networks" (Baudrillard, 1988, p. 27), a volatile refraction of the ImCon. A bit less hyperbolic, Augé (1999) described it as "the fictional self":

> The fictional self, the peak of a fascination which is begun in any *relationship exclusive to the image, is a self without relationship* and as a result without any basis for identity, *liable to be absorbed by the world of images* in which it believes it can rediscover and recognise itself. (pp. 116–117; e.a.)

The imperative of this "world of images"—the global ImCon—is to render the consumer-subject not only "liable" to, but indeed fully absorbed, produced, and constituted by, their flow: its trend of total colonization means that all consumers ought to become fictional commodity-signs, in complete massification. As social life is defined by (partial or full) identity with the ImCon, we insert ourselves in the dream-world of consumerism by becoming commodities, by buying, wearing, displaying, showing off signs, trying to mold them into "unique", hyperreal performances, that is, by becoming unchained commodity-signs—*by dreaming the same dream*.

Put another way, consumers are socialized by becoming atoms of the ImCon, parts of the commodity-discourse: by living like moving images in urban or virtual advertisements, displaying full-time what Arendt (1958, p. 332) called "heterogenous uniformity"—a uniformity that is spectacularly heterogeneous in appearance: mirroring the infinite variety of commodities, the images with which we identify are infinitely varied, yet they are one thing only, commodity-signs. And, the more standard and homogenized the commodity-subjects become, the more "individuality" (uniqueness, difference, distinction) and meaning become not merely a demand but a craving to be satisfied through sign consumption, which is never satisfied, for the sign is empty. The more massified society and subjects get, the more the consumer will crave for difference: massification and consumerism (as provider of difference through the code) are two parallel forces; the latter depends on the first.

5.4.6 The Consumer-Commodity as an Empty Self

Within the perspective of a total colonization of the subject, what one has is not a self that is merely decentered, distributed, flexible, fragmented, saturated—what has been described as the postmodern self (Gergen, 1991; Spears, 1997; Wetherell & Maybin, 1996). As the sign is empty, the end product of *participation mystique* with it is an *empty self* (Cushman, 1990). My proposal is that such idea is behind some subjective phenomena that have been much discussed in our consumption societies. The empty self is a self whose *unconscious* feeling of emptiness is accompanied by everlasting restlessness and insecurity or fear, which are constantly fed by the ImCon. The main effect of such feelings appears as a Pantagruelic *desire* for consumption: an extreme longing for sensations, instant stimuli, constant overexcitement, and pleasure—a *craving* for full immersion in the dream-world of commodities and images that provides fast meaning and sense, instantaneous fulfill of the emptiness by signs and their technicolor phantasmagoria, consumerism's oneiric opiate or *soma*. Without which—without the *participation mystique*—life seems empty, for the self feels empty: there seems to be no interaction with the outside world; meaninglessness and feelings of dreary aridness and vapidity[32] might ensue, or else an utter incapacity for feeling anything or desiring anything, a pervasive numbness, in sum, a ghostly sense of inner, corroding *vacuum*, of non-existence.

This condition (which can, of course, assume many other forms) corresponds to what Bernard Stiegler (2006) described as *disindividuation*, resulting from "the addictive system of consumption" and its "symbolic misery":

> At this stage, consumption releases more and more compulsive automatisms, and the consumer becomes dependent on the consumption hit. He suffers, then, from a disindividuating syndrome that he only manages to compensate for by intensifying his consumer behaviour, which at the same time becomes pathological.

In simple terms, both reality and self seem empty, hollow. Consumption and its imaginary then offer strong doses of unreality: their core best-selling promises are the transcendent beliefs that *there is no reality* and that the consumer can be anything; every subjectivation is possible; "consumer society offers the individual the opportunity for total fulfillment and liberation" (Baudrillard, 2001, p. 12). Mirroring the emptiness of the commodity-sign, which allows it to carry *any* sign-value, the consumer-subject flies rootless and ruthlessly through the seemingly infinite possibilities of being promised by the commodity. No roots, no substance, no

[32] What lurks in the unconscious—symptoms, destructive fantasies, and so on—may start to appear more clearly and haunt the consumer. This group of diffuse sensations, when it appears, is labeled as a consumer-commodity *malfunction* (e.g., depression) by the ImCon, and rapidly treated with the ministration of more commodities, which usually include psychiatric medications: more identification, more *participation mystique* and its anesthetic identities, this time guaranteed by a *chemical* colonization of both psyche and body.

limits: an omnipotent yet empty commodity-subject with a firm belief (nay delusion) that he or she is original, unique, free, electing sovereignly his or her lifestyle and personality. Servitude sold as self-fulfillment.

When existence and identity are defined by communion with commodity-signs and the imaginary, if for some reason consuming them is made impossible, or denied (or else if the whole economic system crumbles), then the masses fall back into their emptiness and—without personae made of signs, without the consumption system as a guarantee of existence—may feel they are about to disappear; and Benjamin's "mythic forces" may reemerge catastrophically.

To conclude this chapter, let me summarize it by recalling Lefebvre (1971, p. 131): "We are surrounded by emptiness but it is an emptiness filled with signs". Indeed, and by consuming and identifying with the ImCon, we *become* that emptiness filled with signs. Or, as T. S. Eliot (1925) wrote just before the great catastrophe: *We are the hollow men, we are the stuffed men.* Total consumerism needs and seeks to engineer hollow women and men, atomized, stuffed, and stupefied with dreams of consumption. (In fact, we are now such stuff as consumption dreams are made on; and our little life is rounded with a narcotic sleep.) For the mass of consumer commodities, life then becomes a succession of commodity-dreams, consumed and discarded, in a perpetual dream-world. Under the ImCon, *La vida es un sueño de consumo; y los sueños, mercancías son* (Life is a consumption dream; and dreams are commodities).

References

Adatto, K. (2003). Selling out childhood. *Hedgehog Review, 5*(2), 24–40.

Adorno, T. W., & Horkheimer, M. (2002). *Dialectic of enlightenment: Philosophical fragments* (E. Jephcott, Trans.). Stanford, CA: Stanford University Press. (Original work published 1944).

Appadurai, A. (1996). *Modernity at large: Cultural dimensions of globalization.* Minneapolis: University of Minnesota Press.

Arendt, H. (1958). *The origins of totalitarianism* (2nd ed.). New York: Meridian Books.

Arendt, H. (1963). *On revolution.* New York: Penguin.

Arendt, H. (1998). *The human condition* (2nd ed.). Chicago: University of Chicago Press. (Original work published 1958).
Arendt, H. (2005). The image of hell. In *Essays in understanding: 1930–1954* (pp. 197–205). New York: Schocken Books. (Original work published 1946).
Augé, M. (1999). *The war of dreams: exercises in ethno-fiction* (L. Heron, Trans.). London: Pluto Press.
Balandier, G. (1985). *Le détour: Pouvoir et modernité*. Paris: Fayard.
Baudrillard, J. (1981). *For a critique of the political economy of the sign*. St. Louis, MO: Telos Press. (Original work published 1973).
Baudrillard, J. (1983). *Simulations*. New York: Semiotext(e).
Baudrillard, J. (1988). *The ecstasy of communication*. Cambridge, MA: MIT Press.
Baudrillard, J. (1993). *Symbolic exchange and death* (I. H. Grant, Trans.). London: Sage. (Original work published 1976).
Baudrillard, J. (1994). *Simulacra and simulation* (S. F. Glaser, Trans). Ann Arbor, MI: University of Michigan Press. (Original work published 1981).
Baudrillard, J. (1996a). *The system of objects* (J. Benedict, Trans.). London: Verso. (Original work published 1968).
Baudrillard, J. (1996b). *The perfect crime* (C. Turner, Trans.). London: Verso.
Baudrillard, J. (1996c). Disneyworld Company. *Liberation*. Retrieved from http://www.uta.edu/english/apt/collab/texts/disneyworld.html
Baudrillard, J. (1998). *The consumer society: Myths and structures*. London: Sage. (Original work published 1970).
Baudrillard, J. (2000). *The vital illusion*. New York: Columbia University Press.
Baudrillard, J. (2001). *Selected writings* (M. Poster, Ed., 2nd ed.). Cambridge: Polity.
Bauman, Z. (2000). *Liquid modernity*. Cambridge: Polity.
Bauman, Z. (2001). *The individualized society*. Cambridge, UK: Polity.
Bauman, Z. (2005). *Liquid life*. Cambridge, UK: Polity.
Bauman, Z. (2007). *Consuming life*. Cambridge: Polity Press.
Bauman, Z. (2011, August 12). Foi um motim de consumidores excluídos. *O Globo*. Retrieved from http://oglobo.globo.com/mundo/mat/2011/08/12/foi-um-motim-de-consumidores-excluidos-diz-sociologo-zygmunt-bauman-925126381.asp
Belk, R. W., Wallendorf, M., & Sherry, J. F. (1989). The sacred and the profane in consumer behavior: Theodicy on the Odyssey. *The Journal of Consumer Research, 16*(1), 1–38.
Benjamin, W. (1991). *Gesammelte Schriften* (R. Tiedemann & H. Schweppenhäuser, Eds., Vol. V). Frankfurt am Main: Suhrkamp Verlag.

Benjamin, W. (1996). Capitalism as religion. In M. P. Bullock & M. W. Jennings (Eds.), *Walter Benjamin selected writings, Vol. 1: 1913–1926* (pp. 288–291). Cambridge, MA: Harvard University Press. (Original work written 1921).

Benjamin, W. (1999). *The arcades project* (H. Eiland & K. McLaughlin, Trans.). Cambridge: The Belknap Press of Harvard University Press.

Benson, A. L. (Ed.). (2000). *I shop therefore I am: Compulsive buying and the search for self.* Northvale, NJ: Jason Aronson.

Berry, G. (2010). The mythic element of mass media and its relation to Plato's cave. *PLATFORM: Journal of Media and Communication*, ANZCA Special Edition (April), 72–85.

Buck-Morss, S. (1989). *The dialectics of seeing: Walter Benjamin and the Arcades Project*. Cambridge, MA: MIT.

Buck-Morss, S. (2000). *Dreamworld and catastrophe: The passing of mass utopia in East and West*. Cambridge, MA: MIT.

Calderón de la Barca, P. (2009). *La vida es sueño*. Retrieved from http://www.cervantesvirtual.com/obra/la-vida-es-sueno%2D%2D0/ (Original work written 1635).

Campbell, C. (2004). I shop therefore I know that I am: The metaphysical basis of modern consumerism. In K. M. Ekström & H. Brembeck (Eds.), *Elusive Consumption* (pp. 27–44). New York: Berg.

Cassirer, E. (1946). *The myth of the state*. New Haven: Yale University Press.

Castoriadis, C. (1987). *The imaginary institution of society* (K. Blamey, Trans.). Cambridge: MIT Press. (Original work published 1975).

Charles, M. (2009). *Speculative experience and history: Walter Benjamin's Goethean Kantianism*. Unpublished doctoral dissertation, Middlesex University, London, UK.

Clastres, P. (1989). *Society against the state: Essays in political anthropology* (R. Hurley, Trans.). New York: Zone Books. (Original work published 1974).

Cohen, M. (2006). Benjamin's phantasmagoria: The *Arcades Project*. In D. S. Ferris (Ed.), *The Cambridge companion to Walter Benjamin* (pp. 199–220). Cambridge: Cambridge University Press.

Curtis, A. (Director). (2002). *The century of the self [Motion picture]*. London: BBC Series.

Cushman, P. (1990). Why the self is empty: Toward a historically situated psychology. *American Psychologist, 45*(5), 599–611.

Cypher, J., & Riggs, E. (2001). Colonizing the imagination: Disney's wilderness lodge. *Critical Studies, 21*, 403–423.

Debord, G. (1967). *La sociètè du spectacle*. Paris: Champ Libre.

Deleuze, G., & Guattari, F. (2004). *Anti-Oedipus* (R. Hurley, M. Seem, & H. R. Lane, Trans.). London: Continuum. (Original work published 1972).
Duarte, L. F. B. (1998). O Sono dos Justos: uma interpretação simbólica. *Cadernos de Comunicação (Unisinos-RS), 1*(4), 73–94.
Duarte, L. F. B. (1999). *O Sono dos Justos: elementos para uma metodologia de interpretação de textos culturais*. Unpublished master's thesis, Unisinos, São Leopoldo, Brazil.
Dufour, D.-R. (2001, November 1). Rumo ao "capitalismo total"? *Le Monde Diplomatique*. Retrieved from http://diplo.uol.com.br/2001-11,a121
Eco, U. (1964). *Apocalittici e integrati*. Milano: Bompiani.
Eliot, T. S. (1925). *Eliot's poems: 1909–1925*. London: Faber & Gwyer.
Ewen, S. (1989). Advertising and the development of consumer society. In I. Angus & S. Jhally (Eds.), *Cultural politics in contemporary America* (pp. 82–95). New York: Routledge.
Featherstone, M. (2007). *Consumer culture and postmodernism* (2nd ed.). London: Sage.
Ferguson, C. (Director). (2010). *Inside job* [Motion picture]. US: Sony Pictures.
Freitas, M. G. (1999). Vida simbólica: uma aliança. *Boletim do Centro de Estudos Junguianos C. A. Meier, 1*(1), 1–5.
Gaiman, N. (1989). *The Sandman. Preludes and Nocturnes* (1–8). New York: DC Comics.
Gauchet, M. (2009). *Marcel Gauchet: "nous sommes sous le coup d'une anesthésie"*. Retrieved from http://www.latribune.fr/actualites/economie/france/20090724trib 000403499/marcel-gauchet-nous-sommes-sous-le-coup-d-une-anesthesie-.html
Gergen, K. J. (1991). *The saturated self*. New York: Basic Books.
Gilliam, T. (Director). (2009). *The Imaginarium of Doctor Parnassus* [Motion picture]. Canada, France, UK: Lionsgate/Sony Pictures.
Giroux, H. A., & Pollock, G. (2010). *The mouse that roared: Disney and the end of innocence*. Lanhan, MA: Rowman & Littlefield.
Goldman, R., & Papson, S. (1996). *Sign wars: The cluttered landscape of advertising*. New York: The Guilford Press.
Gruzinski, S. (1988). *La colonization de l'imaginaire*. Paris: Gallimard.
Guattari, F. (2010). *The machinic unconscious: Essays in Schizoanalysis*. New York: Semiotext(e). (Original work published 1979).
Gunter, B., & Furnham, A. (1998). *Children as consumers: A psychological analysis of the young people's market*. London: Routledge.
Hannerz, U. (1989). Notes on the global ecumene. *Public Culture, 1*(2), 66–75.

Hannerz, U. (1992). *Cultural complexity: Studies in the social organization of meaning*. New York: Columbia University Press.
Hetherington, K. (2005). Memories of capitalism: Cities, phantasmagoria and arcades. *International Journal of Urban and Regional Research, 29*(1), 187–200.
Jameson, F. (1991). *Postmodernism, or the cultural logic of late capitalism*. Durham, NC: Duke University Press.
Jameson, F. (1992). *Signatures of the visible*. London: Routledge.
Jhally, S. (1989). Advertising as religion: The dialectic of technology and magic. In L. Angus & S. Jhally (Eds.), *Cultural politics in contemporary America* (pp. 217–229). New York: Routledge.
Jhally, S. (Ed.). (2006). *The spectacle of accumulation: Essays in culture, media, and politics*. New York: Peter Lang.
Kellner, D. (2009). Jean Baudrillard. In *The Stanford encyclopedia of philosophy* (Winter 2009 ed.). Retrieved from http://plato.stanford.edu/archives/win2009/entries/baudrillard/
Klein, N. (2000). *No logo*. London: Flamingo.
Langman, L. (1992). Neon cages: Shopping for subjectivity. In R. Shields (Ed.), *Lifestyle shopping: The subject of consumption* (pp. 40–82). New York: Routledge.
Lasch, C. (1984). *The minimal self: Psychic survival in troubled times*. New York: W.W. Norton.
Lash, S., & Lury, C. (2007). *The global culture industry: The mediation of things*. Cambridge: Polity Press.
Lefebvre, H. (1971). *Everyday life in the modern world*. New York: Harper & Row.
Maffesoli, M. (1990). *Aux creux des apparences: Pour une éthique de l'esthétique*. Paris: Le livre de Poche.
Maffesoli, M. (1993). *La contemplation du monde: Figures du style communautaire*. Paris: Grasset.
Maffesoli, M. (2008). *Iconologías: Nuestras idolatrías postmodernas* (J. Terré, Trans.). Barcelona: Península.
Marcuse, H. (1964). *One-dimensional man: Studies in the ideology of advanced industrial society*. Retrieved from http://www.marxists.org/reference/archive/marcuse/works/one-dimensional-man/index.htm
Marx, K. (1847). *Wages*. Retrieved from http://www.marxists.org/archive/marx/works/1847/12/31.htm
Marx, K. (1990). *Capital: Critique of political economy* (B. Fowkes, Trans., Vol. 1). Harmondsworth: Penguin. (Original work published 1867).

Marx, K. (1993). Das Kapital: Kritik der politischen Ökonomie. Der Produktionsprozeß des Kapitals. In *Karl Marx Friedrich Engels Werke, Band 23*. Berlin: Dietz Verlag. (Original work published 1867).

McConnell, F. (2002). Preface. In N. Gaiman & E. Kramer (Eds.), *The Sandman: Book of dreams* (pp. 2–5). New York: HarperTorch.

McLuhan, M. (1959). Myth and mass media. *Daedalus: Journal of the American Academy of Arts and Sciences, 88*(2), 339–348.

McLuhan, M. (1994). *Understanding media: The extensions of man*. Cambridge, MA: MIT Press. (Original work published 1964).

Molnar, A. (1996). *Giving kids the business: The commercialization of America's schools*. Boulder, CO: Westview Press.

Nordström, J., & Riddestråle, K. (2005). *Karaoke capitalism: Daring to be different in a copycat world*. Westport: Praeger.

Norris, T. (2006). Hannah Arendt & Jean Baudrillard: Pedagogy in the consumer society. *Studies in Philosophy and Education, 25*, 457–477.

Ovid. (1806). *Les Métamorphoses* (G.T. Villenave, Trans.). Paris: Gay & Ghestard.

Osborne, P. (2005). *How to read Marx*. London: Granta.

Poster, M. (2001). Introduction. In M. Poster (Ed.), *Jean Baudrillard: Selected writings* (2nd ed., pp. 1–9). Cambridge: Polity.

Retort. (2004). Afflicted powers. *New Left Review, 27*. Retrieved from http://www.newleftreview.org/?page=article&view=2506

Ritzer, G. (2001). *Explorations in the sociology of consumption: Fast food, credit cards and casinos*. London: Sage.

Rolnik, S. (2006). *Entrevista a Suely Rolnik*. Retrieved from http://lavaca.org/notas/entrevista-a-suely-rolnik/

Schor, J. (2004). *Born to buy: The commercialized child and the new consumer culture*. New York: Scribner.

Silva, J. M. (2007). O silêncio do objeto: uma lógica hiper-espetacular. In J. Melo & O. Morais (Eds.), *Mercado e comunicação na sociedade digital* (pp. 159–163). São Paulo: Intercom; Santos-SP: Unisanta, Unisantos & Unimonte.

Spears, R. (1997). Introduction. In T. Ibáñez & L. Íñiguez (Eds.), *Critical social psychology* (pp. 1–26). London: Sage.

Stiegler, B. (2006). *The disaffected individual in the process of psychic and collective disindividuation*. Retrieved from http://arsindustrialis.org/disaffected-individual-process-psychic-and-collective-disindividuation

Thussu, D. K. (Ed.). (1998). *Electronic empires: Global media and local resistance*. London: Hodder Arnold.

Tomlinson, A. (1990). Introduction: Consumer culture and the aura of the commodity. In A. Tomlinson (Ed.), *Consumption, identity and style: Marketing, meanings, and the packaging of pleasure* (pp. 1–27). London: Routledge.

Vieira, A. G. (2003). *Imagem, símbolo e narrativa na Psicologia Analítica de C. G. Jung*. Unpublished doctoral dissertation, Universidade Federal do Rio Grande do Sul, Porto Alegre, Brazil.

Virilio, P. (1994). *The vision machine* (J. Rose, Trans.). Bloomington, IN: Indiana University Press.

Wachowski Brothers (Directors). (1999). *The matrix* [Motion picture]. US: Warner Bros. Pictures.

Ward, G. (2009). *The politics of discipleship: Becoming postmaterial citizens*. Grand Rapids, MI: Baker Academic.

Weir, P. (Director). (1998). *The Truman Show* [Motion picture]. US: Paramount Pictures.

Wetherell, M., & Maybin, J. (1996). The distributed self: A social constructionist perspective. In R. Stevens (Ed.), *Understanding the self* (pp. 219–279). London: Sage.

Williams, R. H. (1991). *Dream worlds: Mass consumption in late nineteenth-century France*. Berkeley: University of California Press.

Zukin, S. (1991). *Landscapes of power: From Detroit to Disney World*. Berkeley: University of California Press.

6

Dreamscapes: The Dream-Worlds of Shopping Malls, McDonald's, and Disneyland

Die Welt wird Traum, der Traum wird Welt.
Novalis[1]

Overview
This chapter explores the *dreamscapes*—the scenarios of the night dreams—as dream-worlds of consumption, discussing how they symbolize particular aspects of the ImCon and its typical forms of colonization of culture and subjectivity, in a dialog with the sociological theories of McDonaldization and Disneyization.

The night dreams analyzed in this work share common scenarios, or what I called *dreamscapes*: McDonald's, Disneyland, and shopping malls.[2] There is ample volume of scientific literature on the cultural roles, meanings, and significations these consumerist icons embody. However, the purpose of this short chapter is confined to discussing briefly some aspects

[1] "The world becomes the dream, and the dream becomes the world" (Novalis, 1802/1923, p. 319).

[2] It is important to remind the reader that I employ "Disneyland" meaning Disney thematic parks in general; and the category of "shopping malls" can also encompass giant department stores and hypermarkets.

M. Xavier, *Subjectivity, the Unconscious and Consumerism*,
https://doi.org/10.1007/978-3-319-96824-7_6

of such meanings and roles that are germane for interpreting the night dreams. In this sense, it advances the process of *amplification*, which is part of the hermeneutics of dream interpretation discussed in detail in the next chapter. Thus it focuses on some of their aspects that are important *symbolically*: what they embody within the social imaginary—as ideas, paradigms, icons—that constitute them as typical forms of colonization by consumerism: colonization of cultures, practices, and social spaces, but especially of subjectivity.

The fundamental idea is that, within collective consciousness, they represent and signify *dream-worlds of consumption*, in the senses delineated in the previous chapter: they are global symbols of the ImCon and its transcendental ideology. As semiotic worlds, they embody the utopia of consumerism: what Benjamin (1999) called a "dream life" in a "primeval landscape of consumption" (p. 827). In the same way that Benjamin took "arcades, winter gardens, panoramas, wax museums, casinos, rail road stations" (p. 405) as the nineteenth and twentieth centuries' *dream houses of the collective*, in this work I take malls, Disneyland, and McDonald's as the postmodern signs and spaces that signify and condense the phantasmagoria of our society, of our cultural imaginary, and their colonial power and logic. Such proposal is justified not only because it is logical, but because the night dreams themselves employ them in the same sense.

As argued, such dream-worlds represent the imaginary *signifying structures* (Langman, 1992, p. 41) of consumption society, and thus embody the ways it produces and confirms its social subjects as consumers (or commodities). Indeed, they can be seen as *microcosms* of consumer society, in the same way Benjamin wrote in relation to the arcades: "an arcade of this kind is a city, indeed, *a world in miniature*" (Benjamin, 1986, pp. 146–147). Different authors have in fact proposed such idea: Baudrillard (2001) considers Disneyland as a microcosm of the United States; for Fishwick (1983), McDonald's (or "the world of Ronald McDonald") is a cultural microcosm; and for Hankiss (2001), "The mall is much more than a simple building. It is the symbol of the universe, an *imago mundi*, as medieval cathedrals were" (p. 130). As microcosms, they all share some common characteristics that are typical of consumerism and its imaginary. First, they all represent "commercially produced fantasy worlds"

(Langman, 1992, p. 40). Physically and architectonically, however, these worlds of fantasy are controlled environments absolutely centered on consumption; in them consumption is the *idée force*, the imperative, the rite. That takes us to their mythic, religious aspects: they represent the contemporary *temples of consumption.* Like the arcades, which for Benjamin were materializations of the phantasmagoria, "temples in which goods were worshipped as fetishes" (Featherstone, 2007, p. 72), these dreamscapes can be viewed as consumerism's desacralized sanctuaries, wherein consumers venerate and adore the commodity phantasmagoria and *participation mystique* with the ImCon is reached and celebrated.

All of them are typically American; they represent the ImCon in its American genesis and format. Superficially, they condense the three aspects that define American consumerism: "(a) an American way of doing business, (b) an American way of consuming, and (c) American cultural icons" (Ritzer, 2005, p. 33). Yet, they have also become ubiquitous icons of *global* consumerism. Whether one adheres to the theories of grobalization, glocalization, or Americanization, it is indubitable that such dream-worlds are among the most well-known forms of global colonization by consumer-capitalism. And that is why sociological theories on globalization center on their images and logic, as McDonaldization, Disneyization, and "malling[3]": they also represent the typical forms the imaginary of consumption assumes in its process of global cultural conquest. Accordingly, each form can be seen as distinct from the others; each presents some particularities (which will be discussed next). However, very often even such particularities are blurred; as they are all part of the same totalizing ethos, they combine, mix, and overlap: ironically, McDonald's can be seen as a Disneyized institution (Bryman, 2003), and malls are said to have become McDonaldized or Disneyized; McDonald's franchises are usually found within the physical space of malls and theme

[3] The surreal proliferation and colonization of spaces (and even towns) in the United States by shopping malls has been called "malling of America". Sen (2005) comments, "shopping malls have become a way of life in America. There are more shopping centers than movie theaters, school districts, hotels or hospitals. There are more malls than cities, colleges or television stations. (…) By 2000, there are more than 45,000 shopping malls in the United States." This colonial trend, as with the others, is typically American but also seen globally (especially in China). However, to my knowledge, there is no sociological theory on malling that is equivalent to McDonaldization or Disneyization.

parks; Disneyland spaces are sponsored by corporations (including McDonald's), and corporations and malls use Disney characters and imagery, and so on. That is, they are self-referential worlds that feed off each other, or *consume* each other, profiting mutually; thus even what presumably distinguishes them becomes dedifferentiated. Yet, in order to understand how they appear in the dreams, some of their particularities are discussed in what follows.

6.1 Shopping Malls

More than any other dream-world of consumption, the malls should be seen as the contemporary version of Benjamin's arcades. In our social imaginary, accordingly, they stand as the major "cathedrals of consumption" (Fiske, 2000; Ritzer, 2000, 2001). Although the term was popularized by George Ritzer, Kowinski (1984) had already used it, and condensed its meaning thusly: "malls are sometimes called cathedrals of consumption, meaning that they are the monuments of a new faith, the consumer religion, which has largely replaced the old" (p. 218). The main idea here is that, in the global imagination, the mall figures as the prime temple of consumerism as a simulacrum of religion. Indeed, metaphysical and religious expressions abound in the literature: the mall represents "the Great Consumer Paradise" (Kowinski, 1984), "a shopping nirvana" (Wilson, 1985, p. 154), the "City of Heaven" (Backes, 1997, p. 6); for Hankiss (2001), "the shopping mall is, or is supposed to be, the holy center and shrine of our consumer civilization" (p. 130). Feinberg and Meoli (1991) conclude that "In today's consumer culture the mall is the center of the universe" (p. 426).

Like the arcades, therefore, the mall is unique in that it condenses perfectly the "universe" of consumption, its social world (Lewis, 1990)—its *imaginary*. As Simon (1992) observes, "to walk in the contemporary palace of pleasure, the shopping mall, is to walk through the avenues of the postmodern mentality. What we see, neatly symbolized and codified, are both the promises and problems of commodified life" (p. 248). Yet, it is Langman (1992) who summarizes the ideas that are more central for us:

> In the contemporary world, the signifying and celebrating edifice of consumer culture has become the shopping mall, which exists in pseudo-democratic twilight zone between reality and a commercially produced fantasy world of commodified goods, images and leisure activities that gratify transformed desire and provide packaged self-images to a distinctive form of subjectivity. (p. 40)

For Langman, malls are *neon cages* where consumers *shop for subjectivity*: where they are instituted and confirmed as consumers- or commodity-subjects through consumption. That is, malls embody the imaginary world of consumption, its *dream*.[4]

6.2 McDonald's and McDonaldization

Here we can discuss McDonald's as a symbol through the concept of McDonaldization: how it embodies a paradigm of globalization, of cultural colonization. The central idea, however, is that such paradigm also applies to the colonization and production of *subjectivity* and that such production has a symbolic specificity.

McDonaldization is "the process by which the principles of the fast-food restaurant are coming to dominate more and more sectors of American society as well as the rest of the world" (Ritzer, 1993, p. 1), that is, is a form of capitalist-consumer colonization with distinct principles and imaginary, that annexes wide areas of the *Lebenswelt*. Its four main principles are described by Ritzer as (1) *efficiency*; (2) *calculability*, or reduction of everything to quantity (reification); (3) *predictability*, everything must be uniform and standardized; and (4) *control* by non-human technology.

[4] The experience they represent is obviously dream-like: they are usually built as fully enclosed, self-contained worlds, microcosms of consumption isolated from any external reality; inside, everything seems artificial, a world made of surfaces, all consumable and desirable, a vertigo of moving images, desires, and lights. In fact malls are designed to produce disorientation and keep consumers strolling and *inside* (hence "neon cage"): a dream in which we abandon reality and ourselves to the control of images and their fetish. As Kowinski (1984) wrote, "the essence of the mall is control" (p. 201).

In this sense, McDonaldization is more aligned to the principles of rationality, modernity, and Fordism (Bryman, 2004b). In sum, it denotes rationalization (a Weberian *Zweckrationalität*) as a colonial force, which is translated as strict scientific management, standardization, automatization, and control of mass production and consumption—of both workers and consumers. Its more interesting aspect, however, is what Ritzer (1998) called the *irrationalities* of such rationalization: dehumanization and homogenization.

Both rational and irrational principles can be understood as some general phenomena and paradigms of the ImCon that are signified and (in dreams) symbolized by McDonald's. McDonaldization thus would be seen as a particular form of *mass production of subjects*, based on rationality, in which subjectivity-production replicates commodity-production. "McDonaldization does not solely produce consumer goods, but also good consumers. (...) the ideal McConsumer is one who behaves as predictably and efficiently as the Mcworkers who cook there, and as the Mcfood they prepare" (Gottschalk, 2008, p. 56). I think this quote condenses the main idea: McDonaldization as the production of consumer-subjects that are as automatized, controlled, and *dehumanized* as the mass production of Mcfood, and in fact as the commodity itself. Thus what Kellner (1999) writes about Mcfood can be applied perfectly well to the general process of consumer subjectivation it signifies: "McDonald's is the paradigm of mass homogeneity, sameness, and standardization, which erases individuality, specificity, and difference" (p. 199).

However, as a *symbol*, McDonaldization can also be seen as more specific. McDonald's embodies the principles of a fast-food restaurant: its main theme is *food*. Symbolically, food represents *energy*: very broadly, *libido*, instinct, the irrational. More specifically, food is archetypically connected to the world of *emotions*, feelings, and affects, and how they are cultivated, transformed, and experienced. Cooking, as a symbol, means the transformation of affects and emotions,[5] and eating, as a social act, represents the ways emotions are shared, exchanged, and lived

[5] This idea is beautifully and poetically illustrated by the movie *Como agua para chocolate* (Arau, 1992).

socially; in sum, food and eating represent sociability, the way we interact emotionally and organically with the world and others, and "feed" them and off them.

Therefore, symbolically, McDonaldization would essentially represent the rationalization, mechanization, homogenization, and massification of *emotions*, of how subjects react and relate to the world and to themselves emotionally: predictably, mechanically, as *automata*. Ritzer argues with his concept of McDonaldization that is achieved through *rationalized* means of production and consumption. More pertinent to this work, however, is the idea that the irrational, the imagery, the fantasy—in one word, the imaginary—also plays an important role for such. McDonald's embodies the logic of commodifying "emotional experiences", reduced to the illusion of *fun* and *entertainment*, and commercializing them as an imaginary world of fantasy through advertising. Its slogans explicitly reveal this process: "I'm lovin' it", "Havin' fun", and so on: what it sells is fantasy and fun (an imaginary), not food—its business is *show business* since its very inception (Kroc, 1987). The main icon that represents such imaginary is Ronald McDonald: he embodies the dream-world of mindless and childish fun, of synthetic experiences and amusement, that is typical of consumerism. In fact, if seen as a *symbol*, Ronald reveals the image of the perfect *consumer-subject* McDonaldization seeks to produce: a homogenized, cloned clown—always the same everywhere—embodying and inciting the same mass-reproduced emotions, the image of a *fun automaton*, a completely predictable puppet.

In fact, along with Ronald, McDonald's also has its signifying dream-world, called *McDonaldland*[6]: a magical world of fantasy analogous to Disneyworld, inhabited by fairy tale, fantastic characters that represent commodities and are used in marketing. Until some years ago, its characters and narratives were almost omnipresent in American culture and were used as the basis for equipment in McDonald's playgrounds. Created by ad imagineers, McDonaldland was a copy of a copy (i.e., a simulacrum), largely based on *H. R. Pufnstuf*, a hugely successful, old television show: a boy and his talking flute lost forever in the Living Island, the *fairy tale land*. In other words, McDonald's also built its own commodified

[6] See http://en.wikipedia.org/wiki/McDonaldland

simulacrum of a symbolic imaginary, following the logic of imagineering. Of course, such imaginary is massively advertised and aimed mainly at children. The end result is that "96% of American children recognize Ronald, slightly less than the number who recognize Santa Claus" (Smith, 2006, p. 231).

Therefore McDonaldization combines *rationalization* (a modern automatization and homogenization of behavior) with the commodification of *imagination* and fantasy (a postmodern fabrication of an imaginary typical of Disney[7]), as a typical form of colonization and production of subjects—and, in fact, of the *world*. Benjamin Barber's (1995) concept of *McWorld* is illuminating in that regard. Barber employed it to describe the globalization of the principles of consumerism-capitalism, and the role megacorporations play in it: a totalizing globalism engendered by:

> onrushing economic, technological, ecological forces that demand integration and uniformity and that mesmerize peoples everywhere with fast music, fast computers, and fast food—MTV, McIntosh, McDonald's—pressing nations into one homogeneous theme park, one McWorld tied together by communication, information, entertainment, and commerce. (p. 6)

That is, Barber's concept is in line with what I argue in this work: like many night dreams analyzed here, he chose McDonald's as the cultural sign that defines contemporary consumerism-capitalism as a *totalizing imaginary*, a global colonial force.[8]

---

[7] The analogy with Disney was mentioned by Fishwick (1983): "This appeal to children and to the child taste and mentality strongly links Disney with McDonald's. The comic fantasy characters of Mickey Mouse and Ronald McDonald are the iconographic mascots. Their fantasy lives, as rich with the promise of instant gratification in the almost-instantaneous delivery of fantasy and food, are closely allied" (p. 116).

[8] In this sense, I believe Barber's (1995) assessment of the issue Jihad x McWorld is basically wrong. Jihad and McWorld are not "so intractably antithetical"; they do not "operate with equal strength in opposite directions" (p. 5). What Barber fails to see is that it is rather the opposite: both share precisely the same goal, *total domination of world and human beings*; they have the same totalitarian ethos. Jihad represents the *shadow* side—truly barbaric and mythic—of the totalizing force that consumerism-capitalism has become, and that is why it can so effectively make use of capitalism, even mesmerizing it: because both share this fundamental affinity.

6.3 Disney, Disneyization, and Disneyland

As many pertinent characteristics of the ImCon have already been discussed using Disney as main trope, this final section only presents a few important remarks that are important for analyzing the dreams.[9]

First of all, Disney and Disneyland radicalize virtually *all* the elements discussed above in relation to malls and McDonald's. Culturally, Disney represents the megacorporation and brand that is the metonym for imagineering, or what Mitroff and Bennis (1989) termed the "unreality industry", and its process of colonization of imagination *and* imaginaries; it is the global icon for the great *factory* of a hyperreal, totalizing imaginary, which, hypostatized as the original and greatest dream-world of simulacra ever, corresponds to Disneyland.

In relation to the logic of imagineering, it is important to mention what has been called the *Disneyfication* of symbolic cultural products such as fairy tales, myths, and so on: it refers to their bowdlerization, commodification, and mass production as distinct Disney products. As argued, the logic of this process is behind the colonization of symbolic imaginaries and their replacement by a regime of simulacra. Basically, these Disney products (characters, narratives, celebrities, etc.) turn into the imaginary *models* for the institution of subjects: they function as *représentations collectives*, which are instrumental for the colonization and fashioning of consumers' mentalities since childhood. As Eric Smoodin put it, "Disney constructs childhood so as to make it entirely compatible with consumerism" (as cited in Giroux, 1995, p. 28). Such ideological construction is made through Disney's dream-worlds—through its fabricated imaginaries. This idea had already been hinted at in Dorfman and Mattelart's (1971/1991) classic, *How to Read Donald Duck*:

> the true impulse behind the manufacture of the Disney characters, and the true danger they represent (...) derives not so much from their embodiment of the "American Way of Life", as that of the "American Dream of Life". It is the manner in which the US dreams and redeems itself, and then imposes that dream upon others (...). (p. 95)

[9] The reader can find a very good and comprehensive analysis of Disney, its imaginary, and the way it fabricates subjectivity (including children's) in Giroux (1995).

Such "Dream of Life" is fully accomplished in and globally signified by Disneyland; and the "imposition" of such dream upon others—the *world*—is now called Disneyization.

Disneyization (Bryman, 1999, 2003, 2004a, 2004c) refers to "the process by which the principles of the Disney theme parks are coming to dominate more and more sectors of American society as well as the rest of the world" (Bryman, 1999, p. 26). It is meant as a parallel concept to McDonaldization; it refers to the same global colonization by "the culture-ideology of consumption" (Bryman, 2004c, p. 158), but under more or less different principles: (1) *thematization*, applying a narrative external to the object, which grants it a fetish character; (2) *dedifferentiation* of consumption, or *hybrid* consumption; (3) *merchandising* (of everything, everywhere); and (4) *emotional and performative labor* (Bryman, 1999, 2004c).

Therefore, Disney theme parks embody the imaginary of consumption; they also function as microcosms[10] built on its principles. However, in relation to malls and McDonald's, they seem to embody more perfectly the logic of simulation and hyperreality, the ultimate goal of colonization and *fabrication* of reality. More than microcosms, they are *worlds* in which tradition, history, archetypal narratives, symbols, myths—every form of imaginary, of human production—are commodified and turned into sellable simulacra, and *every* kind of experience is designed as a commodity for consumption. In this colossal bricolage, all referents—the originals—are eventually effaced: we are left with *a totally fabricated imaginary*, which replaces reality. Disneyland thus stands as the imaginary world that functions as "a perfect model of all the entangled orders of simulation" (Baudrillard, 2001, p. 174): the capitalist fairy tale actualized.

In terms of subjectivity, the experience there is equivalent to near-complete colonization (of consciousness and body). Rather than being merely pervasive, as with the semiurgy proliferated by advertising and mass media, these worlds represent a *full immersion* in an imaginary of commodity-signs. In Disneyland, Benjamin's *Traumschlaf*, the collective dream of the phantasmagoria, becomes a magic kingdom—a fantasy world in which everything is spectacularized and mechanically or technologically

[10] For Baudrillard (2001), Disneyland, a "deep-frozen infantile world", is a microcosm of the United States: "All its values are exalted here, in miniature and comic-strip form"; it is a "digest of the American way of life, panegyric to American values" (p. 174).

controlled, yet must present a fake enchantment—paradise of faux happiness all around, "happiest place on earth". Everything being decontextualized, consciousness is overwhelmed: it becomes almost impossible to discriminate. The character of *dream* and fantasy is endlessly repeated: dedifferentiation of real and imaginary; "what is real, what is dream" is rendered meaningless. In sum, a dream in which every experience—and hence also psychic functioning—is mediated by consumption.

Thus, if there is a place in which *participation mystique* with the ImCon is ecstatically reached in full, it is Disneyland. Accordingly, its significance as a religious or sacred site for consumption society has been pointed by many cultural analysts. (An excellent discussion of this theme is found in Chidester, 2005). For instance, Belk, Wallendorf, and Sherry (1989) actually consider its sacred aspect not metaphorically, but as tantamount to the old religious practices:

> Worship of the pure, uncrowded natural site recalls naturistic religion. *There are also new sacred sites*, including such playful centers as Disneyland and Walt Disney World. The nostalgic motifs of these centers are designed to convey the visitor into a sacred time (...) by evoking what Durkheim calls a nostalgia for paradise. (p. 12; e.a.)

A sacred paradise wherein the consumer-subject can again experience life under an absolute, omnipotent, invisible force: Disneyland is a "technologically totalized environment" (Harvey & Zibell, 2000, p. 19) in which all activities and experiences are controlled,[11] and consumption is the only imperative and rite. That Mickey, a rodent, presides over this universe, is not coincidental: it is designed as a behaviorist world in which all subjects must "behave" like mindless, dehumanized, happy consumer-rats in a Skinner box—or, to use the Weberian image, a *dream cage*.

Disneyland thus represents the closest one can get to the concretization of the idea of fabricating reality as a totalitarian[12] dream-world unified by the ideology of consumerism and the religious, mesmerized ritual

[11] "In Disneyland social control is refined to an art, the art of moving crowds by their own motivation instead of coercion. D-land represents the ideal in this regard. It is the perfection of subordination: people digging their own fantasy graves" (Gottdiener, 1982, p. 140).

[12] The logo of Walt Disney World, a Mickey Mouse-shaped *globe*, renders explicit its ethos of global colonization. In this sense, it is probably significant that Hitler was very fond of Mickey Mouse, Disney, and Hollywood... (see Laqua, 1992).

of endless consumption and entertainment; it embodies the ImCon as a hyperreality. As a symbol, it represents at once the palace of the imaginary (Baudrillard, 1996), and the great corporate utopia: paraphrasing Novalis, there the world becomes the consumption dream.

References

Arau, A. (Director). (1992). *Como agua para chocolate [Motion picture]*. Mexico: Arau Films.
Backes, N. (1997). Reading the shopping mall city. *The Journal of Popular Culture, 31*(3), 1–17.
Barber, B. (1995). *Jihad vs McWorld*. New York: Crown.
Baudrillard, J. (1996). Disneyworld Company. *Liberation*. Retrieved from http://www.uta.edu/english/apt/collab/texts/disneyworld.html
Baudrillard, J. (2001). *Selected writings* (M. Poster, Ed., 2nd ed.). Cambridge: Polity.
Belk, R. W., Wallendorf, M., & Sherry, J. F. (1989). The sacred and the profane in consumer behavior: Theodicy on the Odyssey. *The Journal of Consumer Research, 16*(1), 1–38.
Benjamin, W. (1986). Paris, capital of the nineteenth century. In P. Demetz (Ed.), *Reflections: Essays, aphorisms, autobiographical writings* (pp. 146–162). New York: Schocken.
Benjamin, W. (1999). *The arcades project* (H. Eiland & K. McLaughlin, Trans.). Cambridge: The Belknap Press of Harvard University Press.
Bryman, A. (1999). The Disneyization of society. *Sociological Review, 47*, 25–47.
Bryman, A. (2003). McDonald's as a Disneyized institution: Global implications. *American Behavioral Scientist, 47*(2), 154–167.
Bryman, A. (2004a). Disneyization. *Encyclopedia of social theory*. London: Sage. Retrieved from http://www.sageereference.com/socialtheory/Article_n81.html
Bryman, A. (2004b). McDonaldization. *Encyclopedia of social theory*. London: Sage. Retrieved from http://www.sage-ereference.com/socialtheory/Article_n187.html
Bryman, A. (2004c). *The Disneyization of society* (2nd ed.). London: Sage.
Chidester, D. (2005). *Authentic fakes: Religion and American popular culture*. Berkeley: University of California Press.
Dorfman, A., & Mattelart, A. (1991). *How to read Donald Duck: Imperialist ideology in the Disney comic* (4th ed.). New York: IG Editions.

Featherstone, M. (2007). *Consumer culture and postmodernism* (2nd ed.). London: Sage.

Feinberg, R. A., & Meoli, J. (1991). A brief history of the mall. In R. H. Holman & M. R. Solomon (Eds.), *Advances in consumer research* (Vol. 18, pp. 426–427). Provo, UT: Association for Consumer Research.

Fishwick, M. W. (1983). *Ronald revisited: The world of Ronald McDonald.* Bowling Green, OH: Bowling Green University Popular Press.

Fiske, J. (2000). Shopping for pleasure: Malls, power, and resistance. In J. B. Schor & D. B. Holt (Eds.), *The consumer society reader* (pp. 306–330). New York: The New Press.

Giroux, H. A. (1995). Animating youth: The Disnification of children's culture. *Socialist Review, 24*(3), 23–55.

Gottdiener, M. (1982). Disneyland: A utopian urban space. *Journal of Contemporary Ethnography, 11*(2), 139–162.

Gottschalk, S. (2008). All you can eat: Sociological reflections on food in the hypermodern era. In L. C. Rubin (Ed.), *Food for thought: Essays on eating and culture* (pp. 48–65). Jefferson, NC: McFarland.

Hankiss, E. (2001). *Fears and symbols: An introduction to the study of western civilization.* New York and Budapest: CEU Press.

Harvey, C. W., & Zibell, C. (2000). Shrinking selves in synthetic sites: On personhood in a Walt Disney World. *Ethics and Information Technology, 2*(1), 19–25.

Kellner, D. (1999). Theorizing/resisting McDonaldization: A multiperspectivist approach. In B. Smart (Ed.), *Resisting McDonaldization* (pp. 186–206). London: Sage.

Kowinski, W. (1984). *The malling of America: An inside look at the great consumer paradise.* New York: William Morrow Co.

Kroc, R. (1987). *Griding it out: The making of McDonald's.* New York: St. Martin's.

Langman, L. (1992). Neon cages: Shopping for subjectivity. In R. Shields (Ed.), *Lifestyle shopping: The subject of consumption* (pp. 40–82). New York: Routledge.

Laqua, C. (1992). *Wie Micky unter die Nazis Fiel: Walt Disney und Deutschland.* Hamburg: Rowohlt.

Lewis, G. H. (1990). Community through exclusion and illusion: The creation of social worlds in an American shopping mall. *Journal of Popular Culture, 24*(2), 121–136.

Mitroff, I., & Bennis, W. (1989). *The unreality industry: The deliberate manufacturing of falsehood and what it is doing to our lives.* New York: Birch Lane Press.

Novalis. (1923). Heinrich von Ofterdingen. In J. Minor (Ed.), *Novalis Schriften* (Vol. I). Jena: E. Diederich. (Original work published 1802).

Ritzer, G. (1993). *The McDonaldization of society*. Thousand Oaks, CA: Pine Forge.

Ritzer, G. (1998). *The McDonaldization thesis*. London: Sage.

Ritzer, G. (2000). *The McDonaldization of society* (New Century ed.). Thousand Oaks, CA: Pine Forge.

Ritzer, G. (2001). *Explorations in the sociology of consumption: Fast food, credit cards and casinos*. London: Sage.

Ritzer, G. (2005). September 11, 2001: Mass murder and its roots in the symbolism of American consumer culture. In M. L. Andersen, K. Logio, & H. Taylor (Eds.), *Understanding society* (2nd ed., pp. 33–39). Belmont, CA: Thomson Learning.

Sen, A. K. (2005, March). The malling of America. *Span Magazine*, pp. 3–7.

Simon, R. K. (1992). The formal garden in the age of consumer culture: A reading of the twentieth-century shopping mall. In F. Wayne & M. Steiner (Eds.), *Mapping American culture* (pp. 231–250). Iowa City: University of Iowa Press.

Smith, A. F. (2006). *Encyclopedia of junk food and fast food*. Westport, CT: Greenwood.

Wilson, E. (1985). *Adorned in dreams: Fashion and modernity*. Berkeley: University of California Press.

Part II

Empirical Study

7

Method

Overview

The methodological design consisted in an eminently qualitative and exploratory multiple-case study having night dreams as data, which were interpreted through Jungian hermeneutics. The process of interpretation and theory-generation followed a hypothetico-deductive approach.

7.1 Design

The case study method is defined as the intensive investigation of a single unit (Gilgun, 1994; Hamel, 1993; Runyan, 1982; Yin, 2002), and is considered useful to study problems in depth (Gilgun, 1994). In comparison with other research methods, it is more indicated when the research addresses (a) contemporary events in which the relevant behaviors cannot be manipulated, and (b) a descriptive question (*what* happened?) or an explanatory question (*how* or *why* did something happen?) (Yin, 2002, 2005, 2012). When the study has not only an exploratory or descriptive purpose, but also an explanatory one, the case study method can also be employed; in such case, the researcher has to propose

M. Xavier, *Subjectivity, the Unconscious and Consumerism*,
https://doi.org/10.1007/978-3-319-96824-7_7

concurrent explanations for the same set of events, and point out how such set of explanations can be applied to other situations and events.

Yin (2002) stresses the importance of defining the design's unit or units of analysis, for they will define the research object and the case itself. In the classic case study, the individual is both the case and the primary unit of analysis. However, the secondary units of analysis can be *embedded*, that is, the individual appears as principal unit of analysis and adjoining factors serve as secondary units; for instance, the meaning of a cultural factor for the individual studied, together with its expressions. Thus, the secondary units of analysis are inherently relevant to answer the main research question.

Another important requisite for the development of a case study is the establishment of theoretical propositions to guide data collection and analysis. The theoretical propositions at the outset of the inquiry lead to the possibility of generalizing the results—for, rather than being statistical, generalization here is limited to the theoretical level (i.e., to expanding and generalizing theories). Such approach, called "analytical generalization" by Yin (2002, p. 37) as opposed to "statistical generalization", implies that the case study has to be considered as an *experiment*, rather than as a sample; therefore multiple-case studies correspond to multiple experiments, following a *replication logic*. Broadly speaking, the generalizability of the case study findings is demonstrated through showing the connections between the findings and prior knowledge; that is, the findings from a single case are tested in their congruence (pattern-matching) with other cases—in a *comparison of cases*—and with patterns predicted by theory, or with previous research and theory (Gilgun, 1994).

Based on such epistemological and methodological discussion, this work uses a multiple-case study design in which each dream is considered as a *critical case* (an entity that may demonstrate the tenets of a theory: Putney, 2010). The primary unit of analysis is the dream itself; based on my theoretical presuppositions, which inform the research questions, the secondary units of analysis are the forms through which the dream represents and signifies processes of *colonization* (of the subject, of subjectivity, but also of culture) by the imaginary of consumerism. The design thus entails a *comparison of cases*: a comparison between the dreams' motifs, themes, and general narratives, and, more broadly, a comparison of their (symbolic) *meanings*—in terms of *patterns*—in themselves and in relation to the research question, reached through interpretation. Perhaps such approach can become clearer through a commentary of mine (inserted in brackets) on Clifford Geertz, whose epistemological and hermeneutic affinity with Jungian psychology was pointed by Vieira (2003):

> (…) the essential task of theory building here is not to codify abstract regularities but to make thick description possible, not to generalize across cases but *to generalize within them*. To generalize within cases is usually called, at least in medicine and depth psychology, clinical inference. Rather than beginning with a set of inferences and attempting to subsume them under a governing law, such inference begins with a set of (presumptive) signifiers and attempts to place them within an intelligible frame. Measures are matched to theoretical predictions, but symptoms (…) are scanned for theoretical peculiarities—that is, they are diagnosed. In the study of culture [and of *dreams*] the signifiers are not symptoms [nor *signs*], but symbolic acts [and symbolic images] or clusters of symbolic acts, and the aim is not therapy but analysis of social discourse [through the *unconscious discourse*]. But the way in which theory is used—to ferret out the *unapparent* import of things—is the same. (Geertz, 1977, p. 26)

7.2 Data and Data Collection

The corpus consisted of two sets of data from different sources: dream series and individual dreams collected from the internet and dream series from patients. From such sets 16 dreams were selected (15 from Americans, 1 from a Brazilian) and used as main data for this work. However, many other dreams (including dreams from historical personalities) are also mentioned and interpreted, though usually not as extensively. A discussion on collection, selection, and final interpretation is presented in extenso below.

7.3 Hermeneutics and Interpretation

The interpretation of data, and more generally the whole outlook of this research, followed the symbolic-hermeneutics proposed by Jung in his work. Following such hermeneutic method entails the application of a *hypothetico-deductive approach*, which Føllesdal (1979/1994, p. 234) defines thusly:

> As the name indicates, it is an application of two operations: the formation of *hypotheses* and the *deduction* of consequences from them in order to arrive at beliefs which—though they are hypothetical—are well supported, through the way their deductive consequences fit with our experiences and with our other well-supported beliefs.

That is, the internal validity of such method derives from the testing of interpretative hypotheses, generated from a pre-existing theoretical framework (the interpreter's perspective), and the enrichment and transformation of such perspective through them. Therefore, in this work, the interpretative hypotheses and theoretical assumptions were always kept open to correction. That is, the data (the oneiric texts) and the interpretative hypotheses generated in the effort to understand them continually modified the theory (my theoretical perspective), in a constant dialectic formation. The gradual "discovery" (insights) about deeper layers of meaning in many dreams presented here forced me to question the theoretical presuppositions I held, and to think of different ones. From this constant testing of hypotheses, in relation to both the interpretations and the theoretical perspectives that could be used to understand then, arose the more or less coherent (albeit far from complete or finished) theoretical corpus, the dream interpretations, and the conclusions that are presented here. My interpretative and comparative use of cultural products, such as movies, ads, books, and so on, follows such hermeneutic approach of comparing the original text (dreams) with different but related texts, in order to substantiate the validity of the interpretations. For instance, if a person dreams with Ronald McDonald, one compares such image to the texts and images that are socially or culturally connected to it (in this case, the corporative marketing discourse that comes to be the imaginary fabricated around such sign, the image of the clown, etc.). Moreover, whenever possible, I used analogous dreams from other persons and from *different historical and cultural contexts* in order to compare how the symbolic representations and their meanings appeared then and now. For instance, the prototype dream was interpreted in comparison with similar contemporary dreams, but also with a dream by Walter Benjamin, which showed a completely different context and meaning (and which underlined the context and significance of the form of colonization effected by consumerism in the prototype dream and others). Such procedure, representing what one may call "historical and cultural symbolic hermeneutics", arises from the theoretical perspective that the individual symbolic production, the dream, is also cultural and historical because it stems from a substratum that is cultural and historical, and common to all humanity: the archetypes of the collective unconscious. As Vieira (2003, p. 214) put it, in a beautiful paragraph:

> It is impossible to read the symbolic thought by taking into account only the ontogenetic development, the person's life history. The symbolic thought only produces meaning/makes sense[1] when we consider it in its relation to the history of humanity's symbolic production. (…) The theory of archetypes therefore allows for an individual symbolic production to resonate humanity's symbolic production. What is produced individually here is analogous to what is produced collectively there, and such analogy is due to the fact that we are all human, that we all perceive and try to ascribe meaning to the world in ways that are human.

The dreams collected were interpreted psychologically according to the hermeneutics of dream interpretation proposed by Jung in his *oeuvre*, in dialog with elaborations and developments made by authors from the Porto Alegre Jungian School (Duarte, 1998, 1999; Freitas, 1991; Vieira, 2003, 2006), and articles written by myself (Xavier, 1999, 2001, 2005). The theoretical perspective that guided such hermeneutical interpretation was the theoretical corpus developed in this work. The research questions, transformed into objectives, guided the interpretation; the main objective of the interpretation process was to identify patterns in the dreams—not in terms of their *content* per se but in terms of their *meaning*.

[1] "Faz sentido" (hace sentido).

As mentioned, some cultural products—books, advertisements, movies, and so on—were also interpreted in the same way, as a form of illustrating arguments and in comparison, or contrasting, with the dreams. Some of such products illustrated what I called "consumption dreams" and "dream-world of consumption", discussed above. The logic of such procedure follows both the hermeneutical requirement of "using different but parallel texts in order to elucidate the meaning of the original text" (Welman, 1996, p. 170), that is, the intertextuality of dreams and cultural texts, and Jungian dream hermeneutics.

7.4 Jungian Hermeneutics

Jungian hermeneutics of dream interpretation[2] can be summarized into a few methodological steps: assessment of the dream as drama or narrative; thematization; consideration of the dreamer's ego attitude; contextualization, association, amplification, and serialization; interpretation on the subjective level and on the objective level; consideration of the finalist, self-regulatory, compensatory, and prospective functions of the dreams.

1. *Dream as drama*: As discussed in Chap. 2, it refers to assessing the dream according to a dramatic or narrative structure—exposition (which presents a specific problem, or the *theme* of the dream), development, culmination or peripeteia, solution or *lysis*.
2. *Thematization*: It means an attempt at understanding to what main *theme* the dream is referring, without, however, undervaluing its secondary themes. In some typical dreams (e.g., flying or being naked in a public place), thematization is a relatively easy task; in others, it is more difficult, especially when the dream presents a very complex plot. In this work, the dreams refer broadly to the themes studied (colonization of subjectivity by the consumerist imaginary); thematization here will therefore refer to what psychological aspect is being colonized, in what ways, through what, and so on.

[2] Given its complexity and the different ways through which Jung explained it in his publications, what follows is a didactic and concise way of understanding it. As some of these themes have already been discussed in the theoretical framework, here I focus on the practical way of applying such steps.

3. Consideration of the dreamer's *ego attitude*: To consider how ego consciousness (the dreamer, in the dreams) positions itself actively or passively in relation both to the problems posited by the dream (which can be of a cultural nature) and to the whole oneiric narrative. The oneiric drama usually changes due to the ego attitude or passivity, and this is what has to be considered.
4. *Contextualization*: Confronted with a symbolic unconscious product (e.g., the oneiric narrative), one must proceed as if it were an unknown or fragmentary text, like a philologist dealing with a strange language, and consider its context (Jung, CW12). The subjective context depends on knowing the dreamer's life history, that is, *who* had the dream, and on considering the specific moment in his or her life in which the dream appeared. As discussed below in "Limitations", unfortunately such procedure was impracticable with some dreams analyzed here.
5. *Associations*: The psychological context also refers to the web of associations in which the oneiric expression is naturally embedded. Personal associations refer to those in which the dreamer associates a dream-image (an object, person, event, place, etc.) to something in her life and/or her personal assessment of the image (e.g., a person in the dream is associated to a celebrity who the dreamer admires, yet such person appears as a certain friend who the dreamer strongly dislikes). In this work, at times, such associations were given in the written dream narrative; at other times, it was not possible to collect important associations (because the dreamer was unreachable).
6. *Amplification*: in this work, it refers to the associations of a more collective or impersonal character. It constitutes fundamentally an "elaboration and clarification of a dream-image by means of *directed* association and of parallels from the human science (symbology, mythology, mysticism, folklore, history of religion, ethnology etc.)" (Jung, MDR, p. 410). Drawing from the tradition of hermeneutics of cultural texts, association and amplification sometimes appear as two aspects of the same process in Jung, which he described thusly:

> The essence of hermeneutics, an art widely practised in former times, consists in adding further analogies to the one already supplied by the symbol: in the first place subjective analogies produced at random by the patient,

> then objective analogies provided by the analyst out of his general knowledge. This procedure widens and enriches the initial symbol, and the final outcome is an infinitely complex and variegated picture the elements of which can be reduced to their respective *tertia comparationis*. Certain lines of psychological development then stand out that are at once individual and collective. (Jung, CW7, §493)

That means that the interpreter must try and find in culture (not only his or her own, or the dreamer's, but *all cultures*) the parallel forms in which the oneiric images and symbols appear or have appeared—in symbolic cultural productions such as religious systems, myths, fairy tales, and so on, but also in works of art, literature, movies, and, in this work, even mass media products such as advertisements. Such parallel images and narratives furnish the cultural context of the oneiric discourse. Therefore, "Culture enters the process of meaning construction of the fantasies [and dreams] as a context that is subjacent to the context furnished by the patient's [dreamer's] associations and his/her history" (Vieira, 2003, p. 153). This cultural contextualization, as it were, is important especially when the dreamer cannot furnish analogies (associations), or when the dream material is manifestly collective or cultural; that is, when the oneiric symbol is not taken as exclusively personal, the interpreter can and ought to find cultural parallels. Such proposition is obviously grounded in the concepts of archetype and collective unconscious. As mentioned above, the method for dream interpretation used here also included comparison with other dreams, from different cultural and historical contexts, that were analogous (in form and/or meaning) to the dream interpreted.

It is important to differentiate the processes of association and amplification from the Freudian "free association" method. In Jungian hermeneutics, the parallels found must be *closely related* to the *specific* dream-image; as Jung put it, "always stay with the image" (Jung, SCD, p. 381). For instance, if the dream-image is a *giant*, the interpreter has to found cultural parallels for the giant motif; it will not be interpreted as, for example, "the father", unless the dream points in that direction (e.g., in the dream the giant leaves the father's room, etc.)

7. *Serialization*: It refers to considering the dream as part of a dream series (from one dreamer). This process allows for identifying and comparing typical themes and symbols (motifs), which can appear under different forms, across a number of dreams. The meaning of the themes and dreams then presents itself more clearly. "The series is the context which the dreamer himself supplies. It is as if not one text but many lay before us, throwing light from all sides on the unknown terms, so that a reading of all the texts is sufficient to elucidate the difficult passages in each individual one" (Jung, CW12, §50–51). That means that a particular dream-image is clarified when seen against the broader context of the unconscious discourse across a period of time, which renders explicit the dreamer's psychological development, main problems and questions, and individuality. That is, the analysis of a long series of dreams can be a substitute for the subjective contextualization, or personal associations, for in a series the meanings of oneiric ideas and themes become clear:

> [We] adopt the method we would use in deciphering a fragmentary text or one containing unknown words: we examine the context. The meaning of the unknown word may become evident when we compare a series of passages in which it occurs. The psychological context of dream contents consists in the web of associations in which the dream is naturally embedded. Theoretically we can never know anything in advance about this web, *but in practice it is sometimes possible, granted long enough experience*. (Jung, CW12, §48; e.a.)

The series of dreams thus guarantee "a relative degree of certainty" (Jung, CW16, §322) for the interpretation.

8. *Interpretation on the objective level*: It takes the dream-images concretely, that is, in dreaming with a person or object that the dreamer knows, the dream is referring to them concretely. In Jung's proposal of an *interpretation on the subjective level*, the oneiric and unconscious materials are considered as tendencies or parts of the dreamer's psyche. Such materials are not interpreted concretely, but *symbolically*, and are seen as a true hermeneutic symbol (Vieira, 2003). However, depending on the dream, often both levels can be applied tentatively (i.e.,

they are not mutually excluding, but complementary), which is actually the proposal in this work. Theoretically, the dream can be seen as the unconscious discourse regarding the dreamer's conscious and unconscious context (the subjective level) but also regarding the culture in which the subject is embedded and which largely defines him or her. Both levels of interpretation therefore aim at understanding how the oneiric text is related to, or articulated with, the dreamer's psychic system and life—the dreamer's subjectivity—and their cultural context.

9. Finally, the dreams must be considered according to the principles that characterize Jung's theory on the unconscious: One must adopt a finalist view and ask *what is the purpose of this dream? What effect is it meant to have?* (Jung, CW8, §462). And, relating it to (7), *why did it choose specifically such dream-image, or symbol? With what objective?* Such question is related to the self-regulatory character of the unconscious and its products, which works through the compensatory and complementary functions; hence, one must ask *what is being compensated by the dream?* As mentioned, the dream may reflect the prospective function of the unconscious and outline the solution of a conflict. The related question here is, *how is the dream trying to solve a problem or conflict?*

Three last important considerations seem necessary at this point. First, the Jungian hermeneutics discussed above is in accordance with, and follows, the hermeneutic tradition and its hypothetico-deductive method: every interpretation must be considered as a hypothesis. "Every interpretation necessarily remains as an 'as-if'. The ultimate core of meaning may be circumscribed but not described" (Jung, CW9i, §265). Second, it must be emphasized again that, in principle, each dream shall be taken as a *possibility*, not as a determinism; the dream (usually) shows a picture of the dreamer's psychic situation at a given moment and points at problems and alternatives. However, in dream series, when such situation does not change, or consistently changes for worse, then one can affirm that it has been crystallized as a psychological *fact*. In addition, based on the theory discussed before, the dream is seen as capable of revealing both collective and individual realities. According to the objectives set for this work, interpretation will attempt to identify in the dream narratives the interrelationships between (1) the collective realm: as *sociocultural* factors pertaining to the social imaginary of consumption, its collective consciousness; (2) the individual-subjective realm: how the dreams represent the dreamer's subjectivity in relation to such social imaginaries. More specifically, all these guides for interpretation will necessarily be subordinated to the main interpretive objective, namely, to establish and understand the oneiric, symbolic *patterns of meaning* with which the unconscious represents processes of colonization of subjectivity that are typical of the *ImCon.*

7.5 Procedures

Given that the process of data collection and interpretation of dreams presented in this work went through considerable difficulties, and might perhaps be viewed as controversial, it seems necessary to provide a more detailed narrative of the procedures and trajectory undertaken in order to build this dissertation. Presently, I believe such difficulties and limitations stem mainly from the problems involved in researching *dreams* in depth with a hermeneutic method, in a foreign country (i.e., not in a clinical setting[3]), and in the scientific context of social psychology research. In my perception, that is due to the fact that the ideal form of researching night dreams from an in-depth, symbolical-hermeneutic perspective is through the elaboration of complete case studies, which requires access to the dreamers' case history, their detailed personal associations (regarding the dream-imagery), and with long series of dreams. Dreams are also a difficult and elusive subject for research: they are usually considered very personal and intimate; the associations required from the dreamers would often involve the disclosure of life details of a very personal nature; and, finally, most people do not remember nor write down their dreams. Therefore I have concluded that such ideal form is only possible in a clinical setting: it requires strenuous effort from dreamer and researcher, a relationship of deep mutual trust, *time*, openness, and so on; in sum, it represents a huge demand on the participant.

[3] I was not entitled to practice as a psychotherapist in Spain.

Nevertheless, I persisted with my objective of researching dreams. In what follows, the trajectory of collecting and selecting the dreams, and finally interpreting them, is divided into an initial exploratory stage, an intermediary stage, and a final stage.

7.5.1 Initial Stage

Initially, I tried to research dreams and fantasies as a form of collaborating with the Kofarips research coordinated by Professor Blanch, focusing on the roles of the unconscious, the oneiric, and the symbolic for work subjectivation. Data (dreams and fantasies) were collected through a question in the paper-and-pencil Kofarips questionnaire and in its semi-structured interview protocols, both of which were applied to academic and health personnel in Spain and South America. The question was formulated thusly: *Tell us some dream or fantasy about your work (that you elaborated awake or had during sleep).*

The analysis of such data (from more than 300 participants) and its elaboration took a long time. I finally concluded that the data did not allow for in-depth exploration and symbolic-hermeneutic interpretation; analysis remained confined to a sort of content analysis. Such work resulted in a published article (Xavier, 2011).

7.5.2 Intermediary Exploratory Stage

Having given up that initial project, I had to face the main problem of researching dreams: how to collect dreams (and dream series) that *focused on certain themes*, with information on the dreamers and their associations—without having the possibility of doing so in a clinical setting, with patients. The obvious way to circumvent such difficulty was to explore dreams from different sources: (a) dreams posted spontaneously on the internet, (b) series of dreams I already had in my possession, (c) dreams occasionally told to me by colleagues and their friends, and (d) dreams from literature (in a broad sense: not restricted to scientific literature on dreaming). For a number of reasons, (c) and (d) did not work.[4]

[4] Respectively, only few dreams were told to me in the first way, and potential case studies did not follow through with my requests for dream collection; and dreams from literature usually focused

So I concentrated on collecting and analyzing dreams from the internet (entertaining the possibility of asking users for any dreams they had that were related to my research object), and exploring and analyzing the series of dreams I already had.

As I had not managed to define clearly my research object and problem (though I was not aware of this), my focus for their collection and interpretation was exceedingly broad: the *psychic ethos* of contemporary consumption capitalism (in terms of *total capitalism*), and the forms of *subjectivity* it produces—from the viewpoint of the dreams, that is, of the unconscious. The procedures for such collection and interpretation were as follows:

1. Dreams collected through the internet:
   (a) Selection of seemingly reliable forums and websites, and exploration of websites suggested by dream forum users (see Appendix A). The majority of such websites and forums was in English, but those in Portuguese (frequented mainly by Brazilian users), Italian, and Spanish were also consulted. However, it turned out to be much easier to find dream specimens from American dreamers; this is probably due to the many factors that characterize the United States (millions of inhabitants with internet access, a culture found of posting personal information on the web, interest in dreams, the "old" and more popular forums on dreams being in English, etc.). Also, many of their dreams were clearly related to the imaginary of consumption.
   (b) In two forums (dreamtalk.hypermart.net and dreamoods.com), I left a message explaining I was a PhD candidate researching dreams related to consumption, consumerism, and their "social icons" (McDonald's, K-Mart, Disney, shopping malls, etc.), and asking the users for dream narratives related to such themes (and also for suggestions). Unfortunately, only two users provided me dreams.[5] One user had a very interesting dream "in response" to my request, which is interpreted here (even though it does not feature such icons).

on only one theme (which did not coincide with mine), or else did not provide context or associations.

[5] Such response discouraged me from insisting on that procedure for collecting data.

   (c) Around 800 dreams were thus selected and organized in Word files (according to their themes and provenience).

2. Dreams collected from other sources:

   (a) I read through a fairly rich number of dreams (around 850) I collected from former patients, during clinical work (psychotherapy) across 10 years. From this corpus, 24 dreams were selected as potential data.

Such process, which one might term an ethnography of dreams, provided an enormous volume of dreams. A process of "immersion in the data" (Ritchie & Spencer, 1994, p. 178) followed: reading and interpreting the dreams, further selecting possible cases and discarding others. Whenever possible, dreamers were contacted by email or through internet forums and asked if they could provide more information on their dreams. Confidentiality was emphasized. Few dreamers answered the request; associations and other information were thus collected.

From such data, 254 dreams were analyzed in depth,[6] according to the hermeneutics discussed above. Many were part of dream series, which were studied in their entirety as well. Many dream series were part of *dream diaries*. There is an extensive tradition of research using such kind of data (for their use in contemporaneity, see Plummer, 1983). However, the scope of the proposed research was still immense; it had to be delimited somehow. I decided to concentrate on a few symbolic themes or contexts that had repeatedly appeared in the dreams (and which I had also used as keywords when searching for more dream material): McDonald's, Disney (and McDonaldization and Disneyization), shopping malls, supermarkets, and so on. The reasons for such procedure are: (1) the first dreams I analyzed (including the prototype dream) revolved around such themes and scenarios; (2) subsequently, I came upon many

[6] In fact, the processes of constructing the research problem and data collection were even more complicated than what I describe here. For instance, a whole corpus of dreams (around 150) had by users of antidepressants and other psychiatric medications was collected and interpreted; and also many dreams related in one way or another to the theme of totalitarianism. The first corpus was discarded because I already had too much dream material and it did not seem to fit well with the overall proposal (as the dreams showed what can be seen as a *neurochemical* colonization of the psyche). However, I intend to write a couple of articles discussing such material.

dreams that dealt with the same themes and were exceedingly meaningful; (3) a further rationale was that they represented a form of dialog with sociology and social sciences (which discuss McDonald's, Disney, shopping malls, etc., in relation to consumerism and self, as typical forms of consumerism and colonization), and their research corpus, and as a means for contributing with new material and theory (as the colonization forms appeared through dreams).

Another important reason for such procedure is that it is very difficult to collect or search for dreams (even with the wealth of material I had) that deal only, or mainly, with one broad *theme* (especially a more or less technical one, such as colonization or commodification). Dreams usually present us with a full panoply of interrelated individual and collective themes and problems. For that reason, research on dreams (and their collection) usually focuses on one type of *population* (students, patients suffering from a specific pathology, etc.), or studies an individual's dreams (single case study), or else searches specifically for one pattern or archetype (*form*) in the dreams. Thus, although the dreams were selected according to a pre-defined symbolic *content* or dreamscape (representations of McDonald's, etc.), their *forms* (oneiric narratives) and wealth of meaning (other *contents*) varied immensely. However, the research questions I had proposed were still too ample (viz., how the consumerist ethos, subjectivity, and colonization of the unconscious—and their interrelations—appeared in the dreams). At this point, following a suggestion from a colleague, Dr. Miguel Sahagún, a second delimitation of the focus of research was undertaken, based on such extensive interpretation of data, the main themes resulting from it, and practical considerations: to focus on how the unconscious represented, and reacted to, processes of colonization of subjectivity by the consumerist imaginary—through night dreams. This focus was then slightly modified and elaborated as the final research question and objectives, which concentrate on the empirical material (dreams) rather than the theoretical concepts (unconscious) behind them. Due to the limits of this work, a final selection of 40 dreams had to be undertaken, according to the following criteria: (1) dreams had to focus on the themes mentioned: representations of some form of colonization related to consumerism and its imaginary (in the context or under the guise of McDonald's and McDonaldization, Disney and

Disneyization, shopping malls, etc.), and of some form of autonomous reaction (from the unconscious); (2) their clarity of meanings and patterns; (3) dreams had to belong to a series (i.e., not isolated dreams), and the personal associations from the dreamers had to be available; (4) their relevance, meaningfulness, uniqueness, and information-richness (Patton, 1990).

Sometimes not all criteria were fulfilled, but the dream was nonetheless chosen due to its meaningfulness and uniqueness. A number of dreams illustrate typical patterns found across many other dreams. Selection of dreams therefore did not follow any quantitative criteria. The final series, with eight dreams[7] from the same person, was included because of its wealth of meaning and its clarity, and for being part of a larger series (of more than 300 dreams), which provided a rich context for the dreams studied.

7.5.3 Final Stage

It involved the interpretation in depth of the final corpus of dreams (and the *series* in which they were embedded), comparing the dreams' motifs, patterns, structures, meanings, and dynamics, according to the theoretical propositions and hermeneutics discussed above, and the comparison of the dreams with other cultural texts and other dreams. The interpretations were iterative; moreover, they were exhaustive from my point of view, that is, they represent the best and most complete form of interpretation I have managed to reach. I have no doubt, however, that I did not cover all the wealth of symbolic meanings they have—which, in fact, is impossible.[8] As mentioned above, while such process of continuous interpretation was realized based on a previous theoretical framework, the dreams and the hypothetical interpretations they elicited also forced me to develop other theoretical propositions, to modify the theory I had, in

[7] This series was originally intended as a single case study composed of 22 selected dreams. Their interpretation in depth was nearly complete, yet due to lack of time and other considerations (lack of space, varied dream themes), I had to use only a few dreams of hers.

[8] Some (if not *all*) of the dreams presented in this work testify to the wealth of symbolic meanings and relevance that can be found in dreams and in the unconscious. Each of them could originate long monographs.

a dialectical process. (Actually, in the end the dreams forced me to come up with a *new theory*—elements of which I ended up finding in a more or less similar form in other authors—centered on the *participation mystique* with the commodity-sign and on the colonization of imaginaries.)

7.6 Ethical Considerations

With the exception of one dream (the "prototype dream"), all dreams analyzed here were collected from *public* sites on the internet or from literature (i.e., they were in the public domain); therefore, no informed consent was asked from the dreamers. The dreamers' personal details were largely withheld (unless they were absolutely essential for the interpretation). In the few cases personal associations from the dreamers are mentioned, they were modified so as to ensure anonymity. In relation to the "prototype dream", the dreamer was contacted via email and advised about all ethical considerations regarding the research and her participation (voluntary and confidential nature of her participation, the research themes and objectives, how her dream, associations, and personal information would be used, etc.). She signed voluntarily an informed consent form and sent it to me. Her dream narrative was modified in order to preserve anonymity and confidentiality.

7.7 Reliability

One problem regards the veracity, or the degree of reliability and objectivity, of the dreams collected on the internet. Even though the use of secondary sources (internet, newspapers, mass media, etc.) for collecting dreams is not very common in the literature, some recent researches were based on it. For instance, Edgar (2011), Edgar and Henig (2009), and Valtonen (2011) researched dreams collected from newspapers and the internet. Jung himself published extensive analyses of children's dreams as seminars (Jung, SCD), and of dreams and fantasies of an American woman (his classical *Symbols of Transformation*, CW5), that were collected from secondary sources. Freud's classical *Interpretation of Dreams* contains a number of dreams collected from diverse secondary sources. Based on my experience working with dreams, I have no reason to believe that the dreams presented here were invented, distorted, or "enhanced" in any significant way. Quite otherwise, there are many reasons for thinking they were really dreamt as reported:

- Regarding dreams collected in internet forums: In relation to the final selection of dreams interpreted here, as far as I was able to grasp, no dreamer had reasons to invent such dreams, and none received any form of "gratification" (whether emotional—admiration, attention, etc.—or of any other kind) for publishing them; quite the opposite, some dreams analyzed here are obviously terrible experiences[9];
- Many dreamers did not seem to understand their dreams in the least, and some expressed explicitly their incomprehension;
- The majority of the dreams harshly criticize the dreamers, revealing ethical, personal, social, and familiar problems, the disclosure of which would represent an *embarrassment* to the dreamers (rather than a source of any sort of positive stimuli for their conscious concoction), were they aware of their full significance. In other words, the dreams would be sources of opprobrium rather than praise;
- Many dreamers were puzzled, surprised, and at times frightened by their dreams, and some reported them on the internet explicitly seeking answers and help;
- Analysis of *series* of dreams from the same dreamers revealed patterns and dynamics that were clearly unconscious, that is, that could not have been invented or enhanced consciously. Therefore, even if a dream, or a dream-image or narrative, were distorted more or less consciously, such distortion would be corrected by seeing it in comparison with the other dreams and their analogous images.

Another question related to the objectivity of the dreams collected regards their possible alteration, or modification, in the process of consciously remembering and recording them. My argument is: the *totality*

[9] One website (dreamjournal.net) could be an exception: it gives stars for "lucidity" and "cohesiveness" to the dreams published. However, judging from the 250 dreams I read there, the stars did not seem to be conducive to bias or falsification in dream reporting. At any rate, I chose not to analyze "lucid" dreams, or dreams from dreamers who attempted to be "lucid" while dreaming, in this work.

of *any* experience (be it conscious or unconscious) always remains ineffable by definition; the experience is always "modified" to some extent in the process of *narrating* it, of formulating a narrative of the experience. Perhaps dreams, being complex, symbolic, and emotional experiences, may be seen as somewhat more prone to such modification, especially because they are often easily forgotten. In remembering and writing them, in becoming aware of their narrative and the emotions and feelings experienced in them and turning them into a verbal narrative, the dreamer always modifies the original unconscious experience.[10] In that, dreams are no different from any other narrated human experience, but only in that aspect, for their symbolic value and wealth of meaning remain more or less untouched. What Geertz (1977) said regarding anthropological texts is also valid for the dream narrative: it is also a *fictio*, that is, something *constructed*—in a way, it is already an interpretation (Vieira, 2003, 2006). However, and reiterating, the dreams analyzed here present such strange images and strong criticisms—of the dreamer and culture—with many carrying strong emotional tones, that it makes it fairly safe to say that they constitute objective expressions of the unconscious and were reported as such.

7.8 Limitations

The method employed in this work has some pros and cons. On the one hand, collecting dreams from secondary sources such as the internet allowed for amassing an enormous amount of data whose quality was not affected by the researcher. On the other hand, not knowing the dreamer personally is a major disadvantage: it presents problems for the collection of associations and other materials that would greatly help in the interpretation; and discussing how their subjectivity is portrayed in the dream becomes much more hypothetical and risky.

[10] As Guattari and Rolnik (2006, p. 281) put it, the dreamer is always confronted with "[the] contrast between the discovery of the complexity, wealth and differentiation that can come about through an oneiric experience, and the poverty of means, when waking up, when one tries to express such oneiric production through remembrance, writing or drawing".

Regarding the social context: The fact that the dreams originated from American and Brazilian persons, that is, from contexts that are in principle socioculturally different, together with my relatively scarce knowledge of their specific sociocultural backgrounds, may present serious limitations. However, two things should be borne in mind here. One, the dreams themselves, the focus of this work, seen as embedded in series, provided the needed context. Two, regardless of social and cultural context, the dreams presented striking similarities and analogies—which attest to the growing homogeneity of contemporary culture and individuals.

Regarding the associations: For some dreams, I did not have the chance to collect the personal associations of the dreamers in relation to the dreams (and in some cases did not know their personal context, their conscious situation at the time of the dream, nor their life histories in depth). On the one hand, this represents a serious limitation on the validity of my interpretations (as the same dream can have completely different meanings for two persons with different life situations, personalities, etc.). On the other hand, as discussed above, the series of dreams provided both the personal context and the "associations" needed. The dreams interpreted here often employ typical symbols in typical narratives; in comparing them with each other, the cultural critique that emerges is rather clear, or, in other words, my interpretations gain in probability largely because of the comparative affinity in their *collective* or social meanings. Also, more often than not I did not mention associations explicitly in the text (due to the space it would require), even though I took them in consideration when interpreting the dream.

Amplifications: Some amplifications could (and should) be very long and detailed, but this would compromise the succinctness of the text. Given the limits of this work, I have had to summarize the process of amplification while pointing to more sources wherein the amplification is given in much more detail. Such amplifications point to symbolic patterns found across cultures, which, theoretically, are based on psychological patterns (the archetypes of the collective unconscious) for the formation of symbols.

References

Duarte, L. F. B. (1998). O Sono dos Justos: uma interpretação simbólica. *Cadernos de Comunicação (Unisinos-RS), 1*(4), 73–94.

Duarte, L. F. B. (1999). *O Sono dos Justos: elementos para uma metodologia de interpretação de textos culturais.* Unpublished master's thesis, Unisinos, São Leopoldo, Brazil.

Edgar, I. R. (2011). *The dream in Islam: From Qur'anic tradition to jihadist inspiration.* Oxford: Berghahn.

Edgar, I. R., & Henig, D. (2009). The cosmopolitan and the noumenal: A case study of Islamic jihadist night dreams as reported sources of spiritual and political inspiration. In D. Theodossopoulos & E. Kirtsoglou (Eds.), *United in discontent: Local responses to cosmopolitanism and globalization* (pp. 64–82). Oxford: Berghahn.

Føllesdal, D. (1994). Hermeneutics and the hypothetico-deductive method. In M. Martin & L. C. McIntyre (Eds.), *Readings in the philosophy of social science* (pp. 233–247). London: Bradford. (Original work published 1979).

Freitas, M. G. (1991). *Taipas e toupeiras.* Porto Alegre: Fonte Phi.

Geertz, C. (1977). *The interpretation of cultures.* New York: Basic Books.

Gilgun, J. F. (1994). A case for case studies in social work research. *Social Work, 39*(4), 371–380.

Guattari, F., & Rolnik, S. (2006). *Micropolítica: Cartografias del deseo.* Madrid: Traficantes de Sueños.

Hamel, J. (1993). The case study in sociology: The contribution of methodological research in the French language. *Canadian Review of Sociology & Anthropology, 30*(4), 488–509.

Patton, M. Q. (1990). *Qualitative research and evaluation methods.* Newbury Park: Sage.

Plummer, K. (1983). *Documents of life.* London: Allen & Unwin.

Putney, L. G. (2010). Case study. In *Encyclopedia of research design.* London: Sage. Retrieved from http://www.sage-ereference.com/researchdesign/Article_n39.html

Ritchie, J., & Spencer, L. (1994). Qualitative data analysis for applied policy research. In A. Bryman & R. G. Burgess (Eds.), *Analysing qualitative data* (pp. 173–194). London: Routledge & Kegan Paul.

Runyan, W. M. (1982). *Life histories and psychobiography: Explorations in theory and method.* New York: Oxford University Press.

Valtonen, A. (2011). We dream as we live – Consuming. In R. W. Belk, K. Grayson, A. M. Muñiz, & H. J. Schau (Eds.), *Research in consumer behavior* (Vol. 13, pp. 93–110). Bradford, UK: Emerald.

Vieira, A. G. (2003). *Imagem, símbolo e narrativa na Psicologia Analítica de C. G. Jung*. Unpublished doctoral dissertation, Universidade Federal do Rio Grande do Sul, Porto Alegre, Brazil.

Vieira, A. G. (2006). *A interpretação do brincar na caixa de areia*. Porto Alegre: Armazém Digital.

Welman, M. (1996). *Death and gnosis: Archetypal dream imagery in terminal illness*. Unpublished doctoral dissertation, Rhodes University, Grahamstown, South Africa.

Xavier, M. (1999). *Dream interpretation in Jung's theory: A comparative analysis*. Retrieved from http://www.cgjungpage.org/index2.php?option=com_content& do_pdf=1&id=107

Xavier, M. (2001). *Religiosidade e problemas com o álcool: Um estudo de caso*. Unpublished master's thesis, PUCRS, Porto Alegre, Brazil.

Xavier, M. (2005). Religiosidade e problemas com o álcool: um estudo de caso. *Psicologia Ciência e Profissão, 25*(1), 88–99.

Xavier, M. (2011). Trabalho e sonhos: desejos e pesadelos de professores e trabalhadores da saúde na era do capitalismo organizacional. *Cadernos de psicologia social do trabalho, 14*(1), 93–110.

Yin, R. K. (2002). *Case study research: Design and methods* (3rd ed.). Thousand Oaks: Sage.

Yin, R. K. (2005). Case study methods. In J. Green, G. Camilli, & P. Elmore (Eds.), *Complementary methods for research in education* (3rd. ed., pp. 111–122). Washington, DC: American Educational Research Association.

Yin, R. K. (2012). *Applications of case study research* (3rd ed.). London: Sage.

8

Interpretation and Discussion

After discussing the methodology employed in this work, the following chapters are dedicated to presenting its proper empirical study. It consists in the application of the theoretical framework developed in Part I to the interpretation and discussion of the empirical material: the night dreams, focusing on how subjectivity appears colonized in them, how consumer culture and its imaginary seem to be criticized by them, and the general implications that they seem to show in relation to both subjects and culture. Interpretation and discussion therefore also reveal and present the research findings, which are later recapitulated and summarized in the final chapter with the conclusions.

Thus each chapter that follows discusses the dreams according to their respective *dreamscapes*, seen as distinct yet interrelated metaphors for the imaginary of consumerism: first the reader is presented with a few dreams related to McDonald's, interweaved with different archetypal dreams; then two complex and significant dreams related to Disneyland; and finally a long series of dreams that have shopping malls and department stores as their scenarios, which is concluded with a series of dreams from the same person.

Before we probe into such dream-worlds, however, a few comments are needed. In condensing and reporting the dreams already written in

M. Xavier, *Subjectivity, the Unconscious and Consumerism*,
https://doi.org/10.1007/978-3-319-96824-7_8

English, and, alternatively, in translating some other dreams into English, I have tried to preserve the original way they were told to me or written. With few exceptions, all the dreams have been abbreviated.[1] In interpreting the first dream, the hermeneutic procedures—for example, the use of associations, amplification, and so on, and also how the dream is seen according to a dramatic or narrative structure, and how that is useful for the interpretation—are discussed in more detail. For the other dreams, for reasons of space, I have taken for granted that the reader will bear in mind such procedures, and apply them to the dreams (and so they are not detailed). Concluding the interpretation of each consumption night dream, there is a brief summary of how the dream and its interpretation answer some specific research questions of this work, namely, (1) *what* psychological factors, domains, or realms are colonized in the dream; (2) *how* colonization is effectuated; and (3) the possible *effects* of colonization.

Reiterating, rather than searching for patterns in terms of images (i.e., motifs) or concepts, interpretation, and discussion focus on the patterns in *meaning* revealed by the dreams. This warning is particularly important as regards the concepts with which one discusses subjectivity. As mentioned, usually the dreams do not refer directly to the dreamer's "unconscious psyche", "identity", "symbolico-religious function", and so on. These latter are interpretations and translations of symbolic images into psychological concepts, translations that, by definition, should be viewed as somewhat forced and incomplete in relation to the original dream symbol, but which are necessary for discussing the dreams rationally and psychologically. Furthermore, the dream-images often have multiple and varied symbolic connotations; only some of such connotations—the ones that are clearly related to this study's objects of research—are discussed here. As with any true symbol, one must accept that part of its connotations and meanings always remains concealed, opaque, and untranslatable. Therefore, each summary at the end of each dream interpretation should be seen merely as an approximate, abridged formulation of how the dream seemed to answer the specific questions posed by the specific aims—through its interpreted meanings, translated into

[1] In this I follow Jung's procedure in his case study of Wolfgang Pauli (Jung, CW12, §47).

psychological concepts. Thus the summaries have a tentative character, and represent a mere attempt at deciphering and comprehending the symbolic worlds of meaning the dreams naturally portray—worlds which should indeed be the reader's main focus of attention.

9

All That Is Sacred (and Symbolic) Is Commodified: The McChurch™ Dreams

Although processes of colonization by the ImCon in the guise of McDonaldization appeared under many different forms in the oneiric narratives, the dreams presented and interpreted in this chapter were chosen because of some of their common particularities. First, because they are impressive and employ some *typical* symbolic images, for which I was able to find parallels in (equally impressive) dreams of other people, from different historical moments and places. This allowed for comparative interpretations, which not only helped to illuminate both sets of dreams, but also, and importantly, substantiated the idea that there is a fantastic and *historical* mutation of imaginaries under way in our global consciousness. Such mutation is conveyed in the title of this chapter, and is related to the second particularity of the dreams here. With the exception of the last dream, which depicts the totalizing logic of colonization, all these dreams are related to the human domains of the religious and the sacred. They portray one specific form of colonization: the ImCon functioning as a simulacrum of religion, or of religious imaginary, which, drawing from the symbols some dreams employed spontaneously, I called the *McChurch*. It signals how the ImCon's semiotic ideology—embodied by McDonald's—colonizes and commodifies "all that is sacred", and takes

M. Xavier, *Subjectivity, the Unconscious and Consumerism*,
https://doi.org/10.1007/978-3-319-96824-7_9

its place; it pictures dramatically the mutation of imaginaries as "the loss of the symbolic and the passing over to the semiological" (Baudrillard, 1973/1981, p. 98) and, in fact, to the order of simulacra.

For the first dream, the prototype dream, it seemed adequate to provide a longer and more detailed interpretation, rendering explicit its hermeneutic steps and giving more attention to symbolic minutia and subjective functioning. Such procedure aimed at fulfilling two of the objectives of this work, namely, to illustrate clearly how the Jungian symbolic-hermeneutic method is applied to dreams, and to discuss more in depth the theme of *subjectivity*, demonstrating and drawing from the wealth of meaning dreams can offer for such. In this respect, this first interpretation gets closer to a *clinical* perspective. However, all the other interpretations are more concise.

9.1 The Prototype Dream: A McChurch

Dream had many years ago by a Brazilian female student in her early 20s.

> *It was an impressive dream. I was with my teenage sister looking for a Catholic church. That church would be a future McDonald's [franchise] that we were going to open. We pass by a street behind the church. The church is big and old, with a round, dirty roof with fallen twigs on it. There were huge apartment buildings [what we call "dovecots"] very closely surrounding the church's grounds, which were small. We enter the church; a mass, or prayer, is taking place, and some elderly ladies and the priest stare at us as we enter. There were three floors, and we climb the stairs quickly, embarrassed; I think [to myself], "To transform a church into a McDonald's is kind of a sin … and the church is so beautiful, full of little saints…" The place looked abandoned, one would have to make many reforms [renovations]. We climb to the second floor and look at the first floor from behind a small fence.*

To introduce the interpretation, the hermeneutic steps are presented:

1. *Context*: the dreamer's personal details and context are withheld for reasons of secrecy. One important detail can be mentioned, though the dreamer exhibited a definite *childishness*.

2. *Associations* (made by the dreamer):

    (a) Sister: a young teenager, very attached to their parents, and more childish than the dreamer.
    (b) Church: religion, religiosity. The dreamer said that she used to go to church quite frequently with her family, but such practice (along with other Catholic familiar customs) had somehow been abandoned over the years by the family. She used to like going to church.
    (c) McDonald's: a nice place that she frequented.

    It must be noted that, in Brazil, McDonald's seems to have built an image in the national imaginary that is fairly different from its image in the United States and Europe: it is relatively expensive, has an upper middle-class status for consumers, and is not commonly associated with messy, dirty venues (quite the opposite). In sum, it embodies consumerism as entertainment, fun, and the "American way of life"—as a consumption dream with a more expensive patina (see Fontenelle, 2006).

    Amplification of some symbols (e.g., dovecots) is given across the interpretation.
3. *Serialization*: I had access to several of her dreams, as dream series. The problem shown in this dream appeared in different forms in subsequent dreams, which grounds my interpretation of it and makes it more certain. (However, in the following, I do not mention other dreams of this same dreamer).
4. *Dream as a drama:*

    (a) Dramatis personae: the dreamer, her sister, a group of elderly ladies, the priest.
    (b) Time and space: they are not given, but one can assume it was the present (then, more than 15 years ago), and in her hometown (or at least in her country).
    (c) Dramatic structure of the dream (abbreviated):

    Exposition: *I was with my sister looking for a Catholic church. That church would be a future McDonald's. We pass by a street behind the church. The church is big and old, its small ground surrounded by huge apartment buildings.*

Development (*Desis*): *We enter the church; a mass is taking place; elderly ladies and priest stare at us.*

Conflict or crisis (*Peripetia*): *We climb the stairs quickly and embarrassed; I think, "To transform a church into a McDonald's is a sin, and the church is so beautiful". The church looked abandoned, in need of renovations. We climb to the second floor and look at the first floor from behind a small fence.*

Solution (*Lysis*): There is no *lysis*, because there is no individual attitude on the part of the dreamer regarding the problem posed by the dream, only a quasi-realization of it.

Let us proceed first with an interpretation on the *subjective level*. In the exposition of the dream, she is with her sister, looking for a church, and they have a plan (a more or less conscious intention): to transform the church into a McDonald's franchise. That is the *theme* of the oneiric drama, its "common focal point of meaning" (Meier, 1987, p. 122). Such plan indicates that the interpretation on the subjective level is appropriate, for objectively (i.e., in reality) it would be impossible for her to concrete the plan. Then, what do the main elements in the exposition symbolize? She is with her *sister*. According to her own association, her younger sister represents a deeper identification with the parents,[1] which results in a more acute childishness (in comparison to her own). Thus, their being together symbolizes still living in a childish way, in partial identity with the parents (and thus with the unconscious); such identification and childishness are at the roots of the problem the dream posits, the transformation of the church.

The church, according to her associations and to common sense, represents primarily her religiosity or spirituality, which is Catholic and institutional in its (familiar) origins. Thus the church as a symbol in her dream is consistent with the way she describes her religiosity in her life and in her family: it looks abandoned, and thus "dirty", unkempt. However, her abandonment of her religiosity does not extinguish its traditional and imposing character: it looks big and old, perhaps because it

[1] That is, she is a symbol of the dreamer's shadow complex.

is based on an age-old, traditional institution, a cultural, symbolic imaginary that somehow still works within her, in her unconscious.

It seems there is not enough room for that religiosity to live through her, though: the grounds are small and seem to be under the pressure of the *buildings* surrounding it. Such apartment buildings are called "dovecots"[2] because they are huge, with a number of very small apartments in which, often, large families reside—making them resemble dovecots, which are small in our country but contain an incredible number of doves, who live there with almost no space between them, and amidst their excrements and food. That is a vivid image of a social way of living that is extremely *collective* in nature, so much so that the expression "dovecots" alludes to beast-like, massified life, and that seems to be why the dream employed it as a symbol: it is apt to describe a form of living and a mass mentality that, as buildings, seem to occupy more and more space. So the image the dream chose conveys further meaning: her religiosity is not only abandoned and unkempt because of her carelessness, but is also oppressed and encroached upon by *massifying*, dehumanized collective consciousness, which appears to choke, so to speak, the already diminutive space the sacred and the symbolic have in her personality and life.

Such symbolism implies that she is *identified* with collective consciousness to a large extent; it seems to expand and colonize her psychic system. Her identification is clearly seen in her *plan*: in the same way that the buildings (collective consciousness) seem to threaten the church (religiosity) with absorption or burial, her disposition is to colonize the church; she is the McDonaldizing factor herself.

The dream continues, there is a development: they enter the church. One may assume she still wants to carry the plan out. Despite being menaced and left aside, surprisingly the church still *functions*: there is a religious activity, a rite, being conducted there. The people attending the ceremony and the priest are important elements: they are *elderly*. This

[2] To be honest, after this interpretation was written a doubt arose: I am not sure whether the dreamer herself provided this association of the buildings with the expression "dovecots", or it was *my own* association (to her dream-image); my clinical notes from that time are not clear in that regard. At any rate, the reader should thus take the discussion on the symbolic meaning of "dovecots" in this dream cum *grano salis*.

representation is probably a *compensation* for her (and her sister's) childishness: while her ego consciousness (represented by herself in the dream), her identification with her sister, and her plan are portrayed as identified with collective consciousness, and thus infantile (i.e., not individual, undifferentiated), the elements representing the religious function, the elderly ladies and the priest, compensate, through their age and seriousness, her childish ego and her sister. No wonder they stare at the dreamer and her sister: in the oneiric drama, it is as if they wanted to convey, "These childish brats disrupt our sacred rite and even want to transform the holy church into a McDonald's! The audacity!" Symbolically, this might mean that her unconscious, non-actualized adult aspects stand in opposition to her childishness (and everything it represents: her plan, her identification with consumerism, etc.).

Two ideas are of utmost importance here. First, there is an active, unconscious, and autonomous religious function in her—functioning in spite of and *against* her ego consciousness and her will. This recalls Jung's theory of an autochthonous, natural religious function in the psyche, a "religious instinct" (Jung, CW12, §14). As discussed, such religious function is connected to symbolic- and dream-thinking—the psychic form of imaginative, creative activity, expression of the unconscious psyche, its archetypes and instincts: the basal origin of "all that is sacred". In her unconscious, it somehow still functions (at least partially, in a relatively small portion of her psychic space) through the Catholic imaginary of old.

Second, the dream implies that the possibility of a conscious actualization of her religious function is connected to transcending her childishness, her identification with her parents, and thus to the natural process of growing up, of becoming an adult.[3] In her, it represents a very different attitude toward life, and consequently toward herself and the collective: it stands in opposition to consumerism, to the ImCon and its colonial force.

However, her conscious (ego) attitude regarding this problem is still unsatisfactory. Confronted with the stare of the ladies and the priest, she (and her sister) gets embarrassed. No wonder, given her plan. They seem

[3] Because adulthood is represented in this dream as the elderly ladies and the priest, i.e., some part of her psyche (her still unconscious subjectivity) that can fulfill, practice, and give importance to the religious aspect of life.

to try to escape the problem, or perhaps to look at it from a distance, by running up the stairway. Then the *ethical problem*—the *conflict* in the oneiric drama—is enounced by her for the first time: "To transform a church into a McDonald's is kind of a sin ... and the church is so beautiful, full of little saints...."

That is the central problem presented by the dream. It contains the unconscious' critical depiction of the relationship between the individual (subjective) and the collective (sociocultural) realms: here the subjective and objective levels of interpretation have to be seen together. The cultural realm (or collective consciousness) is portrayed as two forms of imaginary: as an old religious order (the church) and as a new imaginary, total consumerism as a colonial power (McDonald's). The dreamer's subjectivity is criticized and confronted with an ethical choice: how she will position herself in relation to the social world and to her own (psychological) life.

In this dream, therefore, colonization of subjectivity (its McDonaldization) appears as a *possibility*, a plan. Perhaps at this point the dream interpretation can focus more explicitly on this work's research questions. First, *how* the dream represents the possible colonization? It appears as the dreamer's unconscious *identity* with collective consciousness, with the ImCon and its ideology: as mentioned, she is herself the agent of McDonaldization. Such identity is "religious": it can be seen as *participation mystique* with the ImCon. Moreover, it seems to follow her identity with childhood and the parents: in a way, here the magical world of childhood is co-opted by the dream-world of consumerism, both working through the same dynamics of *unconscious* identification—something that is taken for granted and happens automatically. With her plan, she would merely reproduce *by default* the collective imperative, the colonizing trend, the ideology—becoming mimetic with them.

The second question is, *what* psychological domains are colonized? As she would replicate a process that is sociocultural and global, interpretations on both subjective and objective levels are interrelated. The core idea is that her dream symbolizes the colonization of the foundations of both the individual and culture: the *church as the signifying edifice of "all that is sacred"*—for her, in her own psychic system—and as what *used* to be such symbolic edifice for Western culture, a representation of its symbolico-religious imaginaries.

Thus, seen on the *subjective level*, what seems to be menaced by McDonaldization is, broadly, her "inner" imaginary, the *représentations collectives* that form part of her own psyche; what in her and for her still functions as truly mythic and *religious*: a symbolic regime of signification connected to old culture, to a traditional (Catholic) social imaginary, that guides and expresses her unconscious functioning, her emotional and irrational psyche, her archetypal foundation. Thus, more specifically, what is in jeopardy is her very religious function. Her identification with the regime of consumerism illustrates that, by colonizing and replacing symbolic thinking and fantasy, the ImCon institutes a magical-religious thinking that replicates its fetishist ideology, and shapes her psyche accordingly. Just like Christianity, it can become a totalizing template for psychic functioning and behavior, thus commanding or influencing the whole of her life by *signifying* it.

The *interpretation on the objective level* would thus see the dream as symbolizing what was discussed in the theoretical part of this work as a mutation of imaginaries: proceeding with her "plan", the dreamer would simply be replicating, in her own life and psyche, the *cultural* colonization of symbolic imaginaries and of "all that is sacred" effected by the ImCon, followed by its institution as a simulacrum of religion: collective consciousness defined as a new church of consumption, the McChurch.

In fact, such colonization can be seen as reflective of a general commodification of religion, which includes a *concrete* McDonaldization of the Catholic Church itself as an institution. Drane (2001, 2008) contends that precisely that has happened on an international (globalized) level: according to him, the Church has largely adopted and is functioning according to the McChurch's dogmas of efficiency, calculability, predictability, and control. Lyon (2001) analyzes the same phenomenon, but from the perspective of a cultural *Disneyization* of religion.

Seen culturally, the dream-image also illustrates the ImCon's logic of colonization as that of the *simulacrum*: if McDonald's represents the totalizing semiotic order and its process of commodification, its taking the church over signifies the replacement and eventual disappearance of the symbolic order. No more symbols: only logos and signs. All that is symbolic has to be commodified and replaced—within both culture and psyche.

Finally, the third research question refers to the *effects* of colonization. As in this dream colonization remains a *possibility*, one might only infer its effects, and in a very general way. The central idea and image is that the ImCon would function as an "inner church" for the dreamer. Psychologically, she would present the dynamics of unconscious identification, that is, of *participation mystique* with the imaginary, discussed in Chap. 5. First of all, consumerism would become "sacred" for her, her *faith*, a totalizing worldview; the dream-world of consumption becomes her religious world. Thus consumerism would further shape and define her ego and her unconscious psyche—her imagination, emotions, desires, dreams. Put simply, if her ego and especially her unconscious *irrational functioning* are McDonaldized, then her reality and her life are McDonaldized—in a way, she will function psychologically like a McDonald's, replicating its ideology, according to its logic, following its dogmas: automatization and dehumanization resulting from the reduction of life to consumption and profit; behavior and emotions defined by consumption, homogenized, massified, reduced to the motifs of entertainment and fun; an ethics of spectacle, in which appearance is all that counts; and so on and so forth. Furthermore, because participation mystique is an unconscious, infantile state, she would remain childish, not autonomous, and dependent from constant consumption of dreams and images. In addition, one might predict that a psychic *split* would become more acute: within her psyche, a full separation from, and clash with, what is "elderly" in her, the principle that impulses her to grow into adulthood and its correspondent libido. Lastly, her "subjectivity" would be reduced to being another massified consumer—a consumystic, a faithful devotee of the McChurch of consumption.

Nevertheless, and to return to the dream narrative, the dream ends with the *perspective* of colonization: an ethical problem, the dilemma presented her by the unconscious. She half acknowledges ("kind of") that her plan is *sinful*—an expression that reveals that she still functions according to the old religious imaginary; and she sees the beauty (and possibly also the sacredness) of the church. The saints probably represent many things here, but some hypotheses seem more appropriate: they are symbolic *models* of conduct and development that stand in complete opposition to McDonaldization; they personify the religious attitude toward life had by unique *individuals*.

Being conscious of the problem, she had the chance, through her *will* and *action*, of changing it, of giving it a different solution. That was the purpose of the dream: that she acknowledged that "the place looked abandoned, [and] one would have to make many *renovations*". In thinking that, she still showed a truly religious attitude—which would have to be renovated instead of commodified. What was seemingly required by the unconscious was the adoption of an active stance *against* the collective gradient: symbolically, she would have to choose not to transform the church into a McDonald's, but rather to preserve the church, cleanse it, reform it, and participate in its rites. The church symbolized the possibility in her of constructing a *new meaning*, not one based on simulacra and total consumption. New meaning which entails reconnecting to her symbolic and religious roots. Seen on the subjective level, the dream points that such possibility is inside her—it is in her unconscious religious function. The recovery of which can only be built by consciousness and action, by the *individual* standing against the forces of commodification: standing *contra culturam*.

The consequences of the opposite attitude—of actualizing the plan of colonization—may be seen in the dream-image that appears *parallel* to McDonaldization: as the church was menaced by dovecots, transforming it into a McDonald's means that, symbolically, it *becomes* a dovecot, a deposit for atomized and dehumanized animals, who can only eat (consume) and excrete (dispose of) *en masse*. The dove here no longer is a symbol of the spirit (or of the soul); rather, it represents the McDonaldized consumer-subject as a perverted Pavlovian animal, the instinct debased to automatic response to stimuli. If I am not taking the dream-image too far, this would represent that, according to the dream criticism, living under the McChurch of Consumption™ means becoming an automatized pigeon-consumer amidst a mass of other identical pigeons: the perversion of both individual and social desires.

What is colonized: subjective identity; symbolico-religious function and imagination (dreamer's "church"); her unconscious psyche.

How it is colonized: identity (*participation mystique*) with the ImCon as simulacrum of religion; dreamer replicates collective consciousness and the cultural mutation in the imaginary (new church is consumption).

Effects of colonization: general effects of *participation mystique*; massification and dehumanization; infantilization and dependence.

9.2 The Massive Temple Dream

This dream, written by a married American woman in her 30s, is analogous to the prototype dream; however, here what is menaced by McDonaldization is quite different.

> *I dreamt of a massive stone temple, like the ones that you see as the Mayan ruins. Instead of going up into it, though, you went down into it, like a hole in the ground. It went down for levels. It was simple. No electricity. Just torches, and a simple chamber at the bottom with a stone altar. I felt wonderful there, I felt like I belonged there. I remember this feeling very distinctly. It was so overwhelming that I wanted to cry. The temperature was warm, not cold. I left the temple and was searching "someone" out, to share this or get some clarification about this place. When I returned, a group of people had bricked over the entrance, and I was very stressed. I was sneaking around looking for a way in. I recall that I thought I was going to be caught "by the Christians". The "coming soon" sign was a McDonald's (???). They were going to build a McDonald's over the entrance to this temple. I told "them" as they were starting to lay boards over the bricks, that something/someone (I can't remember exactly) was down there and we couldn't leave it down there, that it would die. They let me down there very reluctantly, and all I could think was that now they couldn't keep me from this place. I woke up, both stressed and happy.*
>
> *There are a few dreams that really stick in my memory. Most fade within a few minutes of waking. This one sticks.*

It is easy to see that the theme of this dream is the same of the previous dream: the "massive stone temple" and its McDonaldization, that is, the colonization of the sacred, the symbolico-religious function, and the unconscious psyche itself by the aura of capital and the imaginary of total consumption. However, this dream presents some specific characteristics, which are well worth of our attention. Let us follow the dream narrative and its sequence to understand those characteristics.

The exposition presents a peculiar temple, massive, underground, that invites the dreamer into the depths. The dream does not refer to institutionalized and contemporary religion, as in the church, but rather to something archaic, "massive" yet simple, that seems to have been forgotten (i.e., it is unconscious). Its massiveness is analogous to the *grandiosity* of the church in the previous dream. Its material, stone, presents an enormously rich symbolism.[4]

Chevalier and Gheerbrant (1969/1990, p. 751) mention the fundamental connection of the stone symbol with the psyche: "There is a close relationship between the soul and the stone." As an archetypal symbol, the stone stands for the stable, objective, perennial, even immortal foundations of the psyche (*soul*), which are always religious, that is, symbolically connected to the sacred and divine (and chthonic), and appears as such in virtually every religion and culture worldwide. In the West, its symbolism reaches its pinnacle in alchemy, where the stone (*lapis*) is the symbol of both the divinity and the possible *wholeness* of the human being (thus, a parallel symbol to Christ and the process of individuation). In sum, it is a symbol of the *Self*.[5] Von Franz (1964) further amplifies the stone symbol, mentioning some elements (which I emphasize) that are parallel to this dream and the dreamer's experience: "The alchemical stone (…) symbolizes something that can never be lost or dissolved, something eternal that some alchemists compared to the mystical experience of God *within one's own soul*" (p. 210; e.a.). It represents the solid, archaic, and "eternal" (i.e., suprapersonal, transcendental) foundations of the psyche, its wholeness: "a unity that merely exists, that was and is always there, unchanging. In this sense the stone symbolizes perhaps *the simplest* and at

[4] For extensive amplifications and analyses of this symbolism, see Jung (CW13, especially "The stone symbolism", pp. 94–101; and CW12), and Chevalier and Gheerbrant (1969/1990, pp. 751–758).

[5] Discussing the stone symbolism in alchemy, Jung wrote: "The attributes of the stone—incorruptibility, permanence, divinity, triunity, etc.—are so insistently emphasized that one cannot help taking it as the *deus absconditus* in matter. This is probably the basis of the lapis-Christ parallel (…) The lapis may therefore be understood as a symbol of the inner Christ, of God in man" (CW13, §127).

the same time *most profound* experience of the eternal and immutable a person can have" (Von Franz, 1997, p. 336; e.a).

The association with Mayan religion further stresses the archaic character: a 2000-year-old religion that defined and was the foundation of all aspects of life and reality, indeed, a very rich and truly symbolic religious imaginary that was *colonized* by Christianity under its imperialist form—the Spanish *conquistadores*.

The fact that the temple is underground points to a connection with the earth and nature, to its natural roots; moreover, it is something that is buried, unconscious, and secluded from normal and social life. In fact, what the dreamer does finds correspondence in the mythological motif of the *nekyia*,[6] the archetypical hero journey: descending into the depths, returning transformed, sharing the acquired knowledge.

Therefore, she descends into the unconscious depths—not only *her* personal unconscious but the *collective* unconscious, primeval, mysterious, historical, religious. Correspondingly, she enters upon an absolutely *symbolic* setting: archaic, autonomous, and autochthonous. There is no electricity, no man-made devices, and no people there; the torches, the light, and warmness (= libido) seem perennial as well, for they do not depend on human action—an autonomous dynamism, in stark contrast with the human deeds and the semiotic setting above.

Her feeling tone is very important: she obviously feels warm and belonging, for it is her inner roots—and at the same time mankind's—that she is discovering. It is noteworthy that she is *alone*, that is, as an *individual*, rather than amidst the mass. This discovery and experience has always been religious and *numinous* ("overwhelming"); one can say her *nekyia* is of an initiatory kind. The altar—as the place of sacrifice, ritual, consecration: of human relationship with the divine—stands as

---

[6] A *nekyia* involves a descent into hell, or into the underworld or the depths of the sea, that is, into the unconscious, "and a quest for the 'treasure hard to attain'" (Jung, CW9i, §311). However, in this dream there is a *discovery* of the inner treasure, and the quest is not *in* the depths: it consists rather in protecting them from colonization from "above". As an archetypal motif, the *nekyia* appears in the most different cultures and times: for instance, in the Sumerian Gilgamesh; in Greek hero myths such as Heracles's, Dionysus's, Hermes's, and Odysseus's; in the apocryphal accounts of Christ's descent into hell; in Buddha's descent into hell; in Jonah's journey in the depths of the sea, the hero devoured by the monster-whale; in Dante's *Divine Comedy*; and in Goethe's *Walpurgisnacht* in his *Faust*.

the solid religious function and foundation deep inside her unconscious, the center of the stone temple.[7] It is interesting that she does not see a divinity; one can think it is a *deus absconditus*, yet to be revealed and faced by her; or, alternatively, that "the center was empty".[8] In sum, she discovers (is initiated), alone and individually, her archaic religious function, a manifestation of the Self: the dream does not depict institutionalized religion, as in the church, but archetypal, and at once individual, religion—the autochthonous religious function of the psyche as the experience of her own symbolic roots: simple, perennial, giving a sense of integration, "wonderful".

Then she leaves the temple. Her intentions are typical: like people who undergo a numinous experience, or have a "big dream" (i.e., an archetypal dream), her natural reaction is to share that experience and try to understand it. Then she is faced with collective consciousness: the crowd. She does not seem to find anyone with whom she could share her experience. Instead, the crowd (standing for the mob, "mass mentality": consumerism's collective consciousness) blocks access to that kind of experience and all it entails, and seeks to take its place, in an analogous image to the dovecots of the previous dream. The dreamer has a different attitude here, though; instead of going along with the crowd, identified with it and thus being instrumental for the colonization and destruction of the temple (church), as the first dreamer "planned" to do, she feels or senses the value of such experience and runs *against* the crowd, getting very stressed—stress resulting from her resistance, the effort of an *opus contra culturam*.

Interestingly enough, the menacing mass mentality that blocks access to natural, archaic religiosity was personified by "the Christians": it is as if the primeval symbolic experience of the divinity that was once channeled and made possible by the Christian religion had become *perverted*.

---

[7] The altar here is the innermost symbol of the Self. To give a Christian parallel: "There the *rock* was Christ; for to us that is Christ which is placed on the altar of God" (St. Augustine, as cited in Jung, CW13: §313, note 6). The rock = the stone, symbolically.

[8] This is too long and a complex discussion to be dealt with here. However, to sum it up: Jung interprets the frequent appearance of such image in two possible manners—as the Tao, an oriental historical image of the Self in which the center is indeed empty, and as a consequence of the bankruptcy of the Christian system of symbols, which can no longer express the unconscious original contents, thus making the center empty.

The association with Mayan religion comes to mind: an archaic symbolic religion, in which the individuals and the whole culture were "linked by myth with the world of the ancestors, and thus with nature truly experienced and not merely seen from outside" (Jung, MDR, p. 114), colonized by a Christianity that was more and more perverted, brutal, and imperialistic—that, in fact, was sustained by a colonial totalitarianism, the Inquisition. Then, finally, the menace appears in its final, concrete form: what buries such primordial religious experience is once again McDonald's.

However, McDonaldization in this dream does not transform and colonize something already instituted but rather blocks access to something primal, individual, and symbolic, covering it with *signs*: simulacra of consumption disfiguring and burying the symbolic, religious function—in fact attempting to subjugate and replace *the unconscious itself*, the archetypal foundations that are the very source of religion and symbol.

In other words, this dream places *McDonaldization as parallel and analogous to Christian colonization*: as the Mayan religion encompassed *all aspects of life*, now McDonald's—the ImCon itself—aspires and tries to do the same: to become a totalizing imaginary. It is a symbolic image of a *mutation* or *colonization of imaginaries*. Augé (1999, p. 5) points that the historical roots of such aspiration, its genealogy, are the same: "the Church's active efforts—throughout a period which Jacques Le Goff has described as a 'long Middle Ages'—to alter the dreams and re-fashion the imagination of peoples imbued with paganism." That is, colonization of the dreams and imagination—of the symbolic systems, the imaginary—was an integral part of colonialism since the very beginning; through it, a thorough psychological reconfiguration of the conquered peoples was effected. That is what is represented in the dream—although now minds and imagination are colonized by simulacra and ideology, rather than by different symbols and gods and narratives. Therefore the *dream recapitulates a historical fact*, and warns the dreamer that it can happen to her, for it is happening globally: just as the Mayan culture was conquered and enslaved by Christianity through the forceful remaking of their animist, archaic imaginary and religion, now she is confronted with the colonization of every kind of imaginary, in fact of the inner source of the imaginary, the archetypal well, by the new simulacrum of "Christianity": the McChurch of Consumption, the ImCon.

Through this dream, we can see again the ironic criticism of our age formulated autonomously by the unconscious, and the confrontation of imaginaries it depicts. What is "coming soon" is not the Messiah, redemption, or religious rebirth. It is the second coming of capitalism, the parousia of total commodification—the last days of religion and individuality, apotheosis of the sign and simulacra: the eschatology of final and total consumption.

That is the kernel, or main problem, of the dream. In comparison with the prototype dream, here the overwhelming process of colonization seems to happen *automatically*, by default, like the functioning of a mass mentality. "Christians" here are already McDonaldized: Christianity has been effectively replaced by the McChurch.[9] Again, in relation to the first dream, here the *attitude* of the dreamer in relation to colonization is different (and shows that individual choice and action can, and do, change the situation, the conflict): she senses (unconsciously) that there is "something/someone" *alive* down in the temple and that it would *die* as a result of McDonaldization. "Something/someone" is an appropriate expression for what she experienced but that was not personified or apparent in the temple: for the Self (and its religious function) can appear personified (anthropomorphized), or as "something" impersonal (a stone, a diamond), a mandala, or as the divinity (see Jung, CW9ii). At any rate, she *knows* that it was something of the utmost importance. Thus the solution (*lysis*) of the dream narrative is positive: she *goes against* the gradient presented by the massified collective mentality (which embodies the colonizing force of total consumption, crystallized in the McDonald's sign) and manages to descend once more to her profundity, to her archaic, *ancestral*[10] symbolico-religious center, the very origin of

[9] Perhaps this image reflects a difference in cultures (American and Brazilian), in that consumerism is much more "total" (and thus "religious") in the United States than in Brazil.

[10] Indeed, seen symbolically, Mayan religion and culture can represent at once her own ancestral roots *and* her culture's. As Jung interprets, speaking of an analogous dream in which a symbol of the spirit appears: "Why should it be Mexican? (…) She is an American woman. Yes, [together with the Indians] these are her ancestors who are connected with the soil (…) her spiritual ancestors" (SVI, p. 1046).

numen and value, to her Self as her innermost individuality and source of dreams.

The feeling tone she wakes up to is in harmony with her correct attitude: now she knows there is such a place, such experience; she knows and will not forget the value of such living thing, and that it ultimately *depends on her individual attitude*, and thus she feels happy. We have reason to believe that, like the first dreamer, she did not understand consciously the dream—in fact, she was astounded by the dream-imagery, as her many question marks after "McDonald's" indicate, in her narrative of the dream. Yet the feeling tone does not need to be understood to be effective. Indeed, this dream presents many of the characteristics of a "big dream": an archetypal dream.

What is colonized: symbolico-religious functioning; dreamer's own unconscious psyche, including the collective unconscious, and in fact her Self—her innermost individuality.

How it is colonized*: signs* cover and replace the symbolic; reflects cultural process of colonization of imaginaries and institution of consumption as a totalizing "religious" imaginary (as a mass mentality).

Effects of colonization: analogous to the previous dream, but here the dream indicates that the symbolico-religious function and the Self would *die* in her—they would be effaced.

Next two archetypal dreams are presented, dreams had by historical figures, Walter Benjamin and C. G. Jung, in different historical and cultural (European) contexts. Although they do not refer directly to consumption and its imaginary, they present images, symbols, and meanings that are analogous to the others' dreams in this chapter. Furthermore, they also portray the *opposite* of colonization: like in the beginning of the dream above, they symbolize the rediscovery and possible rescue of the symbolic and religious—both within the person and in culture. Thus, comparing and contrasting how the oneiric symbolic representations and their meanings appeared then, in their context, and now, in the contemporary consumption dreams, can be useful for understanding and illuminating further the historical character and the enormous significance of the colonization of "all that is sacred".

9.3 Underground Works: *Walter Benjamin's Dream*

This dream-image is found in Benjamin's *Einbahnstraße*, from 1928; to my knowledge, he never published any interpretation or commentary on it. The title, "Underground Works", is his.

> *In a dream, I saw barren terrain. It was the marketplace at Weimar. Excavations were in progress. I, too, scraped about in the sand. Then the tip of a church steeple came to light. Delighted, I thought to myself: a Mexican shrine* from the time of pre-animism, *from the Anaquivitzli. I awoke laughing. (*Ana = ἀνά; vi = vie; witz *[joke] = Mexican church [!]).* (Benjamin, 1928/1996b, p. 455)

Having only this short oneiric narrative and a few associations, it is difficult to ascertain an interpretation. Yet, its main theme seems clear and is parallel to the "massive temple" dream: here Benjamin discovers the temple, the *sacred*—what he called "mythic forces"—in its primordial form (pre-animist), also underground, underneath the marketplace. One might venture the idea that, in the same way that McDonald's stood for consumerism in the previous dream, here the temple is *buried* under the signifying *market*: it is capitalist culture that overlays the original symbolico-religious foundations.

Weimar obviously represents Benjamin's immense German cultural heritage: the main historical origin, foundation, and apogee of his contemporary collective consciousness. Thus it is meaningful that even Weimar appears as a barren terrain: it is as if the marketplace—the establishment of capitalism—had dried up even such symbolical and cultural wealth, at least on the surface: it establishes itself atop all that is sacred, feeding off the very spring of culture and leaving the colonized soil arid, sterile, without *seeds*. This image seems analogous to the previous dream, in which the symbolico-religious spring would actually *die* if buried (colonized) by total consumerism.

Such spring is symbolized as a church that, fantastically enough, again appears in the guise of an archaic Mexican temple, this time pre-animist. The concept of pre-animism comes from the British anthropologist R. R. Marett, and refers to the primordial and universal stage of religion characterized by belief in and emotional reaction to the supernatural, impersonal, and dynamic power, *mana*. Therefore the characterization of the temple as "pre-animist" in Benjamin's dream confirms what was argued in relation to the "massive temple": both temples refer symbolically to the source of primordial *mana*, or *numina*—the archetypal-symbolic foundation, the collective unconscious as archaic ontology of all the sacred and the psyche.

Moreover, the temple being "Mexican" symbolizes the same as "Mayan" in the previous dream: according to Kraniauskas (1994), Benjamin's interest in ancient Mexican culture was mainly associated with the imperialism and colonialism to which it was subjected. That is, his dream-image repeats the theme of *colonization* of the sacred and its primeval source by capitalism, and presents the same analogy with Christianity's colonialism of religious imaginaries.

Based on such hermeneutic discussion, the interpretation of Benjamin's dream can be summarized under two complementary forms. An interpretation on the *objective level* would propose that Benjamin, through his dreams, view, and works (his archaeological "excavations"), finds in his *culture*, underlying all the history and cultural wealth of Weimar,[11] its original and primeval religious origins—what gives birth to all culture: the archetypal symbol. On a more *subjective level*, the dream is quite similar to the previous one: the archetypal shrine represents *his own* underground religious function. That is, underneath the whole cultural legacy that constituted Benjamin's psyche (the German collective consciousness within him), he, like the previous dreamer, finds and brings to light the *sacred*, buried in the depths of the unconscious: the primordial pre-animistic religious function, the holy foundation of his psyche.

Common to both interpretative levels, however, is the idea that, from a seemingly barren cultural terrain, Benjamin unearths the *archetypal*: the *seed* that represents the "suppressed past" (Benjamin, 1940) of mankind, the symbolico-religious capacity in each one's psyche that virtually contains our entire history. A beautiful image, the typical Benjaminian task: to rescue the symbolic seeds of the past, the origins of the sacred—both

[11] In fact, the etymology of "Weimar" points to a religious foundation: *wih*, holy + *mari*, standing water (Günther, Huschke, & Steiner, 1993, p. 494). "Holy water" = the unconscious.

in himself, in the profundity of his psyche, and in his specific culture. The effects that such discovery of the inner sacred grounds causes seem analogous to the previous dreamer's experience—Benjamin is delighted and wakes up laughing, probably touched, having discovered life, the sacred,[12] in the undergrounds.

Thus, if Nietzsche had denounced that the gods had been "murdered in the marketplace"—the archetypal-symbolic killed by a rationalist capitalist culture—Benjamin, in his epoch, could still discover the gods *underneath that same marketplace*.[13] For, *contra* Nietzsche, the "gods" never die; as long as there exists a human psyche, the source of their numinosity and symbol will be there, deep down, autonomous, and alive. As in the previous dream, here the gods are not dead: they have just been buried.

Thus, if seen on a cultural level, both dreams represent the colonization of imaginaries in their different epochs—both depicting how capitalism-consumerism buries and conquers the sacred, the symbolic imaginaries, *following the colonial ethos of Christianity*, and assumes their places and roles. In fact, such symbolic image is also historical: colonization traditionally involved the conquerors building their temples on top of the conquered people's sanctuaries—the main sign and reminder of conquest and subjugation for the colonized people was, therefore, that their religious-symbolic imaginary had been erased and replaced.

This historical and ontological relation between capitalism and Christianity as colonizing imaginaries, symbolized by the dreams, was in fact theorized by Benjamin: "The Christianity of the reformation period did not favour the development of capitalism, but *transformed itself into capitalism*" (Benjamin, 1921/1996a, p. 290). The corollary of

[12] Unfortunately, I did not understand his comment about "Anaquivitzli", the underground shrine, and could not find any enlightening commentary about it in the literature. Perhaps its meaning has to do with this idea: "ana" = on board, upward, on; "vie" = life; "witz" = wit, joke, humor (laugh). It might mean that such primeval numinosity, symbolized as the Mexican church, represents to be fully "on board" life, to live in connection with the archetypal roots, within a symbolic imaginary—a sacred and humorous life, warm and happy like the previous dreamer felt when in touch with its roots.

[13] The comparison with the previous dreams is striking: in our epoch, it seems that anything sacred and symbolic—in both culture and the individual—is menaced by *automatic* commodification and absorption into a system of signs (i.e., by compulsory McDonaldization).

this post-Weberian theory is that capitalism became a religion—a cultic religion that, as argued regarding the ImCon, *subjugates all meaning and signification*: "Capitalism is a pure religious cult, perhaps the most extreme there ever was. Within it everything only has meaning in direct relation to the cult"—a cult celebrated "sans trêve et sans merci" (p. 288). In some sense, Benjamin described what all the dreams above symbolize: cultic capitalism-consumerism burying the mythico-religious imaginaries, taking their place "as a sort of diabolic religion" (Löwy, 2010)—a phantasmagoric, *ideological* imaginary that intoxicated collective consciousness.

And, if these dreams portray essentially the same phenomenon in distinct epochs, it is indeed vital to remind of its historical consequences for Benjamin's time and culture. As mentioned, the outcome of such mutation of imaginaries was devastating: capitalism as a religion mutated into Nazism—a truly totalitarian imaginary based upon the manipulation of religious and mythic forces, of the *irrational*, the German collective unconscious. Then ideology really became a nihilistic religion. Only a few years after Benjamin recorded this dream, the archaic "mythic forces" buried in the German psyche—the ghosts of the marketplace reawakened with the *Traumschlaf* of capitalism—would take Weimar and almost all of Europe by storm. No more pre-animist shrines: Weimar became Buchenwald.

9.4 Underground Divinity: *Jung's Dream*

Jung published this dream,[14] which he had around 1880, in *Memories, Dreams, Reflections* (Jung, MDR). However, as the published version has been heavily edited and is too long, here I provide Shamdasani's (2009) condensed account of it, emphasizing the symbols that are analogous (or even identical) to the symbols in the "massive temple" dream narrative.

[14] The title "underground divinity" is my invention. Alongside its parallel symbology to the last two dreams, this dream is analyzed here especially because it is essential for the discussion of the next dream on McDonaldization.

> *[Jung] found himself in a meadow with a* stone-*lined* hole in the ground. *Finding some* stairs, *he* descended into it, *and found himself in a* chamber. *Here there was a golden throne with what appeared to be a tree trunk of skin and flesh, with an eye on the top. He then heard his mother's voice exclaim that this was the "man-eater." He was unsure whether she meant that this figure actually devoured children or was identical with Christ. This profoundly affected his image of Christ. Years later, he realized that this figure was a penis and, later still, that it was in fact a ritual phallus, and that the setting was an* underground temple. *He came to see this dream as an* initiation *"in the secrets of the earth."* (p. 194; e.a.)

Jung had this dream when he was only four years old; it deeply affected him and occupied him all his life. The parallels to the massive temple dream are obvious.[15] The mysterious, numinous atmosphere is the same (although probably much more pronounced in Jung's dream), as well as the character of initiation. The main difference is that here there is absolutely no hint of *colonization* of the temple.

On the contrary, there occurs an actual *epiphany*. Instead of an empty altar, and instead of what Jung called the failed symbol of "Lord Jesus", here the divinity becomes manifest in the guise of the *phallus*, which "seems to be a subterranean God 'not to be named'", the "underground counterpart" (Jung, MDR, p. 28) of the Christian divinity: the archetypal symbol of chthonic and masculine creative force. The symbolism of the phallus, being archetypal, appears across all cultures and ages. "The phallus is the source of life and libido, the creator and worker of miracles, and as such it was worshipped everywhere" (Jung, CW5, §147). In the ancient Hindu imaginaries, for instance, it had (and still has) a fundamental role as the omnipresent *lingam*.

One can notice that this dream also presents a problematization of Christianity. Indeed, the broad historical (and actually *familiar*) context of Jung's dream was the ruin of Christianity and its faiths, the volatilization of the sacred announced by Marx. Hegel and Nietzsche had announced the death of God; as Benjamin contended, Catholicism was turning into the desacralized religion of capitalism. Thus, whereas the

[15] Another parallel image is in Jung's own dream narrative: "It was fairly light in the room, although there were no windows and no apparent source of light" (Jung, MDR, p. 12).

gods were dead for culture—its symbolic imaginaries vanishing, decaying, withering away—the dream revealed their very sources in the depths of the psyche, of Nature (the "meadows") within us: the unconscious,[16] our archetypal psychic rhizome.

Compared with Benjamin's dream, in which he had to excavate culture, in Jung's late nineteenth-century Europe, it was still possible to find the sacred in *Nature* (both without and within), untouched, un-colonized, uncommodified: pure symbol and mana, pure archetype. Far from representing the barren terrain instituted by the market, here the meadows hide the archaic procreative power itself, enduring and eternal. Neither Jung nor Benjamin, however, ever dreamed that a day would come when such roots would be in jeopardy of being seized and replaced by consumerism in the spectacular form of McDonaldization.

The presumable subjective effects that such colonization—of the archetypal foundation underground and its manifestations—would represent can be seen in all the dreams analyzed so far. Yet, they become clearer if one *compares* them to the way such foundation appeared in Jung's dream, and the importance it had for him.

Seen theoretically, what appears in the underground is the *archetype* that organizes and impulses libido, as creative energy, and thereby the whole psyche. It is manifest as a god-image, one of the transcendental dominants that, as religious symbols, have always guided all human action. It simply symbolizes one's own *living roots within*, the connection with Nature, the basal foundation of *being*.

Accordingly, this dream of an archetypal creative divinity defined Jung's theory, practice, and, in fact, his whole life.[17] To understand the fact symbolized by the dream—that our psychic roots are archetypal and *universal*—and to formulate a whole psychological theory grounded on it came to constitute his life task, indeed, his *destiny*.

Can destiny be colonized?

---

[16] As the German Romantics held, the unconscious *is* Nature within us.

[17] He wrote that such dream "laid the foundations for everything that was to fill the second half of my life with the stormiest passion" (Jung, MDR, p. 30). In fact this dream also condenses the enormous and crucial distance between his worldview and theory, and Freud's, who would see the *phallus* as concrete penis, biological sexuality, and so on, thus representing the very destruction of the symbolic and religious—in culture and in the psyche—by determinist, materialist ideology.

9.5 Underground Divinity II: *A Ronald McDonald Dream*

This dream was published some years ago by a young American male. He was clearly astonished by it and still did not understand it.

> *I had this dream when I was very young … about 4 or 5. I went downstairs in my basement before carpet was put in; it was dark. All of a sudden there appeared this giant column (like the ones at the White House). The strange thing about the column was that a giant head was on it. It wasn't just any head, it was Ronald McDonald's head. It looked like a robot. The Ronald McDonald suddenly said in a robot voice, "You may go … now". So I ran upstairs and I was freaking out.*

Quite frankly, I found this dream specimen one of the most meaningful and telling dreams I have ever seen. The parallel with Jung's dream is astounding: both dreamers had the dreams at more or less the same age[18]; their imagery and narratives are quite analogous; and their meanings could not be more apart.

The oneiric narrative begins with the motif of *descent*, this time into the basement: here it is in his house, rather than in Nature. As a symbol, the house represents his personality, his psyche.[19] Yet, being a five-year-old child, and the house being in fact the parents' house, it also represents his family's *mentality*, its specific psychological atmosphere[20] that shapes and informs the child's psyche, for he is part of it, in *participation mystique*. The basement is obviously the unconscious, what is underneath and dark, analogous to "the underground" in the other dreams: the hidden foundations. However, being immediately below normal everyday

[18] The fact that the dreamer remembers in detail a dream from his very early childhood obviously means that it was experienced as something very important and charged emotionally (i.e., numinous), like Jung's dream.

[19] And also his body. This is archetypal symbolism: see Jung (MHS). See also Jung (MDR, pp. 170ff) for an important dream of Jung's, had when he was going to the United States with Freud, in 1909, in which the house represented his psyche (including what he later saw as the collective unconscious and its prehistoric layers).

[20] Formed mainly by the parents (and extended family), in their conscious and unconscious psyches and relations (i.e., their complexes).

consciousness, it probably stands for the more personal unconscious—as seen in Chap. 2, the complexes that, reflecting the *représentations collectives*, form the psychic layer that functions as the connection with the archetypal-instinctual foundation, and *expresses* it.

At any rate, it is in these inner psychic recesses that, like Jung, the dreamer is confronted with a similar and sudden epiphany of an underground divinity. It appears as a column, presumably made of stone, with a giant head on top. If one proceeds with a thorough *amplification* of such symbol, the parallels with the previous dream (including the "divine" character of the apparition) become clear.

A stone pillar or column with a head on top is an archetypal image. While the head usually represented a deity, the conjunct had a *phallic* character, representing the invigorative, creative energy of nature that, as a "column" or "pillar", sustains and structures life. Being an archetypal motif, the parallel forms under which it materializes in different cultures and epochs are innumerous. For the Ancient Greeks, it appeared as the *stele*, originally connected to Hermes:

> *stele*, the pillar with the head on top, is supposed to have given the name to this peculiar god. (…) But Hermes is also phallic, his first statues in Greece were just phallic poles. A stele (…) with a head on top was called a *herm*. And in the archaic tradition, they were always characterized by a phallus in the center [and were] worshiped in the way of a lingam, or phallus. (Jung, SVI, pp. 910–924)

In Hebrew these sacred stones or pillars are called *matzevot*; they appear in several places in the Old Testament. In Genesis (28:18, 31:45, 35:14, 35:20), for instance, it is said that Jacob erected four matzevot. Deuteronomy 16:22, however, later connects them to a prohibition: "You shall not erect a stone pillar" (a matzevah), "for such the Lord your G-d detests": the pillars came to be the structures that signified idol-worship, that is, they essentially symbolized *idolatry*, the worship of *false* deities—of images that were simulations.

This last meaning provides the key for interpretation. The dream seems to use the symbol of column with head in all three senses, of stele, god-image, and matzevah: it symbolizes a *false god*, a simulation in the form of image. Ronald McDonald, and the dream-world it signifies, does not bear any relation whatsoever with any true religious symbols, gods, or referents: it is a creature of imagineering, a simulated replacement for the sacred. Thus, instead of a numinous, invisible presence, as in the massive temple dream, and instead of an archetypal phallus, as in Jung's dream, here the underground divinity is *a simulacrum of god*, one of the maximum signifying *idols* of consumerism as a simulation of religion.

If this interpretation is correct, then this short dream appears to condense, in a symbolic narrative, some central problems of consumerism and postmodernity: the interrelationships and the crucial effacement of distinctions between imaginary, dream, and reality; truth and falsehood; human, inhuman, and artificial; symbol, sign, and simulacrum; and *the highest symbol and referent*, God. With this dream,

> the question returns to *religion and the simulacrum of divinity*: "I forbade that there be any simulacra in the temples because the divinity that animates nature can never be represented." Indeed it can be. But what becomes of the divinity when it reveals itself in icons, when it is multiplied in simulacra? Does it remain the supreme power that is simply incarnated in images as a visible theology? Or does it *volatilize itself in the simulacra* that, alone, deploy their power and pomp of fascination—the visible machinery of icons substituted for the pure and intelligible Idea of God? (Baudrillard, 1981/1994, p. 4; e.a.)

Having volatilized and colonized all that is sacred and symbolic, in the dream technological capitalism-consumerism seemingly answers Baudrillard's essential question: "But *what if God himself can be simulated*, that is to say can be reduced to the signs that constitute faith? Then the whole system becomes weightless, it is no longer itself anything but a gigantic simulacrum" (p. 6; e.a.). As argued, such weightless machinery of icons corresponds to the imaginary of consumption as a religion of simulacra—symbolized in a child's dream as an artificial clown, an unchained and tremendously fun *commodity-sign*. A sort of ominous oneiric confirmation of Baudrillard's claim: "God is not dead, he has become hyperreal" (p. 159).

Again, if such hypothetical interpretation makes sense, in this dream the ImCon's totalizing ideology seems to function as an inner psychic deity, or *dominant*. Just like in Jung's dream, it operates as a primordial image "underground"—like the numinous archetypes, "the foundation *stones* of the psychic structure" (Jung, CW9ii, §40; e.a.), here it appears as a structural ("column") foundation of the child's own psychic "basement" (which is in fact his family's unconscious mentality, which reproduces a tendency of his whole *culture*).

Even though a dream is only a possibility, one can imagine the mighty subjective *effects* this kind of colonization can represent. In essence, they would be equivalent to those mentioned in relation to Jung's dream: functioning like an archetype, the ideology defines the dreamer's whole psychic functioning—it coordinates, organizes, and directs his perception, his libido, his creativity, his goals, his *psyche*; it precedes reality. That is, it possibly defines his destiny.

But, returning to the specificity of the dream, it is Ronald McDonald that embodies such ideology, manifest as a phantasmagoric automaton, "a neo-Orwellian, mechanical" (Mestrovic, 1997, p. 26) deity. Thus what characterizes the McDonaldization of psyche here is not merely what Ritzer (2000) called "instrumental rationality", but the *automaton*: the mechanization and automation of the psyche. As it rules over the basement (the foundations), it is an apt symbol for Guattari's (1979/2010) *machinic unconscious*. Therefore everything that was discussed (in Chap. 6) about the McDonaldization of the emotional, the imagination, the irrational, and so on applies to this dream symbol and can be seen as possible effects. However, Ronald seems to rule *from* the unconscious: it is a "giant *head*" that *commands* the dreamer ("You may go now"), which probably means that the goal is ruling the whole psyche, the *mind*. That would imply mutating the dreamer into a head that is a commodity-sign and functions automatically, only expressing itself (its voice) mechanically, reproducing (echoing) the ImCon's industrialized discourse, its ideology, like a robot.

Yet, perhaps the most important effect is what is more specific to Ronald: it symbolizes the totalization of *emotions* as automatized *simulations*. It is like having Chief Happiness Officer as a dominant in your underground psyche: you shall *always* be happy, fun, and mightily entertaining. That is, a consumer-subject whose emotions are reduced to "I'm lovin' it" and "havin' fun", a commodified being who automatically replicates a "postemotional society" (Mestrovic, 1997) characterized by the "McDonaldization of emotion, the abolishment of the boundaries between authentic and inauthentic feelings" (Vester, 1999, p. 26), the mass production of dead, abstracted, prepackaged emotions as "happy meals" (Mestrovic, 1997, p. xi).

To summarize, the dream alerts that the dominant unconscious force for the child is to become a consumer as an automaton-clown: an identification that is not merely dehumanizing, but *inhuman*. In fact this image means not mere ego identification, but *mimesis* with the imaginary, at the level of simulacra. It starts with the unconscious psyche being colonized: here it effectively becomes an underground temple of consumption, a McChurch—the foundation of a *consumer as homo simulacrum*. As McDonald's 2001 slogan in Canada ran, *There's a Little McDonald's in Everyone*. Indeed.

Lastly, some final words comparing these last dreams in cultural terms. As André Vieira (Feb 2012, personal communication) pointed, juxtaposing Jung's and Benjamin's dreams with the other consumption dreams (and especially with this last dream) unveils an enormous difference of societies and epochs: through their symbols, they reflect social worlds and historical moments (Europe at the end of the nineteenth century and beginning of the twentieth century; and America and Brazil at the beginning of the twenty-first century) that seem amazingly different, even antagonistic. As argued throughout this work, such juxtaposition appears to illuminate a thorough *mutation of imaginaries*. In this last dream, such mutation may be seen condensed in the *column*, symbolizing the (social and symbolic) *structuring* role for each subjective psyche: it is associated with the White House but appears as an *icon* of a global megacorporation. Perhaps this means that, within consumption society (but especially in the United States), the mythic power, the main signifying and structuring institution, foundation stone, or *dominating imaginary*, is obviously not religion or the Church any longer, but not even the state (= White House), where it used to be projected: it is in the *image*, in the psychic control or "government" it effectuates both without and within. The social power to command is in the imaginary of consumption: not in a pre-animist religious source, not in the archetypal creativity of a divinity; the gods have disappeared, and what governs and defines the subject is McChurch and Ronald McDonald.

If that is so, then the fact that the dream shows the underground deity as a simulacrum reflects *culture*, the ImCon as a simulacrum of religion and its pantheon of icons. It hints at an ontological mutation of the subject (becoming a simulacrum) that mirrors a cultural mutation (a culture of simulacra) that is typically American, but clearly going global (as McDonaldization, indeed a McWorld).

Of course this is just *a dream*, a child's dream—but, if seen with the other dreams presented here, it begs the frightening question: is it possible that such religion of signs and simulacra may indeed be becoming the totalizing definer of our culture, and as such be replacing every historical, symbolical, and cultural root in the psyche? That would mean that, like this dreamer's psyche, minds are being colonized from the cradle by the market divinities, their absolute simulacra enshrined *within*. A structural colonization of the psyche since early childhood: the dream of mass-producing subjects as McConsumers.

What is colonized: unconscious psyche (personal unconscious, but also archetype, primordial image); emotions; libido; hints at possible colonization of *mind*, of whole subject.

How it is colonized: ImCon appears to function as a deity, an archetype (within the unconscious); structural colonization of the psyche.

Effects of colonization: ideology defines psychic and emotional functioning as if it were an archetypal substratum; replication of the ImCon, as machinization and automation of the subject.

9.6 McDonaldization of the Country

Dream had some years ago by an American male, in his early 20s.

> *I am watching the news when they announce that McDonald's is being nationalized. Then I am out driving around, and I come to this big fortified McDonald's, which was just like a big army base. I knew that someone had to do something or else McDonald's would take over the country ... so I attacked the McDonald's armed only with a spork.*

This dream seems fairly self-explanatory. Again, the interpretations on the subjective and objective levels can and ought to be seen as complementary and interrelated: one mirrors the other. The dream theme is McDonald's "taking over the country". Thus, seen on the objective level (i.e., culturally), it symbolizes the possibility of a complete McDonaldization of the whole of American culture, the entire country; all its imaginaries, its collective consciousness *totalized* by the imaginary of consumption. Surprisingly, the ImCon's imperialist colonial power is shown as a *military* one. This image is probably analogous to the association with the White House in the previous dream: the main institutions that used to signify sociocultural power (the state, the army, the Church) appear McDonaldized; again, what holds power (or governs) now is the image—and consumption.

On an interpretation on the subjective level, the dream means that the ImCon is about to take over the dreamer's psychic "country"; his psychological *Lebenswelt* is in danger of being McDonaldized. In fact the dream implies a forceful colonization of his whole psychic system, a full identification with collective consciousness; but, given his ego attitude of resistance, perhaps one can assume that what is in danger is primarily his ego. Nevertheless, as some of his other dreams revealed a deep identification with cultural icons (i.e., with commodities from the culture industry), both hypotheses should be considered. At any rate, the value of this dream lies more in its depiction of the cultural colonization (i.e., on its cultural critique; on its meaning on an objective level).

It is noticeable that total colonization is just announced as a normal fact—and through mass media. The dreamer's immediate response is to *move*, to do something (drive around); this foreshadows his later reaction (to resist). Then the power of McDonaldization is revealed as equivalent to the army in a war of conquest. Contrasting with its imaginary of mindless fun, fantasy, and food, here it is presented as a fortified war *machine*, hierarchical, ruthless, rational, and so on which as a matter of fact it also is.

The dreamer attempts to resist by fighting such colossal power with the *spork*: the dream (i.e., the unconscious) is again being sarcastic. Fighting with useless weapons is a typical dream motif (Jung, CW18, §477). What should be a *symbol*, the weapon against the semiotic imaginary, uniting different meanings and the opposites (spoon and fork, thrown together into "spork"), here has already been commodified into an InCom *sign*: a tool used to *consume* their products. The fact that he is "armed" with it means that *he can only be another McConsumer*. There are only signs; there is no way out, "all forms of escape are eventually co-opted" (Mestrovic, 1997, p. 147). If one can only fight back with the tools of colonization, there is no possible movement *contra culturam*: total colonization is inexorable.

However, perhaps the dreamer can still attempt to resist precisely because the colonization, however total, remains on the *surface*, in contrast with the previous dreams. That is probably why the dream does not mention any religious aspects (which would be related to the *depths*, to the unconscious psyche), but more of a war-like scenario above—a war of images and signs. Regardless, there is no *lysis*, no solution: the likely *effect* is that everything will be colonized, and the dreamer is foredoomed to becoming a citizen of McCountry. We can presume it will be a fully entertaining and fun experience.

What is colonized: the whole "country". Psychologically, ego consciousness.

How it is colonized: as a natural fact (it simply happens), but also "militarily"—the imaginary appears as a supreme power (like the army).

Effects of colonization: total colonization (it is portrayed as a total imaginary). For the subject,: it becomes impossible to resist, to live differently.

9.7 Final Remarks

Reiterating, the dreams analyzed in this chapter focused on forms of colonization by the ImCon related to the psychic symbolico-religious function—that is, to imagination and fantasy, to the *unconscious psyche*. However, several other dreams researched presented many other instances of McDonaldization. For example, in two of them the dreamers were to celebrate their *marriages* at McDonald's,[21] which, just like in the dreams

[21] Actually I wrote the interpretations for these dreams, under the subtitle "*McMarriages at the McChurch:* I'm lovin' it", but decided against including them in this work, for they were not clear

above, did not appear as a real church, but *functioned* as one. Thus they can be seen as a complementary depiction of the McDonaldization of cultural rites and institutions, of the *sacred and symbolic*, and of the automation and commodification of *emotions*, in fact of our main symbol of emotional relationship, of love as a sacred institution. In other dreams, McDonald's also appeared as destructive technological artifacts (in one dream it appeared as a *toy*) that "possessed" consumers (possesses = commands, takes full control of the psyche); in a dream it shares the scene with Wal-Mart, signifying devastating invasions by aliens or animal monsters. There were also an incredible number of dreams in which Ronald McDonald appeared as a scary, at times terrifying, image. Some were reoccurring nightmares, had since childhood,[22] in which Ronald figured as a source of evil, or as a ghost, a menacing invisible presence (a phantasmagoria). A particularly meaningful dream showed the characters of McDonaldland, including Ronald as a mighty giant, as *demigods* in a childish world, with whom the dreamer identified, fascinated. This McDreamworld of consumption apparently became the dreamer's own imaginary: later he dreams frequently that he *lives* alone in a secluded, empty part of a dark *shopping mall*.[23]

However, the McChurch dreams above were chosen because, in my opinion, they represented the deepest and most important form of colonization: the ImCon becoming a simulacrum of religion within the

---

enough and would require mentioning many personal details from the dreamers.

[22] In order to understand such phenomena, one ought to take into consideration that Ronald can also appear simply as a *clown* symbol, in its negative, shadow aspect: like in Nietzsche's *Zarathustra*, as the jester or buffoon, and in many movies and cultural products, the clown also denotes tragedy, violence, primitivity, etc., all of which, together with the ubiquity of McDonald's signs in the United States, would represent impressive material for the suggestible imagination of children. What I want to convey is, such dreams do not necessarily have *consumption* as their *main* theme; but they do show how ubiquitous the ImCon is.

[23] This represents another instance of identity with the ImCon (here appearing as McDonald's simulacra *and* the mall), which produces a consumer characterized by what Augé called a fictional self: "The fictional self, the peak of a *fascination* which is begun in any relationship exclusive to the image, is *a self without relationship* [alone] and as a result without any basis for identity, *liable to be absorbed by the world of images* [the shopping mall, McDonaldland] in which it believes it can rediscover and recognise itself" (Augé, 1999, pp. 116–117; e.a.). Here the dreamer lives what the band The Clash sang decades earlier: *I'm all lost in the supermarket/I can no longer shop happily/ I came in here for that special offer/ A guaranteed personality* (Strummer & Jones, 1979). These dreams also show how the unconscious employs related symbols, or dreamscapes, alternately—McDonald's, shopping malls, department stores—for what is essentially the same colonization dynamics.

subjects' psyches. An attempted colonization of their *inner* worlds, aiming at turning their lives into McDreams, their psychic structure and functioning determined by the ideology of consumption. As the last dream portrays, such process happens alongside the colonization of the "outer" world; both are essential for the globalitarian objective of consumerism: in dominating the "country" (the whole of culture) *and* its subjects (as a mass that reproduces its ideology), everything becomes an ImCon dreamscape—a totalizing imaginary.

References

Augé, M. (1999). *The war of dreams: exercises in ethno-fiction* (L. Heron, Trans.). London: Pluto Press.

Baudrillard, J. (1981). *For a critique of the political economy of the sign*. St. Louis, MO: Telos Press. (Original work published 1973).

Baudrillard, J. (1994). *Simulacra and simulation* (S. F. Glaser, Trans). Ann Arbor, MI: University of Michigan Press. (Original work published 1981).

Benjamin, W. (1940). *On the concept of history* (D. Redmond, Trans.). Retrieved from http://www.marxists.org/reference/archive/benjamin/1940/history.htm

Benjamin, W. (1996a). Capitalism as religion. In M. P. Bullock & M. W. Jennings (Eds.), *Walter Benjamin selected writings, Vol. 1: 1913–1926* (pp. 288–291). Cambridge, MA: Harvard University Press. (Original work written 1921).

Benjamin, W. (1996b). One-way street. In M. P. Bullock & M. W. Jennings (Eds.), *Walter Benjamin selected writings, Vol. 1: 1913–1926* (pp. 444–488). Cambridge, MA: Harvard University Press. (Original work published 1928).

Chevalier, J., & Gheerbrant, A. (1990). *Dictionnaire des symboles: Mythes, réves, coutumes, gestès, formes, figures, couleurs, nombres* (11ème ed., revue et corrigée). Paris: Ed. Robert Laffont/Jupiter. (Original work published 1969).

Drane, J. (2001). *The McDonaldization of the church: Consumer culture and the church's future*. Macon, GA: Smyth and Helwys.

Drane, J. (2008). *After McDonaldization: Mission, ministry, and Christian discipleship in an age of uncertainty*. Grand Rapids, MI: Baker Academic.

Fontenelle, I. A. (2006). Ilusões de modernidade: o fetiche da marca McDonald's no Brasil. *Psicologia & Sociedade, 18*(2), 38–46.

Guattari, F. (2010). *The machinic unconscious: Essays in Schizoanalysis*. New York: Semiotext(e). (Original work published 1979).
Günther, G., Huschke, W., & Steiner, W. (1993). *Weimar: Lexikon zur Stadtgeschichte*. Weimar: Böhlau.
Kraniauskas, J. (1994). Beware Mexican ruins! 'One-way street' and the colonial unconscious. In A. Benjamin & P. Osborne (Eds.), *Walter Benjamin's philosophy: Destruction and experience* (pp. 139–154). London: Routledge.
Löwy, M. (2010). Capitalism as monstrous religion. *Logos Journal, 9*(1). Retrieved from http://www.logosjournal.com/anticapitalist-readings-of-webers-protestant-ethic.php
Lyon, D. (2001). *Jesus in Disneyland: Religion in postmodern times*. Malden: Blackwell.
Meier, C. A. (1987). *The meaning and significance of dreams*. Boston: Sigo Press.
Mestrovic, S. G. (1997). *Postemotional society*. London: Sage.
Ritzer, G. (2000). *The McDonaldization of society* (New Century ed.). Thousand Oaks, CA: Pine Forge.
Shamdasani, S. (2009). Introduction. In C. G. Jung & S. Shamdasani (Eds.), *The red book: Liber Novus* (pp. 193–221). New York: Philemon Series & W.W. Norton.
Strummer, J., & Jones, M. (1979). Lost in the supermarket. [The Clash]. On *London Calling* [record]. New York: CBS/Epic.
Vester, H.-G. (1999). Emotions in postemotional culture. In J. Schlaeger & G. Stedman (Eds.), *Representations of emotions* (pp. 19–28). Tübingen: Narr.
Von Franz, M. L. (1964). The process of individuation. In C. G. Jung (Ed.), *Man and his symbols* (pp. 208–210). Garden City, NY: Doubleday.
Von Franz, M. L. (1997). *Archetypal dimensions of the psyche*. Boston: Shambhala.

10

Disneyized Dreams: Imaginary Models of Simulation

In this chapter, only two night dreams are presented and interpreted; they are rather complex and rich in details and meanings. Both depict the possible colonization of subjectivity happening through identity with certain *models of being*: models that used to function as symbolic, even archetypal *représentations collectives*, but here appear as Disneyized simulacra. While they unveil some dark, dehumanizing aspects of the ImCon, it is also possible to discern a rather ironic cultural critique in them: they criticize the whole of consumerist culture through its icon, Disney. As the Disney Epcot logo ran many years ago, "If we can dream it, we can do it".

10.1 A Reoccurring Nightmare: Evil (or, Disneyization by Walt Disney Himself)

Dream related by an American male student, 17 years old (at time of dream), attached to his parents. I have kept the temporal order in which the dream was reported. The main title is his (but the part in parenthesis is mine). He also called this dream, along with some others, "night terrors", which underscores its emotional character.

M. Xavier, *Subjectivity, the Unconscious and Consumerism*,
https://doi.org/10.1007/978-3-319-96824-7_10

This dream kept happening—I kept going to Epcot at Disney and going into this castle, in the Japan part of the park. You'd go up an elevator, then into this "celebrity deathmatch" show, fight 7 people, and if you won you could pick a celebrity or a normal person to give you a tour of the castle. I wanted to go back and save this celebrity because I kept having the dream, and finally I went back and did with one of my friends—even though just a few dreams ago I was captured by Walt Disney himself, and forced to do Simba's voice in The Lion King *and Koda in* Brother Bear. *My friend took pictures of the castle after we left—it was black bats and a black aura all around it that only her camera could see. It made me terrified—then I woke up.*

In the interpretation that follows, the oneiric narrative is made more linear. In fact we have more than one dream here: the first dream is with Walt Disney and the movie characters (which he had "a few dreams ago"), and then the reoccurring dreams. Recurring dreams usually reveal a very important problem, which the unconscious "presses" continually upon the ego, forcing him to become conscious of it. According to Jung, they happen particularly in youth; often they are very impressive, highly emotional dreams "which convince one that they 'must surely have a meaning'" (Jung, CW8, §536).[1]

Such meaning is centered on the dream's main theme or problem. At a first glance, its theme does not seem clear at all. However, considering that he is a teenage male, and that the symbols and symbolic meanings employed by his dreams are more or less typical, it seems that the dream problem is related to *rites of passage*, or puberty rites: the coming-of-age narratives and myths that symbolize the process of becoming a *man*, an adult. Thus behind these dreams and their emotional and frightening character is the *telos* of individuation of the unconscious libido, which tries to impulse him into adulthood. But what elements in the dreams would allow us to affirm such? First, the Disney movies mentioned: *Lion King* and *Brother Bear* are essentially coming-of-age stories; their main characters, Simba (a cub) and Kenai (an Indian Inuit boy turned young

[1] The dreamer's reaction is typical, and in fact appropriate: incomprehension and dread. "What do these dreams mean? They have terrified me! One made me immobile after I woke up, and one scared me so bad I woke up crying. These are night terrors, not just celebrity dreams. What do they mean??"

bear), undergo "archetypal"—albeit thoroughly Disneyified—rites of passage. And, second, the fight ("deathmatch"), which involves saving someone, would correspond to the typical deadly battles and tasks, integral parts of such rites, that the initiated (hero) has to endure.

Therefore, the main idea for interpretation is that these dreams depict a general colonization of the *cultural forms* under which such rites originally appeared: the *représentations collectives*—archetypal narratives, mythological models, and rituals—are replaced by simulacra fabricated through imagineering. That is, the typical process of Disneyization that happens culturally—and institutes a totalizing imaginary—here materializes in the dreamer's psyche.

Thus, to understand the dreams we need a few words on such type of rite. The rite of passage, and especially the puberty rite, is a principal rite of initiation. According to Vierne (1987), it is a *commencement* of a state that must lead the human being into maturity; "an education [*Bildung*], that is above all a modification of the ontological *statut* of the subject into an initiated being" (pp. 7–8). As Eliade (1959, pp. 10ff) puts it, it consists in "an ontological mutation of the existential regime (…). Initiation introduces the neophyte in the human community and in the world of spiritual values at once". Accordingly, in primitive societies, the life of the subject and the community wholly depended upon such rites; they condensed their *représentations collectives*, and for many tribes were simply the most important ceremonies (Campbell, 1997, p. 82), a fundamental part of their symbolico-religious imaginaries.

Eliade (1959) mentions a structural *solidarité* between and within all forms of initiation and rites of passage, which reflects the fact that they are archetypal formations, translated into symbolic rituals that are exceedingly charged emotionally. Such rites typically involve the myth of the *hero*: the hero is the symbol (the archetypal *model* with prescribed actions) for the emancipation from the father and mother imagos, from the unconscious world of childhood, and initiation into the sociocultural and spiritual world. It is a second birth, a new, complete life: a spiritual, symbolic, and social life—thus in complete connection with the "world of dreams", *altjeringa* (Campbell, 1997; the term comes from the Australian Aranda tribe), the eternal, transcendental world (i.e., the collective unconscious). Its symbols and numen translate culturally into drastic and complicated ceremonies, fights, and quests—sometimes of a very gruesome and possibly deadly nature—which the child has to overcome just like the hero did, that is, *identified* with the hero symbol. If the child succeeds, he receives a name (a social identity) and becomes an adult human being, fully integrated in the adult social world, but also, and most importantly, with the spiritual, transcendent world, which is the basis of life.

Now we can proceed with the interpretation proper. In the first scene, the dreamer is captured by Walt Disney himself. Staying first with the image of Walt, it is possible to interpret it positively and negatively. Positively, he would represent the adult or elder, the hugely successful, self-made businessman; in a capitalist culture, he would represent the *adult model* the dreamer should identify with. This model-symbol coerces him into identifying with the characters that do undergo the rite of passage and apparently become adults. So Disney would personify an attempt of the unconscious to "force" the dreamer into becoming an adult.[2]

However, the details, the whole emotional atmosphere, and the end of this dream point to a rather negative interpretation. First, in the global imaginary, Disney is by no means just an adult model; he represents as much a commodity-sign, a manufactured *myth*, as his characters.[3] Besides embodying the Great Capitalist, he represents the creator of a dream-world which is clearly *infantilizing*, dehumanizing, and totalitarian. In sum, he personifies—like no one else—the imaginary of consumption as a totalizing subjectivation force. And that is why and *how* the dream employs his image: he *captures* the dreamer, forcing him to become his creature, another Disney character, a *commodity*. Ironically, the dream employs Walt Disney himself as a symbol of forceful Disneyification.

Thus, the "passage" here is not into adulthood: it is the danger of pure commodification. That appears as the dreamer being forced to do Simba's and Koda's voices. As argued, these movie characters (and their respective movies) appear as the surrogate *représentations collectives* for the initiation

[2] In fact this is a possible interpretation too—in the sense that, within our consumption society, to become a consumer-commodity *is* being adapted and "adult".

[3] Watts (1997) mentions that "Disney mythologized his past and presented it to the public" (as cited in Wasko, 2006, p. 7). For an interesting analysis of the Disney myth, see Wasko (2006).

into adulthood. In the dream, it is Disney's fantasy world, its "myths" and *rites*—as commodity-narratives—that determine the social imaginary's rites of passage, forcing its models upon the dreamer. Again, these models pertain to an order of simulation. Both movies employ narratives from fairy tales and typical hero myths, and *Lion King* uses themes from biblical tales (Joseph and Moses). However, they do not refer back to any of these referents; they *become* the referent, erasing any original—simulacra that replace symbolic models.

Amplifying both movies and their characters would be too long and involve too many details. Instead, the interpretation can be limited to what the dream symbolizes as two of the main effects of such models. If the original rites of passage created, through the symbol, a transformation of the purely instinctual, infantile state into full human adulthood, here the Disney characters represent the opposite: infantilization and dehumanization.

Symbolically, animals usually represent the instincts. Thus, in the dream, the dreamer is forced to identify with childish lion and bear images. But more than that, *Brother Bear* starts with a *regression* to a state of animality; the hero, the "primitive" human (Kenai), is transformed into a bear. He then undergoes the passage, becoming adult, yet *remains a bear*. Koda, the one that appears in the dream, in fact is not the hero but the baby bear that *does not grow*—he stays attached to his (dead) mother.[4] Therefore they represent a *regression*, or reversal, into infantilized, animal instinct. Beyond that, such forceful identification means dehumanization in the sense that the dreamer is ontologically transformed into a commodity-simulacrum, a Disney product. It is not even a persona: what remains of him is only the *voice*, fabricated, infantilized; like Echo in the Narcissus myth, he is condemned to reproduce the discourse of the commodity, of the Disney imaginary, as a mere image. The dream implies that such "evil" rite means not adulthood but *mimesis* with the ImCon—replicating its simulacra and becoming a virtual screen.

That prospect sets the emotional tone for the recurring dreams, which take place in Walt Disney World. The initial scenery, mixing Epcot,

---

[4] In turn, Simba is the cub that does grow to be an adult lion, i.e., there is an actual passage into adulthood.

Japan, and castle, is the typical Disney dream-world: hybridized, dedifferentiated, a hyperreal bricolage of cultures, imaginaries, and themes—a commodified fairy tale, in lieu of the symbolic "world of dreams" of primitive rites of passage. The castle actually reminds one of fairy tales, the hero and his quests (save the princess, redeem her and himself, become the king, etc.); it is a symbol linked to rites of passage. But why Japan? It might represent symbolically the *antithesis*, the opposite Eastern culture, with a traditional history that celebrated and valued its initiatory rites.[5] Seen together with the castle image, it is an attempt of the unconscious to search for a different cultural model of rite, a different imaginary. At the same time, it shows that all old traditions and old imaginaries have been Disneyized; all that is left are simulacra: they are part of *Epcot*, the prototype of a future society, a utopic self-enclosed *world*[6] in which virtually everything is ruled by hi-tech consumption—the perfect embodiment of its techno-imaginary.

It is in the castle, however, that the dreamer will be repeatedly confronted with the initiation quest: the hero's struggle, or deadly fight. Henderson (1964) mentioned how, *in his epoch*, the fantasies and dreams of young people often reproduced historical (i.e., archetypal) patterns of initiation rites. The commonest of these patterns is the ordeal, or *trial of strength*, which fits our oneiric narrative:

> The novice for initiation is called upon (…) to submit to the ordeal. He must be willing to experience this trial without hope of success. In fact, he must be prepared to die; and though the token of his ordeal may be mild (…) or agonizing (…), the purpose remains always the same: To create the symbolic mood of *death* from which may spring the symbolic mood of rebirth. (Henderson, 1964, pp. 131–132; e.a.)

However, under the contemporary ImCon, instead of an archetypal pattern, it is "celebrity deathmatch"—a hyperreal television show—that

[5] Rites of passage were exceedingly important in Japan, and still bear a certain aura: "Coming of Age Day" (Seijin no Hi) is a national holiday, with its traditional ceremonies. However, just like in Epcot, they seem to have been commodified. For instance, in some Japanese cities, such ceremony for 20-year-olds has mutated into getting free tickets to Tokyo Disneyland.

[6] Epcot is the acronym for *Experimental Prototype Community of Tomorrow.*

stands as the simulacrum of ordeal. Its semiotic mood of death is made more thrilling: the dreamer has to fight celebrities, in order to save another celebrity—a spectacle to die for. But why does the dream employ such image? In the imaginary, the celebrity is the great commodity-sign that personifies a simulacrum of *individuality*: a representational identikit with codified referents for lifestyle, worldview, sexuality, creativity, political position, and so on. Its numen and fascination lie in the visibility, fame, and power it promises. As such, it stands among the ImCon's most coveted, desired commodities—the image of a unique individual permanently fulfilling a plethora of consumption dreams. Such fetish establishes their role in the ImCon pantheon: veneration and admiration of celebrities is one prevalent practice of consumer culture (Marshall, 1997; Turner, 2004); their worship, an important part of its liturgies. Being manufactured and managed as spectacles by what has been called the celebrity industry (mainly PR, Hollywood, and mass media), they, just like the Disney characters before, represent creatures of imagineering that replace mythological models and symbols. As Kellner (2003) puts it: "Celebrities are the icons of media culture, the *gods and goddesses* of everyday life" (p. 4; e.a.). To sum it up, in the dream the celebrities replace the mythic *hero* model, with which the dreamer has to identify—a commodified image of self—a simulacrum.

As for the "celebrity deathmatch", it is an MTV show, an animation with clay characters that depicts celebrities fighting each other in a wrestling ring, in which at least one always dies gruesomely. Basically, it is a spectacle of commodified hyperviolence; it simply never creates anything but grisly, extremely bloody violence and death, in the celebration of which the ephemeral heroes of consumption society consume themselves.

Also like creatures of imagineering, these heroes are not even human celebrities but "clay characters": inhuman, moldable, resembling the celebrity personae who phantasmagorically stamped the book on "personal branding" whose cover appears in Chap. 5 of this work. Moreover, the whole spectacle is a satire of the pro-wrestling format, which is already a (hyperreal) travesty: it is a parody of a parody, a farce of a farce, a simulacrum of a simulacrum. Actually, this is a pattern that is repeated in the whole dream: it portrays the *precession of simulacra*, typical of postmodernity and best symbolized by Disneyworld.

Returning to the narrative, the dreamer seems to be presented with a choice of identity, which he can save: a celebrity or a normal person. He chooses a celebrity. However, it seems that whatever he chooses, he will just get a *tour*: the dream hints that such an "initiation" has only one possible result—to remain in the fantasy castle, never leaving the dreamworld. It is an initiation into *participation mystique* with the ImCon.

Yet the dreamer eventually saves the celebrity—completing the task, the "rite" forced upon him by the dreams—with the help of a female friend,[7] a real person. This changes the dream completely; the *lysis* is strikingly dissimilar to the rest of the narrative—which can probably be attributed to the appearance of a real, *human* relationship in this world of simulations. It is only then that they can finally leave the Disney imaginary. She is the one with the camera that *can see*—symbolically—the pictures are *real representations*, which reveal the reality of Disney signs and simulacra. That is, at this point the dream de-sanitizes the Disney consumption fairy tale and the imaginary it symbolizes—not merely as the magical world of eternal childhood, which the dreamer must leave, but somehow as an "evil, reoccurring nightmare".

The symbols that signify this uncanny reality are the black bats and black aura. To understand their significations, one must *amplify* them and see how their cultural meanings fit into this image. Chevalier and Gheerbrant (1969/1997) provide the central meaning of the bat symbol for this dream: "as a *nocturnal flying mouse*, the bat represents a blindness to the most patent truths, and it hangs in accretions of filth and moral deformity" (p. 72; e.a.). Thus the bat symbolizes the *dark*, hidden counterpart of Mickey, the great icon of this imaginary—its shadow side. Like an actual rat, it is "an unclean beast", but also stands as a "symbol of idolatry and fear" (p. 70). The image of the "beast" can be connected to what was discussed in relation to the movie characters: it means to remain

[7] The fact that the friend is a female is very important symbolically and for the subjectivity of the dreamer (and his process of growing up). However, those are more clinical aspects which cannot be dealt with here.

"animalized", a regression into beast-like instinct. The character of "idolatry" fits well with a total imaginary based precisely on the idolatry of commodity-signs (e.g., celebrities) and is analogous to the meaning of *matzevot* in Ronald McDonald's dream. Another peculiarity of the bat is that it lives *upside down*, an image of reversion or perversion: in a sense, the symbol turns the luminous, fantastic Disneyworld imaginary upside down, revealing it as a perversion. The black aura that it exudes seems to confirm this idea: instead of the aura, the glowing seduction of such imaginary, the dream reveals its *phantasmagoria*. In a sense, Disney's magic world is portrayed as black magic[8]: operatic transformation of fantasy and imagination by capital and technology. To recall Walter Benjamin's theory, in the dream the Disney imaginary appears as the *phantasmagoric world* of commodity capitalism—for the dreamer, an *evil* world.

This last oneiric image seems to summarize the unconscious' view about the Disney ImCon and its models of subjectivity—models which it not only colonizes and manufactures but actually forces upon individual psyches, bludgeoning them into identification. Such models appear as simulacra of rites of passage—which are shown "upside down" by the dream, revealing the possible colonization of the dreamer's subjectivity. As in the symbolic rites of passage, they institute an *ontological mutation*—one in which the dreamer would not become an adult human, but rather be initiated as another dehumanized, "animalized" consumer-commodity. A mutation that implies full identity with a simulation: in an image that is even more clear than the one in the Ronald McDonald dream, the subject here is *forced* to turn into a *homo simulacrum*. A mutation that entails remaining infantile, in full mimesis with the Disney ImCon, with its "deep-frozen infantile world" (Baudrillard, 2001,

[8] The reader can connect this idea with the Faustian image of *Sorcerer Mickey*, which represents the imagineers and the whole Disney imaginary: an attempt at conjuring up (and totally dominating) reality as a hyperreal phantasmagoria. Black magic replacing "all that is sacred"—the climax of what *The Communist Manifesto* had already announced in relation to capitalism: "Modern bourgeois society (…) is like the *sorcerer* who is no longer able to control the powers of the nether world whom he has called up by his spells" (Marx & Engels, 1848; e.a.). Berman (1982), who quotes this fragment, analyzed modernity and capitalism through this Faustian lens.

p. 2004): a totally Disneyified subject. The dreamer's emotional reaction is consistent with these possibilities: he is scared, terrified, and clueless. Through the dreams the unconscious actually immobilizes him, for it is his future life that is at stake.

To summarize all this interpretation, let us juxtapose this Disneyized dream-image of initiation with the forms under which original symbolic rites *used* to appear in dreams (before the advent of total colonization). For such, we can compare it with a description given by Jung while discussing the *archetypal dreams* of a child:

> they undoubtedly contain *representations collectives* and they are in a way analogous to the doctrines taught to young people in primitive tribes when they are initiated into manhood. At such times they learn about what God or the gods or the "founding" animals have done, how the world and man were created, what the end of the world will be, and the meaning of death. (Jung, CW18, §536)

Thus, in the "reoccurring nightmare", the *représentations collectives* and the "founding animals" are simulacra fabricated through imagineering (celebrities, Disney characters); the *doctrine* is that given by the Disney/ImCon imaginary, the totalizing ideology of consumption; what appears as God is Walt Disney himself, the Capitalist Demiurge who created the Disneyworld; the "meaning of death" is that broadcast by an MTV farce, completely and purposefully meaningless; and finally, mentioned not by Jung, but in my discussion of rites of passage, the communion with the "world of dreams", *altjeringa* (the spiritual-symbolic world, the collective unconscious), appears as full identity with the imaginary of consumption embodied as Walt Disney World: "where dreams come true".

What is colonized: the dreamer's psychological identity, his "existential regime".

How it is colonized: forceful identification with ImCon simulacra, as representational models of subjectivity, in the context of simulated rites of passage.

Effects of colonization: immediate effects (elicited by dream) are fear and terror. Possible effects—full unconscious identity with the ImCon; Disneyification of the subject; infantilization and dehumanization.

10.2 Zombie-Moms at Disneyworld

Dream reported by an American female, in her late 20s, professional (her work has to do with creativity and technology). The dream title is hers; she considers it as a nightmare. It is a very detailed dream; due to the limits of this work, some symbolic details will not be dealt with. Unfortunately, the dreamer did not reply a request for associations and other relevant information on the dream. Interpretation thus had to be based on her series of dreams; some dream symbols remained unclear because of this.

I'm in a park, talking to a female friend of mine. Across the way on an island are oil refineries (?), shaped roundly and looking somewhat like guitars done by an abstract sculpture. I'm admiring them. And can't believe how big they look up close—the island is maybe a mile away over water.

It turns out I am in Disneyworld and I want to check out some things and go inside a tall tower. Every floor is a different theme—Sleeping Beauty, Little Mermaid, etc. *It is very narrow, it looks run-down—paint chipping. On the Little Mermaid floor I see the girl playing Ariel fixing her makeup in a tiny bathroom with the door open. She looks slutty. The next floor is maybe Sleepy Beauty. I'm with my mother. This is near the top of the tower, and I realize it is a ship on water. The higher you get up, the more it teeters. The tower is moving back and forth and the floor isn't steady. Very unstable. We are suddenly chased by a group of totally normal-looking middle aged women who think they are zombies. The rest of the dream is me being chased by people pretending to be zombies who can stop chasing me anytime they want, and running from them. Oddly, no children in "Disneyworld".*

The dream presents two distinct parts, or dramas, that take place in analogous scenarios: a normal park and the Disneyworld park. They correspond to two possibilities, two symbolic attitudes the dreamer can have toward herself and life, two aspects of her psyche in its relation with the social, which the dream contrasts employing analogous symbols. Such attitudes are related to the central themes of this dream, which, broadly, are *being a woman* (feminine identity, including motherhood) and *creativity* (creative libido and its relation with the unconscious psyche). It is easy to see that the dream is about femininity—all its dramatis personae are female figures. The theme of creativity, related to such feminine, is subtler; but it already shows up in the first scene. It must be said that each symbol in the first drama has to be understood in contrast with the way it appears in the second drama (and vice versa).

The first dreamscape is the park. It represents a more *natural* scenery (especially if seen together with the island, water, etc., that appear later), but at the same time a public, *social* space. Such landscape can be understood in two complementary ways: subjectively, it represents a part of her psyche, of her subjectivity; objectively, it denotes part of her social world. Placing both of them together, it signifies her attitude toward the social world, her positioning in relation to it—how she is, how she moves about or *lives* in it—which, here, seems to be more connected to nature, to an open, "natural way". She is conversing with a female friend. As we do not have associations for the friend, and do not know who she is, she ought to be seen in the context in which she appears: she probably represents a female image, or model, that is connected to such "natural" ways of being. Subjectively, she is a shadow figure, that is, she stands as a symbol for a part of the dreamer's psyche. Thus she probably has to do with the dreamer's individuality and *creativity*, for it is conversing (= being together, exchanging) with her that produces the next image.

The dreamer then admires the oil refineries on an island. This image is parallel to Disneyworld as a tall tower, standing on a ship over water, in the second drama. Its symbolism is the most important one in the first part. Oil symbolizes a condensed form of energy, originating from the depths and from the water: libido, psychic energy, in its pure unconscious form—again, the unconscious appears as the original spring underground. Such form of libido is "crude"—dark, raw, unrefined, *natural* energy: instinctual libido as creative force. The means for refining it, the oil refineries, appears in a curious and different way (and that explains the dreamer's feeling of strangeness, noted as a "(?)" in her text): not as an industrial, technological process, artificial and signified by *consumption*—but as artistic human artifacts, symbolized as guitar and sculpture. They represent art and culture as *refinement* ("culture" comes from cultivation): the artistic cultural form the unconscious libido takes through human *creativity*—and through a true *symbol*, which unites oil refinery, roundness, guitar, and sculpture, into one meaningful image. Thus the dream weds a concept of *culture*—the humanist concept, *humanitas*, discussed in Chap. 2, as the creative and symbolic transformation of Nature, *feritas*—with a model for *creative life* for the dreamer, an *identity* that depends on her creation.

The symbolic edifice for this model is on an island, on firmly established land surrounded by water. On a subjective level, this would signify a consciousness sitting on the vast resources (oil) of the unconscious, and feeding from their energy through refinement and artistic cultivation. This is pictured as a solid, direct connection with the unconscious forces and instincts, which provides a stable foundation—a *creative* foundation, which psychologically translates into fantasy, dream-thinking, and imagination. Its signifying edifice, like the temple symbols[9] seen in previous dreams, appears gigantic and imposing to her, eliciting admiration. It seems that, in reality, she is a bit far (a mile away) from it, but the dream gets her "up close" to such possibility.

Immediately after that, however, the dream contrasts it symbolically with Disneyworld: it stands as the signifying edifice for a different form of "culture"—the totalizing consumer culture and its imaginary. The image, a tall tower, is the opposite of the round refinery on an island. However, and to advance the main idea for interpretation, it symbolizes the same things, but as a "refinery of the imaginary": a purely capitalist industrial process, strictly technological, non-human, and artificial, destined only for consumption. It represents how consumer society "refines" culture, art, the unconscious, and nature; "creativity" here can only mean "imagineering".

In contradistinction to the grandeur of the oil refinery, this imaginary is pictured as "very narrow and run-down". In fact this is a pattern seen in many of the dreams analyzed; in them the edifices of the ImCon lose their fantastic grandiosity and fascination, being variously depicted as derelict, poor, dirty, narrow, and oppressive. This may be seen as the *reductive function* of the unconscious at work—it depreciates and dissolves the artificial aura of the ImCon; it "chips the paint", the fetishist makeup of its signs.

---

[9] In this dream, however, there is no mention of any religious aspect or image.

There the dreamer finds *thematized* floors, which is a characteristic of Disneyization (Bryman, 2004). Each "theme", in lieu of creative refinement, represents a ready-to-consume *identity*. Here the dream symbolizes, through Disney, the whole ImCon as a supermarket of thematic female models: prepackaged identikits of femininity, of how to be a woman. The two models that appear in the dream—Little Mermaid and Sleeping Beauty—follow the pattern mentioned in the previous dream: they are *simulacra*, products of the Disneyification of fairy tales, cultural symbolic narratives and its archetypal models and referents, which are imagineered as commodity-signs and commodity-narratives.[10]

As consumption dreams, the Disney characters personify the mythic ideology of consumerism; they are the "very embodiment of consumer-fetishism" (Byrne & McQuillian, 1999, p. 23). In the case of this dream, to amplify thoroughly the symbolic meaning of the two characters would take us too far, so the discussion will be short (the reader can find a wealth of material on it in Bell, Haas, & Sells, 1995; Byrne & McQuillian, 1999; Ray, 2009). One symbolic characteristic that is common to both characters seems to be important for us: they both "live" in unconsciousness, outside of reality—Ariel is a creature of the sea, and Sleeping Beauty is literally unconscious. In their original fairy tales, they symbolize the need for an *ontological transformation*[11] of this condition: to overcome unconsciousness, be redeemed, and become fully human and feminine. The mermaid is particularly meaningful for us in that regard: her unconsciousness and *animalitas* is "below", the fish tail; that is what has to be transformed, *refined*, humanized, an analogous image to the oil refinery. And, of course, both share the stereotypical Disney beauty and sex appeal.

However, the dreamer stays on the Little Mermaid floor (i.e., this character seems to be the more significant one in the dream). Ariel, the mermaid, embodies a particular model of consumer-woman as a heroine (Bell et al., 1995; Ray, 2009): her main concern being material

---

[10] They both are *Disney Princesses*. According to the Disney Corporate website (disney.com), the Disney Princess brand is a "powerful *lifestyle* brand" that "touches every aspect of girls' lives"—that is, a totalizing package for womanhood.

[11] In this sense, they are close in meaning to the characters that appear in the previous dream.

objects, she displays a real fascination for the glitz of consumption, especially of looks and appearance.

Her *desire* seems to be unbound: she always "wants more" and goes to dangerous lengths to buy and seek possessions from the human world. Even the prince, Eric, is revealed as an (aesthetic) object for her collection; "love" here means passion for possession. She personifies an "I want more and can't get enough" lifestyle, rebellious and dangerous; very sexualized looks and aggressive seduction are her weapons, indulging in selfish desires something that defines her. In fact, perhaps the main ideological message of the movie, conveyed through her, is that *to be human is to be a consumer*: Ariel exchanges her individuality, her *creative, artistic voice*, for the role of being another human consumer in their world of objects. In this sense she also represents the deindividuation that appeared in the previous dream: not to have a voice means not to have a discourse, a personality, and merely echo Disneyified lines; it means not to create at all—to be debased to automatic replication.

The girl playing Ariel, which the dreamer sees next, seems to confirm this interpretation. Symbolically, she represents the *identity* with the ideological role: to incorporate the artificial identity, wear the mask of the model, and be a consumer-woman like Ariel. The mention of makeup refers to that pure persona. She appears in parallel to the image of the dreamer's friend and the park in the previous part; the contrast seems evident: instead of an open space connected to nature, she represents a tiny life, tiny bathroom, no privacy anywhere—it represents living and working inside the Disneyworld park. No wonder she looks "slutty": it is an oneiric symbol for *selling* one's energy and character, like Ariel herself, selling her voice in her movie, not a transformation of libido into creative art, but its full commodification. Thus, such identity model means no individuality and no *creativity*: a prefabricated role, a Disney character—it means identifying with a simulacrum, in an image that is analogous to those in the previous dream (i.e., identity with Disney characters and clay celebrities).

Yet, it must be noted that, as in the first scene, the dreamer merely *observes* these models, as *possibilities* of identity; it is not like in the previous dream, which points clearly to the dangers of full identification. However, whereas Ariel still is an aggressive model, the "next" model,

Sleeping Beauty, would represent complete passivity and unconsciousness—she is not even *alive*. Strangely enough, precisely at this moment, the dreamer is with her *mother*: there is some connection between her mother (as the mother complex) and the symbols of Ariel and Sleeping Beauty. Unfortunately, I do not have elements to ascertain any interpretation regarding the mother. However, as a symbol, the mother stands for feminine *creativity* itself—the power to create new life. Judging from the specific moment and place in which she appears in the dream, the mother seems to represent the opposite of such creativity. As a hypothesis, one can think that buying into those prepackaged consumer models somehow represents for the dreamer to remain in the sphere of the mother complex, *unconscious*, not being herself; perhaps the mother is very identified with consumerism. The next scenes indicate this possibility.

Typically, when the mother enters the oneiric stage, the dream changes and gets more dramatic—she introduces the *peripeteia*. Here the tower is revealed as the very opposite of the refinery; it seems to symbolize both the ImCon and the dreamer's psychic condition if she identifies with it. The imaginary is seen not as an island but rather as a teetering artificial construction *in the air*, fluctuating—the antipode of being on the ground, firmly established, in connection with the unconscious forces. Being on "top of the tower" means the possibility of full identification with the ImCon. As the imaginary stands as a replacement of the symbolic unconscious manifestations and its natural creativity, identifying with it (with its models) entails a *disconnection* from the unconscious grounds. Correspondingly, the floor is not steady, which symbolizes psychological instability: the more one identifies with the imaginary, the *higher* one gets—on its simulacra, the surrogate fantasy, the artificial unconsciousness—and the more one teeters, rootless up above, floating on the phantasmagoria of consumption dreams.[12] The reader can recall that the Disneyworld logo conveys exactly that the castle representing the dreamworld of consumption floats on clouds.

[12] As Dorfman and Mattelart (1971/1991) wrote, the "fantasy world of Disney systematically *cuts the earthly roots of his characters* (...) a suppression of real and concrete factors; that is, their personal history, their birth and death, their whole development in between" (p. 34). Identification with such models does the same to the consumer.

Then the dream reveals its image for such condition and the possible effects of identification: the *zombie-moms*. They can be seen as the last "model" for womanhood that appears in the dream; if we amplify the symbol of the zombie, its relations with the themes discussed so far become clear. A ubiquitous image in the contemporary cultural industry, especially in the United States, the zombie symbolizes an extreme image of the *consumer* as a product of consumerism. The idea of *ontological transformation*, present in both dreams in this chapter, finds in the zombie another expression, but as a perversion: it symbolizes the unconscious forces below—the creative libido, the instincts—thoroughly dehumanized and reduced to a mindless, bestial *desire* for consumption, in the form of an extreme compulsion, a perennial craving for consuming what is *human* (flesh, brains, bodies, etc.). It personifies the other side of "consumption" that comes to define society: *consumere*, to waste away, use up entirely—a principle "equivalent to destruction, waste, decay—in short, to a death-directed process" (Williams, 1991, p. 6). Differently from what Sleeping Beauty symbolizes in this dream, the zombie is not merely "sleeping"—the anesthesia or "collective dream" of consumer society; it stands for an extreme form of numbed unconsciousness that is not even alive, *possessed* by the imperative of consuming. That is one central aspect of its symbol: the complete *external control* of mind and body; their defining and only behavior is that of the dehumanized automaton, completely alienated from any instincts or reason. In this sense, they can also be seen as cultural personifications of the totalizing logic of capitalism-consumerism and its principle of unlimited accumulation and conquest, incarnated as an irrational, uncontrolled, absolute impulse to *devour*.[13]

Returning to the dream, when the distancing from the "water" below, that is, the dark creative libido, reaches its apex, the unconscious energy returns in a perverted form: debased into single-minded consumption. And the irony is not lost: these consumer-moms "think" they are zombies (i.e., are unconsciously identified with the imaginary model), behave like zombies, and at the same time believe they can choose (*homo eligens*) and can stop any time they want, like any normal-looking consumer. That is,

[13] Based on a similar idea, Harman (2009) analyzed our politico-economical system as "zombie capitalism".

the Disney imaginary is portrayed as zombiefying: the opposite of glamorous feminine models, the antipode of *creativity*. This meaning is contained in the dreamer's last comment: oddly enough, no children in Disneyworld. As a symbol, children usually represent what is new, the possibilities, the human "seeds" that can or are about to develop: "The child is potential future" (Jung, CW9i, §278). Their conspicuous absence in the dream hints that this imaginary can only mean no spontaneity, no new, *no creation*. The image seems very meaningful: after all, the zombies are *mothers*—but nothing new can come out of a zombie, for it represents only destructivity and consumption, the very opposite of the image of potential creation at the beginning of the dream. Thus, if the previous dream showed that the utmost danger of identification with the ImCon was to become a simulacrum, here it means becoming a "totally normal-looking" middle-aged mom who is a zombie-consumer.

What is colonized: creative libido (instinct); feminine identity.

How it is colonized: models of femininity that are simulacra of symbolic representations; broadly, identification with the ImCon (as Disneyworld).

Effects of colonization: alienation, control by consumption instead of creativity; becoming a zombie-mom.

References

Baudrillard, J. (2001). *Selected writings* (M. Poster, Ed., 2nd ed.). Cambridge: Polity.

Bell, E., Haas, L., & Sells, L. (1995). *From the mouse to the mermaid*. Indianapolis, IN: Indiana University Press.

Berman, M. (1982). *All that is solid melts into air*. New York: Simon & Schuster.

Bryman, A. (2004). *The Disneyization of society* (2nd ed.). London: Sage.

Byrne, E., & McQuillian, M. (1999). *Deconstructing Disney*. London: Pluto Press.

Campbell, J. (1997). *As máscaras de deus: mitologia primitiva*. São Paulo: Palas Athena.

Chevalier, J., & Gheerbrant, A. (1997). *The Penguin dictionary of symbols* (Trans. J. Buchanan-Brown). London: Penguin. (Original work published 1969).

Dorfman, A., & Mattelart, A. (1991). *How to read Donald Duck: Imperialist ideology in the Disney comic* (4th ed.). New York: IG Editions.

Eliade, M. (1959). *Naissances mystiques*. Paris: Gallimard.

Harman, C. (2009). *Zombie capitalism: Global crisis and the relevance of Marx*. London: Bookmarks.

Henderson, J. L. (1964). Ancient myths and modern man. In C. G. Jung (Ed.), *Man and his symbols* (pp. 104–156). New York: Anchor Press.

Kellner, D. (2003). *Media spectacle*. London: Routledge.

Marshall, P. D. (1997). *Celebrity and power: Fame in contemporary culture*. London: University of Minneapolis Press.

Marx, K., & Engels, F. (1848). *Manifesto of the communist party*. Retrieved from http://www.marxists.org/archive/marx/works/1848/communist-manifesto/index.htm

Ray, E. G. (2009). *Part of their world: Gender identity found in Disney princesses, consumerism, and performative play*. Unpublished master's thesis, Brigham Young University, Provo, Utah, US.

Turner, G. (2004). *Understanding celebrity*. London: Sage.

Vierne, S. (1987). *Rite, roman, initiation* (Deux. éd.). Grenoble, France: Presses Universitaires de Grenoble.

Watts, S. (1997). *The magic kingdom: Walt Disney and the American way of life*. Boston: Houghton Mifflin.

Wasko, J. (2006). Challenging Disney myths. *E-Compós*, Vol. 7. Retrieved from http://compos.org.br/seer/index.php/e-compos/article/viewFile/108/107

Williams, R. H. (1991). *Dream worlds: Mass consumption in late nineteenth-century France*. Berkeley: University of California Press.

11

Dreaming in the Temples of Consumption: Shopping Malls and Department Stores Dreams

"A dream about shopping or being at a shopping mall means that those things that you need (affection, friendship, spiritual support, quality time with people you care about) are available to you. However, you may need to learn exactly where to look, how to select what you need, and how to ask for these things when you need them."[1] This quote is part of a "key" for interpreting night dreams, a dream dictionary that, in reflecting collective consciousness, illustrates how the mall is signified in the imaginary: as the dream-world where literally *everything* one needs is purchasable. But more than that, it unveils how dreams themselves—representing the unconscious psyche—are signified and colonized: their possible symbolic contents and emotional tones are disregarded and replaced by the dominant consumption dream that life is fully available through shopping. Under this ideology, *to dream is to learn exactly how to be a good functioning consumer*, and then everything will be magically provided

[1] Found in http://www.smartgirl.org/dreamdictionary.html

M. Xavier, *Subjectivity, the Unconscious and Consumerism*,
https://doi.org/10.1007/978-3-319-96824-7_11

for.[2] In contradistinction to such imaginary miracle, this chapter offers some rather meaningful and disturbing night dreams that take place in malls and department stores, and present a different view on the temples of consumption and the imaginary they symbolize.

11.1 Another Cathedral of Consumption?

Dream reported by a North American man in his late 30s.[3] It also presents the theme of colonization of the sacred, the symbolico-religious function, but in a different form.

I had a dream of being in a building that was shaped like a cathedral, with nave, transepts and choir. A worship service took place in the front part. Later I found out that the back part was just one gigantic department store, filled with strangers and friends from various eras of my life walking and running around through the aisles. I eventually got upset about this and decided I would chase out each and everyone. I was trying to do this when I woke up.

The dream theme is clearly centered on the symbol of the cathedral and its partial commodification into a department store. Thus, its narrative can be viewed as an oneiric depiction of the concept of "cathedrals of consumption" (Fiske, 2000; Kowinski, 1984; Ritzer, 2000, 2001), the new prime temples of the consumerist religion, here attempting to open business within the dreamer's own psyche.

Initially, we can assume that the symbol of the cathedral-like building represents the same the church symbol did in the prototype dream: the dreamer's religious-symbolic function, which reflects and expresses the functioning of the unconscious. Here too worship is taking place—such function is alive, operative, and effective in him. In contrast with the previous analogous dreams, however, here it appears not under an institutional, cultural form (Church), nor as a primitive temple; it resembles a cathedral, but the dream places the emphasis upon its *shape*.

[2] One recurrent dream with shopping malls illustrates this idea symbolically: "The mall always *has everything included* and commonly I will actually *live* or work in the mall." This same dream-image appeared in other dreams as well (but usually with more emotional, even frightening tones).

[3] This dreamer was rather knowledgeable about dream interpretation (he did not provide any interpretation for this particular dream, though).

Such emphasis, seen alongside other elements in the dream, immediately raises the hypothesis that the symbol is employed with a deeper meaning here. Cathedrals are buildings with *archetypical* geometrical structures that combine harmoniously quadratic forms, the quaternity as a central *cross*, with circular ones—a symbol that unites the opposites as the *quadratura circuli* (see Jung, CW12, §123). In other words, they represent typical mandala-like formations, which stand for an ordered, transcendental totality: as such, they can symbolize the Self,[4] the archetype of wholeness, the virtual totality of the psyche, the very origin of the religious-symbolic function.

In fact, the dreamer himself associated the cathedral to one's "psychic life" in general, and the ways it functions. Thus, the dream represents a possible psychological transformation in him, in this case, a structural one.[5] The building, as his psyche, seems to be in an intermediary state, as it were: once again, the religious-symbolic function of the Self is "alive" but menaced by colonization. On the one hand, it can *become* a cathedral, representing its development into solidity and specificity—a personality that is more individual and integral (and that is why an image of the Self appears). On the other hand, it can be commodified and transformed into a cathedral of consumption, a department store—the ImCon already turning into a *gigantic* colonial power within his psychic space. As in the "massive temple" and the "McDonaldization of the country" dreams, the colonization process seems to be effected automatically and autonomously: it is not his "plan" and does not seem to be forced nor even effected by people. That means that the social imaginary encroaches

---

[4] I quote Jung (CW9ii, §§351–352) in order to explain this point in detail: he mentions some of "the facts that led psychologists to conjecture an archetype of wholeness, i.e., the self. These are in the first place dreams and visions (...) in which symbols of wholeness appear. The most important of these are geometrical structures containing elements of the circle and quaternity; namely, circular and spherical forms on the one hand, which can be represented either purely geometrically or as objects; and, on the other hand, quadratic figures divided into four or in the form of a cross. From [this] circle and quaternity motif (...) analogy formation leads on to the city, castle, church" (as possible symbols of the Self).

[5] Personal information on the dreamer confirmed that this interpretation was correct at the time; interestingly, he mentioned a preoccupation with developing a "more spiritual focus" in life in a "Christian sense" (which fits the cathedral symbol) together with a sort of religious philosophy of life that resembled Buddhist traditions (which would explain why the "cathedral" appears as a non-denominational building).

upon individual psychic life in a surreptitious fashion, "at the back of his mind". It simply happens; it is taken for granted—living within a collective consciousness dominated by consumerism naturally induces an automatic identity with its ideological mentality.

The dream shows that there was some significant part of his psyche that was already colonized—the "friends and strangers". As the dreamer did not provide any personal associations regarding them, one can only speculate. They probably symbolize his own psychic contents—complexes, emotions, experiences, and memories ("from various eras of my life")—that seem to function under the aegis of consumerism; the ideology of consumption there assumes the role of "worship service". That is, if part of his psychic "cathedral" is colonized, the result is commodification of part of his Self, his history and memory.

Although the consumption ideology is depicted as an autonomous and "gigantic" force, the dreamer does not *identify* with it: it upsets him, and his conscious choice, his ego attitude, is to go against the grain—he tries to banish, "to put out of his mind" the consumers, the colonizing influence, or the form of *being* psychologically determined by the ImCon. Analogously to the dreamer's act in the massive temple dream, here the required action *contra culturam*—against the mass of people, the mass mentality—can only be *individual*. The absence of *lysis* is meaningful[6]: the dream ends with the dreamer working hard on his task and decision; it points the task ahead and the necessary effort. His conscious ethical attitude indicates that, like the previous dreamer, he has a lot of work to do in order to defend his cathedral (his psychic *life*) from colonization, but there is room for reaction. Meaningfully enough, the dreamer did not seem to be very religious in terms of institutional creed; yet, his attitude is clearly redolent of Jesus's cleansing of the Temple: "Stop making my Father's house a marketplace!" (John 2, 13–22).

What is colonized: symbolico-religious function; part of Self.

How: it is an automatic colonization (transforming into a department store).

Effects of colonization: possible identity with the ideology of consumption, which takes the place of a religious mentality.

---

[6] Incidentally, this dream follows faithfully a drama structure (but closes without a solution—a *lysis*).

11.2 Sci-Fi Hyper-Business World

This is a very remarkable and peculiar dream. It was actually dreamed and later reported by a North American male "in response" to my request, in an internet forum, for dreams broadly related to consumerism (and also to Disney, shopping malls, etc.). Even though it does not feature such particular icons of the consumerist imaginary, I decided to analyze it here because of its uniqueness. I quote the dream narrative in full.

> *While reading your request, I noted that I never recalled having dreams that included buying anything, and found that to be very interesting. All the resources in the dreams have to be fully funded without the slightest concern for the process of procuring materials, food or objects.*
>
> *Until now.*
>
> *I think that this post created a subtle trigger, and last night I had an intensely Sci-Fi hyper-business city environment dream. One of the main development features was a row of tall wide buildings that had earned a nickname of "The Wall" and the plan to extend The Wall to a great distance was common knowledge among the inhabitants. The characters included hungry consumers, driven by the insatiable curiosity to see and learn about new and novel products and processes. On the other side [of] the social arrangement were the equally hungry sophisticated sales representatives, exercising the most accommodating protocols.*
>
> *My guide and I walked along the pedestrian walkway to one of the established showroom buildings and entered the reception area to wait with two other people for our turns to be personally introduced to the mystery of the new products.*

The dreamer begins by stating that he had never had (or recalled) any dream related to "buying", that is, to consumption, which, therefore, does not seem to be an issue for him or his unconscious psyche, normally. That makes his dream all the more meaningful: certainly it is not a *personal* dream, referring to his subjectivity, but rather what primitives called a "Big Dream"[7]—a chiefly archetypal dream that criticizes *culture* from a

[7] Jung (CW7, CW8) borrowed the term from the Elgonyi tribes of Africa to refer to dreams that often present a numinous quality (Jung, CW9i) and strange, fascinating imagery, wisdom, or hor-

strangely wise point of view, thus having a primarily collective value. Indeed, one can clearly see that there are no subjective elements in this dream. Therefore, it seems that the unconscious "answered" my question, my request, with his dream,[8] and in a very specific symbolic way. He was not able to provide any further personal associations to the dream-images, which is in fact typical of archetypal dreams.

The *theme* of the dream is clearly given in the symbol of the sci-fi hyper-business city. It corresponds to a mythological motif, the Paradise or "heavenly city", which Jung (CW18) considers as a "powerful archetype": "This myth is the time-hallowed archetypal dream of a Golden Age or a paradise on earth, where everything is provided" in abundance for everybody (§563). Two interrelated dominant forces rule this paradise: hyper-business and consumption. Based on these main elements, the core idea for interpretation may be advanced: this dream can be seen as *the symbolical depiction*, autonomously produced by the unconscious, of what was discussed in this work as the *totalizing Imaginary of Consumerism*, and the society or world it institutes: *total capitalism-consumerism*. Both are here revealed as a self-contained world, a totalized microcosm, indeed, an archetypal *dream* that embodies the utopia of consumerism, what Benjamin (1999) called a "primeval landscape of consumption" (p. 827), "the Great Consumer Paradise" (Kowinski, 1984).

This paradise (and the dream itself) is characterized as "intensely Sci-Fi". This expression obviously refers to the role of hypermodern science and technology for the ImCon and consumer society: functional rationality governing and automating protocols, products, processes, and people, under the irrational imperatives of capitalism. Thus the image conveys a perfect marriage of capital (business) and science (technology), producing a *fiction*: a seamless hyperreal dream-world, which resembles more a portrait of the *techno*-imaginary of consumption (Balandier, 1985).

---

ror (Jung, CW17). Being archetypal, Big Dreams were formative of the primitive social imaginaries.

[8] In my experience, that is not uncommon. In fact, seen historically, eliciting dreams is a common practice. Meier (1983/2003) demonstrated that the whole realm of medicine, in Ancient Greece, belonged to the cult of Asclepius, the kernel of which consisted in the appearance of a dream propitiated (or "triggered") by the ritual of incubation.

Next in the dream narrative is the curious image of The Wall, whose meanings seem manifold. First, it appears to institute a fundamental *divide*. In fact The Wall is a common element in symbols of paradise and of the heavenly city, as can be seen in the images below; it defines the paradise in its essential significance as a *closed* world—like a womb, the primeval paradise. Speculating based on this idea, perhaps the divide refers to a fundamental separation from *reality*, from any reality that is not determined by the ImCon, and the idea that there is *no escape* from it, no way out—it consists in an all-encompassing hyperreality. This meaning would fit one essential characteristic of the other dream-worlds of consumption studied here, namely, that they purport to be fully enclosed worlds, or microcosms.

The second meaning is related to the plan to extend The Wall to a great distance, as its normal *development*. This clearly symbolizes the principle of unlimited expansion of capitalism-consumerism and its imaginary. Their colonial imperative already appeared symbolized as tall buildings before, the *dovecots*, and as a tall tower in the zombie-moms dream, a symbol of the Disney imaginary. This interpretation seems to be confirmed by two expressions in the dream: it encompasses the whole *city*; it invades all spaces, to the point that it becomes the *environment*—it defines the *Lebenswelt*, the social order, in a total way. Thus, The Wall and city seem like perfect symbols for an imaginary whose *telos* is the institution of a self-enclosed, *totalized world*, which at the same time expands and colonizes the whole environment.

In this total social order, there are only two possible roles and actions: its sole dramatis personae are the salesman and the consumer and the imperatives, to sale and to buy, which means, to *consume*. Within this fully technological, rational habitat, it is interesting that what drives the subjects are solely irrational forces: hunger and curiosity. Again, this image depicts perfectly the dynamics of total consumerism: the fundamental *vis motrix* of both subjects and world is functional irrationality, *desire* debased into an insatiable hunger for the commodity. In the dream, psychological functioning is reduced to the craving for the novelty engineered by technology and congealed into commodities, and the ravenousness for selling and buying, both commanded by an invisible external force, the imaginary of consumption. That is, a "psychology" very close to that of the zombie, or the rat in a Skinner box.

Besides that emphasis on irrationality, the dream also defines the subjects of such world in an interesting way. Its characters embody what Marx (1867/1990) called *Charaktermasken*: "the economic character masks of persons who encounter each other as their carriers, are only the *personification of economic relations*" (pp. 178–179). Curiously enough, the dream presents *exactly* "two persons in the same character masks, a buyer and a seller (…)" (p. 248). Yet, one crucial difference can be pointed out. Whereas within the modernity that Marx described, work and production, as main social referents, still defined economic relations and thus identities and masks, within both the dream and total consumerism, production, and hence work as a referent, increasingly disappear; as Baudrillard pointed in his oeuvre, what matters is *reproduction*, semiurgy, and consumption. Thereby consuming and selling come gradually to determine all the character masks, the *personae* to which everyone must conform.

However, in the dream these identities no longer seem to be mere masks or personae—they are clearly the only *definers of existence* for the inhabitants, the only thing that seems to differentiate them. In this sense, they are no longer masks; the subject here is a personification of the transcendental law that rules this hyper-business paradise: you shall buy and sell, subsumed under *You shall consume*. Not identity, but mimesis with the law; a being made to the semblance of an invisible market god.

In this peculiar dream, total colonization seems to have been actualized, no longer a process, as in other dreams, but a fait accompli: a dreamworld in which the ImCon and its logic rule absolutely, determining desires and subjects as consumers. Accordingly, and in contradistinction to the other dreams, here there are no symbols, no mention to previous symbolico-religious imaginaries.

Apart from one word: the "mystery". In this environment commanded by sci-fi instrumental rationality, consumerism appears as a *mysterium* whose numen is in the commodity fetish, the rites of consumption and sale, and the fascination and cold enchantment of the technological artifact. Historically, the "mysteries" have always represented the *représentations collectives* (Jung, CW5, §654) of a society; expressions of the main symbolic forces, the numinous myths that determine its functioning. Here they are reduced to *phantasmagoria*: the ideology and logic of commodity and consumption are the absolute laws in this world, its ruling gods. Thus, the showroom building appears as the equivalent to a thoroughly desacralized temple of consumption, where the personalized worship of phantasmagoria—the initiation into the mystery of new products—is celebrated.

Thus the dream ends with the religion of hyper-business. But, if we compare it to the previous dreams, some questions remain. Where is the truly metaphysical factor, the real *mystery*? The symbolic, mythic, instinctual forces, the unconscious underworld—where have they gone? What is *underneath* such business paradise—does it have any foundations? Once again, what I propose is that we look at such questions, and to the dream itself, through a historical parallel. The whole dream, but especially the city symbol, reminds one of a cultural symbolic product: the dream-like movie *Metropolis* (Lang, 1927), which described *symbolically* an analogous situation and psychology.

What is colonized: *society*, or the whole imaginary (it is not a personal dream).

How: the dream-image is a symbol of total colonization, which is no longer in process; ImCon and logic of consumerism-capitalism rule this world absolutely.

Effects of colonization: commodification of subjects; only possible identities are seller and buyer.

11.3 *Metropolis*: The Underground Reactions

The similarities between this last dream and Fritz Lang's *Metropolis* are numerous. The movie presents an intensely sci-fi, futuristic depiction of an archetypal Golden Age, a Paradise or heavenly *city*, as the utopic capitalist world. This world too is dominated by immense rows of tall buildings, which totalize the environment. The main difference for us, however, is that in the movie the divide suggested by the image of The Wall is shown to be the city's very structure: it is based on a fundamental *dissociation*, a schism between above and below. The capitalist paradise is founded upon the domination of the workers, who, enslaved and dehumanized, are the moving force of the city—what feeds the monstrous machinery underlying it in the depths. Seen as a metaphor, they obviously represent the proletariat, the forces of production conspicuously absent from the business paradise. However, if seen symbolically, they reveal what has already appeared in other dreams: psychologically, they personify the *underworld*, the forces of the collective unconscious—the basal *instincts*, alienated and hidden from the life above. Subjugated and colonized, they merely replicate the machine—the workers actually resemble automata.[9]

Like in the dream, this capitalist microcosm too is fruit of a pact between capital and science: the alliance of the bourgeois, Fredersen (embodying the ethos of capitalism[10]) and the mad scientist, Rotwang (personifying science and functional rationality). Both seem to feel empty, due to the death of their common love, Hel. They miss what she represented: the emotion, sentiment, love, and the irrational and feminine element (all of which, incidentally, is entirely absent from the dream above). However, in a cultural, mythic plane, Hel symbolizes something much more profound. She was a Nordic goddess who presided over the underworld (Hel = hell), a chthonic divinity connected to the dark, primeval, terrible aspects of Nature. Thus she embodies the real archaic *mystery*, a symbolic expression of the primitive collective unconscious. In relation to German and Nordic cultures, Hel represented the *shadow* of Christianity: the human elements that used to be contemplated and expressed symbolically by the old pagan imaginary, and thus *lived* through it, and the "barbaric" but profound mythic unconscious forces that were buried by the colonial Christian imaginary, and thus "died"—the Christian imaginary that, as Walter Benjamin indicated, turned into capitalism. As archetypal components of the psyche, however, such aspects never die; they become more primitive and ever more *destructive* the

[9] *Suffering*, miserable automata, who still expressed emotionally their loss of humanity, however Taylorized it had been. The dream, by contrast, depicts the automation effected by consumerism: hungry, curious, energetic consumers, desiring hedonist machines, whose very emotions and affects replicate the imaginary.

[10] And its hubris: like Walt Disney, he represents the capitalist's dream of becoming a demiurge, a demigod, of fashioning a world and a being according to his image. Rotwang symbolizes the mad hubris of science, which is analogous. In fact the motif of hubris is symbolized as the main "tall building" of Metropolis, the Tower of Babel built to reach heaven.

more they are repressed, the more culture fetters them in the underworld of the unconscious. Symbolically, they become demons.[11]

What the alliance of capital (the bourgeois) and science (the mad scientist) then creates is what would happen in Nazism[12] some years later: the movie expressed symbolically what was still dormant, but already arising, in the collective unconscious. Capital and science fashion a mystery, *a simulacrum of divinity*, of a goddess: the automaton, a demonic technological product who is meant to take the place of *reality* (Maria, the real feminine) and cause an upsurge in the workers, the mass below—in the unconscious energies, in what seemed to be dead—the "catacombs", in cultural terms, in the "mob", the mass mentality.

A simulacrum of a goddess means a simulacrum of myth and religion[13]: an artificial substitute, an ideological simulation that has an equal absolute claim, substituting the current imaginary (Maria as a metaphor for the *Christian* feminine). That was the Nazi totalitarian *ideology*: like the automaton, fruit of an alliance of mob, science, and capital, it emancipates from human control and becomes an utterly destructive and apocalyptic myth. An ideology that sought not merely to control the subjects completely, but to *create* an artificial human being, a perverted simulacrum: to produce an *automaton* that was at the same time a "divinity", the all-powerful and inhuman Nazi *Übermensch*—the actualization of the *Übermensch* that Benjamin (1921/1996) said was the *deus absconditus* of the religion of capitalism, "a religion that offers not the reform of existence but its complete destruction" (p. 289).

This simulacrum of religion causes an eruption in the underground mythic forces, unleashing all the chthonic, dark, primitive impulses (=Hel). In the movie, these impulses appeared as a massive *flood* coming from the underground. Water is the primary archetypal symbol for the unconscious energy, libido, and thus for the unconscious itself. It translated into a *human* flood, the workers transformed into a medieval mob, an uncontrolled mass movement possessed by atavistic irrational forces.

[11] Etymology expresses this idea very well: the Greek *daimon*, the autonomous spiritual principle, connected to individuality (i.e., to the Self), became *demon* under Christianity.

[12] Naturally the Nazis were fascinated by the film, and Thea von Harbou, Fritz Lang's wife and writer of *Metropolis*, later became a devoted Nazi (see Minden & Bachman, 2002).

[13] In fact the whole movie is permeated by religious allusions and archetypal imagery.

The movie ends with a romantic, sentimental reunion. Yet, seen as a symbol, it foreboded the destroying deluge that would soon submerge Europe and capitalist society: its final denouement was the collective psychosis of totalitarianism.

To return to the dreams, *Metropolis* can be seen as a representation of the same phenomenon depicted in the dream in which Ronald McDonald's head appears in the basement, but in a *cultural* scale. Both images present a simulacrum of divinity, a totalizing *ideology* (Nazism, and consumerism as McDonaldization, respectively) that simulates a mythic imaginary and functions as such in the hidden underground, that is, in the unconscious. Underneath the dream-like and artificial world of *Metropolis*, the alienated primitive libido, the mythic forces, resurged as a tsunami. Perhaps that is also what is underneath the paradisiac hyper-business dream-world—the ImCon.

Such dissociated, perilous unconscious forces appeared in a number of other dreams with temples of consumption. The form under which they appeared more often was as *animals*: symbols for the unconscious instincts, the "animal" parts of our psyche. For instance, in some dreams they were caged in malls or department stores, at times in their underground deposits—sometimes hidden, sometimes in plain view. These were not pets, which would represent more humanized, or tamed, forms of instinctual libido, but lions, sea turtles, giant fish, an eagle, sharks, and even a killer whale, sometimes injured, sometimes presenting a menace, but always *captive*, incarcerated, and usually viewed and displayed as *commodities*. Of course each dream can have a different meaning, and each animal can symbolize a different psychological aspect; yet, taken as a whole, they may be interpreted as symbols for what has been discussed as the commodification of instinctual libido.

Other dreams revealed enormous animal-like monsters (like Godzilla, or dinosaurs) connected to such temples of consumption, sometimes chasing the dreamers. While being chased by dangerous animals is a typical dream motif (Jung, CW18, §477), in this case the animal monsters probably represent the caged, commodified instinct turned into a primitive, destructive beast. There were some other nightmares as well, in which uncanny, metaphysical forces emerged in malls, frightening dreamers. In two of them, the perverted or colonized instinct was again symbolized as zombies; and in a rather singular dream, *celebrities* turned zombies attacked and tried to devour and kill the dreamer (this time not in Disneyland: in an underground shopping mall).

If we look at these dreams more culturally than subjectively, they seem to reveal some collective forms or patterns through which the unconscious psyche manifests itself and reacts primitively to what the temples of consumption represent—the ImCon.

11.4 Dreams in Malls

To close this empirical part of the study, a collection of unusual dreams had by a woman is interpreted. They were part of a very long dream series, span across ten years, and reported by her with lots of details. She spontaneously published a separate series under the title "Dreams in malls", from which the specimens below were selected. Originally, I wanted to present some 22 dreams from such series but had to limit their number. The dreams chosen focus more on the unconscious' critical *reaction* to colonization by consumerism, and the ways it depicted the latter's effects upon subjectivity (effects which can be seen as fairly typical). Although many subjective aspects and problems—at times of a very personal nature—were revealed with clarity by the dreams, interpretation tried to avoid discussing them in depth. Instead, the discussion concentrates more on the ways they reflect and illuminate sociocultural themes, the problems and pathos of our times, through typical symbols (which at times are decidedly historical). A few other dreams that provide relevant context are mentioned along with the main ones. Dreams are presented in chronological order.

Some words on the dreamer: American female, in her 60s, a bit of a New Age mystic, she may be considered an "extreme case" in some regards. Judging from her occasional comments and from the dreams themselves, it seemed she did not understand the criticisms the latter expressed (in relation to both her and consumer culture). The first dream offers a disconcerting depiction of the shopping mall symbolizing consumerism.

I was working as a supervisor in a very large building and carried a huge ring of Master keys out in the open so everyone knew who I was on sight. I decide to go buy something at Sears and Roebuck, so I went into the sunny street through some big glass doors, turned left and went to the huge mall that Sears was a part of. I went inside and was dismayed. The inside of the mall was very dim, the halls immense, and there were many stores but their shop windows were very dim also. Even worse, the air quality in the mall was so poor with pollution that I could actually 'see' the air.

I decided to go back to my office. I chose an exit, but was confused to where I actually was. The street name started with 'M' like Masters. I could feel my heart pounding very hard. I went down a hill and looked down this large area where I could see tiny houses and vehicles and trees and even tinier people. Not as small as ants, but very small. Some children were playing on the edge of a cliff where their world ended. I was amazed that these two worlds were coinciding precariously and we were creating havoc in their world with our carelessness and allowing our children to destroy their world.

The dream theme is clearly the shopping mall. However, the exposition presents a related theme: work. It appears in many other dreams as the main possible source of *personal identity* for the dreamer, in two interrelated senses: a concrete one—work as labor, having a job, and so on—and a more symbolical one, working on *herself*, cultivating her personality, her libido, in a productive and creative way. Here such work identity is signified by the symbol of the *keys*; they also figure often in other dreams meaning the possibility of a stable identity, of differentiation as a subject.[14] The expressions used denote power and authority, an individuality that stands out (even in a very large building): she is the one who carries the *Master* keys, and thus "everyone knew *who I was* on sight". Although this image is also connected to a *persona* of authority, it exemplifies how work could provide her a feeling of being her own "master", a strong definition of who she was.

However, her desire to buy, to *consume* something (which, meaningfully, she did not need) elicits a change in the oneiric drama. This is also

[14] For an extensive amplification of the key symbol that is in line with this interpretation, see Chevalier and Gheerbrant (1969/1997, pp. 564–566). Because they represent the power to open and shut entrances, to accede to places, to reveal "closed" things, etc., keys are "symbols of power and authority", and symbolize "chiefs, rulers and mystagogues who possess decision-making powers and responsibility" (pp. 564–565).

a recurrent theme in her dreams: they present "work" and "shopping" as antithetic worlds, or *ethe*, for her. She is again and again confronted with an ethical decision: the choice between work and shopping; between a stable identity gleaned from work, and the consumable identities derived from shopping. Her dreams point that she invariably chooses consumption (here, as in many other dreams, symbolized as "going shopping at the mall"); she does not seem able to obtain and cultivate an identity through work. In this regard she replicates her social reality: she mirrors the cultural shift from work ethic to consumption ethic, from being a "worker" to being a "consumer" as the major source of identity, and the colonization of work ("work"—or in fact labor—as merely a means to consume).

She leaves work through transparent doors; reality outside still seems normal, sunny even, for here it is seen from the standpoint of ego consciousness. She wants to go to Sears, which represents an icon in American capitalist culture since the 1900s; it is the "archetypal" department store as cathedral of consumption. Then she turns to the *left*, to the unconscious,[15] and things change radically: there appears the mall seen from the standpoint of the unconscious—its autonomous *critical view* of the dream-world of consumption. Contrasting with the latter's typical spectacularity and bright opulence, the unconscious unveils through the dream a completely different, even shocking, reality; no wonder she is dismayed. What is usually a profusion of lights and neon, the seductive, fantastic, incessant flow of shining commodity-signs and consumers, now appears as a hazy, empty, immense edifice. This single oneiric image seems to offer a whole panoply of meanings—indeed, the mall here is a true symbol. One curious element there is the blurring of distinctions, an overwhelming dedifferentiation: quality, meaning, value, image, representation—everything seems to have *dissolved* into air. Or, to recall Marx, within this mall all culture—all that is solid and sacred—has been "consumed" and volatilized into pollution, *waste*, which befogs and blurs all perception. If the mall represents a consumption world made of

[15] See, e.g., Jung (CW12), and Chevalier and Gheerbrant (1969/1990, pp. 369–372), entry "Droite (gauche)", for extensive amplification. The left as a symbol of the unconscious psyche is an archetypal motif; it is the sinister unknown side: *la siniestra* (Spanish), *la sinistra* (Italian), *sinister* (Latin).

appearances, here they all disappear; it seems to turn into a dim, opaque, one-dimensional world. There is no one there, no form of life: a radical depiction of the mall as inhuman "non-space" (Augé, 1995), a "nowhere zone" (Kroker, 1992), in which there are neither social bonds, nor differences, nor life. There is an uncanny supernatural quality to it: it *is* an immense temple of consumption, but empty and devoid of humanity.

Thus we arrive at the key idea for this interpretation: that the dream discloses an *objective critique* of consumerism and its imaginary, both of which it symbolizes as the shopping mall—which does not appear as the dream-world representing the "dominant mode of social cohesion" (Kroker & Cook, 2001, p. 21), nor merely as a "neon cage" (Langman, 1992, p. 40), nor as the sardonically named but truth-revealing "lifestyle center". From the unconscious perspective, "the signifying and celebrating edifice of consumer culture" (ibid.) is revealed as an immense, polluted, and empty *phantasmagoria*.

Presumably spooked by the vertigo and *horror vacui* of such spectacle, the dreamer tries to leave. However, the phantasmagoria seems to have a confusing effect, even outside; she does not know where she is, or where she stands. In the dream, the ideology of consumerism is disorienting, transfixing, *intoxicating*; once she is identified with it, it is difficult to "exit" it, and she cannot return to the world of "work". The name of the street, resembling "Masters", is important. If the keys represented an identity and personal autonomy, here it is as if the unconscious asked, "who is really the Master?"—and answered, it is the commodity phantasmagoria. The emotional impact of this revelation is manifest by the heart pounding.

The dream then discloses that such consumption-smog does not limit its impact to her, or to the mall: it diffuses itself and affects the previously "normal" reality—in fact, it seems to mutate and colonize *all her social reality*, in an invisible way, like an atmosphere, or an *imaginary*. Like in the hyper-business city dream, it ends up totalizing the whole environment, by default. Consumption is airborne. The effect: the "normal" people and world outside the mall have been *atomized*. Symbolically, they represent everything in her psychic system that is (or in fact *was*) not related to consumption. The image presents an asymmetrical relationship: whereas the mall (consumerism) is immense and devoid of life, the human *Lebenswelt* (all the rest of her life) grows very small, withering, atomized, an image of (almost) total colonization.

If the mall was the crucial symbolic image before, here the *children* are most important. They symbolize essentially the same that was discussed in the "zombie-moms" dream: the spontaneous, creative, instinctual, natural functioning of the psyche, with all its possibilities. However, it seems that they too have been "poisoned", or *perverted*, by the corrupting ideology: instead of representing natural *creation*, they become destructive, and their "world" can end. This symbolic image can be connected to the zombie-moms dream, in which "children" are replaced by zombies—creative libido turned into compulsive devouring. However, this same dynamic can be seen culturally, in the movie *Metropolis*: at the end of the movie, the workers' children apparently die in the inundation that floods the machine city underground; stricken with grief, the workers become a rampaging medieval mob. Actually, the analogy can be further extended: in this dream too there are "*two worlds* coinciding precariously", and again it is the world *below* that is menaced by havoc and destruction, the world "above", represented by the mall, presumably taking its place. This image points to a possible dissociation[16] in the dreamer's personality, which becomes clear in some other dreams.

What is colonized: personal identity; ego consciousness.

How: through ideology of consumerism, depicted as *phantasmagoria.*

Effects of colonization: unconscious identity; disorientation, dissociation.

The next dream is mentioned because it presents an image of the results of such process of totalizing expansion by consumerism, and her identification with its phantasmagoria:

I lived in a huge house that included its own shopping mall.

[16] Jung points up a typical pattern of the child symbol that is in line with this interpretation: "In the manifold phenomenology of the 'child' we have to distinguish between the *unity* and *plurality* of its respective manifestations. Where (...) numerous (...) boys [or children] appear, having no individual characteristics at all, there is the probability of a *dissociation*. Such forms are therefore found especially in schizophrenia, which is essentially a fragmentation of personality. The many children then represent the products of its dissolution" (CW9, §279). Of course such dissociation cannot be ascribed only to consumerism, and identification with it; but in this dream consumerism clearly stands for the main etiological factor.

The dream symbolism is very clear: as mentioned before, the house represents the dreamer's personality, her own psyche, the way she lives habitually. Like the "huge mall" before, her house is now "huge", "immense": the mall, and all that it symbolizes, colonizes and commodifies her psyche. So part of her own psyche becomes a temple of consumption; her subjectivity and her inner life are more and more defined by *participation mystique* with the ImCon and its ideology, and dependent upon them. If the mall before was essentially empty, that is how a significant part of her personality becomes now: an *empty self*, she will constantly need to fill it artificially with the meanings, values, and identikits offered by commodities—to inflate it artificially with the mall phantasmagoria, so that she can feel "immense".

This interpretation is confirmed by another dream, which I mention briefly here also because it presents a symbol that will reappear in the last dream of this chapter. It is a rather complex and long dream; the parts that interest us are abridged and simplified in what follows.

The dreamer shuts herself off in a shopping mall, where she seemed to live, covering the long hallway she was in with a huge screen. She eventually reaches a shop in a corner. "I then saw a box of jewels which were on necklaces. I wanted one desperately". She then steals a diamond, pushing it down her shirt.

Here the dreamer again lives in a mall, though it is no longer her own house: what was personal and subjective seems to shrink (like the social world outside the mall, in the previous dream) and disappear; all that is left is the mall. Covering it with a screen may represent that, in a way, she seals herself off from any other form of reality, or life, and also that she becomes a *screen*, merely reflecting the imagery and signs of the mall, that is, of the ImCon—a process of full mimesis with it; she turns into its refraction. Yet the most significant part is the last one, with the jewels and the diamond: they represent symbols of the Self, of an individual personality. Such symbols are archetypal, and their meanings analogous to what was discussed before about the symbol of the *stone*—in this case, precious stones. Jung amplifies the symbol of the jewel as it appears in typical mythologems:

> the dragon guards the jewel that has been lost, the jewel being the symbol of the innermost value of man, individuality or the self. That myth is to be found nearly everywhere in the world. The great jewel in Buddhism, the

> *mani* (...) was originally the magic jewel which was hidden in the sea and then brought up to the surface by the gods. Buddha himself is called the *mani*. (Jung, SNZ, p. 264)

And also, "Many myths and images are concerned with the relation to the Self, the lost jewel, for instance, or the precious stone which fell out of the crown and vanished, or the recovery of the treasure" (Jung, SVI, p. 1304). The diamond represents the most precious stone, the symbol of brightness, solidity, perfection, immortality, incorruptibility, of the "true nature" (Chevalier & Gheerbrant, 1969/1997, pp. 291–292), that is, of the perennial *lapis*—the Self. All these meanings embodied by the diamond make it stand as the absolute *antithesis* of the mall phantasmagoria: it is a symbol of true individuality, and that is why the dreamer craves for it "desperately". She thinks she can buy (or in fact steal) it as if it were another merchandise in a shopping mall; that is, she identifies completely with a central ideological belief of consumerism: that individuality is a commodity.[17] In the dream, it is a theft.

What is colonized: dreamer's own personality; her Self.

How: by becoming a mall (full participation mystique with the ImCon); by identifying with (and stealing) a commodity that represents a simulacrum of Self.

Effects of colonization: possible ones—full identity with the imaginary; alienation from life "outside" of consumption (the mall).

The next dream has also been abridged. The hypothesis of a possible dissociation in the dreamer's personality is confirmed; it seems to constitute an essential problem—for her and for consumer culture.

> *The dreamer tries to go to a mall, but is not sure where she is. She has no money and no keys, and walks stiffly, as if her feet moved slowly but were not followed by her mind and the rest of the body.*
>
> *"I got a big shock then: I came out into a brightly lit underground shopping mall. They had everything down there. It seemed like I had been in this place before and had forgotten it was here". In a more dimly lit area, "a person sat alongside a seemingly stuffed animal bigger than life: the purple Barney. I knew*

---

[17] This interpretation was also confirmed by other dreams in which the symbol of the jewel appeared with the same meanings.

> *these were security guards in case there was trouble. Next to them were a restaurant and a jewelry shop. You could buy anything down here in this completely underground mall. I really wanted to buy something but had no money, so I decided I'd go home, get some money and come back and shop. Just as I turned around, one of the security guards got up from the table and came over to me. It was a woman, threatening and intimidating. She asked strongly, 'I need to see your picture I.D.!' I said twice, 'I'm sorry, but I didn't bring it with me nor any money!"*

The narrative starts with the same theme: "going shopping", which, for the dreamer, means communion and identity with the imaginary of consumption. The effects portrayed are similar: she seems lost and disoriented; again she does not have keys, that is, no *identity*—symbolizing a state of alienation from herself. However, here it appears not as mere alienation, but rather clearly as a dissociation of the personality: what is *below* (feet) moves independently from what is above (mind and body). The reader might recall that the children and the world "outside" the mall were *below*, that is, the foundations, the contact with the soil and reality, are split from the rest of the personality (which once again seeks a mall).

In fact this split in her psyche appears even more bluntly in a preceding dream, which, being rather complicated, can be summarized thusly: she faces the choice between "work" and "shopping" and again chooses shopping. Then she has no keys but insists on reaching the mall. Yet, typically, the unconscious puts her in another place: she suddenly realizes she is driving through the "wild country"—dark, uncanny, weed and flowers invading, an image of an abandoned, uncultivated area. The road is called "Schism Way"; it grows narrower and narrower, turns into sand, until she cannot go any further. That is, the schism is between her "ways"—the mall, her almost total identity with the dream-world of consumption, and the "*wild* country", what is below: the chthonic, Nature, instinct; in sum, the unconscious psyche in its more wild, primitive form, her *shadow*. That is what she is forced to confront, stuck in Schism Way. However, she tries to evade the problem and leave. The dream ironically places a sign in her way, with "Thanks for sightseeing at Schism Way" written on it, meaning, this is *your* split life, your ways are dissociated, schizoid, and yet you treat it as if you were just sightseeing.... At the end of the dream, the unconscious again forces her to face the shadow, which this time appears as a *black snake*, connected to the word "devil". That is also typical: here it is no longer only her personal shadow (the split parts of her personality that remain in the unconscious) but the archetypal, collective shadow: the "devil", an image that signals a very deep schism, indeed, one that reaches the collective foundations of her psyche, one that mirrors the historical schism in our culture. The same symbol appeared in Jung's analysis of a patient:

> The [black] snake, like the devil in Christian theology, represents the shadow, and one which goes far beyond anything personal and could therefore best be compared with a principle, such as the principle of evil. It is the colossal shadow thrown by man, of which our age had to have such a devastating experience.[18] (Jung, CW9i, § 567)

Let us return to the main dream: the dreamer is then shocked by the spectacle of the underground shopping mall. Symbolically, it is almost obvious: it represents the colonization of the *underground*, of the unconscious psyche itself—which becomes a paradisiac dream-world of consumption. Subjectively, it is the radical concretization of what appeared in the massive stone temple dream as a possibility. However, one should also consider an interpretation on the objective level: isn't this dream revealing a process that is also cultural? In that case, it would mean that the "underground temple"—the symbolico-religious unconscious—is replaced by a shopping mall. Theoretically, it would symbolize the cultural colonization of the collective unconscious—the very source of symbols and the imaginary—by the ImCon, which takes its place.

At any rate, what appears in the underground is an unexpected, even bizarre *cultural* image: the purple Barney dinosaur, a cartoon character—a commodity-sign typical of the ImCon. But why does the dream employ such odd image? It can only be explained by considering that Barney is in fact a *tyrannosaurus*. As a cold-blooded, dangerous reptile, it is a reappearance of the black snake—the most primitive, archaic instinctual sphere, the chthonic foundations of the unconscious psyche:

[18] Jung was referring to the evils of totalitarianism.

> the snake is the commonest symbol for the dark, chthonic world of instinct. It may—as frequently happens—be replaced by an equivalent cold-blooded animal, such as a dragon, crocodile, or fish. (Jung, CW9ii, §385)

The facts that such dark chthonic powers were connected with the devil, in the previous dream; that Barney is a typical image of mass consumer culture; and that it is in the depths of consumerism's signifying edifice all point to the idea that Barney symbolizes not merely the dreamer's personal shadow but the *collective* shadow of consumerism: the atavistic instinctual forces of the collective unconscious. As the reader may recall, the alienation, colonization, and perversion of the instinctual foundations appeared before—under many forms, but especially as destructive animals and animal monsters. In this dream, it appears as the most dangerous, voracious, and primeval predator—but absolutely infantilized, commodified, and bowdlerized: Barney is a stuffed animal that hosts a television show for children, a typical representative of the global ImCon, therefore, another creature of imagineering, but one that comes to life through a child's *imagination* (thus representing it). In fact, the dream could not have chosen a more perfect symbol for the cultural bowdlerization and commodification of both imagination and the primeval instincts. Like other similar cultural signs that appeared in the dreams (Disney characters, Ronald McDonald, etc.), Barney is another *model* for the mass production of consuming *children*—who, of course, unquestioningly follow him in his show. He basically embodies an always happy, anesthetized, alienated consumer. His voice is "dopey" and he does not display any facial expressions other than a toothy grin; he is self-centered and saccharine and lives in a paradise in which conflicts and negative feelings and emotions simply do not exist. As Levy (1994) puts it, "the real danger from Barney is *denial*: the refusal to recognize the existence of unpleasant realities" (p. 192)—the denial of reality that characterizes both consumerism and the dreamer, denial that allows for living permanently in a condition of sedated happiness, within a childish dream-world—the world of Barney, the shopping mall, the dream-world of consumption. Levy adds: "along with his steady diet of giggles and unconditional love, Barney offers our children *a one-dimensional world* where everyone must be happy" (p. 191; e.a.).

Thus Barney represents the undergrounds of the one-dimensional world of consumption as its "security guard": the dark, primitive collective forces (the black snake) seemingly under total control, the instincts thoroughly commodified and turned to consumption.[19] However, behind the façade of stupefied elation, *it is still a Tyrannosaurus Rex*—and that is precisely why the dream employs him as a symbol. Put simply, it is the dinosaur, that colossal, ferocious, primeval animality that seems to be *extinct* but somehow resurfaces, an atavistic force of which neither the sci-fi dream's hungry consumers-salesmen nor the buoyant bourgeoisie in *Metropolis* seemed to present the slightest vestige, because it was *buried in the unconscious*. Meaningfully, in the last two decades, the image of the dinosaur appears to have resurrected as an immensely successful commodity-motif in consumer culture (Mitchell, 1998). One can recall *Jurassic Park*, in which these primeval monsters are unleashed within an artificial thematic park (like Disneyland, a microcosm for technological consumerism and the ImCon). Godzilla, the apocalyptic, gigantic reptile that resurges from the *sewers* and brings collective catastrophe, is another conspicuous example among many others.

To summarize, the key idea is that these symbols represent the shadowy instinctual side in what used to be called the "mass man" (i.e., mass mindedness). Commenting upon a dream had by Hannibal[20] before his conquest of Rome, Jung (SNZ) mentions the typicality of such symbol: "Any organized body of men is a huge snake; one dreams of such things in that form" (p. 598). It is "the crowd within", the foundation underlying mass mentality[21]: the *most primitive side of the collective unconscious*—the instinctual roots which, when not expressed and channeled by symbolic systems and rites, remain untamed, unchecked, inhuman, perverted—even if they appear mesmerized, stupefied, and buried by the ImCon's semiotic system.

---

[19] In this sense, Barney would represent an analogous image to Hobbes's *Leviathan*: it is the way the social order of consumerism subjugates the *lupus* side of human nature.

[20] "It is like that famous dream of Hannibal before he went to Rome: he saw himself with his hosts conquering cities and fighting battles, but then he turned around and saw a huge monster crawling behind him, eating up all the countries and towns" (Jung, SNZ, p. 1296).

[21] "The larger an organization the lower its morality. (…) the largest organized groups are from a psychological point of view clumsy, stupid, and amoral monsters like those huge saurians with an incredibly small brain. (…) they are childish and moody, helpless victims of their emotions [and] stupid to an amazing degree" (Jung, CW18, §§1315–1316). Barney fits this description perfectly.

Continuing with the dream, next the dreamer sees a restaurant (which will reappear in a following dream) and the *jewelry* shop (representing the commodity-self for sale, the ersatz identity). The last scene is meaningful: for her, to have an identity (I.D.) is equal to having money, and thus being able to consume; to be a consumer is now the only possible definition of identity.

What is colonized: unconscious personality, including the primeval instinctual sphere (possible related interpretation—colonization of the collective unconscious in culture).

How: again, by becoming a mall; in relation to the primitive shadow, by being commodified into an ImCon character.

Effects of colonization: full identity with the imaginary; split personality.

The next dream shows the underground mall under a different light: the *reductive function* of the unconscious.

> *I started walking down the hall of my house and it appeared I was inside that underground mall I discovered last week in another dream. I had to walk a long way through the mall. There were lots and lots of jostling people out here. I assumed my office was at the far end. I was having trouble getting through the crowds. It seemed more and more nasty looking. The walls and floors were dirty. There were fewer people here but those I saw looked like bad off drug addicts, drunks, and the really bad off people.*

The image seems to point to the possibility that her unconscious psyche has been nearly thoroughly colonized: if the mall was just *part* of her house before, now the house has been taken over—and also the office (the world of work). That is, almost the whole personality is depicted as being an underground mall; the process of expansion or diffusion of the consumption phantasmagoria, initiated in the first dream, is nearly concluded here. Yet, in contrast with the previous dream, in which the underground mall still appears as the dream-world in which everything is available, here its ideological and fictitious character is fully disclosed. The "mass mentality", or crowd psychology, insinuated before, here appears concretely as a jostling mob. The shadow aspects are typical: the psychic depths appear bad off, "nasty looking", dirty. The character of craving and compulsion related to consumption—the colonized desires and instincts—is personified as addicts and drunks. Her underground psyche, turned into a mall, is disclosed as a dark nightmarish world.[22]

What is colonized: unconscious psyche.

How: again, underground psyche appears as a mall—full identity with the imaginary.

Effects of colonization: split personality; addiction, compulsion.

A surprising development in the dream-images occurs in the next dream, which has been abridged; the interpretation concentrates on its main themes.

> *I was with the owner of a fancy restaurant in the basement of a mall. Many rich people came here. The owner told us that she had created a shrine downstairs of the original kitchen because Hitler used to come there and stand outside a window and paint. We went down the stairs which were deep. I felt really comfortable going down these stairs because I had done it so many times before. Here there was a huge old-fashioned kitchen which had been preserved. Within the shrine, we could stand in the exact spot where Hitler had stood. It was beautiful down there.*

The main theme and scenery is the mall: it reappears the way the dreamer's ego sees it—glamorous, wealthy, fancy, signifying the ImCon's fetishist dream-world. The restaurant owner, a female, is the dreamer's shadow, with whom she identifies. Then there is again the motif of descent; this time she goes further down, reaching what is underneath the basement—seemingly the mall's netherworld, what is "buried" beneath it, deep down: a kitchen. The restaurant and the kitchen indicate the symbolism of food, already discussed in Chap. 5; basically, they refer to the ways one deals with emotions, affectivity, the gut feelings—the *fire*, the passions—and cultivates and transforms them. Considering that the kitchen is deep underground,[23] it is connected to the primeval irrational libido, the visceral unconscious, and its emotional charge (see Jung,

---

[22] This dream-image is reminiscent of the last one in the "reoccurring nightmare", in which the Disney ImCon's *phantasmagoric* face is revealed, and also of the zombie-moms in Disneyland.

[23] Considering also the symbols that appeared before: the black snake and Barney, which point to the primitive instincts.

CW16, §378). This kitchen has a religious connotation, for it has been transformed into a *shrine*. The image recalls the underground temple: the deep-rooted archetypal foundations, source of numen and symbol. Or, put differently, it reminds one of what used to coordinate and transform the primeval libido, the ancient "cultural kitchen", so to speak, the symbolic "recipes" (rites, myths, etc.) of religious imaginaries, natural expressions of the archetypal spring.

Eerily enough, like the Mexican temples in previous dreams, this particular kitchen-shrine has also been "preserved" and is "old-fashioned" and historical. However, what is worshiped there, the divinity one would expect to find, is Hitler: the obvious cultural symbol for a *totalitarian ideology*, here functioning as the enshrined myth that underlies, very deep down, the edifice of consumerism.

This image, taken in isolation, may be interpreted in a number of different ways. However, if we compare it to analogous symbols that appeared in her previous dreams, some ideas stand out as more apposite. First, Hitler appears deep underground, where Barney was: he represents a transformation, or symbolic incarnation, of the devilish black snake. Instead of the stupefied, commodified *Tyrannosaurus Rex*,[24] perhaps what is revealed is its true historical face: the arch *tyrant* himself, the *Führer*, embodying the collective, archetypal shadow. Psychologically, the oneiric image represents the atavistic primeval instincts commanded by the maximum cultural symbol of *totalitarianism*—as ruthless, cruel, and inhuman as a tyrannosaurus. However, both images appear as simulacra: just like the murderous dinosaur appears as the retarded Barney, Hitler assumes the guise of the romantic painter, in a very idyllic, beautiful shrine[25]—in a totally ideological *denial of reality*, which mirrors the imaginaries that both symbols represent (the ImCon and the totalitarian Nazi ideology).

Seen on a subjective level, the dream implies that the ideology of consumerism—the ImCon—finally becomes a totalitarian shrine deep down the dreamer's psychic basement, thus commandeering and ruling her

[24] *Tyrannosaurus* = from Greek *turannos* (tyrant) + *sauros* (lizard). *Rex* = king (replaced by *Führer*, Great Leader).

[25] There are many other psychological elements related to this image and the dynamics it symbolizes—e.g., Hitler, being a man, can be seen as an *animus* figure: the embodiment of the collective unconscious in the woman, her "masculine" psyche, with its characteristic effects and dynamics. However, as in other dreams, interpretation had to leave these more clinical considerations aside.

very instinctual foundations, her archaic libido, from within. An outstanding illustration of the ImCon colonizing the deepest recesses of the unconscious psyche as a simulacrum of religion, and especially of its totalitarian character.

Nonetheless, this dream should also be seen on an objective level. If we consider it in parallel with Benjamin's underground shrine, and also with what was discussed regarding the movie *Metropolis*, isn't it a *possible* depiction of what lies in the psychological undergrounds of (American) consumer culture? Again, the symbols the dreams employ are not personal at all but clearly cultural and collective. Furthermore, they all signify the shopping mall—the dream-world of *consumerism*, not only for the dreamer but rather for the whole globe; and, most importantly, they seem to unveil what is *underneath* consumerism, its very hidden foundations or subterranean stream. If we unite the three parallel depictions of such foundations given by these dreams, namely, the jostling mob and addicts; Barney, the T-Rex; and Hitler, what seems to appear is the colossal collective *shadow* of consumption: a barbaric mass mentality, with religious tones, whose primitive affects and instincts are totalized, stupefied, and controlled by the imaginary as if it were a totalitarian ideology, a transcendent objective power that rules from within. In this sense, the dream would be a strikingly *exact* depiction of a core characteristic of postmodernity, the cultural logic of consumerism: that "It represses its own history (and tendency towards cultural fascism) *beneath* the logic of the shopping mall" (Berry, 2010, p. 77; e.a.). At the same time, it reflects a cultural phenomenon that, according to Baudrillard (2002), is symptomatic of our "current imagination": "a perverse fascination with a return to the wellsprings of violence, a collective attempt to hallucinate the historical truth of evil" (p. 15).

Seen culturally, the dream also presents a curious depiction of what Walter Benjamin (1921/1996) saw as the *deus absconditus* of capitalism as a monstrous religion: the *Übermensch*, the posthuman demigod which Hitler incarnated,[26] appearing here ensconced in the underground shrine of consumer society's edifice. A *Übermensch* for whom everything is pos-

[26] "When Nietzsche wrote his prophetic masterpiece, *Thus Spake Zarathustra,* he certainly had not the faintest notion that the superman [*Übermensch*] he had created out of his personal misery and inefficiency would become a prophetic anticipation of a Führer or Duce" (Jung, CW18, §1333).

sible, because *everything is available*, who, transcending every human boundary, can fashion a world (a hyperreality) and be *anything*—all through consumption. The perfect model of divinity for the mass of *Untermenschen* consumers. In the dream, this model is available as a sort of religious entertainment, that is one can "stand" exactly where Hitler stood, that is, can *identify* with him, standing in his place.

The subjective attitude of the dreamer seems to be precisely a complete uncritical identification, a full *participation mystique* with the totalitarian imaginary: she feels "really comfortable" with it and finds everything beautiful. That she had "gone down the shrine" many times before indicates that such *participation mystique* has been the basis of her psychological functioning for some time; it has come to define her.

What is colonized: the very foundations of the unconscious psyche; whole personality.

How: by replacing such foundations with a totalitarian "cult" (i.e., the ideology of consumption is revealed as totalitarian).

Effects of colonization: full participation mystique with the imaginary.

The last dream concludes this rather unorthodox series of dreams on malls, and may be seen as a confirmation of the interpretations delineated above, especially as regards the dreamer's colonized identity. Her ego attitude and emotional reaction to it can be seen in the commentary with which she introduces the dream: "I love this dream, it is so cool".

> *I was in New Berlin. It seemed like my house, but it was also like a shopping mall. I picked up some jewels. Two of them actually belonged to a woman from church, but now that I had them I was going to have them set into a ring for myself. When I got to the store part of the house, a female friend of mine was there. She told me that she always bought my jewels. I disagreed totally and told her I had my own credit card.*

The house, as a symbol of the personality, again appears as a mall, or indistinguishable from one. However, the name of the place, and of the mall itself, gives away the totalitarian character of colonization by consumerism: in an obvious allusion to the image and meaning of Hitler in the previous dream, here her psyche has been transformed into *New*

Berlin,[27] a new colonial outpost gained by the consumerist regime. The symbol of the jewel also reappears, and with the same meaning: a representation of a fake, stolen Self, the only identity permissible and conceded in New Berlin—that given by a commodity-sign. Once again, the unconscious stresses that such identity does not belong to the dreamer; part of it was from "a woman from church"—possibly a shadow figure, connoting what the dreamer *could* be, a different aspect of her. Yet the dreamer again "steals" it. The mention of a church (which is connected to the "shrine" before) hints that what originally had a truly religious character—the jewel as symbol of individuality and Self, the spirituality of the previous owner, the church itself—is transferred to consumption: the jewel as a fetishized commodity-sign, its worship by the dreamer, and the mall as the church of total consumerism.

The female friend who appears then is another shadow figure, this time representing the *store*, the clearly and utterly commodified part of the dreamer's psyche—analogously to the symbol of the restaurant owner before, she stands for full identity with the ImCon. The friend points critically that the jewels, again, are not the dreamer's: it is not her *own* identity, her self, but a fictional commodity-self bought by someone else. The dreamer's answer to this questioning is revealing: it shows that for her it is not even the jewel, the meaning contained in a concrete product, that confers identity; identity is bestowed solely by the behavior of *buying*, by the *idea* of consuming.

In fact, the dream shows that she follows faithfully the immanent principle of consumerism, its metaphysical foundation: I shop therefore I am. Her existence, her "jewel", her Self are defined by her immaterial purchase power, which finally becomes her "innermost value", her *Master*: the key for actualizing all her consumption dreams. Within this totalitarian consumerism, deeply ingrained in her own mind, *her life and identity are defined by her credit card*. As the American Express slogan ran in 2006, "My Life. [American Express logo]. My card."

Buying is the new being.

[27] "New Berlin" is a shopping mall that appears first in the dream with the black snake, and then in many other dreams of hers.

References

Augé, M. (1995). *Non-places: Introduction to an anthropology of supermodernity* (J. Howe, Trans.). London: Verso.

Balandier, G. (1985). *Le détour: Pouvoir et modernité*. Paris: Fayard.

Baudrillard, J. (2002). *Screened out* (C. Turner, Trans.). London: Verso.

Benjamin, W. (1996). Capitalism as religion. In M. P. Bullock & M. W. Jennings (Eds.), *Walter Benjamin selected writings, Vol. 1: 1913–1926* (pp. 288–291). Cambridge, MA: Harvard University Press. (Original work written 1921).

Benjamin, W. (1999). *The arcades project* (H. Eiland & K. McLaughlin, Trans.). Cambridge: The Belknap Press of Harvard University Press.

Berry, G. (2010). The mythic element of mass media and its relation to Plato's cave. *PLATFORM: Journal of Media and Communication*, ANZCA Special Edition (April), 72–85.

Chevalier, J., & Gheerbrant, A. (1990). *Dictionnaire des symboles: Mythes, réves, coutumes, gestès, formes, figures, couleurs, nombres* (11ème ed., revue et corrigée). Paris: Ed. Robert Laffont/Jupiter. (Original work published 1969).

Chevalier, J., & Gheerbrant, A. (1997). *The Penguin dictionary of symbols* (Trans. J. Buchanan-Brown). London: Penguin. (Original work published 1969).

Fiske, J. (2000). Shopping for pleasure: Malls, power, and resistance. In J. B. Schor & D. B. Holt (Eds.), *The consumer society reader* (pp. 306–330). New York: The New Press.

Kowinski, W. (1984). *The malling of America: An inside look at the great consumer paradise*. New York: William Morrow Co.

Kroker, A. (1992). *The possessed individual: Technology and the French postmodern*. Montreal: New World Perspectives.

Kroker, A., & Cook, D. (2001). *The postmodern scene: Excremental culture and hyper-aesthetics* (2nd ed.). Montreal: New World Perspectives.

Lang, F. (Director). (1927). *Metropolis* [Motion picture]. Germany: Universum Film AG.

Langman, L. (1992). Neon cages: Shopping for subjectivity. In R. Shields (Ed.), *Lifestyle shopping: The subject of consumption* (pp. 40–82). New York: Routledge.

Levy, C. W. (1994, February). The bad news about Barney. *Parents Magazine*, pp. 191–92.

Marx, K. (1990). *Capital: Critique of political economy* (B. Fowkes, Trans., Vol. 1). Harmondsworth: Penguin. (Original work published 1867).

Meier, C. A. (2003). *Healing dream and ritual: Ancient incubation and modern psychotherapy*. Switzerland: Daimon Verlag. (Original work published 1983).
Minden, M., & Bachman, H. (Eds.). (2002). *Fritz Lang's Metropolis: Cinematic visions of technology and fear*. New York: Camden House.
Mitchell, W. J. T. (1998). *The last dinosaur book: The life and times of a cultural icon*. Chicago: The University of Chicago Press.
Ritzer, G. (2000). *The McDonaldization of society* (New Century ed.). Thousand Oaks, CA: Pine Forge.
Ritzer, G. (2001). *Explorations in the sociology of consumption: Fast food, credit cards and casinos*. London: Sage.

12

Conclusions

This concluding chapter presents a condensation and articulation of the major findings of this study in relation to the research objectives proposed, discussing the extent to which this work hopes to have fulfilled them and some of their main implications. The chapter closes with a discussion of the limitations of this work and offers brief recommendations and suggestions for future research.

Recapitulating, the proposal that summarizes this study was formulated thusly: to investigate what night dreams can reveal about contemporary consumerism and its social imaginary, being a subject within it, and how it conditions and institutes such being. Accordingly, its main research aim consisted in exploring how night dreams represented the colonization of subjectivity by the imaginary of consumerism. Such aim was informed by a set of specific objectives; in what follows they are briefly recalled, starting by the more theoretical and epistemological ones.

M. Xavier, *Subjectivity, the Unconscious and Consumerism*,
https://doi.org/10.1007/978-3-319-96824-7_12

12.1 Objectives, Findings, and Implications

Thus, two of the specific objectives were more focused on theory: developing and advancing theoretical propositions, based on a Jungian theoretical framework, in order to interpret and understand the phenomena under study; and recovering and signaling the importance of dreams. Regarding the first objective, it is hoped that this work has produced some evidences of the value and validity of the theoretical propositions and hermeneutic method of analytical psychology as a precious means to understand the dreams, the subject, and the social imaginary in contemporaneity. Also, it trusts that it has accomplished, at least to some extent, its rather ambitious pretension of showing that a different theory on the unconscious psyche can be valuable for social psychology, and psychology in general, in their efforts at understanding the psychological subject. An important part of such theory was confirmed empirically in this work: it has shown that it is not only subjectivity but rather the *whole psyche* that is sociocultural and essentially *historical*—which includes its deepest unconscious layers. Such historicity of the psyche was most clearly manifest in some oneiric images that disclosed their archetypal character: they reveal that the psyche produces autonomously some typical forms that are found across different cultures and ages—a phenomenon evidenced through comparison with parallel cultural and historical symbolic manifestations. That corresponds to two important theoretical propositions, which seemed to be confirmed empirically by the dreams and their interpretation: that the psyche naturally expresses itself through the *symbol* and that the symbol must be considered in its unparalleled specificity—as an irrational totality in itself, which represents a reunion of meanings and values and thus the very possibility of dialectics. Its importance as foundational expression of the psyche is connected to its role as origin and primeval constituent of symbolic imaginaries, and thus of *culture*. Perhaps the most significant theoretical proposition resulting from such considerations is that ultimately the psyche and its products can only be understood in depth through a comparative hermeneutic method, which takes into account both cultures and individuals in their symbol-producing capacity.

Dreams, as the main theme and empirical material of this work, represent the natural expression of such capacity. Their manifold relevance, which is impossible to summarize in a few words, was affirmed and analyzed throughout this study. One of their important qualities that was demonstrated here is that they offer a veritable wealth of *meanings* and *signification*; indeed, as a colleague commented once, they disclose a *world*—the inner world of the unconscious psyche, the symbolic, irrational, nocturnal imaginary in us.

This last assertion renders explicit a central feature of this study, namely, the rather distinct *theory on the unconscious* upon which it is grounded. It is hoped that the relevance and usefulness of such theory have been made clear for the reader. Indeed, it may simply consist in a *different paradigm* for psychology, based on the rescue of a humanist concept of the unconscious, and the symbolic realm, as the primeval *foundation* for both the social (culture) and the subject—and hence of both psychology and social psychology as sciences. Within the dialectics between the subject and the sociocultural realm is inserted an *objective* factor, the unconscious psyche, which is seen as the original foundation and common denominator of both. Moreover, such foundation is the very historical matrix that produces symbols—and thus signification, *meaning*—autonomously in each person.

It is not difficult to imagine the importance that the consideration and understanding of the unconscious mind (especially the collective unconscious) has for assessing and comprehending current contemporary phenomena (both in the social and in the individual). Utilizing such perspective can provide answers to an old problem in social psychology: its social relevance. Indeed, it can generate "a social psychology that is dedicated to the systematic explanation of contemporary phenomena" (Rosés & Gabarrón, 1984, p. 94). Among the latter, one may mention both social change and ideology, most especially in this age of worldwide Islamist terrorism, genocide by ISIS, religious and tribal wars in a collapsing Middle East and Africa, and the menace of a (global?) resurgence of fascism and totalitarianism—all these phenomena require social psychology to address the profound unconscious, mythic, irrational factors that lie at their roots.

Most importantly, such different perspective or paradigm would allow us to deal with a central human aspect: the symbolic realm. One of its most crucial expressions has nearly been forgotten by social psychology, since the latter's inception with Wilhelm Wundt: *myth*. As argued above, myths are all-important elements for understanding both the social and the individual—especially in our epoch of fabricated, consumerist myths.

Such different concept of the unconscious underlies the equally distinct theory on dream employed in this study, which stands in opposition to the more or less prevalent attitudes toward night dreams in the contemporary collective consciousness. Such attitudes may be abridged under two main forms, or paradigms: the dream is seen (1) as an ultimately meaningless *epiphenomenon* of neurobiological structures, (2) through an apotropaic and ideological theory of *fulfillment of wishes,* which is actually the historical predecessor of the mutation of dream into "consumption dream", the fulfillment of desire (wish) through consumption. This work demonstrates that, given the astonishing significance of some dreams, paradigm (1) can only be seen as ludicrous, ahistorical, and ideological. Regarding paradigm (2), in this study there is not a single example in which the monocausal theory of "fulfillment of wishes" would be of much use[1]; nearly all the dreams criticize the more or less conscious "wish" (the dreamer's attitude or desire in the dream), and in the instances in which they do not, the "wish" represents rather *an ethical task* that is portrayed as *contra culturam*.

Against such views, the interpretations made in this study reveal not only that the dreams are profoundly meaningful but also that they offer an *objective* discourse, stemming from a very critical viewpoint, on both culture and individual—a discourse that can be sarcastic, sardonic, ironic, even iconoclastic. Dreams like the "massive stone temple" one, for instance, unveiled cultural, subjective, and even *historical* realities with seemingly inhuman acumen: their source is obviously something that transcends the subjects—what one might deem a "superior knowledge", an *irrational* wit or wisdom: the wisdom of Nature. If one strips oneself of rationalistic and postmodern prejudices, this assertion does not sound

---

[1] And, incidentally, there is not a single dream here that can be seen as having a primarily sexual nature.

surprising or mysterious, and for two reasons. One regards Nature: if the unconscious is Nature in us, it will express Nature's wisdom. The other regards history: dreams have *always* been considered as *messengers of gods*, and of *daimons*, spirits, and so on: in one word, of what transcends the merely human. It is only in our rationalist, secularized, and colonized age that dreams are emptied of their meaning and value. That is, the dream is one of the prime manifestations of the symbolic faculty which is and has always been the expressive form of the transcendental, the suprasensory and *numinous*, that is actually immanent in each one of us. Such transpersonal, natural realm is what seems to criticize, trial, and frighten the dreamers; indeed, at times the dreams seem to express the way a transcendental being, a primitive *divinity*, would speak of our misery, of our vain attempts at being posthuman demigods when in fact our humanity is being lost. The center, the transcendental organizing factor that originates such symbolic expressions, is the Self, an *autonomous ethical center in the unconscious*—which is at the same time the virtual totality of the personality; it is the *foundation* of the psyche and has always been. Ultimately, the dreams showed that the reactions from the unconscious can only be understood as manifestations of such foundation.

Such oneiric manifestations revealed symbolically some typical patterns in meaning, which included typical mutations in the imaginary, typical forms of colonization, and typical reactions from the unconscious. Their discussion was informed by three other research aims of an empirical character, namely, discerning, interpreting, and understanding in such patterns (1) which psychological factors or realms were colonized; (2) how the colonization was effected; and (3) the effects that colonization seemed to entail. It seems appropriate to reiterate two general warnings in relation to such discussion. Firstly, some night dreams allowed for an interpretation on the *objective* level, which did not refer only to psychological subjective factors but rather to the sociocultural realms that condition and institute them. As often as possible, interpretation and discussion took into consideration this possible "sociocultural critique", as it were, offered by the dreams. Secondly, in relation to subjectivity, as mentioned, due to the symbolic nature of dreams, it is often rather difficult to delimit very clearly, in terms of strictly defined concepts, what subjective factors and realms they are alluding to, and even what effects—in psychological terms—they seem to point at. This is one of the main reasons for seeking patterns in *meaning* in the dreams, for they usually do not refer directly to the dreamer's "unconscious psyche", or "split personality", for instance; these are interpretations and translations of symbolic images (such as "the underground", a schism between above and below, feet and head, and so on) into meaningful psychological concepts, translations that always remain somewhat forced and incomplete in relation to the original dream symbol (which, to recall Jung's definition, is the best possible definition of something that is irrational and ultimately unknown).

Thus, in what follows, a brief overview of some important patterns that summarize the most relevant empirical findings is presented, together with some of their implications; it follows the order of the three specific empirical aims mentioned above.

(1) Which realms and factors were colonized in the dreams: First, some dreams demanded an interpretation on the objective level, which seemed to point at a total colonization by consumerism of the *social* realm, appearing, for example, as the whole "city", or "country". In accordance with the theoretical argumentation developed previously, these dreams were interpreted as the oneiric depiction of the imaginary of consumerism taking over culture itself, and turning into a totalizing regime of signification, that is, becoming a homogeneous collective consciousness. In relation to subjectivity proper, taken as a conjunct, the night dreams revealed a general colonization of the *psyche*, which, nonetheless, appeared under a variety of symbolic forms signifying different psychological realms, which were interpreted as, for example, the subject's emotional and affective realms, fantasy and imagination, creativity, desire, "libido", femininity, and others. However, one may summarize such diverse forms under one general idea, namely, that the main colonization was of the dreamers' psychological *identity*. As discussed, identity here is meant in two complementary senses: its common one, as the subjective sense and definition of personhood, and in the Jungian sense, as unconscious identification (with the imaginary). Such colonization of identity appeared in a variety of forms, involving different parts of the personality: the dreams unveiled the ImCon shaping, defining, and colonizing the persona, ego consciousness, the unconscious psyche (and thus what was called unconscious subjectivity), and, in some dreams, even the Self—meaning

the whole personality, its very foundations. Most importantly, many dreams reaffirmed what had been shown by the prototype dream: a colonization by consumerism of what seemed to be the dreamers' religious and symbolic functioning, of what was *sacred* in them and for them. That simply represents the typical and most profound form of functioning of the irrational, unconscious psyche. Accordingly, some dreams revealed more or less explicitly the ImCon taking over and commanding the unconscious' archetypal expressions and primitive instinctual libido—the very "depths" of the psyche, indeed its primeval underground foundations. Such oneiric discourses seemed to confirm the theoretical argumentation that the regime of consumerism in fact aims at psychological *totalization*—at fabricating a mimesis, or homoousia, of the psyche with its ideological imaginary.

(2) How the colonization was effected: In the dreams, colonization appeared under many distinct symbolic forms. Yet, seen in very general terms and in accordance with this study's theoretical framework, the colonization of subjectivity appeared to be effected through the social imaginary: through its hegemony of *social signification*, it institutes and formats the psychological subject. The element that appeared as central for such process is the *symbol*: typical commodity-signs of the imaginary of consumerism appeared in many dreams functioning artificially as if they were symbols. Some dreams revealed clearly a *colonization of symbolic imaginaries* by the ImCon—colonization that appeared as analogous to a historical pattern, that of Christianity and its imperial conquests of other peoples and their imaginaries. In this sense, the dreams confirmed Augé's (1999) anthropological theory on the "confrontation of imaginaries", and depicted contemporarily what Gruzinski (1988) called "colonization of imaginaries", which was engendering the colonization of the dreamer's own imagination and "inner" imaginary. Such phenomenon was understood through the theory that it is indeed central for the totalizing efforts of the ImCon that everything that is symbolic and sacred has to be replaced by the semiotic ideology of consumption and its semiurgy of images, in an "operation of total substitution" (Augé, 1999, p. 1). Many dreams displayed clearly the adequacy of such theory; indeed, in them consumerism is represented as a totalizing ideology, disclosed as what Marx (1867/1993) and Benjamin (1999) theorized as *phantasmagoria*—but in symbolical

form. Startlingly enough, in the last dreams analyzed in this work, the ImCon is unveiled as *fully totalitarian*; through them, the unconscious seemed to confirm one main idea advanced in the theoretical framework, namely, that the *telos* of contemporary consumerism is to become total—to produce and control totally both world and subject.

Besides such radical depiction, the most important form of colonization of subjectivity—which appeared repeatedly—was the *ImCon functioning as a simulation of myth or religion, a simulacrum of symbolic imaginary*. Moreover, the dreams revealed that the enchantment, numen, and fetish of such religion of consumption were *phantasmagorias*, symbolized as dream-worlds reigned over by consumption, and also as semiotic *models* that replaced archetypal, historical symbols. Such kind of functioning was usually portrayed as simply happening, as a "natural", automatic phenomenon that took place in or even invaded by default the dreamer's psyche. Although the dreams were not explicit in this regard, the logical conclusion is that the ImCon colonizes and institutes the psychological subject in the same totalizing way a religion does—as a total regime of signification that is naturalized and taken for granted, creating a form of psychological functioning characterized by unconscious identity with it. That consists in the main theoretical proposition for how colonization is effected, which appeared empirically in several dreams: that the imaginary of consumerism engenders *participation mystique* through its dream-worlds and typical consumption dreams, its models for subjectivity, imagery, myths, and so on, which, functioning as archaic *représentations collectives*, fashion the subject as a consumer, identified (and at times identical) with its transcendental ideology. In the dreams, such mythical *représentations* even appeared as ersatz archetypal "deities". Thus the possible result of such *participation* was revealed as the full *commodification* of subjects and their psyches, which at times were shown to be in danger of becoming mere *replications* of the ImCon and its semiotic representations.

(3) Effects that colonization seemed to entail: The subjective effects of colonization also appeared in an ample variety of symbolic forms in the dreams. What seemed to summarize them well, however, is that most of them could be understood as typical psychological phenomena related to *participation mystique*—as unconscious identity and

projection—which were discussed in depth in Chap. 5. These typical phenomena involved remaining in a state of primordial unconsciousness, characterized as infantile; alienation from subjectivity and individuality—which were exteriorized, fused with the imaginary and its signifying commodity-signs; together with alienation, a state of dependency, and even craving or addiction, in relation to the imaginary of consumption and to consumption itself; and a correspondent massification and homogenization of the subject, identified with mass-produced images and significations. Two other effects related to massification, *dehumanization* and *automation*, appeared under various forms, including the possibility of the subject turning into a zombie, or a robot. Such effect of dehumanization also appeared as another possibility—the consumer-subject becoming identical with an empty commodity-sign. Some crucial effects of such extreme form of *participation*—a replication of the imaginary—had already been advanced theoretically as the production of an *empty self*, or what Augé (1999) called the *fictional self*. One dream was rather explicit in its depiction of the main effect of such production: it represents an anthropological mutation, the fabrication of the subject as *homo simulacrum*.

However, perhaps the most important effect of colonization revealed by a number of dreams was a possible split of the personality—the dissociation from the irrational and unconscious roots of the psyche, the archetypes, and especially the *instincts*. As discussed and predicted theoretically before, the instinctual foundations appeared commodified, reified, and alienated. Yet, they were also shown to be underlying a phenomenon, or effect, characteristic of *participation*: some subjects' underground psychic functioning was revealed to consist of an archaic, compulsive, and *primitive* psychology—unveiled most clearly as a mob mentality. That is, some dreams simply symbolized very clearly what Jung had thus described theoretically:

> The further we go back into history, the more we see personality disappearing beneath the wrappings of collectivity. And if we go right back to primitive psychology, we find absolutely no trace of the concept of an individual. Instead of individuality we find only collective relationship or what Lévy-Bruhl calls *participation mystique*. (Jung, CW6, §10)

Crucially, such mass mentality was shown to be connected to another appearance: what underlies such primitive psychology was revealed to be the chthonic, animal side of the unconscious (*feritas*), the primeval instinctual foundations—this time appearing as *radically* primitive, atavistic, destructive forces.[2] Such important effect of colonization was interpreted as being primarily subjective, that is, as pertaining to the individual dreamers. However, an interpretation on the objective level was also advanced, which generated some important questions. What if this pattern applies to many individuals? Or, put differently, to what extent can it be seen as *cultural*? Is it possible that it may be typical of consumerism's functioning, of the way it fabricates subjects through its imaginary? If so, then there would be a collective pattern of primitive forces prowling in the unconscious, in the subterranean stream of consumer society—underneath its signifying edifices. As pointed a number of times in this work and by the night dreams themselves, such situation needs to be understood *historically*—for such atavistic powers were indeed the shadow of capitalism-consumerism in the past. If we have learned anything from history, we should be aware that, within the mass societies instituted by capitalism, given certain social conditions and catalysts, for example, serious economic crises, which are indeed expected today,[3] the foundations of civilized social life can be shattered, moral barriers collapse, and "the gates of the psychic underworld are thrown open" (Jung, CW18, §581), *collectively*. It need hardly be stated that, when that happened, the results were catastrophic: general upheaval and eruption of what Benjamin called "mythic forces", as mass phenomena and mass movements of a totalitarian nature.[4]

As a matter of fact, investigating what appeared in the subterranean psychological stream of both consumers and the regime of consumerism—and the possibility that it showed such disruptive primitive forces in the collective unconscious—was the hidden objective of this work. Thus, in interpreting and analyzing individual dreams related to the ImCon, this study in fact followed Jung's suggestion:

[2] To recall: as animals, monsters, zombies, and finally a dinosaur (preceding totalitarianism).

[3] As Walter Benjamin (1933/1986) put it in 1933, "The economic crisis is at the door, and behind it is the shadow of the next war" (p. 198).

[4] This is most clearly seen today in the colossal problem represented by global jihadism.

> *the psychopathology of the masses is rooted in the psychology of the individual.* Psychic phenomena of this class can be investigated in the individual. Only if one succeeds in establishing that certain phenomena or symptoms are common to a number of different individuals can one begin to examine the analogous mass phenomena. (…) *we can only discover what the defects in the consciousness of our epoch are by observing the kind of reaction they call forth from the unconscious.* (CW10, §445; e.a.)

And indeed, if one may judge from the very small number of dreams studied here, such reactions may be rather alarming.

The *symbol* remains the most important factor for understanding both the social imaginary of consumerism, its subject, and such reactions. Across the theoretical framework and the empirical study, the reader contemplated a phenomenon that can only be described as the *loss of symbol*: the collapse of symbolico-religious imaginaries and their replacement by semiotic ideology. This phenomenon was summarized in a paraphrase of Marx: all that is sacred and symbolic is volatilized into phantasmagorias. Such a mutation of social imaginaries—indeed, a cultural mutation—has dire consequences and effects. If the symbol is the psychological *vis motrix* and condition of dialectics itself, and the symbolic is effaced—colonized and superseded by signs and simulacra—then the poles that should be synthesized by it remain separated and alienated, and the overwhelming tendency is *dissociation*, both in the individual and in culture, split from archetype and instinct. Jung pointed that out a long time ago: with the eradication of numinous cultural symbols, our "moral and spiritual tradition has collapsed, and has left a worldwide disorientation and dissociation" (CW18, §581). Although he wrote these lines in 1961, one can certainly think that they apply more than ever to our present situation.

> Our consciousness is no longer capable of integrating the natural afflux of concomitant, instinctive events that sustains our conscious psychic activity. This process can no longer take place in the same way as before, because our consciousness has deprived itself of the organs by which the auxiliary contributions of the instincts and the unconscious could be assimilated. These organs were the numinous symbols, held holy by common consent. (CW18, §583)

Such numinous symbols, systematized as religious-symbolic imaginaries, constituted the very foundations of society and its individual subjects. Their volatilization and commodification—indeed, their effacement—entail grave consequences; it is imperative that they be understood psychologically and historically.

> We could have seen long ago from primitive societies what the loss of numinosity means: they lose their *raison d'être,* the order of their social organizations, and then they dissolve and decay. We are now in the same condition. We have lost something we have never properly understood. (Jung, CW18, §582)

The night dreams interpreted in this study generated some insights for such process of understanding. Perhaps the most important insight is that the loss of symbol implies a deep *dehumanization*. As Vieira (2003, p. 212) wrote, based on Jung, Cassirer, and the cultural psychology of Bruner and Valsiner: "language and image are the principal symbolic systems with which the human being constructs her/his world" and *life*, through a narrative. In the symbol—the symbolic language, fantasy-thinking, the *imagination*—rests the common origin of both language and thought. The symbolic faculty enables us to acknowledge and reconnect with the universal roots of the human being; without acknowledging such irrational faculty—worse still, with its obliteration and substitution by ideological semiotic imaginaries—what is lost is the human being's very *humanity*. Or, to put it more radically: what defines us as humans is the fact that we are *homo symbolicus*. If a total colonization of symbol—and all that is related to it—is being effected, if we have moved from a symbolic order to an order of simulation, what we have then is a complete anthropological mutation that is absolutely dehumanizing: that appeared in the dreams as the epiphany of the commodity-subject as *homo simulacrum*.

This work tried to look at such phenomena through the concept of *dream*, signifying the natural symbolic production *par excellence* of the unconscious psyche. Its general conclusion may be summarized in one sentence: to colonize dreams means to colonize the whole symbolic imaginary; and to colonize the imaginary means to conquer imagination and the human psyche, replacing them with a destructive fiction: the totalizing ideology of commodities and consumption.

12.2 Limitations

Many limitations of this work have been pointed out in previous chapters; here a few of them are briefly summarized. Some limitations derive from peculiarities of its main object of study: night dreams. As mentioned, dreams should be taken as indicating *possibilities*; thus the interpretations of their messages, and the consequences that may be derived from them, ought to be seem in the same light. Dreams also tend to exaggerate, compensate, and dramatize; at times it is relatively difficult to ascertain whether they should be taken as hard facts, or rather as being playful and overstating—a difficulty that obviously poses some limits to the validity of dream interpretation.[5] Such exaggerating feature of dreams, in conjunction with the characteristically postmodern literature on consumption used, and the (fantastic, oneiric, imaginary) nature of the themes dealt with in this work, resulted in a style of writing that is often *hyperbolic*, which I did not manage to avoid. Analogously, some assertions, allegations, appraisals, and interpretations here may also seem overcritical, or even a bit "over the top". In a way, all such limitations coalesce into a general warning that is also a limitation: all this work and its possible contributions should definitely be seen as an attempt not at reaching hard, established conclusions, but rather at advancing "ideal types", models and ideas whose importance lies essentially in their heuristic and hermeneutic value.

In relation to that, interpretations here are also limited in that they are inherently hypothetical and tentative; of course, many other different interpretations could also be proposed for the same dreams. The hermeneutic procedures employed also suffer from some limitations, as mentioned,

[5] Regarding possible exaggerations, it should be stressed that dreams, imagination, children's play (i.e., spontaneous productions from the unconscious) do not always portray icons or cultural emblems of capitalism-consumerism—such as Disney characters, or malls, and so on—in the same critical, undermining ways as they appear to do here. For instance, children oftentimes have fairy-tale-like dreams with Disney characters in which they appear as cultural images appropriated and used by the unconscious as symbols for archetypal contents, situations, or motifs. That happens because the form the unconscious content takes is often "sourced" culturally, that is, it is drawn from the subject's cultural imaginary—which does not immediately imply that the subject's psyche is being "colonized" by the latter's ideology (although this obviously constitutes a strong possibility, most especially with children). However, in the dreams analyzed here, that is clearly not the case; in them the cultural images of consumerism are *always* criticized in some way, and the phenomenon of colonization is rather clear.

which are mainly derived from the method used for data collection: gathering complex data such as night dreams from the internet entails a number of problems and shortcomings[6] and is probably one of the major limitations of this work.

Accordingly, the discussions on subjectivity had to be very limited, and in some cases remain hypothetical and speculative; they are basically restricted by the main focus of research, night dreams, by the procedures employed for data collection, and by reasons of secrecy. To study subjectivity in depth through dreams would require building full case studies of a more clinical character. Yet, as discussed before, for a number of reasons I had to disregard to a large extent the dreamers' cultural and individual specificities, their social and individual contexts. Instead, such contexts were taken into consideration in the way they were presented by the dreams themselves.

Another limitation regards the problem of generalizing the findings to other subjects and sociocultural contexts. As most dreamers were American, and the dreams themselves had sceneries or themes that are in principle typically American (McDonald's, Disney, etc.), it remains doubtful whether findings may indeed be seen as typical of global consumerism, and of other consumers that are not Americans. At any rate, given the general limitations of this work and its objective, the possibilities of generalization it offers should, in principle, be confined to *theoretical generalization*—rather than any form of statistical generalization; further comparative research would have to be undertaken in order to confirm the applicability of the theories generated in this work to different subjects from different contexts. Finally, all such limitations should be viewed in the context of what perhaps may be seen as this study's main characteristic: while it is ambitious (and probably overtly so) in its thematic and theoretical scopes, it is also rather *exploratory*, preliminary, and tentative in the results it offers. However, and reiterating, it is hoped that, despite its many limitations, this study may have accomplished to some extent its main initial objective: to offer an original contribution for social psychology, and psychology in general, through advancing *new ideas* for

[6] As mentioned, I did not know personally the majority of dreamers; in some cases personal associations in relation to their dreams could not be collected, as well as further personal information on their lives and social contexts.

understanding our contemporary regime of consumerism and its subject, and especially through showing and discussing different perspectives and forms of understanding the psyche, through one of its most complex and bewildering products: the night dreams.

12.3 Suggestions for Further Research

There are many types and possibilities of further research that can be derived from this work, both in theoretical and empirical terms. This section presents briefly some suggestions for developing research, which focus on the possible use of night dreams as empirical material. Two general recommendations seem adequate: future research should privilege case studies in which each dreamer is a case, with long series of dreams and extensive knowledge of the dreamer's life history. Using both quantitative and qualitative methods, for example, employing hermeneutics in dialog with statistical analysis, may also yield interesting results. Diverse populations of dreamers could be researched. As mentioned, one interesting research would be with users of antidepressants and other psychiatric medications, employing clinical case studies with series of dreams and follow-up, in order to investigate the reactions of the unconscious psyche to the treatment and all it signifies. Case studies with compulsive buyers, or persons "addicted" to consumption, may also be promising. Another possibility that can yield interesting results would be to research comparatively how the ideology and imagery of consumption appear in the night dreams of children—comparing different nationalities, or maybe groups who are heavily exposed to mass media (and publicity) and groups who are not, and so on.

A further possibility for research is to explore other relations that night dreams can have with the imaginary, but without focusing on the theme of subjectivity per se. For instance, one line of inquiry would be to explore how *archetypal motifs* appear in dreams now, under the ImCon. And, finally, different types of dreams could be explored comparatively, for instance, "Big Dreams" like the "sci-fi hyperbusiness city" dream analyzed here: archetypal dreams that seem to formulate an objective discourse upon consumer culture.

References

Augé, M. (1999). *The war of dreams: exercises in ethno-fiction* (L. Heron, Trans.). London: Pluto Press.

Benjamin, W. (1986). Experiência e pobreza. In *Documentos de cultura, documentos de barbárie: Escritos escolhidos* (pp. 195–198). São Paulo: Cultrix/ Editora USP. (Original work published 1933).

Benjamin, W. (1999). *The arcades project* (H. Eiland & K. McLaughlin, Trans.). Cambridge: The Belknap Press of Harvard University Press.

Gruzinski, S. (1988). *La colonization de l'imaginaire*. Paris: Gallimard.

Marx, K. (1993). Das Kapital: Kritik der politischen Ökonomie. Der Produktionsprozeß des Kapitals. In *Karl Marx Friedrich Engels Werke, Band 23*. Berlin: Dietz Verlag. (Original work published 1867).

Rosés, M. P., & Gabarrón, L. R. (1984). *La crisis en psicologia social: Elementos para la discusión epistemológica del concepto de crisis* (Vol. II, pp. 89–100). Quaderns de Psicologia.

Vieira, A. G. (2003). *Imagem, símbolo e narrativa na Psicologia Analítica de C. G. Jung*. Unpublished doctoral dissertation, Universidade Federal do Rio Grande do Sul, Porto Alegre, Brazil.

Appendix A: Some Websites Used as Sources for the Collection of Night Dreams

This short list contains the main websites used for the collection of night dreams; however, many others websites were accessed, including personal blogs.

http://dreamjournal.net
http://dreammoods.com
http://sawlogs.net
http://dreambank.net
http://dreamtalk.hypermart.net
http://groups.google.com/group/alt.dreams/
http://www.orkut.com/Main#Community?cmm=60525
http://www.experienceproject.com/dreams/
http://dromma.org
http://www.opsonline.it/forum/psicologia/la-stanza-dei-sogni/
http://www.sognilucidi.it/forum/viewforum.php?f=11
http://sognicondivisi.forumfree.it/
http://forum.riza.it/forumdisplay.php?f=26

M. Xavier, *Subjectivity, the Unconscious and Consumerism*,
https://doi.org/10.1007/978-3-319-96824-7

Appendix B: Glossary

Archetype Archetypes are collective or suprapersonal psychic elements that are common to all human beings and express the inherited part of the psyche, which, together with the instincts, compose the collective unconscious. They correspond to the psychic representations of instinct—the typical forms through which libido is represented as *symbolic* images. As such, the archetype is an *a priori* formal factor of psychic life, functioning as uniform and regularly recurring modes of apprehension, perception, and representation of reality. Thus it underlies the faculty of symbolic imagination: it organizes and arranges the psychic elements into certain images, representations, and later ideas, according to characteristic motifs that have a mythological character. The ensembles of such symbolic motifs, projected culturally, constitute symbolico-religious imaginaries; that is, the archetypes are the psychological foundation (as structuring patterns, or templates) of both the imagination and social imaginaries.

Commodity-Sign A fusion of commodity and sign, it is at the same time the elemental form of representation of the imaginary of consumerism and the structuring form of consumer capitalism. "The object of this political economy, that is, its simplest component, its nuclear element—that which precisely the commodity was for Marx—is no longer today properly either commodity or sign, but indissolubly both" (Baudrillard, 1973/1981, p. 148). Its mass production follows the logic of advertising, which consists in the manipulation of signs (as atoms of social meaning systems), arbitrarily combining and recom-

M. Xavier, *Subjectivity, the Unconscious and Consumerism*,
https://doi.org/10.1007/978-3-319-96824-7

bining their abstracted, emancipated components (signifier and signified). The sign (as image, or representation) is thus attached to a product, or becomes a product itself, thereby signifying particular relations, experiences, or forms of subjectivity, as a commodity. The commodity-sign therefore stands basically as the representation of reified social relationships; through its consumption, social signification (meaning, value, and difference) is exchanged as sign-value, which is the fundamental dynamics of consumerism.

Consumption Dream Consumption dreams can be defined thusly:

(a) Culturally, they correspond to the matter of *advertisements*: Elaborations of sign-value—social signification artificially attached to some form of consumption or commodity—as fetishized narratives and imagery that articulate cultural fantasies and desires and determine the commodity-forms that promise to satisfy such desire-fantasy (or are at least connected to it).
(b) Subjectively, they stand for the fantasies of *consumers*: The desires, fantasies, daydreams, and ideals about goods and experiences—and, in fact, life in general—that have consumption as their underlying idea or motif. Here the dream is seen as a more or less *personal* or subjective desire or object of desire, image of the future, main goal, the "good life", and so on—all of which are imagined (dreamed) to be reachable, fulfilled, or attainable through consumption.

This work assumes the standpoint that (b) merely replicates (a), that is, consumption dreams are by definition collective: each consumption dream represents, articulates, and communicates the social ideology of consumerism in semiotic form, fabricating *irrational and imaginary* psychic contents (desire, emotions, fantasy, imagination, etc.) in the consumer-subject.

Imaginary The concept of social imaginary denotes the network or system of social-historical significations and meanings of a particular social group, society, or culture, expressed as a corpus of *images* and representations. Historically, the original social imaginaries were *symbolic imaginaries*: ensembles of typical symbolic forms—rites, rituals, myths, religious systems, and so on, and their imagery—that were shared socially. In analytical psychology, the symbolic imaginary represents the cultural expression of the symbolic function of the unconscious and its archetypes; its main constituents are *représentations collectives*. Broadly, the social imaginary corresponds to the concept of collective consciousness, as the typical collective mentality. Seen as the social imagination—the social ways of imagining, organizing, and representing meaning—it institutes social categories of identity and otherness, and thus defines both social relations and subjectivity. In sum, it underpins the identity of both society and social actors; as the psychological (imaginary) foundation of social order, it defines how reality is signified, or, indeed, what is real.

ImCon Acronym that can be read in two senses—as social Imaginary of *Consumption* and of *Consumerism*.[1] It can be defined as a semiotic and ideological social imaginary, whose supraordinate idea, categorical imperative, and absolute principle is consumption. As such, it is meant to encompass some factors that are central for consumer society, for consumption is essentially based on what is *imaginary*—it is founded upon imagery, imagination and imaginary things, and the irrational. The *sign* defines its corpus of images and representations: it is a semiotic and semiological system, a regime of signification whose fundamental elements are commodity-signs and consumption dreams. In the second sense of Imaginary of *consumerism*, the ImCon corresponds to the *mass ideology*, of a totalizing character, that defines our globalized societies and, indeed, our epoch.

Night Dream An autonomous, spontaneous manifestation, in the form of images, of the *unconscious* psyche. As such, the dream represents its most natural product, a creative and imaginative expression of its symbolic language and primeval form of thought, the most primary form of production of symbols by the psyche. Being a natural phenomenon, the dream does not deceive or lie, it does not disguise or distort; it invariably expresses something that consciousness does not understand. Seen as an inner drama, the oneiric narrative can depict the situation of the whole psyche (including its subjective part) from the objective viewpoint of the unconscious, a depiction which is usually not in accord with the conscious mind; additionally, it can also reveal a critical view of sociocultural reality, and its relations with subjectivity.

Participation Mystique Concept derived from anthropology (Lévy-Bruhl) and the study of primitive psychology, denoting an archaic, unconscious *identity*, based on a mystical and emotional connection between subject and object in which both remain non-differentiated or conflated. It corresponds

[1] In English it is rather difficult to come up with a single expression; it may also be called "consumerist imaginary", or "consumer imaginary", yet none of all these formulations is very common in the literature. The French language offers a perfect expression, *l'imaginaire de (la) consommation* (whose translations into Spanish and Portuguese are close enough to its meaning).

to the primordial unconscious state of the infant and the primitive, in which part of the subject's psyche is *projected* upon the object (or environment) and remains bound to it through a symbol (or symbolic system). Being a symbolic phenomenon, it is relatively indifferent to logical, rational contradiction. The forms, emotional tones, and characteristics such identity and projection assume are conditioned by the *représentations collectives*.

Représentations Collectives Concept also derived from anthropology, drawing from theorizations elaborated by Durkheim and Lévy-Bruhl, but employed psychologically. In its more Durkheimian formulation, it refers to the typical *symbolic* forms (myths, rites, legends, religions, etc.) that have social and historical origin and are shared socially. They function as collective mental categories for acting, thinking, and feeling that are taken for granted. Such forms are understood as the culturally elaborated expressions of archetypes, and as such represent the fundamental constituents of the symbolic imaginaries that define cultures. Complementing such formulation with Lévy-Bruhl's contribution, the *représentations collectives* are also understood as supraordinated ideas imbued with intense *emotional* feeling-values and expectations, usually of a religious or *mystical* character. Such ideas work as general categories of imagination that define the way reality is experienced and signified. As symbolic patterns, they function as a cultural system of projections.

Sign Form of representation characterized by the arbitrary relationship between signifier and signified. Its signification is conventional; by definition, it points to something known a priori, and always signifies *less* than what it represents. The sign thus stands for fabricated, artificial signification, that allows for emancipation from what is represented. As pointed above, the sign is the crucial element for the system of consumption; its structure and logic are at the "very heart of the commodity-form" (Baudrillard, 1973/1981, p. 146). The political economy of the sign defines consumerism and characterizes its imaginary (the ImCon) as semiotic and semiological.

Simulacrum The simulacrum represents basically the coupling of a semiotic simulation with the disappearance and effacement of reality. The sign, as a representation of reality, becomes a simulacrum when it is totally emancipated, that is, it bears no relation whatever to reality; it stands for a short circuit of reality—a short circuit between reality (referent) and its representation (signifier and signified)—and the replacement of the latter by a simulation, a semblance that is more real than the real (hyperreal). Thus the level of simulacrum means the substitution of the abstract, artificial signs of the real for the real, engendering a hyperreality without origin or reality: the artificial model or representation takes ontological precedence over reality (precession of simulacra), erasing any distinction between simulation and real, thus superseding and becoming the "real". That is, the copy erases any original: the simulacrum is the copy for which there is no original or referent.

Symbol The symbol is the form of representation that is the best possible expression for something relatively unknown. By definition, it expresses an irrational quantum: "in the symbol, rational and irrational elements are always combined" (Meier, 1987, p. 98). As its etymon indicates, the symbol unites opposite or heterogeneous meanings into one image; it is a whole that expresses homogeneity between signifier and signified. Accordingly, the symbol is one with what it symbolizes; it functions as the psychological form through which instinctual libido (psychic energy) is directed and transformed. It is the natural product and expression of the unconscious psyche, appearing chiefly as symbolic fantasy, imagination, and dream—manifestations of the imaginative function. In analytical psychology, the very language of the unconscious is symbolic: its symbolic function defines the human psyche, and thus what is human (*homo symbolicus*).

Unconscious Psychic domain that encompasses the totality of all psychological phenomena that lack the quality of consciousness. In relation to consciousness, it is autonomous, independent, and inexhaustible. It is composed of two layers: the personal unconscious containing the complexes, which constitute an unconscious subjectivity; and the collective or transpersonal unconscious, which is the source of the instinctual forces of the psyche and of the forms or categories that regulate them, the archetypes (Jung, CW8). The unconscious is understood as a psychic organ, which has a creative and self-regulatory function, and, just like the body, a marked historical character. Its typical functioning is an archaic form of thought called fantasy-, dream-, or symbolic-thinking, which is expressed through the unconscious' typical imagistic, symbolic language. As our psychic matrix of symbols, it is the common origin of symbolic imaginaries.

References

Abraham, K. (1913). *Dreams and myths*. New York: Journal of Nervous and Mental Disease.

Adatto, K. (2003). Selling out childhood. *Hedgehog Review, 5*(2), 24–40.

Adorno, T. W., & Horkheimer, M. (2002). *Dialectic of enlightenment: Philosophical fragments* (E. Jephcott, Trans.). Stanford, CA: Stanford University Press. (Original work published 1944).

Allen, L. (2008). *The Fear* [CD single]. London: Regal Recordings.

Allott, P. (2002). *The health of nations: Society and law beyond the state*. Cambridge: Cambridge University Press.

Álvaro, J. L., & Garrido, A. (2003). *Psicología social: perspectivas psicológicas y sociológicas*. Madrid: McGraw Hill.

Álvaro, J. L., Garrido, A., Schweiger, I., & Torregrosa, J. R. (2007). *Introducción a la psicología social sociológica*. Barcelona: Editorial UOC.

Appadurai, A. (1996). *Modernity at large: Cultural dimensions of globalization*. Minneapolis: University of Minnesota Press.

Arau, A. (Director). (1992). *Como agua para chocolate [Motion picture]*. Mexico: Arau Films.

Arendt, H. (1958). *The origins of totalitarianism* (2nd ed.). New York: Meridian Books.

Arendt, H. (1963). *On revolution*. New York: Penguin.

Arendt, H. (1978). *The life of the mind*. New York: Harvest.

M. Xavier, *Subjectivity, the Unconscious and Consumerism*,
https://doi.org/10.1007/978-3-319-96824-7

Arendt, H. (1998). *The human condition* (2nd ed.). Chicago: University of Chicago Press. (Original work published 1958).
Arendt, H. (2005). The image of hell. In *Essays in understanding: 1930–1954* (pp. 197–205). New York: Schocken Books. (Original work published 1946).
Arendt, H. (2006). *Diario filosófico 1950–1973* (R. Gabás, Trans.). Barcelona: Herder.
Ars Industrialis. (2010). *Manifesto 2010*. Retrieved from http://arsindustrialis.org/manifesto-2010
Augé, M. (1995). *Non-places: Introduction to an anthropology of supermodernity* (J. Howe, Trans.). London: Verso.
Augé, M. (1999). *The war of dreams: exercises in ethno-fiction* (L. Heron, Trans.). London: Pluto Press.
Bachelard, G. (1942). *L'eau et les rêves: Essai sur l'imagination de la matière*. Paris: Corti.
Backes, N. (1997). Reading the shopping mall city. *The Journal of Popular Culture, 31*(3), 1–17.
Bakhtin, M. M. (1984). *Problems of Dostoevsky's poetics* (C. Emerson, Trans.). Minneapolis: University of Minnesota Press. (Original work published 1929).
Balandier, G. (1985). *Le détour: Pouvoir et modernité*. Paris: Fayard.
Barber, B. (1995). *Jihad vs McWorld*. New York: Crown.
Bastide, R. (1966). The sociology of dream. In G. E. von Grunebaum & R. Caillois (Eds.), *The dream and human societies* (pp. 199–211). Berkeley: University of California Press.
Batkin, L. M. (1990). *Gli umanisti italiani: Stile de vita e di pensiero*. Roma: Laterzi.
Baudrillard, J. (1975). *The mirror of production*. St. Louis, MO: Telos Press.
Baudrillard, J. (1981). *For a critique of the political economy of the sign*. St. Louis, MO: Telos Press. (Original work published 1973).
Baudrillard, J. (1983a). *Simulations*. New York: Semiotext(e).
Baudrillard, J. (1983b). *In the shadow of the silent majorities*. New York: Semiotext(e).
Baudrillard, J. (1988). *The ecstasy of communication*. Cambridge, MA: MIT Press.
Baudrillard, J. (1993). *Symbolic exchange and death* (I. H. Grant, Trans.). London: Sage. (Original work published 1976).
Baudrillard, J. (1994). *Simulacra and simulation* (S. F. Glaser, Trans). Ann Arbor, MI: University of Michigan Press. (Original work published 1981).

Baudrillard, J. (1996a). *The system of objects* (J. Benedict, Trans.). London: Verso. (Original work published 1968).
Baudrillard, J. (1996b). *The perfect crime* (C. Turner, Trans.). London: Verso.
Baudrillard, J. (1996c). Disneyworld Company. *Liberation*. Retrieved from http://www.uta.edu/english/apt/collab/texts/disneyworld.html
Baudrillard, J. (1998). *The consumer society: Myths and structures*. London: Sage. (Original work published 1970).
Baudrillard, J. (2000). *The vital illusion*. New York: Columbia University Press.
Baudrillard, J. (2001). *Selected writings* (M. Poster, Ed., 2nd ed.). Cambridge: Polity.
Baudrillard, J. (2002). *Screened out* (C. Turner, Trans.). London: Verso.
Baudrillard, J. (2007). *Forget Foucault*. New York: Semiotext(e). (Original work published 1977).
Bauman, Z. (2000). *Liquid modernity*. Cambridge: Polity.
Bauman, Z. (2001). *The individualized society*. Cambridge, UK: Polity.
Bauman, Z. (2005). *Liquid life*. Cambridge, UK: Polity.
Bauman, Z. (2007a). *Consuming life*. Cambridge: Polity Press.
Bauman, Z. (2007b). Exit *Homo Politicus*, enter *Homo Consumens*. In K. Soper & F. Trentmann (Eds.), *Citizenship and consumption* (pp. 139–153). Hampshire, UK: Palgrave Macmillan.
Bauman, Z. (2011, August 12). Foi um motim de consumidores excluídos. *O Globo*. Retrieved from http://oglobo.globo.com/mundo/mat/2011/08/12/foi-um-motim-de-consumidores-excluidos-diz-sociologo-zygmunt-bauman-925126381.asp
Bauman, Z., & Tester, K. (2001). *Conversations with Zygmunt Bauman*. Cambridge: Polity.
Béguin, A. (1954). *El alma romántica y el sueño*. Mexico: Fondo de Cultura Económica.
Belk, R. W., Ger, G., & Askergaard, S. (1996). Metaphors of consumer desire. *Advances in Consumer Research, 23*, 368–373.
Belk, R. W., Ger, G., & Askegaard, S. (2003). The fire of desire: A multisited inquiry into consumer passion. *Journal of Consumer Research, 30*, 326–351.
Belk, R. W., Wallendorf, M., & Sherry, J. F. (1989). The sacred and the profane in consumer behavior: Theodicy on the Odyssey. *The Journal of Consumer Research, 16*(1), 1–38.
Bell, D. (1976). *The cultural contradictions of capitalism*. New York: Basic Books.
Bell, E., Haas, L., & Sells, L. (1995). *From the mouse to the mermaid*. Indianapolis, IN: Indiana University Press.

Benjamin, W. (1940). *On the concept of history* (D. Redmond, Trans.). Retrieved from http://www.marxists.org/reference/archive/benjamin/1940/history.htm

Benjamin, W. (1982). L'arcobaleno (1915–1916). In G. Agamben (Ed.), *Metafisica della gioventù: Scritti 1910–1918* (D. Regenbogen, Trans., pp. 151–158). Torino, IT: Einaudi. (Original work written 1916).

Benjamin, W. (1986a). Experiência e pobreza. In *Documentos de cultura, documentos de barbárie: Escritos escolhidos* (pp. 195–198). São Paulo: Cultrix/Editora USP. (Original work published 1933).

Benjamin, W. (1986b). Paris, capital of the nineteenth century. In P. Demetz (Ed.), *Reflections: Essays, aphorisms, autobiographical writings* (pp. 146–162). New York: Schocken.

Benjamin, W. (1991). *Gesammelte Schriften* (R. Tiedemann & H. Schweppenhäuser, Eds., Vol. V). Frankfurt am Main: Suhrkamp Verlag.

Benjamin, W. (1996a). Capitalism as religion. In M. P. Bullock & M. W. Jennings (Eds.), *Walter Benjamin selected writings, Vol. 1: 1913–1926* (pp. 288–291). Cambridge, MA: Harvard University Press. (Original work written 1921).

Benjamin, W. (1996b). One-way street. In M. P. Bullock & M. W. Jennings (Eds.), *Walter Benjamin selected writings, Vol. 1: 1913–1926* (pp. 444–488). Cambridge, MA: Harvard University Press. (Original work published 1928).

Benjamin, W. (1999). *The arcades project* (H. Eiland & K. McLaughlin, Trans.). Cambridge: The Belknap Press of Harvard University Press.

Benson, A. L. (Ed.). (2000). *I shop therefore I am: Compulsive buying and the search for self.* Northvale, NJ: Jason Aronson.

Bergson, H. (1919). *L'enérgie spirituelle. Essais et conférences.* Retrieved from http://classiques.uqac.ca/classiques/bergson_henri/energie_spirituelle/energie_spirituelle.html

Berman, M. (1982). *All that is solid melts into air.* New York: Simon & Schuster.

Biocca, F. (Ed.). (1991). *Television and political advertising (Vol. 2): Signs, codes, and images.* Hillsdale, NJ: Lawrence Erlbaum.

Blanch, J. M. (1982). *Psicologías sociales: Aproximación histórica.* Barcelona: Hora.

Blanch, J. M., & Cantera, L. (2007a). El *capitalismo sanitario* como factor de riesgo psicosocial. In C. Guillén & R. Guil (Orgs.), *Psicología social: un encuentro de perspectivas* (Vol. 1, pp. 1075–1080). Cádiz: APPS.

Blanch, J. M., & Cantera, L. (2007b). Efectos colaterales del capitalismo académico. In FES (Org.), *IX Congreso Español de Sociología: Poder, Cultura y Civilización.* Comunicaciones orales sobre sociopsicología del trabajo y de la organización (pp. 12–29). Barcelona: FES.

Blanch, J. M., & Cantera, L. (2011). La nueva gestión pública de universidades y hospitales. Aplicaciones e implicaciones. In E. Agulló, J. L. Álvaro, A. Garrido, R. Medina, & I. Schweiger (Eds.), *Nuevas formas de organización del trabajo y la empleabilidad* (pp. 515–534). Oviedo: Ediuno.

Blanch, J. M., & Stecher, A. (2009). La empresarización de servicios públicos y sus efectos colaterales. Implicaciones psicosociales de la colonización de universidades y hospitales por la cultura del nuevo capitalismo. In T. Wittke & P. Melogno (Eds.), *Psicología y organización del Trabajo: Producción de subjetividad en la organización del trabajo* (pp. 191–209). Montevideo: Psicolibros.

Boltanski, L., & Chiapello, E. (1999). *El nuevo espíritu del capitalismo*. Madrid: Akal.

Borges, J. L., & Ferrari, O. (2005). *En diálogo/I* (Edición definitiva). Madrid: Siglo XXI.

Bourdieu, P. (1984). *Distinction: A social critique of the judgment of taste* (R. Nice, Trans.). London: Routledge & Kegan Paul.

Braidotti, R. (2006). Posthuman. All too human: Towards a new process ontology. *Theory, Culture & Society Annual Review, 23*(7–8), 197–208.

Bruner, J. (1986). *Actual minds, possible worlds*. Cambridge: Harvard University Press.

Bruner, J. (1990). *Acts of meaning*. Cambridge: Harvard University Press.

Bryce, W., & Olney, T. (1991). Gender differences in consumption aspirations: A cross-cultural appraisal. *Social Behavior and Personality, 19*(4), 237–254.

Bryman, A. (1999). The Disneyization of society. *Sociological Review, 47*, 25–47.

Bryman, A. (2003). McDonald's as a Disneyized institution: Global implications. *American Behavioral Scientist, 47*(2), 154–167.

Bryman, A. (2004a). Disneyization. *Encyclopedia of social theory*. London: Sage. Retrieved from http://www.sageereference.com/socialtheory/Article_n81.html

Bryman, A. (2004b). McDonaldization. *Encyclopedia of social theory*. London: Sage. Retrieved from http://www.sage-ereference.com/socialtheory/Article_n187.html

Bryman, A. (2004c). *The Disneyization of society* (2nd ed.). London: Sage.

Buck-Morss, S. (1989). *The dialectics of seeing: Walter Benjamin and the Arcades Project*. Cambridge, MA: MIT.

Buck-Morss, S. (2000). *Dreamworld and catastrophe: The passing of mass utopia in East and West*. Cambridge, MA: MIT.

Butler, J. (2003). *Gender trouble. Continental feminist reader*. London: Routledge.

Byrne, E., & McQuillian, M. (1999). *Deconstructing Disney*. London: Pluto Press.

Calderón de la Barca, P. (2009). *La vida es sueño*. Retrieved from http://www.cervantesvirtual.com/obra/la-vida-es-sueno%2D%2D0/ (Original work written 1635).

Campbell, C. (2004). I shop therefore I know that I am: The metaphysical basis of modern consumerism. In K. M. Ekström & H. Brembeck (Eds.), *Elusive Consumption* (pp. 27–44). New York: Berg.

Campbell, J. (1997). *As máscaras de deus: mitologia primitiva*. São Paulo: Palas Athena.

Caro, A. (2002). *La publicidad de la significación: Marco, concepto y taxonomía*. Madrid: E-prints UCM. (Original work published 1993).

Caro, A. (2007). Jean Baudrillard y la publicidad. *Pensar la Publicidad: Revista Internacional de Investigaciones Publicitarias, I*(2), 131–146.

Carus, C. G. (1846). *Psyche*. Pforzheim, Germany: Flammer und Hoffmann.

Carvalho, V. D., Borges, L. O., & Rêgo, D. P. (2010). Interacionismo simbólico: origens, pressupostos e contribuições aos estudos em Psicologia Social. *Psicologia ciência e profissão, 30*(1), 146–161.

Cassirer, E. (1944). *An essay on man: An introduction to a philosophy of human culture*. New Haven: Yale University Press.

Cassirer, E. (1946). *The myth of the state*. New Haven: Yale University Press.

Castoriadis, C. (1987). *The imaginary institution of society* (K. Blamey, Trans.). Cambridge: MIT Press. (Original work published 1975).

Castoriadis, C. (1997). The "rationality" of capitalism. In *Figures of the unthinkable* (pp. 81–122). Stanford, CA: Stanford University Press. Retrieved from http://www.costis.org/x/castoriadis/Castoriadis-Figures_of_the_Thinkable.pdf

Charles, M. (2009). *Speculative experience and history: Walter Benjamin's Goethean Kantianism*. Unpublished doctoral dissertation, Middlesex University, London, UK.

Chevalier, J., & Gheerbrant, A. (1990). *Dictionnaire des symboles: Mythes, réves, coutumes, gestès, formes, figures, couleurs, nombres* (11ème ed., revue et corrigée). Paris: Ed. Robert Laffont/Jupiter. (Original work published 1969).

Chevalier, J., & Gheerbrant, A. (1997). *The Penguin dictionary of symbols* (Trans. J. Buchanan-Brown). London: Penguin. (Original work published 1969).

Chidester, D. (2005). *Authentic fakes: Religion and American popular culture*. Berkeley: University of California Press.

Christensen, G. (2002). *Mental simulations, anticipations, and dreams: Toward a theory of consumption visions in consumer behaviour*. Unpublished doctoral dissertation, Pennsylvania State University, State College, US.

Clarke, S. (2005). The neoliberal theory of society. In A. Saad-Filho & D. Johnston (Eds.), *Neoliberalism: A critical reader* (pp. 50–59). London: Pluto Press.

Clastres, P. (1989). *Society against the state: Essays in political anthropology* (R. Hurley, Trans.). New York: Zone Books. (Original work published 1974).

Cohen, M. (1995). *Profane illumination: Walter Benjamin and the Paris of surrealist revolution*. Berkeley, CA: University of California Press.

Cohen, M. (2006). Benjamin's phantasmagoria: The *Arcades Project*. In D. S. Ferris (Ed.), *The Cambridge companion to Walter Benjamin* (pp. 199–220). Cambridge: Cambridge University Press.

Corbin, H. (1964). *Mundus imaginalis or the imaginary and the imaginal* (R. Horine, Trans). Zürich/New York: Spring.

Curtis, A. (Director). (2002). *The century of the self [Motion picture]*. London: BBC Series.

Cushman, P. (1990). Why the self is empty: Toward a historically situated psychology. *American Psychologist, 45*(5), 599–611.

Cypher, J., & Riggs, E. (2001). Colonizing the imagination: Disney's wilderness lodge. *Critical Studies, 21*, 403–423.

D'Astous, A., & Deschênes, J. (2005). Consuming in one's mind: An exploration. *Psychology and Marketing, 2*(1), 1–30.

Davis, J. E. (2003). The commodification of self. *Hedgehog Review, 5*(2), 41–49.

Davis, M. (2008). *Freedom and consumerism: A critique of Zygmunt Bauman's sociology*. Hampshire, UK: Ashgate.

De Zengotita, T. (2005). *Mediated: How the media shapes your world and the way you live in it*. New York: Bloomsbury.

Debord, G. (1967). *La socièté du spectacle*. Paris: Champ Libre.

Deleuze, G., & Guattari, F. (2004). *Anti-Oedipus* (R. Hurley, M. Seem, & H. R. Lane, Trans.). London: Continuum. (Original work published 1972).

Descartes, R. (1996). *Meditations on first philosophy* (J. Cottingham, Trans, Ed). Cambridge: Cambridge University Press. (Original work published 1641).

Dorfman, A., & Mattelart, A. (1991). *How to read Donald Duck: Imperialist ideology in the Disney comic* (4th ed.). New York: IG Editions.

Douglas, M., & Isherwood, B. (1980). *The world of goods*. Harmondsworth: Penguin.

Drane, J. (2001). *The McDonaldization of the church: Consumer culture and the church's future*. Macon, GA: Smyth and Helwys.

Drane, J. (2008). *After McDonaldization: Mission, ministry, and Christian discipleship in an age of uncertainty*. Grand Rapids, MI: Baker Academic.

Duarte, L. F. B. (1998). O Sono dos Justos: uma interpretação simbólica. *Cadernos de Comunicação (Unisinos-RS), 1*(4), 73–94.
Duarte, L. F. B. (1999). *O Sono dos Justos: elementos para uma metodologia de interpretação de textos culturais.* Unpublished master's thesis, Unisinos, São Leopoldo, Brazil.
Duarte, L. F. B. (2000). Bakhtin e Jung: Relações dialógicas. *Boletim do Centro de Estudos Junguianos C. A. Meier, 5*(1), 6–9.
Dufour, D.-R. (2001, November 1). Rumo ao "capitalismo total"? *Le Monde Diplomatique.* Retrieved from http://diplo.uol.com.br/2001-11,a121
Dufour, D.-R. (2003, October 1). A arte de reduzir as mentes. *Le Monde Diplomatique.* Retrieved from http://diplo.uol.com.br/2003-10,a763
Dufour, D.-R. (2005, April 1). O homem neoliberal: da redução das cabeças à mudança dos corpos. *Le Monde Diplomatique.* Retrieved from http://diplo.uol.com.br/2005-04,a1098
Dufour, D.-R. (2008). *The art of shrinking heads: The new servitude of the liberated in the era of total capitalism.* Cambridge and Oxford: Polity.
Durand, G. (1963). *Les structures anthropologiques de l'imaginaire.* Paris: Dunod.
Durand, G. (1994). *L'imaginaire: Essai sur les sciences et la philosophie de l'image.* Paris: Hatier.
Durand, G. (1996). *Introduction à la mythodologie. Mythes et sociétés.* Paris: Albin Michel.
Durand, G. (2004). *Las estructuras antropologicas del imaginario: Introducción a la arquetipología general.* Mexico: FSE.
Durand, Y. (1988). *L'Exploration de l'imaginaire: Introduction à la modélisation des univers mythiques.* Paris: L'Espace Bleu.
Durkheim, É. (1982). *The rules of sociological method* (W. Halls, Trans.). New York: Free Press. (Original work published 1895).
Durkheim, É. (1995). *The elementary forms of religious life* (K. E. Fields, Trans.). New York: Simon & Schuster. (Original work published 1912).
Duvignaud, J., Duvignaud, F., & Corbeau, J. P. (1981). *El banco de los sueños: ensayo antropológico del soñador contemporáneo.* Mexico: Fondo de Cultura Económica.
Eco, U. (1964). *Apocalittici e integrati.* Milano: Bompiani.
Edgar, I. R. (2011). *The dream in Islam: From Qur'anic tradition to jihadist inspiration.* Oxford: Berghahn.
Edgar, I. R., & Henig, D. (2009). The cosmopolitan and the noumenal: A case study of Islamic jihadist night dreams as reported sources of spiritual and political inspiration. In D. Theodossopoulos & E. Kirtsoglou (Eds.), *United*

in discontent: Local responses to cosmopolitanism and globalization (pp. 64–82). Oxford: Berghahn.

Eliade, M. (1959). *Naissances mystiques*. Paris: Gallimard.

Eliot, T. S. (1925). *Eliot's poems: 1909–1925*. London: Faber & Gwyer.

Ellenberger, H. (1970). *The discovery of the unconscious*. New York: Basic Books.

Espinosa, O. N. (2009). *El imaginario sociocultural a través del sueño en jóvenes universitarios*. Unpublished doctoral dissertation, UNAM, Ciudad de México, Mexico.

Ewen, S. (1976). *Captains of consciousness: Advertising and the social roots of the consumer culture*. New York: McGraw-Hill.

Ewen, S. (1988). *All consuming images*. New York: Basic Books.

Ewen, S. (1989). Advertising and the development of consumer society. In I. Angus & S. Jhally (Eds.), *Cultural politics in contemporary America* (pp. 82–95). New York: Routledge.

Ewen, S. (1990). Marketing dreams: The political elements of style. In A. Tomlinson (Ed.), *Consumption, identity and style: Marketing, meanings, and the packaging of pleasure* (pp. 29–39). London: Routledge.

Ewen, S., & Ewen, E. (1982). *Channels of desire*. New York: McGraw-Hill.

Fairclough, N. (1989). *Language and power*. London: Longman.

Fairclough, N., & Graham, P. (2002). Marx as critical discourse analyst: The genesis of a critical method and its relevance to the critique of global capital. *Estudios de Sociolingüística, 3*(1), 185–229.

Farr, R. M. (1987). Social representations: A French tradition of research. *Journal for the Theory of Social Behavior, 17*(4), 343–370.

Farr, R. M., & Moscovici, S. (Eds.). (1984). *Social representations*. Cambridge: Cambridge University Press.

Featherstone, M. (2007). *Consumer culture and postmodernism* (2nd ed.). London: Sage.

Featherstone, M. (2010). Event horizon: Utopia–dystopia in Bauman's thought. In M. Davis & K. Tester (Eds.), *Bauman's challenge: Sociological issues for the 21st century* (pp. 127–147). Hampshire, UK: Palgrave Macmillan.

Feinberg, R. A., & Meoli, J. (1991). A brief history of the mall. In R. H. Holman & M. R. Solomon (Eds.), *Advances in consumer research* (Vol. 18, pp. 426–427). Provo, UT: Association for Consumer Research.

Ferguson, C. (Director). (2010). *Inside job* [Motion picture]. US: Sony Pictures.

Fine, B. (2002). *The world of consumption: The material and cultural revisited* (2nd ed.). London: Routledge.

Fishwick, M. W. (1983). *Ronald revisited: The world of Ronald McDonald*. Bowling Green, OH: Bowling Green University Popular Press.

Fiske, J. (2000). Shopping for pleasure: Malls, power, and resistance. In J. B. Schor & D. B. Holt (Eds.), *The consumer society reader* (pp. 306–330). New York: The New Press.

Flanders, S. (Ed.). (1993). *The dream discourse today, The new library of psychoanalysis, 17*. London: Routledge.

Foix, J. V. (2004). *És quan dormo que hi veig clar*. Barcelona: Edicions 62. (Original work published 1953).

Føllesdal, D. (1994). Hermeneutics and the hypothetico-deductive method. In M. Martin & L. C. McIntyre (Eds.), *Readings in the philosophy of social science* (pp. 233–247). London: Bradford. (Original work published 1979).

Fontenelle, I. A. (2006). Ilusões de modernidade: o fetiche da marca McDonald's no Brasil. *Psicologia & Sociedade, 18*(2), 38–46.

Forty, A. (1986). *Objects of desire*. London: Thames and Hudson.

Fournier, S., & Guiry, M. (1993). An emerald green Jaguar, a house on Nantucket, and an African safari: Wish lists and consumption dreams in materialist society. *Advances in Consumer Research, 20*, 352–358.

Freitas, M. G. (1991). *Taipas e toupeiras*. Porto Alegre: Fonte Phi.

Freitas, M. G. (1999). Vida simbólica: uma aliança. *Boletim do Centro de Estudos Junguianos C. A. Meier, 1*(1), 1–5.

Freud, S. (1925). The relation of the poet to day-dreaming. In *Collected Papers, IV*. London: Hogarth Press. (Original work published 1908).

Fromm, E. (1955). *The sane society*. New York: Rinehart & Company.

Gabriel, Y., & Lang, T. (2006). *The unmanageable consumer* (2nd ed.). London: Sage.

Gadamer, H. G. (1975). *Truth and method*. London: Continuum.

Gaiman, N. (1989). *The Sandman. Preludes and Nocturnes* (1–8). New York: DC Comics.

Gaiman, N. (1991). *The Sandman. Dream country* (Vol. 3). US: DC Comics.

Gane, N. (2006). When we have never been human, what is to be done: An interview with Donna Haraway. *Theory, Culture & Society Annual Review, 23*(7–8), 135–158.

Gare, A. (2008). Marxism and the problem of creating an environmentally sustainable civilization in China. *Capitalism, Nature, Socialism, 19*(1), 5–26.

Garin, E. (1973). *L'umanesimo italiano: Filosofia e vita civile nel Rinascimento*. Roma: Laterzi.

Gauchet, M. (2009). *Marcel Gauchet: "nous sommes sous le coup d'une anesthésie"*. Retrieved from http://www.latribune.fr/actualites/economie/france/20090724trib 000403499/marcel-gauchet-nous-sommes-sous-le-coup-d-une-anesthesie-.html

Geertz, C. (1977). *The interpretation of cultures*. New York: Basic Books.
Gergen, K. J. (1991). *The saturated self*. New York: Basic Books.
Gilgun, J. F. (1994). A case for case studies in social work research. *Social Work, 39*(4), 371–380.
Gilliam, T. (Director). (2009). *The Imaginarium of Doctor Parnassus* [Motion picture]. Canada, France, UK: Lionsgate/Sony Pictures.
Giroux, H. A. (1994). *The mouse that roared*. Oxford: Rowman & Littlewood.
Giroux, H. A. (1995). Animating youth: The Disnification of children's culture. *Socialist Review, 24*(3), 23–55.
Giroux, H. A., & Pollock, G. (2010). *The mouse that roared: Disney and the end of innocence*. Lanhan, MA: Rowman & Littlefield.
Giroux, H. A., & Pollock, G. (2011). *How Disney magic and the corporate media shape youth identity in the digital age*. Retrieved from http://truth-out.org/index.php?option=com_k2&view=item&id=2808:how-disney-magic-and-the-corporat e-media-shape-youth-identity-in-the-digital-age
Goldman, R. (1992). *Reading ads socially*. London: Routledge.
Goldman, R., & Papson, S. (1996). *Sign wars: The cluttered landscape of advertising*. New York: The Guilford Press.
Goodman, D. (2004). Consumption as a social problem. In G. Ritzer (Ed.), *Handbook of social problems*. London: Sage. Retrieved from http://www.sage-ereference.com/hdbk_socproblems/Article_n14.html
Gottdiener, M. (1982). Disneyland: A utopian urban space. *Journal of Contemporary Ethnography, 11*(2), 139–162.
Gottdiener, M. (1996). *The theming of America: Dreams, visions, and commercial spaces*. Boulder, CO: Westview Press.
Gottschalk, S. (2008). All you can eat: Sociological reflections on food in the hypermodern era. In L. C. Rubin (Ed.), *Food for thought: Essays on eating and culture* (pp. 48–65). Jefferson, NC: McFarland.
Graham, P. (2006). 'Capitalism' as false consciousness. *Studies in Language & Capitalism, 1*, 57–76.
Gruzinski, S. (1988). *La colonization de l'imaginaire*. Paris: Gallimard.
Gruzinski, S. (1990). *La guerre des images*. Paris: Fayard.
Guattari, F. (2010). *The machinic unconscious: Essays in Schizoanalysis*. New York: Semiotext(e). (Original work published 1979).
Guattari, F., & Rolnik, S. (2006). *Micropolítica: Cartografias del deseo*. Madrid: Traficantes de Sueños.
Gunter, B., & Furnham, A. (1998). *Children as consumers: A psychological analysis of the young people's market*. London: Routledge.

Günther, G., Huschke, W., & Steiner, W. (1993). *Weimar: Lexikon zur Stadtgeschichte*. Weimar: Böhlau.

Hamel, J. (1993). The case study in sociology: The contribution of methodological research in the French language. *Canadian Review of Sociology & Anthropology, 30*(4), 488–509.

Hamelink, C. T. (1983). *Cultural autonomy in global communications*. New York: Longman.

Hankiss, E. (2001). *Fears and symbols: An introduction to the study of western civilization*. New York and Budapest: CEU Press.

Hannerz, U. (1989). Notes on the global ecumene. *Public Culture, 1*(2), 66–75.

Hannerz, U. (1992). *Cultural complexity: Studies in the social organization of meaning*. New York: Columbia University Press.

Haraway, D. (1991). *Simians, cyborgs and women: The reinvention of nature*. New York: Routledge.

Harman, C. (2009). *Zombie capitalism: Global crisis and the relevance of Marx*. London: Bookmarks.

Harvey, C. W., & Zibell, C. (2000). Shrinking selves in synthetic sites: On personhood in a Walt Disney World. *Ethics and Information Technology, 2*(1), 19–25.

Haug, W. F. (1987). *Commodity aesthetics, ideology and culture*. New York: International General.

Hearn, A. (2008). 'Meat, Mask, Burden': Probing the contours of the branded 'self'. *Journal of Consumer Culture, 8*, 197–217.

Hebbrecht, M. (2007). The dream, anno 2007. *Tijdschrift voor Psychiatrie, 49*(12), 877–886.

Henderson, J. L. (1964). Ancient myths and modern man. In C. G. Jung (Ed.), *Man and his symbols* (pp. 104–156). New York: Anchor Press.

Henderson, S., & Petersen, A. R. (Eds.). (2002). *Consuming health: The commodification of health care*. London: Routledge.

Hetherington, K. (2005). Memories of capitalism: Cities, phantasmagoria and arcades. *International Journal of Urban and Regional Research, 29*(1), 187–200.

Hirschman, E. C., & Stern, B. B. (1999). The roles of emotion in consumer research. *Advances in Consumer Research, 26*(1), 4–11.

Hobbes, T. (1651). *Leviathan, or the matter, forme, & power of a common-wealth ecclesiasticall and civill*. London: Yale University Press.

Hubert, H., & Mauss, M. (1909). *Mélanges d'histoire des religions*. Paris: Alcan.

Huws, U., & Herrman, C. (Eds.). (2008). *The new gold rush: The new multinationals and the commodification of public sector work*. London: Work Organisation, Labour and Globalisation.

Illouz, E. (2009). Emotions, imagination and consumption: A new research agenda. *Journal of Consumer Culture, 9*(3), 377–413.

Jacobs, J. (1984). *The mall: An attempted escape from everyday life*. Prospect Heights, IL: The Waveland Press.

Jameson, F. (1981). *Narrative as a socially symbolic act*. New York: Cornell University Press.

Jameson, F. (1984a). Postmodernism: Or the cultural logic of late capitalism. *New Left Review, 146*, 53–92.

Jameson, F. (1984b). Postmodernism and the consumer society. In H. Foster (Ed.), *Postmodern culture* (pp. 111–125). London: Pluto Press.

Jameson, F. (1991). *Postmodernism, or the cultural logic of late capitalism*. Durham, NC: Duke University Press.

Jameson, F. (1992). *Signatures of the visible*. London: Routledge.

Janet, P. (1890). *L'automatisme psychologique*. Paris: Alcon.

Jha, P. S. (2006). *The twilight of the nation state: Globalisation, chaos and war*. London: Pluto Press.

Jhally, S. (1989). Advertising as religion: The dialectic of technology and magic. In L. Angus & S. Jhally (Eds.), *Cultural politics in contemporary America* (pp. 217–229). New York: Routledge.

Jhally, S. (Ed.). (2006). *The spectacle of accumulation: Essays in culture, media, and politics*. New York: Peter Lang.

Jodelet, D. (1991). *Madness and social representations*. London: Harvester/Wheatsheaf.

Jovchelovitch, S., & Gervais, M. (1998). *The health beliefs of the Chinese community in England: A qualitative research study*. London: Health Education Authority.

Jung, C. G. (1994). *Los complejos y el inconsciente* (J. L. Pacheco, Trans.). Madrid: Altaya. (Original work published 1933).

Jung, C. G. (2002). *Cartas de C. G. Jung* (Vol. II). Petrópolis: Vozes.

Kellner, D. (1999). Theorizing/resisting McDonaldization: A multiperspectivist approach. In B. Smart (Ed.), *Resisting McDonaldization* (pp. 186–206). London: Sage.

Kellner, D. (2003). *Media spectacle*. London: Routledge.

Kellner, D. (2009). Jean Baudrillard. In *The Stanford encyclopedia of philosophy* (Winter 2009 ed.). Retrieved from http://plato.stanford.edu/archives/win2009/entries/baudrillard/

Klein, N. (2000). *No logo*. London: Flamingo.

Knights, D., & Wilmot, H. (2006). *Introducing organizational behaviour & management*. London: Thomson Learning.

Kowinski, W. (1984). *The malling of America: An inside look at the great consumer paradise*. New York: William Morrow Co.

Kracke, W. (1987). Myths in dreams, thought in images: An Amazonian contribution to the psychoanalytic theory of primary process. In B. Tedlock (Ed.), *Dreaming: Anthropological and psychological interpretations* (pp. 31–54). Cambridge: Cambridge University Press.

Kraniauskas, J. (1994). Beware Mexican ruins! 'One-way street' and the colonial unconscious. In A. Benjamin & P. Osborne (Eds.), *Walter Benjamin's philosophy: Destruction and experience* (pp. 139–154). London: Routledge.

Kroc, R. (1987). *Griding it out: The making of McDonald's*. New York: St. Martin's.

Kroker, A. (1992). *The possessed individual: Technology and the French postmodern*. Montreal: New World Perspectives.

Kroker, A., & Cook, D. (2001). *The postmodern scene: Excremental culture and hyper-aesthetics* (2nd ed.). Montreal: New World Perspectives.

Lacher, H. (2005). International transformation and the persistence of territoriality: Toward a new political geography of capitalism. *Review of International Political Economy, 12*(1), 26–52.

Lair, D. J., Sullivan, K., & Cheney, G. (2005). Marketization and the recasting of the professional self: The rhetoric and ethics of personal branding. *Management Communication Quarterly, 18*(3), 307–343.

Lang, F. (Director). (1927). *Metropolis* [Motion picture]. Germany: Universum Film AG.

Langman, L. (1992). Neon cages: Shopping for subjectivity. In R. Shields (Ed.), *Lifestyle shopping: The subject of consumption* (pp. 40–82). New York: Routledge.

Laqua, C. (1992). *Wie Micky unter die Nazis Fiel: Walt Disney und Deutschland*. Hamburg: Rowohlt.

Lasch, C. (1979). *The culture of narcissism*. New York: W.W. Norton.

Lasch, C. (1984). *The minimal self: Psychic survival in troubled times*. New York: W.W. Norton.

Lash, S., & Lury, C. (2007). *The global culture industry: The mediation of things*. Cambridge: Polity Press.

Laval, C., & Weber, L. (Orgs.). (2002). *Le nouvel ordre éducatif mondial*. Paris: OMC, Banque Mondiale, OCDE, Commission Européenne.

Lears, T. (1983). From salvation to self-realization: Advertising and the therapeutic roots of the consumer culture, 1880–1930. In R. Fox & T. Lears (Eds.), *The culture of consumption: Critical essays in American history, 1880–1980* (pp. 1–38). New York: Pantheon Books.

Lebowitz, M. (2003). *Beyond 'Capital': Marx's political economy of the working class* (2nd ed.). Basingstoke: Palgrave Macmillan.

Lefebvre, H. (1971). *Everyday life in the modern world.* New York: Harper & Row.

Levy, C. W. (1994, February). The bad news about Barney. *Parents Magazine*, pp. 191–92.

Lévy-Bruhl, L. (1985). *How natives think* (L. Clare, Trans.). Princeton: Princeton University Press. (Original work published 1910).

Lewis, G. H. (1990). Community through exclusion and illusion: The creation of social worlds in an American shopping mall. *Journal of Popular Culture, 24*(2), 121–136.

Leys, C. (2007). *Total capitalism: Market politics, market state.* London: Merlin Press.

Lillie, A. (2003). *India in primitive Christianity.* Whitefish, MT: Kessinger Publishing. (Original work published 1893).

Lincoln, J., & Seligman, C. G. (1935). *The dream in primitive cultures.* Retrieved from http://books.google.es/books?id=wH9qj79iU00C&printsec=frontcover&hl=es

Liodakis, G. (2010). *Totalitarian capitalism and beyond.* Surrey, UK: Ashgate.

Löwy, M. (2010). Capitalism as monstrous religion. *Logos Journal, 9*(1). Retrieved from http://www.logosjournal.com/anticapitalist-readings-of-webers-protestant-ethic.php

Lukács, G. (1971). *History and class consciousness* (R. Livingstone, Trans.). London: Merlin Press. (Original work published 1923).

Lyon, D. (2001). *Jesus in Disneyland: Religion in postmodern times.* Malden: Blackwell.

Maffesoli, M. (1988a). *Le Temps des tribus. Le déclin de l'individualisme dans les sociétés de masse.* Paris: Méridiens Klincksieck.

Maffesoli, M. (Ed.). (1988b). *The sociology of everyday life.* London: Sage.

Maffesoli, M. (1989). Jeux de masques: Postmodern tribalism. *Design Issues, IV*(1–2), 141–151.

Maffesoli, M. (1990). *Aux creux des apparences: Pour une éthique de l'esthétique.* Paris: Le livre de Poche.

Maffesoli, M. (1993a). *El conocimiento ordinario: Compendio de sociología.* Mexico: FCE.

Maffesoli, M. (1993b). *La contemplation du monde: Figures du style communautaire.* Paris: Grasset.

Maffesoli, M. (2008). *Iconologías: Nuestras idolatrías postmodernas* (J. Terré, Trans.). Barcelona: Península.

Marcuse, H. (1964). *One-dimensional man: Studies in the ideology of advanced industrial society*. Retrieved from http://www.marxists.org/reference/archive/marcuse/works/one-dimensional-man/index.htm

Marcuse, H. (1966). *Eros and civilization*. Boston: Beacon. (Original work published 1955).

Markus, H., & Nurius, P. (1986). Possible selves. *American Psychologist, 41*, 954–969.

Marshall, P. D. (1997). *Celebrity and power: Fame in contemporary culture*. London: University of Minneapolis Press.

Martín-Barbero, J. (1987). *De los medios a las mediaciones: comunicación, cultura y hegemonía*. Barcelona: Ediciones Gili.

Martins, J. S. (Org.). (1996). *(Des)figurações: a vida cotidiana no imaginário onírico da metrópole*. Hucitec: São Paulo.

Marx, K. (1847). *Wages*. Retrieved from http://www.marxists.org/archive/marx/works/1847/12/31.htm

Marx, K. (1978). Grundrisse. In R. C. Tucker (Ed.), *The Marx-Engels reader* (2nd ed., pp. 222–293). New York: WW Norton. (Original work published 1858).

Marx, K. (1990a). *Capital: A critique of political economy* (S. Moore & E. Aveling, Trans., Vol. 1). Retrieved from http://www.marxists.org/archive/marx/works/1867-c1/index.htm (Original work published 1887).

Marx, K. (1990b). *Capital: Critique of political economy* (B. Fowkes, Trans., Vol. 1). Harmondsworth: Penguin. (Original work published 1867).

Marx, K. (1993). Das Kapital: Kritik der politischen Ökonomie. Der Produktionsprozeß des Kapitals. In *Karl Marx Friedrich Engels Werke, Band 23*. Berlin: Dietz Verlag. (Original work published 1867).

Marx, K., & Engels, F. (1848). *Manifesto of the communist party*. Retrieved from http://www.marxists.org/archive/marx/works/1848/communist-manifesto/index.htm

Mauss, M. (1903). *Esquisse d'une théorie générale de la magie* (l'Année Sociologique, 1902–1903). Retrieved from http://classiques.uqac.ca/classiques/mauss_marcel/socio_et_anthropo/1_esquisse_magie/esquisse_magie.html

McConnell, F. (2002). Preface. In N. Gaiman & E. Kramer (Eds.), *The Sandman: Book of dreams* (pp. 2–5). New York: HarperTorch.

McCracken, G. (1988). *Culture and consumption: New approaches to the symbolic character of consumer goods and activities*. Bloomington: Indiana University Press.

McLuhan, M. (1959). Myth and mass media. *Daedalus: Journal of the American Academy of Arts and Sciences, 88*(2), 339–348.

McLuhan, M. (1994). *Understanding media: The extensions of man*. Cambridge, MA: MIT Press. (Original work published 1964).

Meier, C. A. (1977). *Jung's analytical psychology and religion*. Carbondale, IL: Southern Illinois University Press.

Meier, C. A. (1986). *Soul and body: Essays on the theories of C. G. Jung*. Santa Monica: Lapis Press.

Meier, C. A. (1987). *The meaning and significance of dreams*. Boston: Sigo Press.

Meier, C. A. (1989). *Consciousness*. Boston: Sigo Press.

Meier, C. A. (Ed.). (2001). *Atom and archetype: The Pauli/Jung letters, 1932–1958*. Princeton: Princeton University Press.

Meier, C. A. (2003). *Healing dream and ritual: Ancient incubation and modern psychotherapy*. Switzerland: Daimon Verlag. (Original work published 1983).

Mestrovic, S. G. (1997). *Postemotional society*. London: Sage.

Minden, M., & Bachman, H. (Eds.). (2002). *Fritz Lang's Metropolis: Cinematic visions of technology and fear*. New York: Camden House.

Mitchell, W. J. T. (1986). *Iconology: Image, text, ideology*. Chicago: University of Chicago Press.

Mitchell, W. J. T. (1998). *The last dinosaur book: The life and times of a cultural icon*. Chicago: The University of Chicago Press.

Mitroff, I., & Bennis, W. (1989). *The unreality industry: The deliberate manufacturing of falsehood and what it is doing to our lives*. New York: Birch Lane Press.

Molnar, A. (1996). *Giving kids the business: The commercialization of America's schools*. Boulder, CO: Westview Press.

Moore, A. (1980). Walt Disney World: Bounded ritual space and the playful pilgrimage center. *Anthropological Quarterly, 53*(4), 207–218.

Moscovici, S. (1988). Notes towards a description of social representations. *European Journal of Social Psychology, 18*, 211–250.

Navarro, V. (1976). *Medicine under Capitalism*. New York: Prodist.

Navarro, V. (1993). *Dangerous to your health: Capitalism in health care*. New York: Monthly Review.

Nietzsche, F. (1974). *The gay science* (W. Kaufmann, Trans.). New York: Vintage Books. (Original work published 1882).

Nietzsche, F. (1984). *Human, all too human: A book for free spirits* (M. Faber & S. Lehmann, Trans.). Lincoln: University of Nebraska Press. (Original work published 1880).

Nordström, J., & Riddestråle, K. (2000). *Funky business: Talent makes capital dance*. Harlow, UK: Pearson.

Nordström, J., & Riddestråle, K. (2005). *Karaoke capitalism: Daring to be different in a copycat world.* Westport: Praeger.

Norris, T. (2006). Hannah Arendt & Jean Baudrillard: Pedagogy in the consumer society. *Studies in Philosophy and Education, 25*, 457–477.

Novalis. (1923). Heinrich von Ofterdingen. In J. Minor (Ed.), *Novalis Schriften* (Vol. I). Jena: E. Diederich. (Original work published 1802).

Osborne, P. (2005). *How to read Marx.* London: Granta.

Otto, R. (1917). *Das Heilige: Über das Irrationale in der Idee des Göttlichen und sein Verhältnis zum Rationalen.* Breslau: Trewendt und Granier.

Packard, V. (1961). *The status seekers: An exploration of class behaviour in America.* Middlesex: Penguin.

Parker, I. (2007). *Revolution in psychology: Alienation to emancipation.* London: Pluto Press.

Pasolini, P. P. (Director). (1969). *Medea* [Motion picture]. Italy: San Marco SpA.

Patton, M. Q. (1990). *Qualitative research and evaluation methods.* Newbury Park: Sage.

Pawlett, W. (2008). Against banality: The object system, the sign system and the consumption system. *International Journal of Baudrillard Studies, 5*(1). Retrieved from http://www.ubishops.ca/baudrillardstudies/vol5_1/v5-1-article13-Pawlett.html

Pessoa, F. (1995). *Poesias* (15th ed.). Lisboa: Ática. (Original work published 1924).

Piedras, E. R. (2006). *Sonho de consumo: a publicidade na intersecção entre o consumo material e o simbólico, pelo olhar do receptor.* Anais do XV Encontro da Compós. Bauru, SP, Brazil.

Piedras, E. R. (2007). *Publicidade, imaginário e consumo: Anúncios no cotidiano feminino.* Unpublished doctoral dissertation, PUCRS, Porto Alegre, Brazil.

Plummer, K. (1983). *Documents of life.* London: Allen & Unwin.

Poster, M. (2001). Introduction. In M. Poster (Ed.), *Jean Baudrillard: Selected writings* (2nd ed., pp. 1–9). Cambridge: Polity.

Putney, L. G. (2010). Case study. In *Encyclopedia of research design.* London: Sage. Retrieved from http://www.sage-ereference.com/researchdesign/Article_n39.html

Pykett, J., Jones, R., & Whitehead, M. (Eds.). (2017). *Psychological governance and public policy: Governing the mind, brain and behaviour.* London: Routledge.

Radice, H. (2005). Neoliberal globalization: Imperialism without empires? In A. Saad-Filho & D. Johnston (Eds.), *Neoliberalism: A critical reader* (pp. 91–98). London: Pluto Press.

Ray, E. G. (2009). *Part of their world: Gender identity found in Disney princesses, consumerism, and performative play*. Unpublished master's thesis, Brigham Young University, Provo, Utah, US.

Reiser, M. F. (2001). The dream in contemporary psychiatry. *The American Journal of Psychiatry, 158*(3), 351–359.

Retort. (2004). Afflicted powers. *New Left Review, 27*. Retrieved from http://www.newleftreview.org/?page=article&view=2506

Riesman, D. (1969). *The lonely crowd: A study of the changing American character*. New Haven: Yale University Press. (Original work published 1950).

Ritchie, J., & Spencer, L. (1994). Qualitative data analysis for applied policy research. In A. Bryman & R. G. Burgess (Eds.), *Analysing qualitative data* (pp. 173–194). London: Routledge & Kegan Paul.

Ritzer, G. (1993). *The McDonaldization of society*. Thousand Oaks, CA: Pine Forge.

Ritzer, G. (1998). *The McDonaldization thesis*. London: Sage.

Ritzer, G. (2000). *The McDonaldization of society* (New Century ed.). Thousand Oaks, CA: Pine Forge.

Ritzer, G. (2001). *Explorations in the sociology of consumption: Fast food, credit cards and casinos*. London: Sage.

Ritzer, G. (2002). *McDonaldization: The reader*. London: Sage.

Ritzer, G. (2005). September 11, 2001: Mass murder and its roots in the symbolism of American consumer culture. In M. L. Andersen, K. Logio, & H. Taylor (Eds.), *Understanding society* (2nd ed., pp. 33–39). Belmont, CA: Thomson Learning.

Roberts, R. (2015). *Psychology and capitalism: The manipulation of mind*. Washington: Zero Books.

Rocha, E. P. G. (1990). *Magia e capitalismo: Um estudo antropológico da publicidade* (2nd ed.). São Paulo: Brasiliense.

Rocha, E. P. G. (1995). *A sociedade do sonho: comunicação, cultura e consumo*. Rio de Janeiro: Mauad. Retrieved from http://books.google.es/books?id=vYVf_ll8jX4C

Rocha, E. P. G. (2006). *Representações do consumo: estudos sobre a narrativa publicitária*. Rio de Janeiro: PUCRio/Mauad.

Rolnik, S. (2006). *Entrevista a Suely Rolnik*. Retrieved from http://lavaca.org/notas/entrevista-a-suely-rolnik/

Rosés, M. P., & Gabarrón, L. R. (1984). *La crisis en psicologia social: Elementos para la discusión epistemológica del concepto de crisis* (Vol. II, pp. 89–100). Quaderns de Psicologia.

Ross, D. (2004). Escape from Wonderland: Disney and the female imagination. *Marvels & Tales: Journal of Fairy-Tale Studies, 18*(1), 53–66.
Runyan, W. M. (1982). *Life histories and psychobiography: Explorations in theory and method*. New York: Oxford University Press.
Schor, J. (2004). *Born to buy: The commercialized child and the new consumer culture*. New York: Scribner.
Segal, R. A. (2007). Jung and Lévy-Bruhl. *Journal of Analytical Psychology, 52*(5), 635–658.
Sen, A. K. (2005, March). The malling of America. *Span Magazine*, pp. 3–7.
Sennett, R. (1998). *The corrosion of character: The personal consequences of work in the new capitalism*. New York: W. W. Norton.
Sennett, R. (2006). *The culture of the new capitalism*. Yale: Yale University Press.
Shafton, A. (1995). *Dream reader: Contemporary approaches to the understanding of dreams*. Albany, NY: State University of New York Press.
Shamdasani, S. (2003). *Jung and the making of modern psychology: The dream of a science*. Cambridge: Cambridge University Press.
Shamdasani, S. (2009). Introduction. In C. G. Jung & S. Shamdasani (Eds.), *The red book: Liber Novus* (pp. 193–221). New York: Philemon Series & W.W. Norton.
Silva, J. M. (2007). O silêncio do objeto: uma lógica hiper-espetacular. In J. Melo & O. Morais (Eds.), *Mercado e comunicação na sociedade digital* (pp. 159–163). São Paulo: Intercom; Santos-SP: Unisanta, Unisantos & Unimonte.
Simon, R. K. (1992). The formal garden in the age of consumer culture: A reading of the twentieth-century shopping mall. In F. Wayne & M. Steiner (Eds.), *Mapping American culture* (pp. 231–250). Iowa City: University of Iowa Press.
Slater, D. (1997). *Consumer culture and modernity*. Cambridge: Polity.
Slaughter, S., & Leslie, L. L. (1997). *Academic capitalism: Politics, policies and the entrepreneurial university*. Baltimore: Johns Hopkins University Press.
Slaughter, S., & Leslie, L. L. (2001). Expanding and elaborating the concept of *Academic capitalism. Organization, 8*(2), 154–161.
Slaughter, S., & Rhoades, G. (2004). *Academic capitalism and the new economy: Markets, state and higher education*. Baltimore: Johns Hopkins University Press.
Smith, A. F. (2006). *Encyclopedia of junk food and fast food*. Westport, CT: Greenwood.
Spears, R. (1997). Introduction. In T. Ibáñez & L. Íñiguez (Eds.), *Critical social psychology* (pp. 1–26). London: Sage.
Stephens, J. (1990). *The Italian renaissance: The origins of intellectual and artistic change before the reformation*. New York: Longman.

Stiegler, B. (2006). *The disaffected individual in the process of psychic and collective disindividuation*. Retrieved from http://arsindustrialis.org/disaffected-individual-process-psychic-and-collective-disindividuation

Strauss, S. (1924). Things are in the saddle. *Atlantic Monthly, 134*(5), 577–588.

Strummer, J., & Jones, M. (1979). Lost in the supermarket. [The Clash]. On *London Calling* [record]. New York: CBS/Epic.

Taylor, C. (1989). *Sources of the self: The making of modern identity*. Cambridge, MA: Harvard University Press.

Taylor, C. (2002). *Varieties of religion today: William James revisited*. Cambridge, MA: Harvard University Press.

Taylor, C. (2004). *Modern social imaginaries*. Durham and London: Duke University Press.

Taylor, M., & Saarinen, E. (1994). *Imagologies: Media philosophy*. London: Routledge.

Tedlock, B. (Ed.). (1992a). *Dreaming: Anthropological and psychological interpretations*. Santa Fe: School of American Research Press.

Tedlock, B. (1992b). Dreaming and dream research. In B. Tedlock (Ed.), *Dreaming: Anthropological and psychological interpretations* (pp. 86–104). Santa Fe: School of American Research Press.

Tester, K. (1993). *The life and times of post-modernity*. London: Routledge.

Thomas, J. (Ed.). (1998). *Introduction aux méthodologies de l'imaginaire*. Paris: Ellipses.

Thomson, I. T. (2000). *In conflict no longer: Self and society in contemporary America*. Lanham: Rowman & Littlefield.

Thussu, D. K. (Ed.). (1998). *Electronic empires: Global media and local resistance*. London: Hodder Arnold.

Todorov, T. (2002). *Memoria del mal, tentación del bien* (M. S. Crespo, Trans.). Barcelona: Península.

Tomlinson, A. (1990). Introduction: Consumer culture and the aura of the commodity. In A. Tomlinson (Ed.), *Consumption, identity and style: Marketing, meanings, and the packaging of pleasure* (pp. 1–27). London: Routledge.

Turner, G. (2004). *Understanding celebrity*. London: Sage.

Valsiner, J. (1989). *Human development and culture: The social nature of personality and its study*. Massachusetts: Lexington Books.

Valsiner, J. (2002). Forms of dialogical relations and semiotic autoregulation within the self. *Theory and Psychology, 12*(2), 251–265.

Valtonen, A. (2011). We dream as we live – Consuming. In R. W. Belk, K. Grayson, A. M. Muñiz, & H. J. Schau (Eds.), *Research in consumer behavior* (Vol. 13, pp. 93–110). Bradford, UK: Emerald.

Vester, H.-G. (1999). Emotions in postemotional culture. In J. Schlaeger & G. Stedman (Eds.), *Representations of emotions* (pp. 19–28). Tübingen: Narr.

Vieira, A. G. (2003). *Imagem, símbolo e narrativa na Psicologia Analítica de C. G. Jung*. Unpublished doctoral dissertation, Universidade Federal do Rio Grande do Sul, Porto Alegre, Brazil.

Vieira, A. G. (2006). *A interpretação do brincar na caixa de areia*. Porto Alegre: Armazém Digital.

Vierne, S. (1987). *Rite, roman, initiation* (Deux. éd.). Grenoble, France: Presses Universitaires de Grenoble.

Virilio, P. (1994). *The vision machine* (J. Rose, Trans.). Bloomington, IN: Indiana University Press.

Virilio, P. (2001). From modernism to hypermodernism and beyond: An interview with Paul Virilio. In J. Armitage (Ed.), *Paul Virilio: From modernism to Hypermodernism and beyond* (pp. 25–57). London: Sage.

Von Franz, M. L. (1964). The process of individuation. In C. G. Jung (Ed.), *Man and his symbols* (pp. 208–210). Garden City, NY: Doubleday.

Von Franz, M. L. (1997). *Archetypal dimensions of the psyche*. Boston: Shambhala.

Von Schubert, G. H. (1814). *Die Symbolik des Traumes*. Leipzig: Brockhaus.

Wachowski Brothers (Directors). (1999). *The matrix* [Motion picture]. US: Warner Bros. Pictures.

Waitzkin, H. (2003). *At the front lines of medicine: How the health care system alienates doctors & mistreats patients … & what we can do about it*. New York: Rowman & Littlefield.

Ward, G. (2009). *The politics of discipleship: Becoming postmaterial citizens*. Grand Rapids, MI: Baker Academic.

Warwick, K. (2000). *I, Cyborg*. London: Century.

Wasko, J. (2001). *Understanding Disney: The manufacture of fantasy*. Cambridge: Polity.

Wasko, J. (2006). Challenging Disney myths. *E-Compós*, Vol. 7. Retrieved from http://compos.org.br/seer/index.php/e-compos/article/viewFile/108/107

Weber, M. (1958). *The Protestant ethic and the spirit of capitalism*. New York: Scribners. (Original work published 1905).

Wee, L. (2010). Personal branding and the commodification of reflexivity. *Cultural Sociology, 4*(1), 45–62.

Weir, P. (Director). (1998). *The Truman Show* [Motion picture]. US: Paramount Pictures.

Welman, M. (1996). *Death and gnosis: Archetypal dream imagery in terminal illness*. Unpublished doctoral dissertation, Rhodes University, Grahamstown, South Africa.

Wetherell, M., & Maybin, J. (1996). The distributed self: A social constructionist perspective. In R. Stevens (Ed.), *Understanding the self* (pp. 219–279). London: Sage.
Williams, R. (1976). *Keywords*. London: Fontana.
Williams, R. H. (1991). *Dream worlds: Mass consumption in late nineteenth-century France*. Berkeley: University of California Press.
Williamson, J. (1978). *Decoding advertisements*. London: Boyars.
Williamson, J. (1986). *Consuming passions*. London: Boyars.
Wilson, E. (1985). *Adorned in dreams: Fashion and modernity*. Berkeley: University of California Press.
Wunenburger, J.-J. (1997). *Philosophie des images*. Paris: PUF.
Xavier, M. (1999). *Dream interpretation in Jung's theory: A comparative analysis*. Retrieved from http://www.cgjungpage.org/index2.php?option=com_content& do_pdf=1&id=107
Xavier, M. (2001). *Religiosidade e problemas com o álcool: Um estudo de caso*. Unpublished master's thesis, PUCRS, Porto Alegre, Brazil.
Xavier, M. (2005). Religiosidade e problemas com o álcool: um estudo de caso. *Psicologia Ciência e Profissão, 25*(1), 88–99.
Xavier, M. (2006). O conceito de religiosidade em C. G. Jung. *Psico, 37*(2), 183–189.
Xavier, M. (2011). Trabalho e sonhos: desejos e pesadelos de professores e trabalhadores da saúde na era do capitalismo organizacional. *Cadernos de psicologia social do trabalho, 14*(1), 93–110.
Xiberras, M. (2002). *Pratique de l'imaginaire: lecture de Gilbert Durand*. Quebec: Les Presses de l'Université Laval.
Yates, F. (1996). *Lulio y Bruno: Ensayos reunidos I*. Mexico: FCE.
Yeats, W. B. (1914). *Responsibilities*. Retrieved from http://www.sacred-texts.com/neu/yeats/lpy/lpy080.htm
Yin, R. K. (2002). *Case study research: Design and methods* (3rd ed.). Thousand Oaks: Sage.
Yin, R. K. (2005). Case study methods. In J. Green, G. Camilli, & P. Elmore (Eds.), *Complementary methods for research in education* (3rd. ed., pp. 111–122). Washington, DC: American Educational Research Association.
Yin, R. K. (2012). *Applications of case study research* (3rd ed.). London: Sage.
Zayas, E. C. (2001). *Publicidad y hegemonía: matrices discursivas*. Buenos Aires: Norma.
Zukin, S. (1991). *Landscapes of power: From Detroit to Disney World*. Berkeley: University of California Press.

Index[1]

[1] Note: Page numbers followed by 'n' refer to notes.

M. Xavier, *Subjectivity, the Unconscious and Consumerism*,
https://doi.org/10.1007/978-3-319-96824-7

J

The manufacturer's authorised representative in the EU is Springer Nature Customer Service Centre GmbH, Europaplatz 3, 69115 Heidelberg, Germany. If you have any concerns regarding our products, please contact ProductSafety@springernature.com

Printed and bound by CPI Group (UK) Ltd, Croydon, CR0 4YY
30/09/2026
02225653-0017